C. Allen Merrit

Communications Mgmt.
Conference
Jan 10-12, 1973

The United States and
the Industrial World

The United States and the Industrial World

American Foreign Economic Policy in the 1970s

William Diebold, Jr.

Published for the
COUNCIL ON FOREIGN RELATIONS

by

PRAEGER PUBLISHERS
New York · Washington · London

PRAEGER PUBLISHERS
111 Fourth Avenue, New York, N.Y. 10003, U.S.A.
5, Cromwell Place, London SW7 2JL, England

Published in the United States of America in 1972
by Praeger Publishers, Inc.

Library of Congress Catalog Card Number: 70–96292

For a partial list of Council publications, see pages 461-63.

Printed in the United States of America

To
Percy W. Bidwell,
who set me on this path

Contents

Acknowledgments

"Of the making of many books there is no end." Ecclesiastes—or whoever added these words to what he had written—probably referred to the steady flow of new writing (if he had anything like this modern interpretation in mind at all). Nevertheless, these famous words came back to me often in recent years as I wondered whether there might be no end to the making of this particular book. But, finally, I have found a place to stop, if not precisely a conclusion.

The starting place was in the deliberations of a study group of the Council on Foreign Relations in the latter '50s about how the United States should react to some recent developments. I expected to base a book on the results, but quite a different book from this one. It soon became clear that to deal adequately with a relatively narrow issue it was necessary to understand some much broader ones. And so, instead of a sharply focused study of a more or less clearly defined problem in American policy, I found myself writing a general work on American foreign economic policy as a whole. This book does not comprise quite that much; for reasons set out in chapter 1 it concentrates on the very large segment of American policy that concerns relations with Western Europe, Canada, and Japan, here called for short (but with less than total accuracy) "the industrial world" to distinguish it from the Communist part of the world and from those lands which, again with some inaccuracy, can be called the less developed or developing countries. With these I shall be dealing in two further books.

Chapter 1 also explains why it is that a book that is concerned with policy for the future should look backward to the conception of a desirable world economy that guided American policy at the end of World War II. That backward look—which covers the intervening experience as well—adds considerably to my acknowledgments for help received. It makes the subject matter of this book roughly coterminous with my professional life. During most of the time between 1939 and 1947, I was engaged, at the Council on Foreign Relations and the State Department, first in postwar planning and then in trying to put some of the plans into practice. Since my return to the Council's staff in 1947, my work has continuously concerned the issues dealt with in this book. All this has been very educational. However small my own contribution may have been and whatever narrow slice of the whole occupied my attention at a given moment, I saw and heard a great deal about all parts of the subject and had splendid opportunities both to learn what some of the best thinkers thought and to see how government officials and businessmen, American and foreign, reacted to some of the circumstances with which this book is concerned. Thus I am indebted to many people who can only be thanked collectively and anonymously.

I must, however, make some exceptions. This book is dedicated to Percy W. Bidwell, who was the Council's Director of Studies when I arrived as a Rockefeller Research Fellow in the fall of 1939. With some help from the war, he diverted me from other plans to what became my first book, on American foreign trade policy. From then on, and especially between my return to the Council in 1947 and his retirement in 1958, he was in every sense my mentor in all these matters and remained an adviser and friend until he died in the summer of 1970. In the 6 months that followed, while I was revising the manuscript, two other friends died who had also done much to shape my interests, ideas, and career. Jacob Viner was co-chairman of the group at the Council with which I worked in the '40s to formulate ideas for the postwar period. Clair Wilcox was my teacher when I was an undergraduate and then headed the office in which I worked in the State Department at the end of the war. My association with these men was much deeper than these formal relations might suggest. The impact of Bidwell, Viner, and Wilcox is strong on the pages that follow; I hope I have not fallen too short of their high standards. After the book was all done except for this preface, Philip E. Mosely died. As the Council's second Director of Studies, he supported and helped me during much of the writing of this book; as a friend and occasional colleague from 1940 on, he did much to shape my mind.

If naming these men is an inadequate recognition of what I owe them, not naming some others also fails to acknowledge a large debt. I refer to the immense number of people who by their writing have helped me understand the many subjects that in one way or another are dealt with in the chapters that follow. A critical bibliography such as I have written for earlier books seemed desirable, but I quailed before the prospect of reviewing the whole postwar literature in several different fields and a number of quite specialized sub-literatures as well. Footnote bibliographies—those quick passing references to the "best" books on each subject or the noncommittal "see also"—seemed to me unsatisfactory. Consequently, this book refers to the writings of others only when they are quoted or used as the source for specific data. (Figures not footnoted come from standard sources.) The result is to leave unmentioned most of the people whose writings over the last few decades have informed me about many subjects and influenced my judgment by their analysis and argument. For this I am truly sorry and apologize in advance to the many who could expect to see their work cited in the discussion of a field to which they may have contributed a great deal.

My departure from scholarly custom in this regard is not meant to stake false claims to originality, nor would I go so far as Jorge Luis Borges, who says in the preface to *Ficciones* that it is sometimes "a better course of procedure" to pretend that certain "books already exist, and then to offer a résumé, a commentary." The reasons for not interlacing references once the book was written were largely esthetic; an extraordinarily large number of footnotes would have been needed and there were enough already. If there is any other advantage to be claimed for what I have done, it is that exposition and discussion are to a degree simplified by treating points of view in a more generalized fashion than would be correct if I were dealing by name with specific authors; then I would have to discuss their particular formulations and consider significant variations advanced by others.

Because this book has been so long in the making, almost everyone who has worked in a similar field at the Council has, wittingly or not, contributed. Among Council Visiting Fellows during this period, I have a special debt to Judd Polk, the late Henry G. Aubrey, and C. Fred Bergsten for the insights they have given me into monetary affairs (and also Stephen V. O. Clarke in a somewhat different capacity). Warren S. Hunsberger's work on Japan first took me deep into the economic relations of that country with the United States; Randall Hinshaw's trenchant approach to American trade with the European Community clarified a number of issues for me. I benefited from my association with authors of studies related to mine prepared for other parts of the Council's program, including Bela Balassa, Harold van B. Cleveland, Richard N. Cooper, John W. Evans, Robert V. Roosa, and the late John O. Coppock. The chairmen and members of discussion and study groups with which I have worked over the years contributed greatly to my understanding of many issues.

It is, of course, the Council itself which has made this book possible. The Council is many people, only a few of whom can be mentioned here. It might seem a formality to thank the Board of Directors, but the fact that at a late stage of this work they were willing to devote part of a meeting to discuss my main conclusions was very encouraging. For years the Committee on Studies, first under the chairmanship of Henry M. Wriston and then of Grayson Kirk, has been helpful, patient and yet subtly prodding, as I periodically reported "progress." George S. Franklin, Jr., the Council's Executive Director during the life of this study, deserves my thanks for many things, not least his tolerance and the confidence on which I believe it was founded. I hope I have justified his faith. My colleagues in the studies program, William J. Barnds, John C. Campbell, Miriam Camps, Andrew J. Pierre, and Richard P. Stebbins, have all helped both with my education on many matters dealt with in this book (sometimes peripherally) and in carrying burdens that might otherwise have fallen to me. They will, I feel sure, agree with me that I owe a special debt to David W. MacEachron, who for a number of years now has made exceptional efforts to permit me to devote most of my time to finishing this book, at considerable expense to his own workload and other activities. Like everyone who works at the Council I have been enormously helped by the library staff under Donald Wasson. For years Lorna Brennan and her staff and, more recently, Jane Lagas have cheerfully and efficiently helped in many ways.

Once the manuscript was in a more or less complete draft, a number of experts on various parts of the subject who were also old friends were generous enough to spend a day at the Council criticizing what I had written. They were C. Fred Bergsten, Harold van B. Cleveland, Emilio G. Collado, Richard N. Gardner, Walter J. Levy, David W. MacEachron, Alfred C. Neal, Judd Polk, Helena Stalson, and Raymond Vernon. Willard L. Thorp acted as chairman of the group. To him I have a special debt, not only for this occasion but much else. One of the many times I have had the pleasure of working with him (going back to days in the State Department) was when he was chairman of the study group in whose deliberations this book had its origins.

Others who were not able to attend the review session but who read the whole manuscript and often gave me detailed and valuable criticisms were Miriam Camps, Richard N. Cooper, Joseph A. Greenwald, Edward R. Fried, John M. Leddy, Gardner Patterson, Frank W. Schiff, and Sidney Weintraub. Isaiah Frank, who was kept from the review meeting by his duties as Executive Director of the staff of the Williams Commission, was good enough to circulate my manuscript among his associates and then permit me to spend the better part of a day exchanging views with him and them. I found this extraordinarily helpful and refrain from listing their names only because they are already public property. I should acknowledge, however, the special attention that Scott R. Pearson gave to my discussion of adjustment problems and Kenneth E. Ogren to agricultural policy. At Chatham House (the Royal Institute of International Affairs in London) a study group under Andrew Shonfield was kind enough to devote one of its meetings to a discussion of an early version of my manuscript. Their critical comments have, I hope, improved my perspective.

Quite a few people with specialized knowledge have been good enough to read individual chapters and comment on them. They include: Saburo Okita and Warren S. Hunsberger (chapter 3); John S. Dickey, John W. Holmes, Sperry Lea, Roy A. Matthews, Richard J. Storr, Paul Wonnacott, and Gerald C. V. Wright (chapter 4); Edmund Wellenstein (chapter 5); John W. Evans and J. Robert Schaetzel (chapters 5 and 8); Jack N. Behrman (chapters 5 and 6); Robert J. van Schaik (chapter 8). Chapter 4 was used as a background paper for a conference sponsored by the Canadian Institute of International Affairs and the Council on Foreign Relations and also was distributed to the steering committee of a continuing study sponsored by the World Peace Foundation and the Centre Québecois de Relations Internationales.

An important part in the preparation of this book was played by those who combined the functions of secretary and research assistant. At the head of the list is Carol Richmond, who has been a mainstay for nearly five years, during which the whole book has gone through two drafts and many more revisions of parts. She typed all this, often several times, carried out many pieces of research, checked most everything, and finally prepared the index. Before her, I had indispensable help from (in reverse historical order): Carol Meadows, Anne Kingston, Mary Williams, Kate Oliver, Ellen Choffin, Antoinette Rogers Willis, Evangeline Tsirkas, and Jean Pearce.

Robert W. Valkenier, the Council's editor, labored in the friendliest and most tolerant fashion over my idiosyncrasies, coped with my stubbornness, and even so managed to improve the manuscript as well as to prepare it for the press.

Helena Stalson, economist on the staff of the Council and an old friend, has made an enormous contribution to this book. Even before I began working on it, she had helped me to understand issues with which it deals. She has kept me honest by challenging many of my statements and kept me accurate by forcing me to look at facts which had somehow taken a different shape in my mind from that which they had in the real world. The research on any number of issues discussed in this book is hers and there must be as much again on matters that do not appear at all in the final version, or perhaps only as general statements. I am very grateful for everything.

It will be seen that I have had an extraordinary amount of help in writing this book. It is only fair to say that I have probably turned down more advice than I have taken, so the traditional formula applies that none of those who have done so much to help me is responsible for what I have finally perpetrated. Another traditional formula applies to my family. My wife and children (especially William, the one remaining full-time resident) have had to put up with a good bit from me over the years. Since at least some of this can be blamed on the book, it is only fair that they, too, should be mentioned here.

*   *   *

At various places in this book I have explained the time perspective in which I am writing. Just a word at the outset will help orient the reader. Since producing books is such a slow process, it is foolhardy to try to deal with current events. The only way to stay "up to date" is to deal with fundamental issues of continuing importance. I was not, therefore, dismayed when, between this manuscript's going to the printer and the final correction of proofs, many things happened which, had they occurred a few months earlier, would have been noted here. For the most part, the things that happened were quite compatible with the analysis of these pages and often, indeed, illustrated points. It was not surprising, for instance, that the AFL-CIO's initiative should be successful in having a bill introduced into Congress that would put quotas on imports and establish controls over investment. Some of the major developments could be foreseen but had to be handled in quite different ways. The Williams Commission report, for example, necessarily dealt with many of the issues considered in this book; it appeared too late for its points to be incorporated in my text in any sensible way, so I have left it aside completely. Raymond Vernon's long-awaited book on the multinational corporation came out too late to cite; but my comments on these matters were already shaped by my exposure to the author's views. The British Parliament voted to join the European Community, as had seemed likely for some time; most of the book is written on the assumption that there will soon be a Community of Ten, but the text is not altogether consistent in this matter and the reader's indulgence is requested for some old-fashioned references to the Six as well as for occasional passages reflecting a prudent hedging against the possibility that even at this late date some slip might prevent, or at least delay, the consummation of the negotiations. The one event that threw doubt on much that had been said in this book was the apparent reversal of some major American policies reflected in the actions announced on August 15, 1971, about ten days after the manuscript went to press. Thanks to the understanding and generosity of the Council and the publishers, I was able to add an epilogue to the book to deal with these matters and also made a few changes in the text, especially in chapter 7, to avoid the most obvious conflicts between the new facts and certain generalizations in my earlier version.

No doubt by the time these words are read something more will have happened that bears on the central issues with which this book is concerned. I can only hope that, as I believe was true of the events following August 15, 1971, it will be something that can be better understood in the light of this book than otherwise.

W.D.
February, 1972

The United States and
the Industrial World

A World That Is Both Old and New

In the middle of the twentieth century the government of the United States had a clear view of the kind of world economy it would like to see created when the destruction and disorganization of war were overcome. For the next twenty-five years American foreign economic policy was largely shaped to achieve those aims. As the last quarter of the century approached, clarity was lost. Uncertainty as to both objectives and methods came not from the failure of the earlier efforts— though some of them had failed—but from the changes that had taken place in the world economy and in what people expected of it. Some of those changes were the result of the policies initiated just after World War II, and some were the cumulative effect of a large number of separate, though often related, private and public initiatives, scientific and technological developments, and the reaction of people to both sets of forces. While the impact of these changes was world-wide, it was particularly great on the relations among the highly industrialized, non-Communist countries: Japan and the nations of North America and Western Europe.

With one-fifth of the world's population, these countries account for something like two-thirds of its production of goods and services. Decisions made in the capitals and business centers of these relatively rich countries do much to shape the international economy. The United States is by far the biggest and richest of the group but is neither so strong nor so wealthy that it can ignore the others. About two-thirds of American foreign trade is with Canada, Western Europe, and Japan; only a slightly smaller share of American direct investment abroad is located in those areas. It follows that an important part of American foreign economic policy concerns relations with these few countries, and that part is the subject of this book.

It may seem odd to treat such diverse sets of relations as those with Europe, Japan, and Canada as a single segment of American policy, but only in this way can a coherent American policy be devised. To separate this segment from the rest of American foreign economic relations is not arbitrary; the links among the economies of these countries are of a character, scale, and intricacy that do not exist between them and the rest of the world. This does not mean that American policies toward Europe, Canada, and Japan can be shaped without regard to the poor nations and the Communist countries. On the contrary, the segments of policy frequently intersect in significant ways, as will be pointed out in subsequent chapters. But the starting place for a fresh analysis of American foreign economic policy as a whole is quite properly the large, complex, and in many respects novel set of problems and possibilities arising out of its relations with the other non-Communist industrial countries.

Wealth, growth, openness, interpenetration, and change are keynotes of both the possibilities and the problems. Production and consumption in the industrialized countries with which this book deals have reached unprecedented heights. Trade among them has grown faster than world trade as a whole, and its patterns have become more complex as new industries have grown up and the structure and character of old ones have changed. A great volume of foreign investment, much of it American, has altered ownership and control, intensifying familiar problems and creating new ones. The international monetary system differs from any known in the past, has changed significantly in the last decade, and will be further altered in the next. Even agriculture, in many ways the most tradition-bound part of any economy, is undergoing major changes in these countries which, in spite of their marked industrial character, still produce a substantial share of the world's food.

The relaxation of governmental restrictions on trade and payments, the increased speed and ease of communication and transportation, and the increasing mobility of capital have made the economies of the industrialized countries remarkably open to one another. National policies have to be sensitive to what happens in other countries. Private economic activities are increasingly international or transnational. But political power, and therefore policy, remains deeply rooted in nation states. How it is exercised and what forms and degrees of international cooperation are possible are matters that are significantly influenced by the fact that the strength and power of Europe and Japan have grown greatly since the framework of postwar cooperation was built under American leadership.

That framework was intended to accommodate and, indeed, to promote change. Naturally, there was also emphasis on reconstruction and the rebuilding of national economies. International economic relations, however, were to be different from what they had been in the interwar period. Barriers were to be lowered, restrictions removed, and narrow nationalism curbed. International cooperation was to replace the beggar-my-neighbor policies of the '30s. How these aims were to be achieved was quite fully thought out and embodied in fairly definite proposals, most of which were put into practice. The immediate postwar years saw some major additions to the program, notably the Marshall Plan and the move toward Western European integration. Later there were other changes and some shifts in emphasis, but the main lines of American foreign economic policy have remained those laid down between 1943 and 1950. The question Americans have to ask themselves is whether it can possibly make sense to try to cope with the changing world of the '70s and the '80s in the same way.

The quick negative that such a question elicits is not an adequate answer. That an old policy is being followed in a new situation is not necessarily a ground for indictment. Some elements of the old policy work better today than they did right after the war. There are times when it is better to maintain continuity in direction even at the sacrifice of immediate advantages rather than veer with every change in circumstances. Some of the desirable changes in the world are themselves the product of past policies, and to scrap what is old because it is old may bring retrogression. But it is also possible that in changed circumstances policies that served well in the past will yield no results or bad ones.

One of the aims of this book is to examine the present and future problems of American policy in the perspective of the past to see what blend of change and continuity responds to the needs of the '70s and beyond. More is involved than replacing some elements of policy with new ones while polishing up others, as if one were repairing an engine. The purpose of the machine is also in question. The main policies that have guided American foreign economic relations since 1945 were based on a rather clear and coherent picture of the kind of world economy that seemed desirable coupled with fairly concrete ideas about how one could move toward it. Is that picture still valid? Can an equally good one be drawn for the '70s and the '80s? To provide at least a partial answer to these questions is another purpose of this book.

THE WORLD PICTURE OF 1945

The foreign economic policy that the United States put together during and just after World War II was reasonably clear-cut and fairly consistent. It sought to build a global economy based on intergovernmental cooperation, the equal treatment of nations, and the reduction of barriers to the movement of goods and money. To achieve these aims a number of international economic organizations were to be set up, each the centerpiece of a major agreement binding governments to a code of rules and procedures. Countries with serious balance of payments difficulties or extensive reconstruction needs were to be exempted from the full rigor of the agreements for the time being but were still called on to meet certain standards that were, as a rule, to be internationally supervised.

The outlines of this kind of world economy were suggested in some of the broad statements of the Atlantic Charter, signed by Roosevelt and Churchill in August 1941. A fuller sketch was provided by Article VII of the lend-lease agreement between the United States and Britain signed in February 1942 (and repeated in the later agreements with other countries). Article VII called for "agreed actions . . . directed to the expansion, by appropriate international and domestic measures, of production, employment, and the exchange and consumption of goods, which are the material foundations of the liberty and welfare of all peoples; to the elimination of all forms of discriminatory treatment in international commerce, and to the reduction of tariffs and other trade barriers." A major step toward putting these general ideas into practice was the agreement at Bretton Woods, New Hampshire, in July 1944 to create the International Monetary Fund (IMF) and the International Bank for Reconstruction and Development (IBRD). In addition to establishing a new international organization, the Articles of Agreement of the Fund set the ground rules of a postwar international monetary system. Formation of the Food and Agriculture Organization had preceded the Bretton Woods conference, and work on the economic provisions of the United Nations Charter was going ahead at the same time. Though important, these efforts did less to shape the postwar international economy than the Bretton Woods agreements because they did not impose clear-cut obligations on the signatories. Proposals about postwar trade arrangements were set forth in connection with a major American loan to Britain in 1945 and led to extensive multilateral negotiations in the years that followed. A painfully negotiated Charter for an International Trade Organization (ITO) that would have dealt with a wide range of issues proved unacceptable to the United States, but a more modest General Agreement on Tariffs and Trade (GATT) became a major factor in the postwar world economy. Other arrangements, some bilateral, some involving a relatively small group of countries, some taken *ad hoc*, supplemented these larger efforts. Not all problems were dealt with, but by and large a recognizable picture of a desirable world economy emerged from these efforts.

The initiatives and much of the pressure to act came from the United States government, but many hands had contributed to the shaping of this collection of policies, which, for convenience, I shall call the Bretton Woods approach. Private groups in the United States were very active. People from foreign countries participated as national civil servants, temporary exiles, or members of the Secretariat of the League of Nations (then housed in Princeton), or the International Labor Office (then in Montreal). It was striking how much similarity there was in approach and how wide an area of agreement was finally found beneath a multiplicity of plans, proposals, and differences of view. To an important degree this was a reflection of the almost universal wish to avoid "the errors of last time," meaning not only specific features of the Versailles peace but also the common practices of the '30s and the conditions which gave rise to them. All of this work was conducted under the shadow of the fear that Congress would, in the end, not support far-reaching proposals even if the executive branch decided to make them. After all, one of the important "lessons of last time" was that national and international civil servants with academic advisers could draft enlightened agreements which were then turned down by governments or evaded or broken when the going got tough.

The record of the '40s and '50s proved to be different. There were compromises and qualifications. Some parts of the general scheme were never completed—notably in trade—and some of what was set up was never truly tested before it was adapted to different circumstances. There were failures, inconsistencies, and distortions of what had been agreed on. But by and large the United States and the other leading countries made a striking record both in adopting the main elements of the Bretton Woods approach and in following through with the kind of national action that is essential to keep the cooperation of others.

This thumbnail sketch makes the process seem simpler and smoother than it was. The coherence and consistency I have described were not always apparent to contemporary observers. In the United States there were difficult struggles within the executive, with Congress, and in public debate. National interests were sometimes con-

ceived narrowly instead of broadly. High principles were bent to accommodate interests, pressures, and prejudices. Arrangements such as
the weighted voting in the IMF seemed specially designed for the
benefit of the United States. Other governments, facing quite different
problems, disagreed with Washington as to how the world economy
should be shaped. They sometimes suspected American motives and
agreed to some arrangements with less than their whole hearts even
after long negotiations. Nothing was more infuriating to them than
to be told that something was "impossible because Congress will not
accept it" while they were being asked to take steps that would meet
serious opposition at home. There is no doubt that American economic strength and the need of most countries for help played an
important part in bringing about agreement on the kind of system
the United States was advocating.

It does not follow that the shape of the postwar economy was dictated by Washington. Not just "a decent Respect to the Opinions of
Mankind" but the simple practicalities of reaching agreement made
that impossible. Moreover, a key element in the American approach
was the understanding that no system would last or function well—if
it could get started at all—unless it served the interest of other countries, too. They could not be expected to abide by rules if the rules
did not apply to the United States, and, while some of the rules
seemed to favor the United States, the great bulk of exceptions were
made for the benefit of countries in balance of payments difficulties.
Moreover, it is a mistake to suppose that the reluctance to adopt
American proposals was always an accurate reflection of the true interests of other countries. European governments were preoccupied
with the need to maintain controls over trade and payments and
fearful of commitments to liberalize. Would they really have benefited if the creation of GATT had been postponed until they were
stronger and in consequence the United States had put off reducing its
tariffs? One way or another a balance had to be struck, and,
while there is room for argument about how far the board was tilted
on one issue or another—and even which way—the fact was inescapable that the proposals the United States was making would work
only if other countries regained their economic strength.

CHANGES IN THE WORLD PICTURE

Though the scope of American foreign economic policy at war's end
was large, a major addition was soon made to it: foreign aid. The
Marshall Plan and other forms of aid to Europe and Japan were, in a
sense, an unanticipated implementation of the Bretton Woods ap-

proach. Aid helped these countries to take the place expected of them in the world economy and then dropped out of the picture. Aid to the less developed countries has a different history and remains a central question of American policy in the '70s. Its exclusion from this book, along with the range of other issues concerning American relations with the poor countries, is a mark of their importance, not their unimportance. Those who drew the Bretton Woods world picture were not unaware of the problems of economic development, but they underestimated them. Not surprisingly then, the policy issues that have emerged in this field go far beyond anything with which the Bretton Woods framework was capable of dealing.

Matters were different again in relations with the Communist countries. Those who worked out plans for the postwar world economy knew that it would not be easy, and perhaps not possible at all, to accommodate state-controlled economies in a system of cooperative arrangements built largely on the experience of market economies. They made efforts to provide ways of cooperating with the Soviet Union but were not greatly surprised when that country refused to sign the Bretton Woods agreements or even to take part in the negotiations leading to the ITO and GATT. The omission was not expected to have a great impact on the operation of those agreements. The U.S.S.R. had played a relatively small part in international trade and payments before the war. The problems of domestic reconstruction plus the nature of the Soviet economy made it unlikely that the situation would change rapidly after the war. Though the creation of a Soviet sphere of influence in Eastern Europe and the Communist victory in China enlarged the area that would be outside the Bretton Woods system, the change was not great enough to affect the basic lines of American economic policy.

The great impact was political. The cold war and the fear of worse to come did much to stimulate the will to act and the willingness of governments to cooperate. Economic policies were affected, along with defense measures, and some new problems were created. But, since the aims embodied in the Bretton Woods picture had not in the first place been shaped by hostility toward the Communist world, they were not significantly altered. The economic relations that developed between the Communist countries and others—more with Western Europe and Japan than with the United States—were conducted largely outside the Bretton Woods system. As these relations develop further in the '70s, perhaps in new and interesting ways, the American share in them is likely to grow. But there can be little doubt that, even if the Communist countries are drawn more fully into the general pattern of trade and payments, it will be on rather different terms from those which have evolved among the countries dealt with in this book.

Thus, although the pattern of economic cooperation set in motion in the late '40s was conceived as global, we find it in the '70s very highly developed in relations among the industrialized non-Communist countries and applying in only more limited ways to the relations of those countries to the rest of the world. Even in the sector of world economic life considered in this book there has been a structural change that raises questions about the Bretton Woods aim of constructing a system of multilateral economic relations among separate countries. Since the early '50s a process of partial economic integration has been going on in Western Europe that has already altered the nature of the economic units there for some purposes—for example, the Common Market is a single tariff entity—and may go much further. Fully in keeping with that part of the Bretton Woods prescription that called for an economically strong Western Europe, this development poses other problems, not just for the countries left out of a grouping, including the United States, but for some of the bases on which the original pattern of cooperation was built as well.

Of course, there have been other major changes in the world economy since 1945. Western Europe, in addition to being partially integrated, is strong and prosperous, no longer the object of special solicitude in American policy or heavily dependent on the United States. Japan, whose position in the 1945 picture was rather shadowy, reflecting a greater awareness of past troubles than of future promise, has made its way exuberantly into the ranks of major industrial powers. Canada, whose position in the old picture roughly paralleled that of the United States, with due allowance for differences in size, finds itself drawn even more closely than before to its southern neighbor in a rather special relation which was begun by geography but enhanced by man. The United States itself, still the largest and richest economy in the group, no longer has anything like the preponderance of the immediate postwar years. Its economic position is affected by overseas political and military commitments on a scale not envisaged in the Bretton Woods picture. Not unconnected with both these facts has been a decade of concern about the balance of payments and the position of the dollar in the world, a concern that was completely absent during the first half of the postwar period. For many different reasons, serious doubts have arisen about the willingness of the United States to continue on the course it set so many years ago and, even if it proves willing, about its ability to lead others in the same direction.

There are new features in the relations among the industrialized economies, almost a new tone. The beginning of this chapter alluded to the openness of these economies to one another and their mutual interpenetration; the body of the book has much to say on these matters. The pattern is not altogether uniform. Japan has not opened its economic frontiers as much as the other countries, and the others are not as free in importing from Japan as from one another. American businessmen have shown a greater propensity to invest abroad than foreigners to invest in the United States. In Europe there is greater integration than has been achieved elsewhere, which brings a significant differentiation between those who are in a group and those who are outside. The high degree of integration between Canada and the United States is one-sided and only partially formalized. Close cooperation among the industrialized countries in some matters is accompanied by a primary reliance on national controls and policies in others. And, where there is cooperation, as in monetary matters, there is often also friction. As Jacob Viner said more than once, people who try to work together have more to argue about than those who follow separate courses.

Great as the changes of the last quarter-century have been, there are some features of the world of the '60s and '70s that resemble those of the '40s and '50s. The Kennedy Round of negotiations in the mid-'60s had the same main aims as proposals made by the United States in 1945 and 1946: the reduction of tariffs, the removal of other trade controls, and the maintenance and extension of equal treatment. The threat that new trade barriers will be imposed in the '70s is discussed in language heard often in the '40s and '50s. The need that is felt to attack nontariff barriers reflects the same approach that made tariffs and quotas the targets of past efforts. In agriculture the effort to liberalize trade encounters the same kinds of obstacles that frustrated earlier efforts. GATT is still the main body for dealing with trade problems. The IMF remains one of the centerpieces of cooperation, and fixed exchange rates are the legal norm, although significant innovations have been made in the way the international monetary system operates. Does the persistence of these elements mean that they remain sound, or is it only a matter of time until they, too, must give way to something new? Were the unilateral severance of the link between gold and the dollar and the accompanying indications that the United States felt the need to strengthen its competitive position in the world to be seen as pressure for greater economic cooperation or as a reversion to a world dominated by economic nationalism?

The blend of old and new, and especially the emergence of issues that were either unknown, unimportant, or ignored in the past, must give any observer a sense that relations among the industrial countries are taking on a new and unprecedented cast. Old ways of thinking about these issues, much less old ways of dealing with them, cannot be adequate for the future. But it is for the rest of the book to give substance to these impressions and content to generalization about them.

SOME VALUE JUDGMENTS

Why the United States should have adopted the Bretton Woods approach is a matter about which there can be debate. At the time some Americans thought the position was unnecessarily generous and idealistic. Some foreigners thought the American approach was anachronistic. Free trade was a nineteenth-century idea; was American emphasis on removing controls simply a lack of understanding of the modern world or an attempt to make planning and socialism impossible? Then and now, there were and are those who believed that Washington was trying to clear the way for American businessmen to take control of much of the world's economy. Freedom seemed likely to favor the strong, and, according to this view, American political power was being used to deprive weaker countries of the only defenses they had, economic controls. Another interpretation was that economic policy would pave the way for American political dominance. Some have discerned an effort to hold back the Soviet Union and divide the world even in measures that took shape before it was clear there was to be a cold war. For others, the prominent place anti-Communism came to have in American policy crowds out belief in the broader aims professed by those who did most to shape foreign economic policy.

To ascertain how real, or how important, any of these motives may have been would require a historical study that is not possible within the confines of this book. Fortunately it is also not necessary. Within some reasonable limits the main analysis of this book is compatible with different estimates of the motives of the American government and the relative influence of various groups on its decisions. Such differences need not create much disagreement about a few central propositions: that, in spite of some important discrepancies, there was a certain coherence among a number of major elements in American foreign economic policy from the '40s on; that a primary objective of that policy was the reduction of barriers to international trade and payments; that, with some major exceptions, substantial progress was made in moving toward that objective (whether it is regarded as a good one or not); and that enough changes have taken place in the world so that a framework of policy designed in the '40s (whatever its motivations or merit) needs to be re-examined to ascertain its relevance to the '70s.

Naturally some of the pages that follow will be colored by my own interpretation of the Bretton Woods approach and the way it was applied. The reader can form his own judgment of the validity of my views as he encounters them in the discussion of specific policies. A few generalizations may help to orient him. They apply only to the range of problems discussed here; relations with the poor countries and the Communist countries have to be judged somewhat differently.

The "liberal," or liberalizing, emphasis of American policy was, in my opinion, a sound one, for the United States and the rest of the world. There should be, and has been, more to the policy than simply the removal of barriers. It is inevitable that conflicts should sometimes arise between obtaining the advantages of opening an economy freely to the rest of the world and directing that economy in the pursuit of certain national objectives. To find ways of reconciling the two purposes that can cope with a great variety of circumstances on some reasonably consistent basis was always recognized as a central problem of the Bretton Woods approach. It has been dealt with in ways that are only partially satisfactory. For these and other purposes the effort to build a system of continuing international economic cooperation was essential. The effort could be successful only if the United States made the creation and preservation of such a system an objective of its own policy and did not confine itself to the pursuit of narrower, more conventionally defined, national interests. Finally, I would argue that, in spite of all the setbacks and changed circumstances, there was a good deal of progress in twenty-five years in carrying out the Bretton Woods approach and that, in spite of exceptions, there was a good deal of consistency and coherence in American foreign economic policy.

There is, of course, a kind of anthropomorphic fallacy in speaking of "the United States" and its aims and ideas. This is a convenient convention, however, so long as one bears in mind the complex process it sums up. Political support for measures of foreign economic policy comes from a coalescence of people of different opinions and interests, sometimes conflicting ones. The grouping shifts over time and according to issues. In the process of persuasion, arguments are used which exaggerate the consequences of any action and sometimes lend spurious political coloration to measures that in a more rational world could be decided on their economic merits. To achieve worthy aims, men acquiesce in statements that do not fully reflect their honest judgment and so become parties to misrepresentation. How can such a process produce the relatively high degree of coherence that I think has marked American foreign economic policy during the last twenty-five years? Part of the explanation is that, among people who give close attention to international economic issues, there has continued to be a broad area of agreement on the desirability of the characteristics set by the Bretton Woods approach. There are enough people, in and out of government, who are persuaded of the importance of coherence and continuity in policy to ensure that this aspect of any proposed action (or inaction) is at least taken into account, though it may not prove decisive. Another part of the explanation is that, once a relatively coherent set of long-run aims has been adopted, they are to a certain degree self-reinforcing. Proposals that are "in line with policy" have a certain advantage over those that entail departures from it. Semantics and bureaucratic inertia aside—though they cannot really be left aside—the adoption of one course of action makes some others more logical. Moreover, inconsistency may put what has already been achieved in jeopardy.

Since continuity in policy is not an end in itself, it can be argued that consistency and coherence in American policy must be explained by the fact that the results of the policy have served the national interest. I believe that by and large they have, but the question of how the national interest is to be determined in so complicated a matter as foreign economic policy, which frequently involves conflicts of interest within countries, is better discussed toward the end of this book than at its beginning. In any case, our main concern is not with what has been done in the past but with what ought to be done in the future. In the face of some changes in the world, continuity in policy can become a vice, not a virtue, coherence may become the victim of a partial adaptation of policy, and cogency can be lost either by failing to perceive relevant changes or by exaggerating them.

WHAT THIS BOOK IS

Tempting as it is to try to see how the ideas of the '40s were translated into the reality of the '70s, I write not as a historian but as one who uses history when he can. Some interpretations of what has happened in twenty-five years will appear from time to time in the chapters that follow, but only as they help in understanding the issues of the present and future. A fresh look at policy should not be so fresh that the reader is led to believe that the problems are all completely new. An occasional look backward is a safeguard against seeing the future only in terms of the present. Without assuming that a trend discernible over twenty or twenty-five years past can safely be projected ten years ahead, one ought at least to ask whether vivid contemporary events—say, at the moment of the final revision early in 1972—represent old stirrings, passing phases, or new directions. Some history is essential, too, to an understanding of the place of continuity in foreign economic policy. Of course policy must adjust to changing circumstances, but foreign economic policies of the sort the United States has followed in the postwar years are peculiarly dependent on persistence in the pursuit of aims that cannot be attained in short periods. There is one more reason, of considerable importance, for paying some attention to the development of events. The pursuit of policies rooted in the Bretton Woods approach has itself been a factor in changing some segments of American economic relations with the rest of the world, and especially relations with other industrialized countries. So old policies have contributed to posing new problems that call for either new policies or adaptation of existing ones.

In place of the historian's responsibility for completeness, precise limning, and the exact weighing of evidence, I have put the essayist's right to pick and choose those things that seem essential—or at least enlightening. My approach is similar when it comes to foreign policy generally or to domestic politics, matters that can be neither omitted nor thoroughly discussed. To be free from some of the strictest canons of scientific analysis is a desirable state of affairs in discussing policy, since approximations sometimes have to serve where conclusive evidence is lacking.

Although I speak of foreign economic policy generally, this book has almost nothing to say about transportation, communications, travel, insurance, patents and licensing, films, and a number of other activities.

A book that deals with as many subjects as this one must abound in generalizations, so there is a risk of making accomplishments look too easy and prospects too optimistic, whereas a closer look would show the flyspecks on the picture of the past and the multiple hazards underlying any statement about the future. In suggesting courses of action for the future, I have avoided time-bound speculation about what might be acceptable to one Congress or another (while, I hope, not straining the bounds of credibility either). My conclusions about policy concentrate on directions rather than timetables.

Many of the most difficult problems in policy concern the interconnection of subjects that have to be analyzed more or less separately. Any arrangement of a complex subject matter keeps some things apart that have to be considered together; any alternative slice of the amalgam produces some other arbitrary results. No single ordering, by history, geography, or subject, works as the sole organizing principle;

all three are relevant coordinates on a grid that the reader ought to superimpose on the material from time to time. But *écrire, c'est choisir,* and I have settled on the following arrangement:

The three chapters that follow this one, called, collectively, "The World We Live In," deal with the salient features of American policy toward Western Europe, Japan, and Canada in the postwar period. Though all stress the global economic framework, they are not altogether of a piece. Because so much has been written about Europe, that chapter is shorter than the others. Because there are so many special characteristics of American relations with Japan and Canada, some sections of those chapters look farther into the future than the section title might lead one to expect. The exposition and interpretation of the main segments of American policy, past and present, are spread through these chapters (and occasionally later ones). If a reader wishes to assemble the parts, the index has been designed to help him.

The four chapters of Part II deal with the problems of the '70s in trade policy, investment and the internationalization of business (including the multinational corporation), the monetary system (and the relation of the U.S. balance of payments to it), and that seedbed of perennial trouble, agriculture. In every case, the prognosis is for a growing complexity in the relations among the industrial countries and a broadening of the range of issues once thought of as domestic that will become matters of international concern.

Chapter 9 might be regarded as an appendage of Part II; placed as it is, it becomes a prolegomenon to the conclusion. Read either way, it deals with the future of European regionalism and the question whether some other grouping of the industrialized nations would be desirable. The last two chapters form a kind of double-barreled conclusion. One modernizes the Bretton Woods world picture. The other discusses the implications of the book's analysis for the shaping of American policy in a changing world.

This book closes with an epilogue concerning the dramatic steps in foreign economic policy taken by President Nixon in August 1971 and the subsequent events which led to the agreement among the industrial countries to realign exchange rates, reached just before Christmas that year. The aim is not the futile one of trying to keep a book up to date by adding footnotes but to take this important episode as a whole, appraise it in the light of the book's basic analysis, and suggest some long-run implications of the changes that may have been set in motion. My manuscript was at the printer when the President made his speech of August 15. More than one person asked if I would not have to rewrite the book or at least delay its publication. I thought not, believing that fairly modest changes would best serve the purpose of both taking account of the new events and helping an observer to understand them. Whether I was right or wrong is something for the reader to decide.

In addition to the epilogue, I have made relatively few changes in the text (most of them in chapter 7), not so much to alter my emphasis as to alert the reader to connections between the earlier analysis and subsequent developments. The issue is essentially one of perspective. This is not a book about whether the dollar is worth 10 cents more or less. It is a book about a major part of the world economy—relations among the advanced non-Communist nations—which has characteristics entitling it to be called an international economic system of a special sort, and about the place of the United States in that system as shaper, participant, and potential shaker. The events of August to December 1971 are of potentially great importance to the whole system and may alter it in ways that lead to its destruction, malfunction, or improvement. These possibilities are all contemplated in this book's exploration of the changing character of what I have called "the Bretton Woods approach."

We may not be able to tell for some time whether the period ushered in by President Nixon's speech can properly be likened to a watershed, but it is not impossible to speculate on the sense in which it might be. What waters will flow in different directions from before? Which rivulets may become torrents, and what long familiar reservoirs may be dried up? The epilogue points out some of the ways in which this book casts light on these possibilities.

If there is an excuse for putting quite so many different issues between the covers of one book, it is that, however imperfectly rendered, this complex set of interconnections at least dimly reflects the real world in which governments function, where the consideration of one problem in isolation is permitted only occasionally and then not for long.

PART I

The World We Live In

2

Europe: From One Set of Problems to Another

Because the policy with which the United States emerged from World War II aimed at building a world economy, it was especially concerned with Europe. Without a Europe that could produce, consume, invest, and trade at high levels, a prosperous and well-operating world economy was inconceivable. Indeed, it would be hard to know what meaning could be attached to ideas of liberalized multilateral trade and payments if they did not apply to Europe.

As the Nazi troops were driven back, the liberated areas of Europe were provided with relief in various forms and substantial amounts. But to rebuild would require substantial financial help as well. No one doubted that the U.S. government would give help (but in what form and how much was not clear). The International Bank for Reconstruction and Development was expected to play an important part in the process, and some people thought that private capital would soon flow again. Though many European governments had prewar debts, no mountainous new obligations had been built up during the war—in marked contrast to the situation at the end of World War I.

That result had been achieved by shipping American goods to allies as "lend-lease" aid instead of selling for cash or credit. What the ultimate repayment, if any, should be was left open, but agreements

between the United States and each recipient firmly linked the settlement to negotiations about the postwar world economy. Many people
expected that lend-lease would be continued until other arrangements
were made to finance European reconstruction, but through shortsightedness and lack of coordination the Truman Administration
abruptly ended it in the fall of 1945. In something of a scramble,
ways were found during the rest of 1945 and 1946 to help Europe by
a series of credits covering lend-lease goods still in the pipeline and
the foreign purchase of surplus property held by the United States
abroad, and, of greater importance, by major reconstruction loans to
Britain, France, Holland, and Belgium, and smaller ones to half a
dozen other countries.

The largest of the loans, $4.4 billion to Britain,[1] was intended to
do more than revive the British economy. Americans saw it as a major
step toward creating the kind of world in which the Bretton Woods
approach could operate. Britain had played a central part in the prewar world economy, as importer, exporter, broker, banker, and investor. London housed markets for money and goods. Sterling was
a reserve currency for many countries and the medium for financing
a large part of the world's transactions. Though the past could not be
recaptured, the functions Britain had performed were essential for
the kind of world economy the Americans wanted to build, and there
were no other good candidates for the role. To help speed the result,
the loan agreement provided that sterling soon become convertible
and an effort be made to reduce the threat to its stability from
the large balances held in London by sterling area countries. The
British announced their support of a set of American proposals
(modified after negotiation) for rules to promote multilateral liberal
trade in the world, including some that would reduce the margin of
tariff preferences among British Commonwealth countries dating
from 1932.

While there was significant progress toward these larger purposes
in the two decades that followed, it is hard to attribute much of it
to the economic effect of the British loan. The effort to make the
pound convertible proved grotesquely premature. Many of the loan
dollars passed through London into the hands of foreign holders of
pounds without noticeably strengthening sterling's position in the
world. By mid-1947 Britain had drawn most of the credit; it was still
in serious balance of payments difficulties and far from ready to resume anything like its former place in the world economy.

1. Strictly speaking, it was a line of credit to be drawn on as needed, except for
$650 million which represented credit covering the lend-lease settlement and the
sale of surplus property.

Though the speed of events was shocking, the failure was not altogether surprising. From the beginning there had been many who felt that the loan was too small for what it was supposed to accomplish, or that the proposed removal of controls was too rapid. No matter how one allocated blame, no doubt remained that the task of British recovery had been underestimated. Nor was the problem confined to Britain. The hard winter of 1946–47 dramatized the fact that the Continent, too, had a long way to go before its economy would be functioning at an adequate level. At the rate they were being used, existing loans would be exhausted and imports would fall to a point at which Europe would be pressed for food and fuel.

In February 1947 the British announced that they could no longer carry the responsibilities they had exercised in the past for stability and defense in the eastern Mediterranean. In a series of quick decisions, the United States decided to fill the gap. Economic and military aid for Greece and Turkey was the immediate need; in asking Congress to provide it, the President enunciated the Truman Doctrine, which seemed to promise American help for anyone anywhere who was threatened by communism. While the interpretation of this declaration and the wisdom of its apparent scope were to become matters of continuing debate, there was no doubt that one of the foundations of American aid policy was thereby laid.

The next major step was the Marshall Plan. Its story need not be retold here. It did what it was supposed to do, making a major contribution to European recovery by the provision of American goods and money. Before the Marshall Plan had fully run its allotted course of four years, another task had been added to European recovery and another form of aid inaugurated to support it. When the North Atlantic Treaty was signed in 1949, the European countries were not spending large sums on arms and armies. So that they could play their parts in the new military alliance without imperiling their economic recovery, the United States provided additional massive aid. Most of it took the form of arms and equipment, but there were also civilian supplies called "defense support" to bolster economies and check the inflationary impact of diverting domestic resources to defense. Military aid soon reached a peak and then declined. By the mid-'50s, American aid to Europe continued to be important only for Greece, Turkey, Spain, Yugoslavia, and in coping with special problems such as Berlin and the deployment of NATO forces in Europe.

Though the rebuilding of the world economy had turned out to be a much longer process than Americans had imagined on V-E day, by the late '50s Western Europe seemed in many respects to be filling the place envisioned for it at that time. The countries there were paying their way in the world and building up reserves of gold and foreign exchange. Their currencies were made convertible for non-residents in 1958. The dollar shortage was no longer the dominant fact of international finance; for the first time since the end of the war, the international monetary system looked as if it might function in something like the manner conceived of at Bretton Woods. Fairly good progress had been made in liberalizing trade within Europe; it was possible to talk seriously of speeding the reduction of barriers to trans-Atlantic trade. The period of Europe's gross dependency on the American economy was over. While one should be chary of the word "independent" in international economic affairs, the Western European economy was undoubtedly far more autonomous than it had been at any time since the end of the war, and getting more so.

There were, of course, problems. Rapid rates of growth in Europe raised questions about the economic policies of slower-growing America. For the first time, the United States felt concerned about its balance of payments. Relations with Europe appeared to be contributing to the problem: the cost of paying American troops there added to the outflow of dollars; imports from Europe grew faster than American exports to that area; American investment there was rising rapidly. Greater autonomy in Europe meant that there was more room than before for differences over international questions, and especially the international monetary system. Britain showed no signs of resuming the key role it had had in the world economy.

This combination of new possibilities and new difficulties—which continued in the '60s and '70s and about which more will be said in later chapters—was the not unnatural consequence of the achievement, with about a decade's lag, of some of the aims of American policy of the late '40s. The same cannot be said about the results of the progress toward economic integration made in Europe during the '50s and '60s. This development to an important degree altered the world picture of 1945, posed new issues for the United States, and then required changes in some policies.

How European Integration Altered American Policy

When Secretary Marshall made it clear in his Harvard speech in June 1947 that the Europeans would have to work closely together if they expected to elicit major new American aid, he was reflecting some immediate practicalities and some long-established ideals. To make the most of American aid the Europeans would have to make much better use of Europe's own resources; that meant, in part, arranging for a more efficient exchange of goods among the European countries so that scarce dollars could be husbanded for the things Europe could not provide for itself. It meant more mutual aid among Europeans to carry out national efforts at self-help. There was also a very practical need on the American side. About $10 billion had already been provided for European relief and recovery. Congress would not look kindly on a further parade of separate national requests. The chances of getting adequate funds would be much better if a once-for-all comprehensive program could be drawn up with national efforts fitted together and a total sum of money stipulated.

The old ideal that Marshall evoked by inference was the widely, though sometimes vaguely, held view that the world would be better off if the Europeans got together and put their own house in order. The idea of a "United States of Europe" comes naturally to most Americans. However, there were always some Americans who warned that a unification of Europe would create a consolidation of power that would not be in the interest of the United States. Although such views were expressed by some who advised the U.S. government in its postwar planning, there had been no need to resolve the issue, because, in 1945, European unification did not seem to be practical politics. As time passed, however, more and more people, inside the U.S. government and, more importantly, in Europe, believed that a much higher degree of unity among the Western European countries than had ever existed before was not only desirable but feasible. Soon it became the policy of the United States to foster as well as it was able the drawing together of the Western European countries in economic, political, and military matters.

The Marshall Plan played an important part in shaping that policy and increasing its chances for success, not least because it involved Americans in dealing with problems that could best be solved by closer cooperation among Europeans. By the fall of 1949 Paul Hoffman, the head of the Economic Cooperation Administration (ECA), had gone beyond anything Marshall had said and was urging the Europeans toward "integration," by which he meant the creation of "a single large market" free from quotas, exchange controls, and "eventually all tariffs." "Unification" was a prescription for Europe that found favor in Congress but was avoided by the State Department and the ECA. As a Dutch participant in the work of recovery and integration observed, the executive branch of the U.S. government showed "a definite reluctance . . . to enforce solutions which were not acceptable to all or some of the major participants in the European Recovery Program . . ." This was, he felt, "a wise policy" because "a viable integration cannot be imposed externally."[2] Never-

2. Ernst H. van der Beugel, *From Marshall Aid to Atlantic Partnership* (Amsterdam: Elsevier Publishing Company, 1966), pp. 220-21.

theless there were times when it looked as if the Americans were leading the parade as well as cheering and beating the drum.

When the European governments presented the report that embodied their response to Marshall's speech, they said that its "programme of concerted action . . . marks the advent of a new stage of European economic co-operation."[3] No dramatic changes ensued but the exercise in cooperative arithmetic was followed by the creation of the Organization for European Economic Cooperation (OEEC). Its work in the years that followed contributed greatly to European integration, especially through the liberalization of trade, the multilateralization of payments, and the requirement that each country justify its economic policies to its peers. The French initiative of 1950, the Schuman Plan, which led to the European Coal and Steel Community, started another deeper-going process, but one long limited to six countries. When a proposal to create a defense (and to a degree political) community of the same countries was defeated in 1954, it looked as if the drive toward integration had stopped. This proved not to be the case, as a conference at Messina in 1955 led to the creation in 1957 of the European Economic Community (EEC or Common Market) and an atomic energy community (Euratom). Efforts to create an industrial free trade area comprising most of Western Europe failed, so seven countries outside the Common Market formed the European Free Trade Association (EFTA).

The result was a European configuration quite different from the one Americans supposed they would be dealing with when, in 1945 and thereabout, they worked out a desirable pattern for the world economy. The United States played a part in bringing about this change, or rather several different parts. Under the Marshall Plan, American officials were deeply engaged in the process of European cooperation, not only pressing and prodding, but also proposing measures of integration that were then negotiated with Europeans. American officials played a key part in bringing occupied West Germany fully into the process of cooperation and later had a hand in some arrangements that were important to the acceptance of the Schuman Plan, though the basic decisions about that enterprise were firmly European. The French veto of the European Defense Community showed the limits of American power in trying to shape events in Europe. In that effort the United States was no longer "pushing on open doors," and afterwards Washington conducted itself far more cautiously. The determining role in the creation of the Common

3. Committee of European Economic Co-operation, *General Report* (Paris: Author, September 21, 1947), as transmitted to President Truman, in U.S. Department of State Publication 2930 (Washington: GPO, 1947), p. 3.

Market and in the efforts that followed was plainly European. Like the European economy, the movement toward integration became largely autonomous.

The changes have not all been in Europe. American policy has been altered by European integration. The next section explains how American policy accommodated itself to Europe's efforts to integrate. Then we shall look at an American initiative stimulated by what Europe was doing.

Accommodation

The trade policy with which the United States came out of the war aimed at the reduction of trade barriers, without discrimination, over as much of world trade as possible. Measures to increase trade among the countries of Western Europe so as to reduce the need for any one of them to spend dollars for goods obtainable in Europe implied discrimination. A clash between the global and regional policies was inevitable. The United States favored both and therefore had to find a compromise. This was not too difficult so long as the discrimination was temporary and could be seen to strengthen the European countries.

Part of the problem had been faced before. The Articles of Agreement of the IMF permitted countries in serious balance of payments difficulties to discriminate against the countries with "hard" currencies, notably the United States, Canada, and Switzerland. GATT had similar but quite complex rules. The United States not only accepted the necessity for this kind of discrimination but in the late '40s and early '50s negotiated reductions in its tariff that were of immediate value to others, while the tariff reductions given in return by soft-currency countries meant little so long as their imports were controlled by quotas and exchange controls.

This departure from the cherished idea of "reciprocity" was sensible and also not quite as one-sided as it appeared. The tariff concessions made by other countries became valuable to the United States when quotas and exchange controls were eventually removed; the agreements themselves committed countries to remove the controls when their balance of payments positions improved and provided a certain amount of international pressure to insure that these steps were taken reasonably promptly. Freer access to the American market helped speed European recovery, reduced the need for American aid, and brought nearer the day of balance of payments equilibrium. The immediate impact on the American market was limited because Europe and Japan were not able to export great quantities of goods right away. During the "dollar shortage," the volume of American exports was determined more by how much other countries had to spend than by their trade restrictions (though the United States was not indifferent to the composition of its exports which was affected by the import restrictions). Finally, the alternative of waiting until countries were in easier balance of payments circumstances before trying to tie them firmly into GATT would not have helped the immediate position and might have made future negotiations more difficult.

Part of Europe's problem was that the countries there did not discriminate against the United States and in favor of one another sensibly enough. While almost all their currencies were soft, they were not equally soft; it made a difference whether you held drachmas or pounds. Each country focused on its own dollar problems and tried to get hard currencies for its exports even if that meant importing less than it might usefully have done from neighbors. Bilateral trade and payments agreements were the order of the day, and while they made some transactions possible, they had a constricting effect on Europe as a whole. To meet Marshall's standard of making full use of their own resources, the Europeans had to get rid of some of the barriers to trade among themselves. That was the aim of one of the principal activities of the OEEC, a trade liberalization program under which each year more quotas were removed on trade among its members (while being kept on imports from the United States). The result was a systematic discrimination against the United States which Washington approved and encouraged, though not in every instance. Like the purely national measures of discrimination provided for under GATT, these steps were thought of as temporary, as justified by the dollar shortage, and, indeed, as hastening the day when the European countries could remove more trade barriers and establish equal treatment.

There was, however, a risk that matters would develop otherwise. This possibility led to considerable controversy inside the U.S. government about the proposal for a European Payments Union (EPU). A device of joint American and European manufacture, EPU carried the process of internal liberalization much further than the scheduled removal of quotas could have done alone. Agreed to in the summer of 1950, it provided credit to ease intra-European transactions; payments were settled multilaterally rather than bilaterally, thus giving each country much greater freedom of choice in its purchases; incentives to a rough balance were provided by an arrangement under which the larger a country's debt the greater the share of it that had to be paid in gold or dollars; if a country's accounts with the group were persistently out of balance, an international board might recommend changes in its national policies. This last provision was one source of controversy as a number of people in the U.S. government thought it endangered the already somewhat weak position of the IMF and might lead the EPU to usurp the global organization's jurisdiction over exchange rates.

The rest of the controversy largely centered around the risk that instead of making a contribution to recovery the EPU would strengthen forces that would permanently keep Western Europe somewhat apart from the multinational world economy the United States was trying to build. Roughly, the argument was that by sheltering Europe from the competition of the rest of the world, notably North America, EPU would reduce pressures for the most desirable kind of economic adjustment. Countries capable of making their currencies convertible might be held back by the attraction of a sheltered market in the EPU. By making it easier to buy inside Europe than in the United States, even at higher prices, EPU might make Europe a soft-currency, high-cost area. The burden would ultimately fall on the Europeans themselves but the prospects of building a world economy that required a strong Europe would be diminished. In the end the contrary view won out: that internal competitive pressures in so large an economic area would do much to force adjustment and that Europe's interest in world trade would make it interested in reducing trade barriers. That view very largely proved correct. EPU probably helped the main European currencies move toward convertibility, after which the restrictions established on balance of payments grounds lost their justification and largely fell away.

Thus the first major accommodation of American policy to Europe's recovery needs and some initial, limited steps toward economic regionalism worked well. If there is a general lesson, it would seem to be that the controlled departure from general principles to meet specific conditions is the kind of flexibility that lends strength to policy.

The second accommodation was of a more lasting sort, going beyond recovery to take account of a structural change in the economy of Western Europe. Quite a few aspects of American policy were involved, but the issue presented itself first and most sharply in trade policy. There it involved not a formal or technical change but a significant shift in emphasis.

The emphasis on equal treatment and the most-favored-nation clause in the trading arrangements the United States was advocating was directed not only against the discriminatory bilateral bargains which had marked the '30s but also against the rarer arrangements in which groups of countries systematically gave preferential tariff treatment to one another. A particular target in many American eyes was British imperial preference and a good many man-hours had been spent in wartime and postwar negotiations about the future of that well-established arrangement. A reasonably satisfactory agreement (from the American point of view) had been reached under which no new preferences were to be introduced and margins of discrimination would fall as tariffs were cut. The United States had also begun to phase out its own preferential arrangements with Cuba and the Philippines. There was hardly room for doubt that the United States would firmly oppose suggestions for setting up a permanent preferential trading arrangement in Western Europe.

If, however, the Europeans wanted to form a customs union, they could expect a good reception from Washington. In the "friendly advice" he offered the officials who prepared the response to Marshall's Harvard speech, Under Secretary of State William L. Clayton suggested that they consider this course. No doubt they did, but they did not show much serious interest in the possibility, and the British were not willing to see it stated as even a distant objective.

Some people thought it inconsistent of the United States, the foe of preferences, to look favorably on an arrangement that might be said to create 100 per cent preferences. Tradition was on the American side; customs unions have long been established as exceptions to the most-favored-nation clause. There was more to the position, though, than that. A customs union requires a firm commitment to remove all internal barriers, thus creating free trade within the group; a preferential arrangement is likely to retain a good deal of internal protection and to emphasize the exchange of favors at the expense of outsiders. Customs unions were regarded as definitive changes; preferences could easily be altered. Not everyone accepted these arguments, but the issue did not seem likely to be very troublesome. Customs unions were hard to work out and rare. Those that existed were of minor importance to world trade, often because one of the partners was so small, as in the case of Belgium and Luxembourg. The most famous customs union, the German *Zollverein*, was regarded as something of a special case that had been shaped by Prussian dominance more than the economic interest of the parties. At the same time it was often cited as evidence that customs unions are likely to lead to a political union, another reason countries were not likely to be enthusiastic about them. Postwar experience was limited. During the war the governments-in-exile of Belgium, the Netherlands, and Luxembourg had decided to form a customs union. After the war, Benelux, now aiming at a complete economic union, became a reality but slowly. France and Italy negotiated a customs union treaty but never put it into effect. In any case, the American position was not one of strong advocacy (as for the reduction of trade barriers and equal treatment), but rather of somewhat vague benevolence colored by the thought that if the obvious obstacles could be removed, some countries (not the United States) would gain from joining in customs unions. That attitude seemed natural enough when the prevailing views were that countries ought to cooperate more intensively and that many of them were too small for optimum economic existence, let alone defense. The United States, it was often said, was itself a great customs union.

GATT continued the tradition of recognizing customs unions as exceptions to the most-favored-nation clause but stipulated that the "general incidence" of the new common tariff should be no higher than that of the national tariffs it replaced. The intention was to prevent the internal liberalization from being accompanied by new external restrictions. How fully it would really serve that purpose was not much discussed. It was not until 1950 that Professor Jacob Viner's *The Customs Union Issue* was published, which has done so much to shape all subsequent discussion of customs unions. By distinguishing between trade-diverting and trade-creating effects of a customs union, he showed that the GATT rule offered no guarantee that a customs union would on balance have the effects advocates of trade liberalization wanted or that outsiders would be shielded from damage. But Viner's analysis, as amended by other studies giving greater weight to possible dynamic effects of customs unions, is not clearly translatable into a set of rules of general applicability. The most important factor is the character of the economies forming the union; in that respect Western Europe looked fairly promising. By the late '50s, the customs union question was transformed from a minor and slightly academic possibility to a central, controversial fact of Western European life. By the time that happened, American policy, too, had undergone an important shift in emphasis.

Washington became convinced that the United States had a strong interest in the greatest possible degree of Western European unity. The reasons are familiar enough. A larger unit than the existing nation states offered better prospects of economic, political, and military strength. Such a Europe could resist Russian pressure better than a divided one. If the Europeans worked together, they could overcome the internal rivalries, especially between France and Germany, that had been responsible for two world wars. The division of Germany posed difficult and dangerous problems; by far the best chance of dealing with them seemed to be to start by fitting West Germany as closely as possible into a Western European grouping. Economic integration served all these ends. Essential for purely economic advantages, it was deemed likely to promote political unity as well. That possibility suggested to some people a reconciliation of the conflict between regionalism and multilateralism in American policy: a European Community would be virtually a single entity in a multilateral trading system. European integration might, of course, put outsiders, including the United States, at a disadvantage, but there would be economic as well as political compensations. For example, in spite of the discrimination inherent in a European customs union, the United States would sell more to an economically healthy Europe than to a series of weak national economies. By the time the Common Market became a serious possibility, the rate of growth in Western Europe lent color to the view that the outsiders' gains from expanding demand would outweigh any tariff disadvantage. (To some the logic seemed weak since Europe was showing it could grow rapidly without integration; how much the growth was due to expectations of economic fusion and how much the steps toward integration were made possible, or easier, by the expanding economy were not easy to distinguish.)

It is common to sum all this up by saying that the United States wanted European integration for political reasons and was prepared to pay an economic price if necessary. There is broad truth in this, but as the last paragraph's resumé of the policy rationale shows, the formulation is too crude, especially in implying a sharp distinction between "economic" and "political." It is true, however, that Washington's support of European integration was not made conditional on any demonstration that the results would be good for the American economy. There was a willingness to accept and try to deal with the problems that would inevitably arise from trying to fit into the world economy a new unit made up of imperfectly blended national economies. The first big step in trying to do that required a reanimation of the United States's established policy.

Invigoration

While Western Europe was eliminating trade barriers in an unprecedented fashion, American trade policy seemed to be running down. The United States still subscribed to the aim of a more freely trading world, but its efforts to move toward one were not very striking in the late '50s. The results of the 1960–61 Dillon Round in GATT were modest, largely because of the limits Congress had put on the President's power to lower duties. The balance of payments was beginning to bother Washington; unemployment and slow growth caused the country to worry about foreign competition. Imports were increasing rapidly as Japan and Europe became capable of taking full advantage of past tariff cuts. The government resisted pressure from domestic producers to check the flow of imports, but the escape clause was invoked to raise duties on some items and Japan was pressed to restrict its shipments of a number of products. By giving way on a few points, it could be argued, the first Republican Administration since 1932 made it politically possible to retain the liberal treatment of a far wider range of imports in difficult times. Nevertheless, when the best possible face is put on it, the fact remains that the United States was not exercising a strong influence on world trading policies and was not pointing the way to new measures that the countries of the free world might be undertaking.

It was ironical that this should be the American posture just as most of the advanced industrial countries of the free world were approaching conditions of prosperity, full employment, and convertibility that would put them in a better position than at any time since the end of the war to live up to the liberal rules of GATT and the IMF. The United States had been agreeable to their temporizing while they suffered from dollar difficulties and had recovery as their first task; but now that they could be pressed not only to live up to their commitments but perhaps to move farther ahead, the United States seemed less interested than at any time in the postwar period in what might be achieved by new moves toward liberal trade, less willing to take further steps in a direction in which it had already moved far, and less able than before to equip the President with the powers needed to negotiate effectively with others.

Why the United States was in that curious and unhelpful position was understandable. American tariffs had been substantially reduced while many other countries retained quotas and exchange controls. Such one-sidedness had become irksome to many Americans and tedious to others. The United States had patiently accepted departures from the rules for countries in this, that, or the other kind of difficulty. It had agreed to exceptions that applied almost across the board to everyone except the United States and a few other countries. Americans had been called on by their leaders to be understanding of the problems of others and to adhere, more or less consistently, to the trade principles the United States had propagated. It was not surprising that willingness to persevere in such a course should have worn down when the United States began to have its own problems of adjustment.

Explanation is no substitute for effectiveness. Dynamism in Europe, matched by a holding operation in the United States, might well bring to a stop progress toward the kind of multilateral trading world the United States had sought since before the end of the war. Exporting ever larger amounts, Western Europe had no urgent need to drive down tariffs abroad. It might well become preoccupied with what were now thought of as internal affairs of the Common Market or the EEC's relations with EFTA and push the problems of global trade into the background. The United States, however, had an interest in keeping in play all possible means of influencing events in Europe; in that perspective an inert trade policy began to look like a liability.

The change in administration in Washington and the expiration of the Trade Agreements Act in June 1962 provided the traditional occasions for a debate about trade policy. Whatever action was taken would be regarded as a declaration of intent. If nothing but trade policy had been at stake, it is moot what line the new people in Washington would have taken. They seriously considered simply extending the existing legislation or even letting the Act lapse for a while. Instead they wrote and got through Congress with substantial majorities the most important piece of trade legislation since the original Trade Agreements Act of 1934. Europe made that possible.

"The challenge of the Common Market," one of the tritest phrases of our time (though now no more shopworn than *le défi américain*), had a strong influence on the conception and passage of the Trade Expansion Act of 1962. Some saw the challenge as a threat: The Europeans had embarked on a course that would leave American producers at a distinct disadvantage outside a common tariff wall that enclosed their principal competitors. Others stressed the opportunity: Europe had achieved new levels of prosperity and a sustained rate of growth well ahead of that of the United States; could the United States share the benefits by increasing its trade with Europe? On either view of the challenge the problem for the United States was how to reduce the disadvantage of being outside by getting the Europeans to lower their barriers to American goods. It was hard to find any promising way of doing that except the traditional one of tariff bargaining. That meant the United States would have to give something to get what it wanted from the Europeans. To do that, the President would need substantial new powers and the will to use them.

This economic, or commercial policy, argument was by itself persuasive, but for the Kennedy Administration more was involved than trade. As Europe grew wealthier, stronger and more unified, its relations with the United States were bound to change (as America had hoped since the beginning of the Marshall Plan). Consequently, the United States needed a different kind of diplomacy from that which had served when the disparity between the United States and the divided European countries was as great as during the first postwar decade. Men around the President liked a pattern they called "partnership," a term that at least implied a more nearly equal association between the United States and a united Europe (with its boundaries not clearly defined in advance but certainly including Britain and the Six). Trade policy became the first concrete expression of this idea.

Partly that was an accident of timing: something had to be done about trade policy. More importantly, trade presented an opportunity to express ideas of partnership in a way that other relations did not. Though a kind of partnership could be said to have emerged already in finance as Europe helped the United States meet its balance of payments problems, there were objections to formalizing that kind of cooperation while it was still evolving. Moreover, these partners were not two but four or six or nine or ten, depending on the combination, and some were countries that were not going to be part of a unified Europe. The United States was not ready for partnership in defense if that meant anything like equal control over nuclear weapons. It would have been hard to know how to embody the changing political relations in any kind of framework of "partnership." But trade provided a ready-made opportunity.

Whether the Administration's not fully articulated interest in partnership had much to do with the support its proposals received in Congress and the country is doubtful. However, the idea that there were "foreign policy" reasons for the trade initiative was probably of some help. Hopeful or worried, many businessmen responded to the logic of meeting Europe's challenge. Promises and compromises neutralized some groups that might have opposed the bill. Textile producers were given a separately negotiated arrangement regulating international trade in cotton goods. The import quota on oil was exempted from any action under the new act. Farmers seemed more concerned with access to the Common Market than with the threat of European competition at home. Though he had nothing like the ascendancy over Congress that made it possible for Roosevelt and Hull to put through the first Trade Agreements Act in 1934, John F. Kennedy was helped by an aura of vigor, youth, and new initiative.

Whatever is the proper weight to give each factor, the result was that the Administration bill passed more easily and with greater support than could have been expected. There was also less opposition, or at least vociferous opposition, than was usual for trade measures, lending color to the suspicion that perhaps the tariff had lost its traditional importance for many American businessmen. Were more of them thinking in terms of world markets? Did they realize that the domestic mobility of the American economy, to which they were accustomed, brought greater changes than anything likely to stem from further tariff reduction—except for a few of them? Could it be that the argument that American business lived by competition no longer carried a silent proviso that it did not apply to foreigners? There was no clear answer at the time, and the questions are still with us.

The showing would have been impressive if the issue had been just a simple renewal of trade agreements legislation or a modest increase in the President's power. But the Trade Expansion Act (TEA) of 1962 was much more than that. For the first time, the President was given the power to remove duties altogether on a wide range of products, notably those of which the combined exports of the United States and the European Community amounted to 80 per cent of world exports (excluding trade within the Community and exports to or from Communist countries).[4] Many manufactured goods would be on this list if Britain were a member of the Community; if not, only one or two products would qualify. For other products, the 50 per cent limit on the President's power to cut duties was reestablished in place of the lower limits of recent years. Cuts were to apply to the 1962 rates of duty, most of which had already been cut one or more times and some of which were only 25 per cent of what they had been when the trade agreements program started in 1934.

In short, the TEA put the United States within striking distance of generally low tariff rates and even some free trade. Moreover, there was a strong implication in the TEA that the old practice of refusing to make cuts if domestic industries might be hurt was to be abandoned. This possibility arose from several features of the new law. An old rule was dropped that was intended to make it hard for the President to cut duties below predetermined "peril points" arrived at by estimating the effect on imports of reducing tariffs. The escape clause under which duties could be raised if imports injured domestic producers was weakened, and its use was linked to one of the TEA's major innovations: machinery to provide federal help to those hard pressed by import competition. The aim was not to restore protection but to improve the domestic producer's ability to compete or to help him shift to other lines of work. The TEA was intended, the Administration made clear, to make possible a general reduction of tariff rates. Cutting "across the board" was expected to produce greater re-

4. The others were: products subject to duties of 5 per cent or less; most tropical products, provided the European Community did the same; agricultural products if that seemed desirable as part of an agreement with the Europeans that would promote U.S. exports.

sults than the old method of working out separate bargains item-by-item.

American adherence to most-favored-nation treatment was re-affirmed in the TEA. The emphasis on Europe did not mean tariff discrimination in favor of Europe. Whatever cuts were made would be extended to all others (except those Communist countries to which the United States denied equal treatment). Nevertheless, the focus was undeniably on Europe. That was plain enough in the new and radical power to eliminate tariffs. The effect of the 80 per cent rule was first to distinguish between trade in manufactures and other trade and then to separate those products of which the United States and Western Europe were the world's dominant suppliers from those in which Japan (or Canada) had a prominent position. The use of other provisions to free trade also largely depended on agreement with Europe. There was nothing surprising in this emphasis since it was concern about trade with Europe—and for some people about more than trade—that had prompted the United States to reinvigo-rate its trade policy. But the matter was even more fundamental than that. The fact that Europe in the early 1960s was economically strong and embarked on a process of integration which seemed about to in-clude more countries had forced the United States to put new energy into its flagging trade policy if it was to continue to move in the di-rection it had set earlier and also to do something new: to begin to work out a set of international economic relations that took account of Europe's new position. A new dynamic process had appeared: Eu-rope's approach to the conditions aimed at in the original postwar plan generated a change in the picture of the kind of world that could be achieved. Then it turned out that the world for which the TEA was principally designed did not come into existence when it was expected to.

The Test of the Kennedy Round

A peculiar characteristic of the TEA was that, to an important de-gree, it legislated for a condition that was yet to come. Indeed, the whole idea of "partnership" assumed a partner who did not yet exist and could not be created by anything the United States did. There was nothing basically wrong in being foresighted and at the same time showing that, when a united Europe existed, its relations with the United States would be on a new basis. It was inevitable, though, that when de Gaulle forbade British entry into the Community at the beginning of 1963, many people should conclude that the basis of American trade policy toward Europe had been largely destroyed. This reaction was exaggerated. Partnership was in suspense, or perhaps dead, but trade questions remained. Though few tariffs could be completely removed (because the formula depended upon Britain's being in the Community), the United States was better equipped than it had been for years to negotiate effectively. And it had a clear interest to do so since, even without Britain, the Common Market presented a formidable challenge and opportunity.

The Kennedy Round appeared to many observers to be dominated by negotiations between the United States and the Common Market. The impression may have been exaggerated; had Britain and the main EFTA countries not been willing to engage in serious negotiations, the outcome of the Kennedy Round would have been quite different. Nevertheless, time and again the decisive action, vital to a satisfactory outcome of the whole massive multilateral endeavor, was the agreement between the negotiator for the European Community and the American representative. Even the interest of the other countries in tariff reductions by either the Common Market or the United States contributed to this result since neither of these giants was willing to give the other a free ride, and reductions applied to trade among all the participants.

The degree of liberalization achieved in the Kennedy Round was substantial. The main countries involved reduced their tariffs on more than two-thirds of their imports of manufactured goods and raw materials. Their performance in agriculture was far less impressive (see chap. 8, pp. 257–300). Many of the cuts were the full 50 per cent agreed on at the outset as a probably maximum result. But smaller cuts brought the weighted average down to about 35 per cent for each of the main trading partners. The reduction was less on steel, textiles, and, for the Common Market, pulp and paper and some electronic products in which the American competitive position was strong. Every country had sensitive items that were withheld from serious cutting. In chemicals the basic bargain was a two-stage affair, with one part dependent for completion on the willingness of the U.S. Congress to repeal the law establishing American Selling Price (ASP) as the basis of tariff valuation. Those who thought of the Kennedy Round in terms of the complete removal of tariffs on a number of products that would have been theoretically possible if Britain had been in the Community, or even an across-the-board cut of 50 per cent when that became the maximum, were disappointed in the results. Those who assumed that the results of any negotiation would fall well below the possible maximum were pleased with what was undoubtedly the largest all-round tariff reduction of the postwar period (and probably the largest in history).

The Kennedy Round also proved something about the European

Community's place in world trade. Though statesmen of the Six had repeatedly professed their interest in the expansion of world trade and said the Community would be "outward looking," doubts had persisted. Producers were still adjusting to rapid reduction of tariffs on trade within the Community. Because the common external tariff was an average, some producers (usually French and Italian) had already lost some of their protection against competition from the rest of the world and would resist going further. Though other advantages might be gained later, the immediate concrete reward for member countries was a preferred trading position in the others' markets. The Community's new farm policy was markedly protectionist. All these factors cast doubt on the willingness of the Six to make important tariff concessions to the rest of the world. Hence the Kennedy Round was regarded by many people (inside as well as outside the Community) as a test.

In my opinion, the Common Market passed that test so far as industrial products are concerned. It appears to have done as well as the other major trading countries, and that is the only tenable criterion. No doubt, if the Six had been willing to reduce certain tariffs further, others would have been willing to reciprocate and the total liberalization would have been greater. But that is also true of the United States and other countries. I know of no evidence that the Common Market established the lowest common denominator more often than other countries. No doubt some duties were not reduced because one member or another of the Community was adamant, even though the others wanted or would have agreed to its reduction—for example, aluminum. But there must also be cases in which, as part of an internal bargain, a member agreed to a reduction it would not have made if it were acting independently. At a minimum, and put negatively, the Kennedy Round showed that the Community is not dedicated to protectionism in manufactured goods to a degree beyond the average for the industrial countries of the free world. Putting the matter positively, one is justified in supposing the interplay of protectionist and liberal forces within the Community will permit it to take part in future trade negotiations on an even basis with other countries.

It would not be correct, though, to conclude that the Kennedy Round showed that the Common Market can be thought of as a unit comparable to individual industrialized countries so far as future trade policy is concerned. On the contrary, the fact that the Commission, while negotiating with the rest of the world for the Community, had to negotiate with the member governments at the same time about what to say to the rest of the world was a source of awkwardness and difficulty in the Kennedy Round. Procedurally this situation made for delay, complication, and sometimes the inability to strike a bargain at the psychological moment with the fair assurance a strong national negotiator would have of being backed up at home. Substantively it meant that decisions worked out with difficulty among the Six became fixed positions rather than bases for negotiation which could be altered in the interest of making an advantageous bargain. Maybe these things were more troublesome in the Kennedy Round than they will be in the future because it came at a time when the common external tariff was not fully in effect, when the Commission's power had been checked, and when the assent of all members was needed for tariff changes (whereas in the future majority voting is supposed to govern), and because it was the first time. It cannot be taken for granted, however, that by the time of the next trade negotiations the Community will be so cohesive that its members will find it much easier to agree on positions and alter them flexibly, or so clear about their common economic interest that each will accept what it regards as a nationally disadvantageous tariff reduction without seeking compensation in another part of the tariff structure. Moreover, if future trade negotiations cover more subjects than tariffs, as they almost certainly will (see chap. 5, pp. 117–73), there will be further complications unless the Common Market has made great strides toward the establishment of common policies on matters still principally under national control (like many nontariff barriers).

One could speculate long on such matters. Some judgment about them is necessary to the shaping of future American policy. However, they are best seen not in isolation but as part of the whole complex of issues that has to be taken into account in considering American policy toward the Community in the coming decade, a matter to which we return in chapter 9.

DIVIDED EUROPE

In the end no monument to partnership, the Kennedy Round was nevertheless a major landmark in American trade relations with Europe. Though many of the key bargains were between the United States and the EEC, the other nations of Europe were also major participants, and the results were significant not only for trans-Atlantic trade but for trade within Europe itself. Posing new problems in the first instance for Western Europe, the division of the area into two trading blocs has a bearing on American interests as well.

Though one might argue about the extent to which the Europe of the Six was a "natural" unit, shaped by geography, history, economics, culture, and postwar politics, such a contention about EFTA would not detain one for a moment. The three Scandinavian countries have natural affinities and their economic ties with the United Kingdom are strong, but the grouping of these four countries with Portugal, Austria, and Switzerland was simply a response to circumstances. After the refusal of the Six to form a larger European free trade area, the Seven created EFTA for two main purposes. By stimulating trade among themselves they could gain some material compensation for their exclusion from the Common Market. They hoped, also, to strengthen their position for future bargaining with the Six.[5] This was to be achieved not by making EFTA a single negotiating unit but by putting the Common Market countries at a disadvantage in EFTA markets and so giving them an incentive to negotiate. If this strategy was successful, EFTA might well cease to exist. *Naître pour mourir*, was a Swiss characterization of the situation.

Though agricultural products were dealt with only by special arrangements, the EFTA countries eliminated tariffs on manufactured goods a bit more rapidly than the Common Market did. Trade within the group increased greatly. Useful but limited work was done on other kinds of trade barriers and national practices that affected the conditions of competition. An arrangement that freed trade with Finland was helpful to that country in its difficult spot between Russia and the West. Iceland joined EFTA in 1970. Ireland, though it did not become a member, made a free trade arrangement with the United Kingdom, its principal trade partner. Britain, the most important country in EFTA, created problems for the others when to help deal with its troubled balance of payments in 1964 it imposed import surcharges without consulting them. It had also caused trouble earlier by seeming to give its EFTA relations little weight in its first effort to gain entry to the Common Market. The failure of that effort injected some new life into EFTA, but by the time serious negotiations began again, late in the decade, Denmark and Norway were as quick off the mark as Britain in seeking membership.

Whether the European Community is enlarged by the inclusion of Britain or other countries is a matter of considerable importance to the United States and so are the future relations of the Community, enlarged or not, to the European countries that stay outside it. These subjects are touched on in several places later in this book and then

5. Britain had the added motive of avoiding further discrimination against itself that might result from arrangements between some of the smaller countries and the Community.

the strands are drawn together in chapter 9. Before then more will have been said about the impact on the United States of the dual development of postwar Western Europe: its turnabout from weakness to economic strength and its partial integration. And more than once it will be necessary to ask what difference it would make if the European Community comes to act as a unit in matters other than trade. Thus far the Community has done that only in agriculture. To the resulting problems no solutions have been found, and friction with the United States is increasing.

In monetary affairs, the impact of Europe's accretion of strength was, if anything, greater than in trade and felt sooner. The shift from the dollar shortage of the '40s to the dollar plenty of the '60s was massive. Free to disregard its balance of payments at the beginning of the period—and, indeed, happy to see gold move to Europe because that would make the international monetary system work better—the United States became with the passage of time a country inhibited as others had been by a concern with the deficits in its transactions with the rest of the world. Internationally the process of adapting to this change led to the development of a degree of cooperation, often informal and *ad hoc*, not matched in other fields, but the cooperation was marked by friction and strains of a high order. Several of the Common Market countries played central roles in the process, but they did not act as a unit. Differences in their relations with the United States and differences in view about what ought to be done contributed to the divergence, and the fact that among themselves they had not achieved the same degree of integration as in trade matters was crucial. Nevertheless, they gained power and responsibility, which they are not likely to lose as the international monetary system evolves further. Relations that were never simple have grown more complex.

High on the agenda of the post-de Gaulle Community is the question of monetary integration. The possibility that it will be achieved is one the United States has to take into account. Even partial steps in that direction might have significant implications for the international monetary system of the future. But the United States has also to be prepared to deal with a Common Market that remains divided in these matters. The same is true of European policies toward American investment and the closely related efforts to foster more scientific research and technological development in Europe, nationally and by international cooperation.

Whether the Europe with which the United States has to deal in the '70s is one or many—or different for different purposes—it will be far stronger than the Europe of the '40s and '50s. This is what the

United States wanted when it committed itself to the Bretton Woods world picture, launched the Marshall Plan, proposed NATO, supported European integration, and began in the Kennedy Administration to talk of partnership. At the beginning of the '70s, some Americans are questioning the wisdom of some of these decisions, but they cannot undo them. Still, some choices remain open to the United States. For more than two decades the United States has been adapting its policies to changes in Western Europe's position and the resulting shifts in the world economy. But have the adjustments been as great as the changes require? Is the United States prepared for what may yet come?

The Old World and New Problems

The American decision that a strong, independent Europe was preferable to one that was weaker and more dependent on the United States meant that, if the aim were achieved, the time would come when the United States and Europe might differ seriously on important issues. How could it be otherwise? No matter how much confidence one has in the basic commonality of interests and the durability of close relations based on history, culture, economics, and security, it is inevitable that between two or more complex societies there will be some conflicts of interest, some differences in view as to how problems should be treated, and some differences in behavior arising from the fact that each government responds to a different electorate and a different set of pressures and priorities.

In a broad sense, the structure of international economic cooperation set up at the end of the war took account of these elementary facts. It provided not only principles of behavior, rules of conduct, and a set of organizations, but also means of settling disputes, reconciling or compromising interests, and making possible adjustment to changed circumstances. It was a premise of American policy that that machinery would not work well unless Europe were well enough off economically to play a full part in it. By the '60s that condition was largely met. And, as we have seen, the most visible result is not the easier solution of old problems but the appearance of new ones. Some old, or continuing, problems take on a new appearance, or at least there is a shift in priorities, emphasis, or the balance of interests to be satisfied. The existing framework of rules and organizations may well not be able to function as it did before when it has to accommodate changed participants, notably a stronger, more autonomous, and partially integrated Western Europe. And if integration goes further, still other problems will arise.

Some problems are predictable, some not. The chapters that follow deal with some that are discernible, especially those that stem directly from the removal of old obstacles to trade and the flow of money and from the intensification of economic relations among the industrial countries. It is certain, though, that still others will arise simply because two major complexes of political and economic power occupy opposite shores of the Atlantic. Moreover, not all problems can be resolved by trans-Atlantic cooperation. Japan has become so strong an industrial and commercial power that its participation is essential to the satisfactory handling of an increasingly wide range of issues. Nor is it possible for even this enlarged group of industrial countries to ignore the effect of their actions on the rest of the people of the world, who outnumber them.

3

Japan: Problems of Change

When Americans get fretful about their relations with Europe—when they are annoyed by a de Gaulle, outraged by a trade dispute, frustrated by lack of support for what they consider a common effort— then they are apt to feel that their own government makes too much of Europe. It is a familiar reaction in American history and has something to do with the question whether the people who left their homes and made America really turned their backs on Europe, and also with such matters as the frontier, isolationism, and a possible manifest destiny in the Far East; there are lineaments of it in the Farewell Address, the Monroe Doctrine, and the vision of a hemispheric New World radically different from the Old. Something similar made the debate in the Second World War about giving the European Theater of Operations primacy over the Pacific more than a purely strategic or logistical discussion. The feeling waxed and waned as "the China question" rose and fell in its impact on American opinion and became denser in the atmosphere as the war in Vietnam dragged on with little help and much condemnation from Europe.

Less marked, less emotional, but sometimes clearer, the same attitude can occasionally be discerned in criticisms of American foreign economic policy. An "obsession with the Common Market" has been thought by some to blind the United States to its true broader interests. But if less emphasis is to be put on Europe, where should more emphasis be put? As a rule the critics of economic policy were not championing some other part of the world, but rather a line of policy that put less stress on "strengthening Europe" and more on creating the kind of multilateral world envisioned in 1945. A less widely held view is that if the Europeans are going to subordinate almost everything else to their own integration, the United States might do well to seek some partners of its own. Another form of the argument is simply that the preoccupation with the striking economic growth of the Common Market in the '50s and '60s may blind Americans to the true pattern of their foreign economic interests. For this last contention there is some statistical evidence.

American trade with Canada has long been greater than that with all the Common Market countries put together. Japan is the second largest market and supplier, far behind Canada but still well ahead of the United Kingdom and Germany, the contenders for third place in both exports and imports. But the European Community taken together is a good bit more important than Japan alone, especially for American exports. If you add Britain and the other countries of Western Europe to the Community (as an indicator of what a fully integrated Europe might be), you are dealing with just about one-third of U.S. exports in the late '60s, a little more than went to Canada and Japan up to 1968 and a little less than they took in 1969 and 1970. While the European share declined slightly from the beginning of the decade to the end, the shares of both Canada and Japan increased from just over one-quarter in 1960–61. On the import side, the share of Japan and Canada in U.S. imports has risen from about 30 per cent at the beginning of the decade to 40 per cent at the end, compared with 30 per cent or a little less that has quite consistently come from Western Europe.

Direct investment presents a somewhat different picture. Though there is again a rough balance, Japan plays a minor part in it. Canada is once more at the top of the list with $22.8 billion of U.S. direct investment at the end of 1970, almost 30 per cent of the total. Britain, in second place, had only a third as much, followed by Germany and France. Japan was well down the list with $1.5 billion, 1.9 per cent of the total, about the same as the Netherlands or Belgium and less than U.S. holdings in Australia and several Latin American countries. American investment in the six countries of the European Community taken together came to $11.7 billion, more than in Britain but only half the amount in Canada. The total for all Western Europe was, at the end of 1970, $1.7 billion more than for Canada. But the big difference was in rates of growth. Over the decade, Canada's share in American direct investment fell somewhat while that of Europe as a whole increased by half. Japan's rate of increase was even greater, but the total amount remained small. In another financial dimension, however, Japan was much more important to the United States. During most of the '6os, transactions with Japan provided by far the largest entry in the accounts showing the annual movement of American short-term claims on the rest of the world. Often the figure was well over 40 per cent. Most of the time it registered a net flow of American capital to Japan, principally in the form of bank lending.

It may seem odd to look at figures this way, adding Japan and Canada and comparing the totals with those for a nonexistent "Western Europe" in which EFTA and the Common Market are treated as if they were part of the same thing. But there is a point, the one that emerged most clearly from the first trade figures cited: though Europe looms large in the foreign economic relations of the United States, so do Canada and Japan. They are most of the rest of the industrialized world outside the Communist sphere.[1] Different as they are, the relations of Japan and Canada to the United States have certain things in common which are different from the key characteristics of American relations with Europe. The implications for American policy of having to take account of these different sets of relations is a matter to which I shall return after separately examining American relations with Japan in this chapter and with Canada in the next.

New Japanese Dimensions

In his speech of May 8, 1947, foreshadowing the Marshall Plan, Dean Acheson linked Germany with Japan as "two of the greatest workshops" of the world, which would need rebuilding if the world economy was to function well. Not nearly as important in this respect as Europe, Japan was, nevertheless, a source of manufactured products and technical skills, a major market for food and raw materials, a country that should be capable of making its own way in the world. The American aim was not, however, to put Japan back where it was in the years that led to Pearl Harbor. Tokyo was no longer to rule over Korea, Taiwan, Manchuria, or build its economy on the domination of other areas. Confined to its home islands, Japan would be more dependent than before on foreign trade. Stability and growth, perhaps even peace, would depend on Japan's fitting into a world trading system better than it did before.

As in the case of Western Europe, the nearby expansion of Communist power sharpened the U.S. interest in Japan's welfare and

1. Australia and New Zealand are somewhat special cases not separately treated in this book but touched on at various points.

made its recovery most urgent. Communist domination of China's mainland and Soviet power at Vladivostok made a strong Japan essential to security in the western Pacific. But the strength was not to be in Japanese arms. Military power in that part of the world was to be supplied by the United States. Behind the American shield, the Japanese were to build a self-sustaining economy with American help.

As in Europe, American aid proved essential, but there were big differences from the Marshall Plan. Economic cooperation with neighboring countries was a matter for the future; there was no question of Asian integration. Until 1952, aid to Japan was closely tied to the policies of the United States as the occupying power. By the time the Japanese regained full control, aid was less important as a source of dollars than were American military expenditures, which had increased substantially during the Korean War. These dollars were not given, they were earned; the goods and services the Japanese provided to American troops were (to an economist) "exports" which, moreover, did not press into world markets in competition with American and European products. Some of Japan's imports of foodstuffs continued to be covered by the easy payment provisions of American legislation for disposing of surpluses; cotton and coal were bought against short- and medium-term dollar credits from the Export-Import Bank. Some American aid funds reached Japan when other countries used them to buy Japanese goods. Japan became one of the biggest borrowers from the World Bank. Private capital, too, flowed in as Japanese recovery proceeded, much of it in the form of U.S. bank loans and the purchase of Japanese government bonds.

The growth of Japan's economy has been rapid and impressive. The gross national product showed a ninefold increase, at an annual rate of 14.7 per cent (at current prices), between 1954 and 1970. Even at constant prices, the annual rate of increase between 1954 and 1970 was 10.3 per cent. The expansion of exports was an essential part of the process. They rose very greatly, from $1.6 billion in 1954 to $4 billion in 1960, and $19 billion in 1970. The increase—faster than that of any other sizable country in the world—moved Japan from tenth in the ranks of non-Communist exporting countries in 1954 to fourth in 1970. That during the '70s it will come into third place after the United States and Germany is confidently assumed by Japan's economists. To explain just how this phenomenon occurred is not our present task, but some of its implications for the trade policies of the United States and other Western countries are of major importance. Trade is only part of the story, but it provides the sharpest focus because from the outset basic policy questions were raised that required different answers from those given before the war. The record is one of substantial progress and present uncertainty, which poses important problems for the future with implications for a wide range of international economic relations.

JAPAN IN WORLD TRADE: THE PAST

Between the two world wars, Japanese competition was a familiar problem in world trade.[2] Relatively late industrialization, the development of an indigenous economic and political base without major resort to foreign capital, the associated growth of military strength, and the acquisition of naval power on a scale new for Asian countries, all helped to heighten Japan's impact on the unstable world economy of the '20s and the depression-dominated one of the '30s. Low prices, the ability to deliver large quantities rather quickly, a certain adeptness in meeting demand with reasonable facsimiles of Western products, and a good deal of enterprise in the conduct of business were major elements of what was sometimes thought of as Japan's commercial threat to the West. Linked to those factors—as a source of real concern for some and just a rallying cry for others—was the belief that low wages were the source of the low prices of Japanese goods. And behind that was the troublesome picture of crowded islands with a rapid increase in population providing cheap labor and permanent unemployment. The workers of Europe and North America were held to be threatened by something like the export of low oriental living standards, "social dumping" in the slightly formal phrase. The teeming population pressing on meager resources of food and raw materials made it seem likely that the Japanese drive to export would continue to increase. Racial feeling and, at least in the '30s, political hostility added fuel. A reputation for shoddiness should, in a rational world, have been thought to reduce somewhat Japan's commercial challenge. Instead it added to the sense of cheapness and unfair competition and the feeling that Japan was an outsider who could be treated under a double standard.

Neither the defeat of Japan nor the plans for the rebuilding of a postwar world trading system provided a guarantee that history would not repeat itself. The decision to make a conciliatory peace and give the Japanese responsibility for their own political affairs and economic welfare made it plain that the rest of the world, especially North America and Western Europe where the largest markets lay, would have to expect renewed competition. If Japan was to pay its way in the world, the other industrial countries would have to absorb

---

2. The matter of Japanese emigration, also of concern in that period, has not reappeared as a postwar problem.

large amounts of Japanese goods. Naturally enough the United States had to take the lead in the process of opening doors to Japan. It became not only the pace setter in accepting Japanese goods but something like Japan's advocate before Europe and eventually its sponsor in the cooperative associations of the free world.

Both in its exercise of occupation responsibilities and afterwards in pursuit of policies that would make Japan economically viable, the United States treated imports from Japan more liberally than might have been expected from the prewar record. The process was not always smooth, however. The escape clause in American trade legislation was invoked to raise tariffs on some Japanese goods. The use of "voluntary" export quotas was foisted on Japan, first for textiles, then for other products, to stem not only the flow of goods but the tide of American protectionism as well. The United States was the moving force in the restrictive international cotton textile agreement of the early '60s and by the late '60s was calling for its expansion to products made of wool and synthetic fibers, all important Japanese exports. In its greatest trade initiative—the Trade Expansion Act of 1962—the United States employed a formula that seemed calculated to avoid having to remove tariffs entirely on Japan's principal exports, in contrast to what could be done about goods exported mainly by Europe and the United States. Nevertheless, Japanese exports increased tremendously during the postwar period and more rapidly to the United States, by far Japan's largest market, than to the rest of the world.

Canada, too, was a relatively open though much smaller market for Japanese goods, but sales to Europe developed more slowly. Japan became a member of GATT in 1955 (after being a provisional member since 1953), but most European countries did not extend most-favored-nation treatment to Japanese goods until 1963 or 1964. Even then, Japan was not really put on an equal footing. A number of European countries kept quotas on Japanese products that they imported freely from one another or from the United States. Other quotas were removed only when Japan promised to limit its exports of certain products to European markets, thus extending and formalizing the restrictions first applied informally in trade with the United States.

The limits to Japan's full participation in trade liberalization are not just those imposed by other countries. Japan, too, is a laggard. Although much food and many raw materials come into Japan duty-free, some segments of agriculture are highly protected. There are tariffs on most manufactures, including those which Japan exports in great quantity, and many quantitative restrictions as well. The protectionist tradition is strong and there is less evidence in Japan than in the Western industrial countries of strong domestic interest in tariff reduction. When Japan removed a substantial number of its import quotas in the early '6os, it sometimes increased tariff rates. Coming late to GATT, Japan had been exposed to fewer of the successive rounds of tariff bargaining than the other industrial countries. Consequently, the Kennedy Round became an important test.

Right at the outset the Japanese produced a long list of "exceptions"—products which they were not prepared to subject to the across-the-board tariff cut which it was hoped would result from the elaborate negotiations. Though later shortened, the list led to a reduction in offers by other countries. When the bargaining was over, the Japanese performance compared reasonably well with that of the other major trading countries. A weighted average of tariff reductions on most dutiable nonagricultural goods shows a cut of 39 per cent for Japan, the same as Britain's and slightly more than that of the United States and the European Community.[3] With the cuts fully in effect, the Japanese tariff on manufactured goods averaged 10.7 per cent, not very different from that of the other industrial countries. Before the Kennedy Round about three-quarters of Japan's tariff rates on nonagricultural products fell between 12 and 25 per cent; afterwards the comparable bulge was between 5 and 15 per cent.

The American negotiators were not at all sure that they could strike a balanced bargain with Japan in the Kennedy Round. Although the United States had rather consistently sold more to Japan than it bought there, almost half the American products entered Japan duty-free while Japan sold twice as much in dutiable manufactured goods to the United States as it bought there. Though difficult bargaining brought substantial results, there was some indication that tariffs were reduced less on Japanese-American trade than on trade between the United States and Europe.[4] However, both partners declared them-

---

3. Ernest H. Preeg, *Traders and Diplomats: An Analysis of the Kennedy Round of Negotiations under the General Agreement on Tariffs and Trade* (Washington: Brookings Institution, 1970), Ch. 13, Tables 1 to 4. Definitions and weighting are given in the source. Figures in the following paragraphs come from these and other tables in Chs. 13 and 14.

4. The United States reduced tariffs on 79.4 per cent of its dutiable imports from Japan compared to 84-90 per cent of imports from the Community and Britain. Only two-thirds of these rates were cut in half, compared to over 85 per cent of the others. Japan reduced tariffs on 68.6 per cent of its dutiable imports from the United States while Britain and the Common Market made reductions on 86.5 and 92.5 per cent respectively. However, 87.6 per cent of the Japanese cuts were 50 per cent or more, compared with 35.4 per cent of Britain's and 51.7 per cent for the Common Market (not including further cuts that would be made if the United States eliminated ASP). The figures take no account of commitments to continue the duty-free entry of some products, which cover a substantially larger share of Japan's imports from the United States than of Europe's.

selves satisfied. The United States expected to gain from the substantial cuts Japan made in its chemicals and machinery duties; Japan benefited from American concessions on a wide range of goods even though the reductions in steel and textiles in which it was especially interested fell well below the average for manufactured goods as a whole.

Export and import quotas limit the usefulness of such comparisons. Nevertheless, the reduction of tariffs resulting from Japan's participation in the Kennedy Round seems not to have been vastly different from that of the other major countries. In spite of inhibitions and reservations on both sides, Japan was, for the most part, treated as an equal partner with the other major trading nations in the negotiations. For example, its representatives sat in a small steering committee headed by Eric Wyndham White, the Director General of GATT. This formal equality coupled with something less than equal participation in substance symbolizes the central feature of the next stage of the problem of how Japan is to fit into the world trading system.

JAPAN IN WORLD TRADE: THE FUTURE

In the course of the first UNCTAD conference in Geneva in 1964, as the division between the developed and less developed countries grew sharper, Japan was asked not to attend the Asian caucus and consequently was omitted from the key drafting group. The "news from Geneva was something of a jolt," said a leading Japanese economist, and reached the front pages when the leader of the delegation was called back to Tokyo to report, and presumably to get new instructions.[5] Perhaps that is what Japan as a whole is receiving as a result of the changes in its own economy and in its relations with the world economy: new instructions on how to behave as an advanced industrial nation. The counterpart of Japan's ability to act on these new instructions is the willingness of the other industrial nations to accept Japan as one of them and treat it as an equal.

Part of the difficulty on both sides stems from the speed with which Japan's position has been changing and the inevitable incompleteness of the change. Faust had two souls in one body; Japan has something like two economies in one country. The response of the world, and to some degree of Japan, too, has lagged behind the shift from the old to the new one.

5. Saburo Okita, "Japan and the Developing Nations," *Contemporary Japan,* June 1965, p. 230. Its importance in world trade was finally recognized by election to the continuing UNCTAD Board from the industrialized group.

In spite of growth and high productivity, Japanese living standards are still considerably lower than those of the main Western industrial countries. While some Japanese production is highly capitalized, mechanized, and automated, some still operates on the tacit assumption that Japan's greatest competitive advantage lies in skilled cheap labor. Within the same industry, work at the frontiers of technology co-exists with factory, cottage, and handicraft arrangements reminiscent of the early industrial revolution.

The direction in which Japan is moving is reflected in the changing composition of exports. Before the war, raw silk, cotton and rayon goods, and a host of light manufactures led the list. In 1954, 40 per cent of Japan's exports was made up of textiles and clothing and 12 per cent of machinery and transport equipment. In 1970, this last category accounted for 46 per cent, textiles and clothing for 12. Within the machinery group, the shift has been away from sewing machines toward ships. A moderate increase in the share of "metals and metal manufactures" from 1954 to 1970 conceals a sizable shift from stamped tin spoons to steel bars. While there are still toys, fans, and artificial flowers, Japan's reputation has become a thing of high quality optical goods, electronic equipment, motorcycles, and giant tankers. Even in such a small category as "musical instruments," pianos have replaced pennywhistles.

Along with the shift in composition has gone a shift in markets. In 1954, the United States, Canada, Western Europe, Australia, and New Zealand took 30 per cent of Japan's exports, in 1960, 46 per cent, and in 1970, 55. Asia's share—including the Middle East—fell between 1954 and 1970 from 49 to 31 per cent and Latin America's from 13 to 6 per cent.

More and more the pattern of Japan's exports looks like that of other highly industrial countries. That, of course, is part of the problem: a great surge of competitive products into the markets of the Western industrial countries. The other part of the problem is that the new pattern of Japanese exports does not leave the old one entirely behind. Though the share of such things as textiles and clothing in Japanese exports has fallen, total exports have risen so rapidly that Japanese sales of these products are larger than ever. The new reputation for quality has not eliminated the fact that many Japanese goods are still much cheaper than those produced in the United States or Western Europe. So old trade complaints about competition in consumer goods do not disappear, while the surge of heavier products, not least steel, creates new ones.

There is no doubt about the direction in which Japan is moving, and at a rapid pace. Full employment and sometimes labor shortages combine with a rise in wage rates of nearly 50 per cent from 1966 to 1969. Increases in productivity have not kept pace[6] and, while Japan may have far to go before it becomes a high-wage country, it is clearly on the way. Already Japanese exports have lost ground to transistors and light machinery from Taiwan and Hong Kong, plywood from Korea, along with textiles, toys, and simple manufactures from a number of countries.

Nevertheless, it would be unrealistic to suppose that the bogy of "coolie wages" will not continue to influence Western policy for some time. It strengthens the temptation of governments in Europe and North America to continue to treat Japan differently from the way they have come to treat one another, even though the real problem is how to make room for Japan in the world economy whether its trade advantages come from low wages or something else. At one time it could have been argued that a foresighted course would have been for the United States and Europe to shift resources out of textiles and other "labor-intensive" products, leaving the field to the Japanese. That may still be a sound prescription from which the developed countries could benefit, but it is an inadequate prescription for making a place for Japan. That country is now an efficient exporter of a wide range of products which will continue to grow wider. The brunt of future Japanese competition will be met by Western industries other than textiles, and not necessarily declining ones. Sometimes the immediate impact will come from Japan's ability to keep wage increases behind productivity in modern plants, and as long as remnants of the dual economy persist there will be patches of the old cheap-labor kind of competition. But more and more Japan will lose that advantage to countries like Taiwan, Korea, and perhaps India and become itself much more like Western Europe and the industrial parts of the United States and Canada. For those countries, trading more freely with Japan will become less a matter of meeting the old problems of a particular kind of competition and more the sort of thing they already do by extending the area of liberal trade among themselves. Like those already inside the group, the new major industrial producer brings a mix of talents and resources that creates a peculiar set of comparative advantages. Like theirs, its advantages will

6. "In five of the past eight years [to 1969], wage increases have equaled or exceeded increases in productivity. . . ." *International Commerce*, April 28, 1969, p. 16. Between 1956 and 1968, unit labor costs in Japanese industry rose 24.4 per cent, compared to 16.1 per cent in the United States. *Japan's International Economy* (New York: Morgan Guaranty Trust Co., 1970), p. 35. The figures for Germany and Britain are 29.5 per cent and 30.7 per cent. Between 1964 and 1968, however, the Japanese (and German) increase was only 2 per cent compared to 10.5 for the United States (and 13.9 for Britain).

keep shifting over time, so one more moving part is added to the complex of adjustment and accommodation.

That Japan will be easy to accommodate is unlikely. That the Western nations cannot expect Japan to go on for a long time accepting less accommodation than they themselves expect should be equally clear. One need not wave the assorted bloody shirts of Communism, Japanese imperialism, or a pooling of forces with China to make the point; well short of these extremes there are costs and disadvantages to the free world in a failure to provide for Japan the kind of treatment that is implicit in accepting it as a member of GATT, OECD, the Fund, and the Bank. There is no justification for a double standard so long as Japan lives up to the same standards of behavior as other countries. A frustrated Japan will be a troublesome one. Without the full participation of Japan, the advanced industrial world will be operating without one of its major potential assets and will be poorer and weaker in consequence.

On the Japanese side, the accommodation will also not be easy. Japan still relies quite heavily on import quotas. Although many quotas have been removed, they still applied, in 1971, among other things, to high technology products such as computers, other industrial equipment, some chemicals, certain consumer goods, rice, meat, and dairy products. The resistances to further quota liberalization and tariff reduction come not only from private interests but from at least some parts of the government. In some sectors, it appears to be national policy to provide a protected home market as a basis for industrial expansion and export. Where the dual economy exists, inefficient producers are protected, at least until they can be eliminated by domestic measures. In other sectors, Japanese appear to believe that they must reorganize their industrial structure before they can face foreign competition (and Japan is surprisingly uncompetitive in the production of some goods). What appears to Western eyes as close cooperation among businessmen along with complex government-business relations leads to the suspicion that the removal of overt governmental controls will not in itself produce the results that might be expected in a freer market.

Japanese export policies also worry the West. Having made the promotion of exports a major aim throughout the postwar period, the Japanese government has at one time or another resorted to a variety of incentive schemes, tax concessions, cheap credit, and subsidies. The very rapid expansion of productive capacity—sometimes far ahead of planned targets—combined with "stop-go" policies that sometimes contract domestic demand sharply seem to create spurts in Japanese exports of some products which Westerners find unsettling. The government provides "administrative guidance" as to the proportion of an industry's output that should be exported and the share of new investment that should go into export industries. One hears it alleged that for reasons of national strength and prestige the Japanese government fosters the expansion of such basic industries as steel and shipbuilding in ways that subordinate ordinary considerations of profitability. A number of domestic factors, undischargeable labor and a high ratio of debt to equity for example, make it reasonable for firms sometimes to sell abroad at a loss. The separation of home and export markets makes for dumping.

Few countries have clean hands in all these matters. Trade negotiations in the future will pay far more attention than in the past to pricing, subsidies, and a wide range of government and business practices (see chap. 5, pp. 137–73). It is difficult enough to work out acceptable rules about fair competition for countries with similar institutions and fairly transparent business practices. The complexities of Japanese social organization and practice will make the task harder, but there is no escaping freer discussion and fuller explanations of these matters as part of the process of bringing Japan fully into the group of advanced industrial nations. To discard or alter old practices would not necessarily be bad for Japan and some Japanese would clearly benefit.

While the three interconnected aims of freer access to Western markets for Japanese goods, equal treatment for Japan, and removal of Japanese controls inhibiting imports are not likely to be achieved quickly, they do not seem utopian. Pressed further, the trend of the last decade might well prove adequate for an interim handling of the problem. Even if treatment of Japan falls short of equality, it may be tolerable for some time to come provided Japan continues to gain materially (i.e., to get larger markets even if it is discriminated against and has to withhold exports) and there is some progress toward more complete acceptance of Japan. Though exports are very important to Japan, there is a good bit of evidence that the principal dynamics of Japanese growth lie in the domestic economy, especially in the level of investment but also in the expansion of domestic demand.[7] Growing concern with pollution, land use, and the need for more social expenditure may hold down the pressure to expand investment in export industries. Both government and business in Japan have shown

---

7. The ratio of foreign trade to GNP has been substantially lower in postwar than in prewar Japan. It is lower, too, than that of the major trading countries of Western Europe. Such statistics are, however, an inadequate measure of true dependence, which is a question in part of what is imported and what is exported and what alternatives a country faces if it cannot trade at a certain level.

themselves willing to accept a certain braking of exports when other countries felt under strain. Just how fast the progress toward full acceptance will have to be to keep Japan in this frame of mind is a question about which *a priori* judgment has little value; unpredictable circumstances may be of great importance. As Japan comes to feel its true strength more fully than in the recent past, the pace may have to accelerate to be satisfactory. Much depends on Japan's willingness to liberalize, without which one cannot expect too much from the rest of the world.

The export quotas that Japan has been required to impose are bound to have an important place in future trade negotiations. Evading formal discrimination, they remain the major mark of Japan's second-class membership in the trading system of the industrialized nations. While the hypocrisy of these devices is distasteful, it is worth recalling that as "the homage vice pays to virtue" hypocrisy can sometimes be of some help in making progress. Japanese acceptance of export restrictions prevented American imposition of import restrictions that might have been more stringent or have affected a greater range of products. In some circumstances export controls can be more flexible than import restrictions and may be easier to remove when circumstances change.[8] But events do not warrant too optimistic a view. The European practice of formalizing the export quotas in bilateral agreements reduces the odor of subterfuge that arose from the American use of extra-legal understandings but invites acceptance of the idea that export quotas should be regarded as normal forms of trade restriction, a view that might well encourage a spread of their use. The multilateral agreement restricting world trade in cotton textiles gave additional "respectability" to export controls and probably embedded them more firmly in practice than those that had been bilaterally negotiated. The possibility that export restraints might become more rather than less important was increased by events at the end of the '60s and the beginning of the '70s.

The morrow of the Kennedy Round, with interest in trade liberalization shifting to nontariff barriers, seemed a logical time to reexamine the Japanese export quotas. Most of them dated from the '50s and early '60s and might well seem outmoded by the mid-'70s as a result of the rise in Japanese wages and the changes in the structure of Japanese exports. Fear that their removal would lead to sudden "market disruption" would be allayed by eliminating them gradually, by means of annual increases. The steps might well be linked

8. Why this is so is explained more fully by Warren Hunsberger, *Japan and the United States in World Trade* (New York: Harper & Row, for the Council on Foreign Relations, 1964), pp. 234-39.

with the removal of Japan's own import restrictions. In terms of American foreign policy, which took cognizance of the growth of Japan's power and aimed to encourage Japan to take on more responsibilities in the world, it would be highly desirable to get rid of old marks of inferior status. But instead of moving in that direction, the Johnson and Nixon Administrations reverted to the old patterns and asked the Japanese to hold back on exports under threat of having even tighter restrictions imposed on them.

In the case of the Johnson Administration, the product was steel. The State Department asked not only Japan but the European Community to keep steel shipments in 1969–70 to levels (in tonnage) somewhat below those they had reached in the period 1967–68 so that the Administration could resist the pressure of the American industry for import quotas.[9] The Nixon Administration's problem was with textiles. Though imports of cotton textiles were restrained under the long-term multilateral arrangements negotiated at the beginning of the Kennedy Administration, fabrics and clothing of man-made fiber and woolens were coming into the United States in increasing quantities. Having given a campaign commitment to do something about the problem, the President made it a first order of business to try to get other countries to agree to limit their shipments. The first thought was that this should be done multilaterally, possibly even by extending the existing agreement on cotton products to cover other textiles. Foreign reactions were frosty. Washington then concentrated its efforts on Japan, one of the biggest suppliers and a country against which (it would seem) American officials felt they could bring pressure to bear.[10] But Tokyo bargained much harder than ever before, and the Nixon Administration had to start its third year in office without an agreement.

Washington's position was weakened by the unwillingness to go through any domestic or international procedure to demonstrate to impartial judges how much injury had really been suffered by the American industry. The extent of Japanese resentment was a warning that the political costs of such measures of trade policy had increased. When in March 1971 the Japanese industry made an offer endorsed by its government, Wilber Mills, the Democratic chairman of the House Committee on Ways and Means, who had been instrumental in stimulating the offer, called it acceptable. But President

---

9. Something more is said about steel in chapter 5, pp. 147, 169–71.

10. Taiwan and South Korea, also large suppliers, might be thought even more vulnerable to American pressure, but an agreement with them would exercise less leverage on Japan than vice versa. Because of the importance of the textile problem to the present and future of the less developed countries, I have postponed a fuller discussion to a later volume.

Nixon rejected the proposal as inadequate and called on Congress to give him the power to impose quotas. The Administration continued negotiating with other Asian countries as well as Japan. The surcharge imposed on American imports in August and the pressure on the yen exchange rate that followed the suspension of gold payments by the United States greatly strengthened the hand of the negotiators, and in October agreement was reached. Japan undertook to limit its shipments of man-made textiles to a 5 per cent annual increase for three years (using as the base year the twelve months ending March 31, 1971, when imports were at a record height). For woolens the increase was to be only 1 per cent a year. Higher or lower rates of increase were established for a number of categories with very little shifting permitted among them. About the same time, South Korea, Taiwan, and Hong Kong undertook to provide for somewhat larger annual increases of shipments of man-made textiles for five years.

The textile episode (not yet over as this is written) does not encourage the hope that the United States is ready for a new approach to the problem of Japanese export restraints. On the contrary, it is a continuation of the approach of the '50s and '60s—and indeed of the '30s when the first voluntary quotas for textiles were negotiated—of forcing Japan to act by the threat of imposing more stringent American import controls. There are, however, some facts that may force a change. Longer, harder bargaining than in the earlier cases reflected the growth in Japan's strength. The political element in the dispute was greater than ever before, both in fears of how the struggle over textiles might damage other relations and in the American view that Prime Minister Sato had committed himself to deal with the problem when he and President Nixon arranged the return of Okinawa to Japan. The resistance of the Japanese industry to its government's wishes suggested that other countries could not assume that their problems with domestic interests were always harder than Tokyo's. Despite those warning signals, there was little doubt that other U.S. producers—perhaps those making electronic products—would seek the same kind of protection for themselves. Prudence suggests that foresight in trade policy should include an effort to work out some principles about export restraints that would reduce the acrimony of future confrontation, avoid a great growth of restrictions, and perhaps alleviate the pressure for them.

The starting point for a set of principles would be acceptance of the fact that it is understandable, when there are great surges of trade that "disrupt" domestic markets, for importing countries to want a temporary easing of pressure without giving up the continuing aim of trade liberalization. What is needed is time to adjust to changed circumstances. Exporting countries can help gain this time by slowing the growth of exports, and it may be advantageous for them to cooperate in this fashion, especially if the alternative is likely to be unilateral import controls. To accept such a rationale is to accept the principle that the export restraints should be temporary. Ordinarily an understanding would provide for a maximum annual growth of trade over the level in a base period. The question whether adjustment to changing conditions requires a special program of adaptation with possible government help is a matter for the importing country to decide. Since it would be unreasonable to expect the exporting country to wait indefinitely for a process to take place over which it has no control, some form of time limit appears to be the essential ingredient of an understanding. Knowledge of the deadline would itself be a prod to making the adjustment instead of relaxing behind the assurance of protection. These matters are discussed more fully in chapter 5, pp. 151–67.

When possible, such arrangements should be multilateral so that the country restraining exports should not be doubly penalized by seeing a competitor move into markets it has agreed to forgo. More than equity is involved. Even if Japan is more often than others the exporter which precipitates the problem, a broader agreement, like that on steel, can help reduce the sting of always singling out Japan for less favorable treatment than other countries. If these principles were accepted, it would be logical to apply them not only to future difficulties but to a re-examination of existing Japanese export controls in a process that could be linked with Japanese import liberalization. It is not likely that the unwinding of the Japanese controls would be rapid; others might even be added before all the old ones were eliminated. But a new stage would have opened.

Accommodating Japan in world trade will present problems for the other industrial countries for some time to come. The chief need, however, is to continue the process of insuring fuller Japanese participation in all the economic activities that are central to the relations of the industrialized countries to one another and the rest of the world economy. In that way Japan can be helped to move ahead, partly by being subjected to pressure to live up to its obligations (including those which are not laid down in law), while the other countries will have some means of advancing the interest they have in Japan's following the same course.

FINANCE AND INVESTMENT

Though specific problems take different forms, the relation of Japan to the rest of the industrial world in finance and investment has many of the same characteristics as in trade: for the past, delayed entry; for the present, change; and for the future, the need to find a new balance between Japan's potential role on the one side and the way both Japanese and foreigners have been inclined to behave on the other.

It was only in 1964, three years after the major European countries, that Japan submitted itself to the full obligations of membership in the International Monetary Fund, which it had joined twelve years before. Until then it received the special treatment accorded a country not yet able to make its currency convertible. As a member of the World Bank, Japan received thirty-one loans totaling $857 million between 1952 and 1966. Half of the sum was borrowed in the '60s for roads; the rest, spread over a longer period, was mostly for electric power, steel, and railways, with a small amount going into agriculture and other activities. Amounting to 8.2 per cent of all Bank loans, this was a larger sum than has gone to any other developed country. Only India has borrowed more. The fact that Japan's borrowing stopped in 1966 is one of the indications of the change in its position in world finance. Another is that, early in 1970, the Bank of Japan began buying World Bank bonds, and in 1971 there were two public issues of them in Japan.

Thanks to a forward-looking American initiative, Japan was made one of the Group of Ten, a body in which major steps in monetary cooperation and reform were worked out. Already in 1963, before it assumed full obligations under Article 8 of the Fund Agreement, Japan took part in the creation of the General Arrangements to Borrow, the mutual assistance scheme of that group. It made agreements to swap currencies with the United States and others and was among the creditors providing funds in other international support arrangements, such as those for the pound sterling and the French franc in 1968. After joining the OECD in 1964, Japan took part in the deliberations of Working Party No. 3, another key group dealing with monetary issues. Not a member of the Bank for International Settlements until it was readmitted in 1970, Japan, nevertheless, was represented informally since 1963 at the regular meetings of central bankers in Basle. An outsider cannot render a definitive judgment about Japan's part in the secret deliberations of these bodies, but perhaps it is not a bad guess that it was for long a secondary one, not fully commensurate with the size of Japan's economy or its importance in world trade. It has not been easy for Japan to move quickly into the patterns of international consultation that have grown out of North American and European ways of doing things; the style of cooperative monetary diplomacy has been particularly subtle. A certain dependence on the

United States must have been reflected in Japan's approach along with inhibitions flowing from apprehension over the volatility of Japan's balance of payments.

By the late '60s, however, change was apparent. Except for a dip in 1967, Japan ran a strong surplus in its basic balance of payments (current account plus long-term capital movements) from 1965 through 1970. In spite of a number of measures to cut down the flow (such as repaying debts in advance and increasing foreign aid), Japan's reserves of gold and foreign exchange, which had been a bit over $2 billion during most of the decade, came to $2.9 billion at the end of 1968 and $4.7 billion two years later. When quotas in the International Monetary Fund were revised shortly after the introduction of Special Drawing Rights, Japan's quota, which had been smaller than India's or Canada's, was raised from $725 million to $1,200 million.

Looking forward to that action, the Japanese Deputy Finance Minister said, "The issue is really the size and strength of our whole economy."[11] That was certainly true and the point had been emphasized earlier when, in 1966, it was agreed that Japan's subscription to the Asian Development Bank should be the same as that of the United States, $200 million. The continuing strength of Japan's balance of payments had implications for more than aid and Fund quotas, however. Quite a few people argued in 1969 and 1970 that the exchange rate of the yen should be raised as was done with the Deutschemark, the currency of the other largest creditor country. For understandable reasons, not least the high value they put on their strong export surplus, the Japanese were reluctant to consider such a course. When, at the end of 1971, a major realignment of exchange rates took place, the upward valuation of the yen was greater than that of any other currency. During these years, growing evidence of the need of Japan to contribute to the international adjustment process strengthened the case for accelerating the removal of import restrictions. Indeed, learning to live with a strong balance of payments seemed likely to have quite pervasive implications for Japanese economic policy, domestic as well as foreign, since concern for the balance of payments and a certain fear of what might happen to it had been an important ingredient of the old attitude that Japan was a poor, overcrowded country heavily dependent on imports of raw materials and struggling to make a precarious living in the world. With low military expenditures of its own, Japan has gained foreign exchange from the overseas spending of the U.S. Department of Defense and American troops. Only in 1971 was a major public effort made by Washington to find ways of

11. Yusuke Kashiwagi, at a press briefing in Tokyo, quoted in *The New York Times*, March 10, 1969.

offsetting the annual drain of some half-billion dollars in the U.S. balance of payments.

Strong or weak, Japan's international financial position is closely linked to the dollar. In the press briefing already quoted, the Japanese financial official said, "gold is a good thing to have. We are studying how best to acquire it." Perhaps he was reminding the United States of the need to consult Japan in monetary matters since a hunger for gold instead of dollars has not been a mark of Japanese policy. In the 1960s, an average of about 15 per cent of Japan's reserves (excluding SDRs and IMF holdings) were in gold, compared to nearly 30 per cent for Sweden, the next lowest of the Group of Ten, and over 50 per cent for Germany. While Japan probably values the earnings it gets from dollars instead of gold, there can be no doubt that this ratio also reflects a Japanese wish to cooperate with the United States in this country's handling of its balance of payments problem. There are good reasons for this cooperation. Throughout the postwar period much of the capital flowing into Japan—an important factor in strengthening its balance of payments—has taken the form of American bank lending and the purchase of Japanese securities by American investors. Japan has also been by far the biggest borrower from the United States Export-Import Bank during the '60s. Transactions amounting to $1.6 billion were authorized between 1960 and 1970, some 12 per cent of the Bank's total loans. Short-term cotton credits have been an important part of the total, but the Bank has also financed sales of equipment for power plants, steel mills, chemical plants, motor vehicle plants—major growth points in the Japanese economy—and also the purchase of aircraft.

Not surprisingly the United States's imposition of a tax to discourage foreign borrowing in 1963 caused great consternation in Japan. The Tokyo Stock Exchange went into a "Kennedy Slump"; Japan became an important borrower in European capital markets. Later, from 1965 to February 1970, a limited exemption from the tax was provided, and Japan was in some respects favorably treated in subsequent regulations intended to protect the U.S. balance of payments. Not as comprehensive as the arrangements made with Canada either in the exemptions from the American controls or the corresponding commitment about national policies (see chap. 4, pp. 105–106), the treatment of Japan reflected a different relation from that between the United States and Europe.

The last few paragraphs suggest that, if something like a *"de facto dollar area"* existed in recent decades, Japan was certainly in it. The pattern seems to break down, however, when we look at direct investment. But the fact that less than 2 per cent of American direct investment is in Japan does not mean that other countries have closer ties of this sort with Japan. On the contrary, the $1.5 billion of American ownership at the end of 1970 is a very large part of the total foreign holding in Japan. Of all the developed countries, Japan has the most restrictive and cautious policy toward foreign direct investment with the result that the amount of foreign capital at work in the country is probably between one-sixth and one-quarter of that in the major European countries. To the extent that foreign capital has contributed to Japan's remarkable growth, it has largely taken the form of borrowing, by the government, industry, and the banks, and the foreign purchase of Japanese securities. Much foreign technology, which has been important in the postwar development of Japanese industry, has been acquired through patent licenses and various kinds of technical agreements. It has also been brought in by foreigners as their equity in Japanese companies, but with few exceptions they have received only minority participation in return. The wholly owned foreign companies that stud the industrial landscape of Western Europe and Canada, and are increasingly important in the United States as well, are rare in Japan.

The situation is not new. Probably no industrialized country except the Soviet Union owes as little of its development to foreign investment as Japan. From Meiji times, capital has been borrowed abroad more than it has come in as direct investment. The important role of the government in promoting and financing economic development has been one factor shaping that preference. A kind of cultural nationalism, permeating economic life and government policy, is another. Following the common practice of the '50s, Japan established controls over foreign investment on balance of payments grounds. Not knowing how durable Japan's rapid growth might prove to be, foreign companies were often happy enough to limit their risks by providing technology in return for minority participation. Once the scope and strength of Japanese expansion were fully realized and foreigners became interested in getting into the market on a larger scale, they found themselves confronted with a tight set of restrictions.

The rules were called into question when Japan joined the OECD in 1964. Some were in clear violation of that organization's code for the liberalization of invisible transactions; more generally, the restrictive approach contradicted its aims. Under a transitional arrangement, Japan was given time to make adjustments. Since then other industrial countries, and especially the United States, have pressed Japan, through the OECD and bilaterally, to "liberalize" investment more rapidly than it was doing. The Japanese have responded with a few concrete steps and assurances for the future, but progress, at least to foreign eyes, was slow. Like trade liberalization, the liberalization of investment has become a central question of the pace at which Japan conforms to the practices that have grown up among the well-off industrialized countries. In this case there is an even deeper question, whether Japan will in fact go as far along that road as the others or whether it will develop new patterns of its own.

In addition to the factors that create some resistance to foreign investment in all countries (see chap. 6, pp. 188–96), there are some special obstacles to the liberalization of investment in Japan. History is one. The argument that foreign investment is needed for growth can hardly carry much weight. To suggest that the structure of Japanese industry could be improved by foreigners is to inspire caution in those who like the existing arrangements. Where Japanese industry is not fully competitive, the fear is that foreign companies established in Japan will dominate the market. Where Japanese industry includes modern competitive plants and also small, uncompetitive companies —the dual economy—the fear is that foreigners will be ruthless instead of conforming to the internal arrangements by which weaker firms are shielded from competitive pressure. There is talk of the need for "liberalization cartels." While balance of payments arguments now sound hollow (though less so to many Japanese than to foreigners), it remains true that the Japanese method of managing the economy depends on having firms that respond quickly, effectively, and without too much argument to government wishes. Japanese firms are subject to pressures that foreigners might escape. With debts on a scale that alarms Western observers, Japanese companies are far more vulnerable to monetary pressures than firms would be that had easy access to foreign capital. In other matters, too, concern about fitting foreign enterprises into the Japanese system of social and political control seems to be one of the most deeply rooted objections to too much liberalization. As the president of the largest chemical company in Japan put it, for foreign firms to operate within the Japanese system "requires a willingness to accept government guidance, the honoring of long established labor-management practices, and the respecting of agreements among industrial circles."[12]

The strength of some of these arguments should decline as time passes, especially those concerned with the competitiveness and structure of Japanese industry, just as the balance of payments arguments which were once so important have faded. Others will prove more durable. The probable balance is hard for an outsider to assess, and so is the possibility that Japanese businessmen will become a strong

12. Norishige Hasegawa, president of the Sumitomo Chemical Company, quoted in *The New York Times*, May 7, 1969.

force for liberalization, as some of them predict. The direction, if not the strength, of three sets of outside pressures is clear. First, there is the argument of the governments and business communities of Europe and North America that Japan is not living up to the standards of industrial countries or playing the part it should if it persists in an investment policy better suited to a weak country than a strong one. A lack of Japanese response would be bound to color the general attitude of other countries about Japan's future place in the world. They may well link their own actions on the liberalization of imports from Japan with Japan's liberalization of investment. A second economic pressure concerns Japanese investment abroad. Modest in the past, it is growing rather rapidly and will probably continue to do so. Much of it goes to less developed countries to secure control of raw materials and oil for Japanese industrial expansion. Some goes into manufacturing in Asian countries as Japanese labor costs rise. But there are also investments in North American raw materials; and the expansion of manufacturing, assembling, service, and repair facilities seems a natural concomitant of the expansion of Japanese sales in the industrialized countries. If Japan persists in restricting foreign investment at home, it is hard to believe that Japanese investors will not encounter obstacles to their efforts to invest in America and Europe. The importance of "acting like other industrial countries" will take on new meaning.

The third pressure lies in the Japanese economy itself. There is a question in the minds of some observers whether Japan will continue to be able to meet its needs for the latest technology by the tactics that have worked so far. At the forefront of development in many lines and needing to catch up in others, Japan wants the best and latest, not just the patents that will be licensed because they are on the verge of becoming obsolete. Though Japan is itself a source of inventions and innovations, maximum progress depends on getting the right things wherever they are. If foreign companies continue to be satisfied with half shares, because they put a high premium on getting inside the most rapidly expanding economy in the world, the Japanese are unlikely to offer more. But if the bargaining position changes, Japanese may have to yield more often than in the past.

There are those in the United States who think that Washington should not press Tokyo to liberalize investments because it is unseemly, and a little parochial, to insist that things must be done our way. A deliberate choice by a people that knows what it is doing must be respected, even if it denies foreigners a chance to increase their profits. There are others who think it would be dangerous to the stability of the complex and unique Japanese system to introduce too strong a foreign element. There are some forces at work in Europe and Canada that could lead to more rather than less regulation of foreign investment in the future, a development that would make Japan less of an anomaly. But it is hard to believe that the forces that have made for increased interpenetration of the industrial economies, in which investment has a vital part, will be stopped or turned very sharply aside. In that case, the investment question will continue to be high on the agenda of international negotiation with Japan and, in a more fundamental sense, will remain a key part of the process of fitting Japan into the imperfect union of the industrialized countries.

THE UNITED STATES AND JAPAN

The United States has had an especially important part in Japan's postwar entry into the world economy. This relation has been a factor of some importance in shaping Japanese policy, as we have seen, for instance, in regard to monetary matters. Up to a point it is reasonable to view the future in terms of the unfinished business of the past, but the dynamic growth of the Japanese economy is bringing about some important differences of emphasis. As is so often the case where Japan is concerned, those in trade loom large.

Though Japan's trade has expanded in all directions, the United States remains by far its principal market and chief supplier. In itself, this is nothing new. In the '30s the United States supplied about one-third of Japan's imports and was also its largest market, taking about one-quarter of all sales, until it was displaced by the leased territory of Kwantung; even then it continued to take over one-third of Japan's sales outside the yen area. In 1970 over 30 per cent of Japan's exports came to the United States; while American inflation may have made the figure particularly high for that year, it was over one-quarter in every year of the '60s and appears to be increasing. Not quite 30 per cent of Japan's imports came from the United States in 1970; the figure was more than one-third a decade before and seems to be declining slowly and irregularly.

The structure of trade is very different on the two sides. Ninety-six per cent of Japan's sales to the United States in 1967–70 was made up of manufactured goods, with electrical machinery and iron and steel products leading the list at annual sales averaging about $750 million apiece. Roughly $1.2 billion a year was provided by the next three categories added together: textiles and clothing, automobiles, and nonelectrical machinery. Among Japan's purchases from the United States, in contrast, manufactured goods came to only 40 per cent of the total; food, fuel, and raw materials accounted for the rest. The biggest items on the American sales list were nonelectrical machinery, lumber, coal, coarse grains, oil seeds, and scrap metal. The United States has been supplying Japan with 85 per cent of its imports of soybeans, three-fifths of its coarse grains, and over half of its coal, rather as Manchuria once did.

During most of the postwar period, Japan's imports from the United States exceeded its exports to this country, a fact that has been made much of in Japanese policy. But since 1965, the balance has run the other way, to the extent of over $1 billion a year in 1968–70. Inflation undoubtedly contributed and the deficit fell in 1970. Experience has shown how hard it is to predict Japanese trade, but there is no reason to expect a complete turnabout back to the old pattern. In one segment of its trade the United States faces in the Japanese market the problem less developed countries face in selling to the industrialized countries in general. Although Japan is now the biggest market for American farm exports, their rate of growth is likely to slacken as food consumption usually does not keep pace with incomes once a certain level is reached. Raw materials are used with increasing efficiency; the growth of the chemical industry provides substitutes for natural raw materials. There are also some specific factors. Coal is giving way to oil. Cotton, once the greatest American export to Japan, has been in decline for years as Japan buys from other suppliers, as textiles decline in relative importance in Japan's industry, and as other fibers displace cotton. Much of Japan's rising foreign investment is directed toward acquiring ownership of raw materials supplies, more outside the United States than in this country. Negotiations with the U.S.S.R. look toward a large increase in the shipment of Siberian raw materials to Japan. A policy of diversifying sources of supply for foodstuffs may already be affecting American farm exports. Australia presses its claims as a supplier. Japanese aid to Southeast Asia puts a certain emphasis on agricultural development for the Japanese market.

Though bilateral balancing is bad medicine in trade policy, the United States is more concerned about its exports in the '70s than it was in the past. Japanese import liberalization in manufactures is of substantive importance to the United States, not just a matter of principle. It is also important to Japan as an exporter since support for a liberal import policy in the United States is based in part on the idea that trade is a two-way street. Japan's investment policy is also involved. American businessmen are plainly interested in all forms of access to the Japanese market, and Washington has made liberalization of both imports and investment a combined objective of its economic diplomacy toward Japan, beginning in 1967 with the automobile industry.

This brief analysis of American-Japanese trade supports the conclusion reached on more general grounds that, if it is to fit into the industrial world economy, Japan is likely to have to make relatively greater adjustments in its policies in the '70s than in the '60s. Of course the European countries are also involved, but their interest in the opportunities Japan can offer by liberalization is not yet as great as that of the United States. Japan may, however, be able to invoke reciprocity in an effort to make more headway in their markets. In that process the United States cannot play as much of a role as it did in the '50s. It can support Japanese protests against discrimination but has no bargaining power to spare on Japan's behalf. The idea that other countries should "share the burden" of taking Japan's booming exports may not be a very persuasive one to Europeans, but if Japan presses its interest in growing and diversifying export markets, it will be easier to solve American-Japanese problems. In that respect, as in others, both Japan and the United States have a common stake in measures that continue the postwar trend toward greater openness among the industrialized economies and a multilateral approach to their problems rather than one that concentrates on the special relations of certain sets of countries.

The risk that economic relations between Japan and the United States will become more difficult in the '70s makes it important that people in both countries see matters in proper perspective, taking account of how much has been achieved and of their wide areas of common interest. Both countries, for instance, want to see a reduction in the Common Market's trade barriers. Their interests in an international monetary system that is not too restrictive are largely similar. Their financial ties are close and are of special importance to Japan. As is the case generally among the industrialized countries, capital movements of many sorts are growing in importance and sometimes overshadow trade as a source of problems and in potential contributions to welfare. Neither the United States nor Japan could fit easily into a regional grouping where cooperation was more intensified and more exclusive than it can be among the industrialized countries as a whole.

Though many Japanese are interested in some sort of arrangement with Southeast Asia, its possibilities are greatest in enhancing Japan's role in the development process, rather than in providing potential markets for a prosperous export trade. While Australia and New Zealand are of great interest to Japan, no amount of bloc-building would be satisfactory if it led to a trading arrangement that in any way put

Japan at a disadvantage in the American market. The priorities have been summed up by a leading Japanese economist in this fashion. "The best choice for Japan is to expand and free mutual trade with every trading region." If progress in that direction were blocked and world trade further "compartmentalized," Japan would be interested in "measures for expanding trade on an assured basis through establishing the Pacific Free Trade Area or some other alternative." But, "economic integration without the United States . . . offers less incentive for Japan to join."[13] Japanese interest in a Pacific Area including the United States and Canada has in it a certain element of insurance against undue American preoccupation with an Atlantic Area and the fear some Japanese have that, if Europe unifies, most major decisions about the world economy will be made in a trans-Atlantic *tête-à-tête* from which they are excluded. For the United States, though, it is hard to see sensible arrangements with one part of the developed world that leave out another part, and it is there that Japan's real assurance lies (see chap. 9, pp. 321–27).

China has a very special place in Japanese thought and policy. History, geography, and culture pull the two countries together; history, politics, war, and ideology have pulled them apart. In economics there is a certain complementarity that suggests closer and mutually more profitable relations than have existed since the end of the war. Like manufacturers everywhere, Japanese think of the potentialities offered by hundreds of millions of Chinese consumers. The Chinese drive to industrialization creates a demand for capital goods that Japanese think themselves particularly well placed to supply. At the same time, remembering history, many Japanese think of China as a potentially large supplier of food, raw materials, and coal, a possibility on which other analysts cast doubt. No doubt the growth of Chinese industry would increase the possibilities of trade between the countries, especially if Japan reaches the point of being willing to import the kind of labor-intensive products that once dominated its own exports.

Though Germany and Britain have played an important part in the growth of China's trade with the free world in the '50s and '60s, Japan's share is the largest. Even so, results have consistently fallen short of Japanese expectations. On the Chinese side there has sometimes seemed to be a certain lack of interest coupled with the setting of unacceptable political conditions. At its peak in 1970, the exchange of some $800 million (both ways) remained a small share of Japan's

13. Kiyoshi Kojima, "Japan's Interest in the Pacific Trade Expansion," in Kojima, ed., *Pacific Trade and Development* (Tokyo: Japan Economic Research Center, 1968), pp. 169-70.

trade. In all probability the trade will continue to grow, but it is hard to imagine its becoming so large as to substitute to any serious degree for Japan's trade with the rest of the world. Much the same is true of Japan's trade with the U.S.S.R., though the rate of increase may be greater if long-discussed plans for Japanese participation in Siberian development work out as the Japanese hope they will.

American policy has sometimes been blamed for the failure of Japan's trade with China to grow faster. It is doubtful if Washington's attitude has really been a major factor, though at times the Japanese government has probably not pressed as hard as it might otherwise have done to expand the trade with China because the United States frowned on it. But those days are passing, if they are not already over. As the United States moves to end its own bans on trade with China, it can hardly discourage Japan from doing the same. It may be tempted to try, if economic concessions are thought of as instruments of diplomacy. This is not a promising course, however, and would contribute to American-Japanese friction. It would be better if the American posture were one that helped weaken the argument of "dependence on America," which plays so troublesome a part in Japanese politics. The Japanese show no intentions of letting themselves be exploited by the Chinese in trade. Even if they make mistakes, there is no risk of their becoming seriously dependent on trade with the mainland so long as their opportunities in the rest of the world remain as large as they have been.

JAPAN IN THE INDUSTRIALIZED WORLD

By every test, Japan's interest is in taking a full part in the rather open economy that is evolving in the non-Communist industrialized world. And the American interest is in helping that process along. Like most countries, Japan wants to take part on its own terms as much as possible. For that reason, and because the others sometimes find the impact of Japanese entry jolting, there are difficulties to overcome, as this chapter has made plain. In the terms employed in this book, the difficulties are those of adjustment to something like a Bretton Woods world.

Perhaps, though, Japan will, in the long run, want to go in a different direction. The course charted in these pages and those yet to come is a natural projection not only from the economic evolution of the countries of Western Europe and North America, but also from their social and political history and the interplay of ideas, ideals, and interests that have shaped their past and present. Japan shares much of the economic evolution but only some of the other features and has its own strong characteristics shaped by a different history. It has, as Raymond Vernon puts it, a different "social contract." Its mix of the individual and the collective, of freedom and obligation, of rights and duties is different from that of Western countries. Consequently, there are differences, too, in what is regarded as the proper relationship of business and government, labor and management, buyer and seller, and between one competitor and another. These matters change in some respects but persist in others, even in as rapidly changing an economy as Japan's. There are, of course, differences among the Western countries as well in these respects, some of them very important, but there is discernibly more homogeneity than between Japan and the rest.

That Japan will continue to be significantly different from other countries, or from the "Western world" as a whole, is almost certain, but that is no fundamental obstacle to Japan's taking a full part in the new kind of relationship among the industrial states that is taking shape. No doubt Japan will make its own distinctive contribution to the development of that relationship, a constantly changing process. Certainly there are many forces in Japan working in that direction and many Japanese who wish to further it. More and more one hears Americans and Europeans saying, "We must learn from the Japanese." No doubt "we" must, but one may be gently skeptical as to how many of the secrets of Japanese success, even if discovered, can be translated into usable practices in the rather different societies of North America and Western Europe. Again, the persistence of differences is no proof of incompatibility.

There are, in industrial societies, important forces making for convergence. There are, in each nation, major resistances to those forces. How the contest will play itself out is more than one can confidently foresee. Fortunately, a vision of the ultimate is not needed to show that in the foreseeable future, and perhaps a little beyond, there are possibilities for the closer fitting of Japan into the industrialized world that would continue the trends of recent history, promise mutual benefit, and—as is the nature of change—pose new problems.

4

Canada: A Special Relation

The fundamentals of economic relations between the United States and Canada are simple—far too simple, Canadians might say. Two characteristics dominate all others: the closeness of the two economies and their difference in size.

In trade, each country is by far the other's best customer. Since the mid-'60s over one-quarter of American imports have come from Canada while a slightly lower share of exports has gone there. For Canada the concentration is much heavier: over 70 per cent of both exports and imports in recent years. The proportions have been rising, largely as a result of the automobile agreement of 1965, of which more will be said below. By the end of the '60s, the value of the trade was double the level of the mid-'50s. Throughout the century the United States exported more to Canada than it bought there, often much more, until 1968 when the balance was reversed and in 1970 the American trade deficit reached $2 billion, greater than that with Japan.

Financially, too, the relationship is close. A heavy flow of U.S. capital in a number of forms has been a regular ingredient of Canadian economic life. Nearly 90 per cent of Canada's net foreign indebtedness is to the United States, where about 80 per cent of foreign-owned Canadian government bonds are held. Americans provide two-thirds of foreign portfolio investment in Canada and over 80 per cent of all foreign direct investment. In the mid-'60s, Americans controlled over

73

half the capital invested in Canadian mining and manufacturing (and much more in certain industries). Nearly two-thirds of all Canadian private investment abroad is in the United States.

In an area about 6 per cent larger than the United States, Canada has about one-tenth the population. The American gross national product is thirteen to sixteen times that of Canada.[1]

Inevitably this combination of size and closeness spells dependency to Canadians. American prices, interest rates, inflation, and unemployment push or pull the Canadian economy with results which Canadians must cope with in their daily lives and which their government has to take into account in shaping its policies. Almost any broad movement in the United States economy is bound to communicate itself to Canada. Whether the point is thought of in advance or not, major economic policy decisions taken in Washington (and many minor ones, too) have an influence, often great, on Canada and Canadians.

It is not as if Canada or its provinces were like states of the United States. There are tariffs and other barriers to trade between the two countries, two systems of money, credit, and banking, separate fiscal entities, and two fairly different sets of economic relations with the rest of the world. Foreign trade is about five times as important in relation to GNP for Canada as for the United States. Though it is small compared to the United States, the Canadian economy is sizable in world terms. Though GNP per head is only two-thirds to three-fourths that of the United States, Canada has one of the highest living standards in the world and was the sixth largest trading country in 1969. Much of its trade is with the other industrialized countries besides the United States; though the old focus on exchanges with Britain is waning, trade with Japan is growing. Wheat exports to China have been important in some years; there is a marked interest in Canada in developing economic relations with the poor countries. While farm products and raw materials processed to varying degrees remain important in Canadian exports, the share of manufactured goods is growing. While Canada is capable of producing stimuli to which the United States has to respond, the fact inherent in the size and intimacy of the two countries remains. In the conduct of its national policy Canada has to take far greater account than any other country of the impact of the American economy and American policies, whether to counter them, take advantage of them, adjust to them, or decide that nothing needs to be done.

1. By national methods of calculation, the figures for 1968 are $66 billion and $865 billion; by World Bank methods, which attempt to minimize price changes, $51 billion and $801 billion (all in U.S. dollars).

NEIGHBORLY WORRIES

From the time the American colonists failed to persuade the people north of the Great Lakes and the St. Lawrence to join their war for independence and then failed to take Quebec, Canada has been preoccupied with building an economy of its own. First the decisions were British, then those of Canadians governing themselves under the distant sovereignty of London, then wholly Canadian. But a problem that was always central was to tie the country together by establishing a system of east-west transportation north of the border. The horizontal line of development in the southern margin of Canada has always been subject to a strong pull toward markets and industries in the United States that were closer or richer than Canadian centers. The historical problem of what effort to make and what price to pay to orient the flow of resources from the west to Canadian industrial centers in the east, which was dramatized in the nineteenth century by the building of the Canadian Pacific Railway, has been repeated in the postwar period in the discussions about pipelines for oil and natural gas. The growth of the American market for lumber, paper, and metals was welcome, but the perennial problem was how to do more of the processing at home. Agriculture had to cope with twentieth century agrarian protectionism in the United States and the competition of subsidized American farm exports in third markets.

As they sought to industrialize, Canadians debated the right kind of tariff policy. In the pull between a heritage of free trade doctrine from Britain and the demonstration of Hamilton's and List's ideas south of the border, the latter largely won. Though Britain got preferred treatment in return for keeping its markets open for Canadian products, the target of the Canadian tariff was always both British and American industry. One result, especially after the elaboration of the preferential system in the Ottawa agreements of 1932, was that American firms created branch plants in Canada to get inside a tariff wall that enclosed not only the Canadian market but, for many things, that of Britain and most of the rest of the Commonwealth as well. The development of Canadian resources, including the growth of processing, was to an important degree stimulated by American demand and financed by American capital. While all these steps contributed to Canadian development, they also helped lay the foundations of contemporary worries: too much American ownership, too many fragmented industries with units below the size needed for the most economical production, too few exports of manufactured goods to the U.S. market, too high costs as a result of tariffs on machinery and supplies that had to be imported.

The existence of its large neighbor is a constant stimulus to nationalism in Canada. Many of the problems of Canadian policy translate themselves into conflicts between national feeling and economic interest. World War II increased both economic development and the sense of Canadian nationality. It also intensified economic ties with the United States and weakened those with Britain. The feeling grew that Canada should play a part in the world as a middle power with its foreign policy independent of both London and Washington. A fairly open world economy in which goods and money could move multilaterally seemed to provide the opportunities Canada needed to trade widely, continue its industrialization, and look after its own interests without becoming more dependent on Britain or the United States. On substantially all major issues of the organization of the postwar economy, Canada's position paralleled that of the United States. There was intimate collaboration between the two governments in working out the Bretton Woods arrangements, their trade policy counterparts, and the United Nations. Commensurate with their resources, the Canadians aided European recovery, also making a loan to Britain and helping to found NATO.

The delays in building the kind of world economy the United States and Canada were both after have increased Canada's problems. Economic weakness on the Continent, the dollar shortage, and especially the inability of Britain to resume its former place in the world economy pushed Canada closer to the United States. There was no alternative source of capital for Canadian development, especially as Canadian savers seemed to prefer established outlets (often in New York) to newer ventures. In championing Article 2 of the North Atlantic Treaty, aimed at giving the alliance more economic content, the Canadians registered a hope that was to be disappointed. Few Canadians were as enthusiastic as most Americans about European integration. The Community's Common Agricultural Policy seemed even more of a threat to Canada than to the United States, especially if Britain joined the Common Market. Instead of the multilateral world economy they wanted, Canadians saw a regionalism growing in Europe that made them uncomfortable. If they looked in other directions they saw that the Commonwealth, an association to which many of them had long attached great importance, was losing strength and coherence.

Canadians asked themselves whether they were being left alone in the world. As other countries tied themselves to partners by close economic cooperation, Canada would suffer the neglect of the outsider. Must it, therefore, strengthen its ties with the United States? Would that not mean greater economic dependence? Was it compatible with the effective assertion of an independent Canadian policy and personality in the world? If trade barriers were to be removed, could the Canadian economy stand the competition? And even if closer ties with the United States brought economic advantages, what political or psychological sacrifices were Canadians prepared to make for wealth, comfort, and growth?

The basic questions were old ones in Canadian life. During a stay in Ontario in 1880, Walt Whitman noted:

> Some of the more liberal of the presses here are discussing the question of a *zollverein* between the United States and Canada. . . . It is said that a large proportion of the merchants of Canada are in favor of this step, as they believe it would materially add to the business of the country. . . . Those persons who are opposed to the measure believe that it would loosen the bonds between Canada and England; and this sentiment overrides the desire for commercial prosperity. Whether the sentiment can continue to bear the strain put upon it is a question.[2]

The political issue has changed, the economic issue is not being posed so simply, and the division of opinion may follow different lines, but the basic question is much the same now as in 1880, and at other times before and after that date. The history, in a capsule, is that from time to time over more than a century one group of Canadians asserted the great economic advantages of free trade with the United States and then other Canadians rejected the idea, often vehemently, on the ground that the result would be American dominance and perhaps the political absorption of Canada, or that the Canadian economy would be damaged. Always the verdict has been negative,[3] sometimes after a heavy political battle in Canada and occasionally influenced by American *gaucherie*. (President Taft meant to be helpful when he said that approval of the Reciprocity Agreement of 1911 would be a "parting of the ways" for Canada.) In the United States there has been interest in free trade with Canada, but also opposition and often indifference. Politics, protectionism, and ignorance have played their parts, but often a major conditioning factor has been the general acceptance, sometimes tacit, sometimes shouted, of the sentiment with which Whitman concluded the entry already quoted: "It seems to me a certainty of time, sooner or later, that Canada shall form two or three grand states, equal and independent, with the rest of the American Union. The St. Lawrence

2. *Specimen Days* (New York: Signet Classics, New American Library, 1961), p. 220.
3. I.e., so far as free trade was concerned, except for the Reciprocity Treaty of 1854 which provided for free trade in natural products until it was abrogated by the United States in 1866.

and lakes are not for a frontier line, but a grand interior or mid-channel." That is, of course, just what many Canadians fear.

The free trade idea is stirring again in Canada, this time accompanied by a great volume of research, analysis, and discussion, some focused on the liberalization of trade with a number of countries and some on free trade with the United States alone. What has set off this process is not just the general concern about Canada's possible isolation but also a series of specific events and some serious doubts about the adequacy of past trade policies for the future of Canadian industrial development. And, in the classic cycle, economic nationalism has also intensified. It is not confined, though, to a rejection of proposals for free trade. It is far wider and takes many forms. One of its main targets is American investment. Some of its supporters would not be content just to keep the bonds with the economy to the south from becoming tighter; they would like to loosen them, moved by a sense that American influence on Canadian life—and not just the economy—has grown too great.

New Thinking About Canadian Trade Policy

Responding to the old worry about undue dependence on the United States, John Diefenbaker, whose Progressive Conservative Party came to power in 1957, talked of shifting 15 per cent of Canadian imports from the United States to Britain. How this was to be done was never clear and in the event no such thing happened. Perhaps the futility of this gesture helped to clarify some home truths about the Canadian position. Reducing trade with the United States would have costs in welfare and a lower rate of growth that were not acceptable to Canadians. A 15 per cent shift would have meant a doubling of imports from Britain. When the British government suggested that the way to achieve this was to eliminate tariffs between the two countries (except on agricultural products), the Canadian reaction was one of "shock and alarm."[4]

Even if they doubted whether the British were serious about this unexpected gesture, Canadians had to admit that they themselves were not prepared for anything so radical. But a few years later, when the British government decided to seek entry into the Common Market, the Canadian Finance Minister threatened counteraction against

4. *The Times* (London), October 5, 1957. According to a Canadian journalist, "Diefenbaker was so vehement in condemning the idea that he insisted the final communiqué of the meeting not even mention his reaction." Peter C. Newman, *Renegade in Power: The Diefenbaker Years* (New York: Bobbs-Merrill, 1963), pp. 269-70.

"any tampering with the advantages we have in the British market . . ."[5] and Diefenbaker whipped up Commonwealth opposition to London's move. Many Canadians shared these views, but as time passed (and the British did not get in) a rethinking of Canada's problems (and perhaps Britain's) calmed fears. When Britain tried again, there was little complaint in Canada and a general blessing from the Liberal government of Lester Pearson (who had also supported the first British attempt).

The United States did not consult closely with Canada when it drew up the Trade Expansion Act of 1962. While many Canadians realized that part of the explanation for this departure from past practice lay in the unhelpful attitudes of the Diefenbaker government, they were upset to find that the TEA formula for moving to free trade in some products would leave out some items in which they had a strong export interest. Even though in the end nothing came of the formula, Canada found the Kennedy Round rather awkward. In past GATT negotiations, Canada had been able to get other countries to reduce their barriers to its exports while keeping much of the protection judged necessary for its own industries. But tariff reduction across-the-board, as proposed for the Kennedy Round, would greatly reduce the chance to be selective. The talked-of objective of a 50 per cent cut seemed threatening to many Canadian industries, which would lose protection while their high costs, it was argued, would keep them from taking advantage of the cuts made by others. Consequently, Canada became the largest trading nation to exclude itself from the "linear group"—those subscribing to the 50 per cent aim.

Not surprisingly, Canada appears to have made somewhat smaller cuts in its tariff in the Kennedy Round than other industrial countries, though it is not easy to make close comparisons.[6] Unlike the

5. Donald Fleming at a press conference in London, September 23, 1960, quoted by Newman, same, p. 271.
6. Taking trade as a whole, including goods imported free of duty, Canada reduced tariffs on 14 per cent of its imports, compared to 17 per cent in Britain and the Common Market, and 25 per cent in the United States, and 10 per cent in Japan. For manufactured goods (including semifinished products), Canada's figure remains at 14 but the others rise to 28 per cent for Britain, 31 for the United States and the Common Market, and 34 per cent for Japan. F. K. Liebich, *Die Kennedy Runde* (Freudenstadt: Eurobuch-Verlag August Lutzeyer, 1968), pp. 104-11, 198. These estimates are not comparable to those used in chapters 2 and 3, which refer to dutiable goods only. Among other difficulties of comparison are a reclassification of the Canadian chemical tariff, the use of different rates for products in the same category according to whether each item was produced in Canada or not, and the effect of the antidumping laws on import valuation.

others, Canada's reductions were about evenly balanced between manufactured products and foodstuffs and raw materials, partly as a result of reducing or removing revenue duties on tropical products which are mostly imported duty-free by other industrial countries.[7] On goods of interest to the United States, the Canadian record is better. Duties were cut on products making up 30 per cent of total imports from the United States in 1964, which amounts to 60 per cent of dutiable imports. Half the cuts were less than 25 per cent, but there were a number that were 50 per cent and above, and some duties were entirely eliminated. The tariffs left untouched were either low or fell on products not made in Canada.

For its part, the United States reduced some tariffs of interest mainly to Canada, especially on some agricultural products and aluminum ingots, and eliminated low duties on partly processed materials. In addition, Canada got the benefit of the extensive cuts in duties on manufactured goods that resulted from the United States's negotiations with Europe and Japan. *The Financial Post* of Toronto said that Canada was "one of the big gainers" from the Kennedy Round, "winning much improved access into the U.S. market and giving up relatively little in return."[8] But the Americans professed themselves satisfied (as is incumbent on parties to so complex a trade bargain) and presumably other countries, with less at stake in the matter, reacted the same way. Part of the reason for their satisfaction was Ottawa's adherence to the international dumping code, negotiated during the Kennedy Round, which was intended to end a number of practices that had long troubled Canada's trading partners.

After the Kennedy Round, Canada still faced hard questions about trade policy. The industry that grew up behind Canada's tariff walls is extensive and varied. Where it is related to the processing of Canadian raw materials, or, as in the case of the aluminum industry, uses Canadian water power to process imported raw materials, it often has a strong export position. Some kinds of manufactures also do well in exports, but much of Canada's industry has been built primarily to serve the domestic market, which, while growing, is modest in size. A large number of products are manufactured in relatively small quantities without the benefit of long runs on production lines and other

7. One result of the cuts on raw materials, components, and machinery was that "the average level of effective rates may well have been reduced very little." In one-third of the industries out of a sample covering about one-quarter of Canada's Kennedy Round cuts "the levels of effective rates have actually gone up." James R. Melvin and Bruce W. Wilkinson, *Effective Protection in the Canadian Economy* (Ottawa: Queen's Printer, for the Economic Council of Canada, 1968), p.v. Effective rates are explained in chap. 5, pp. 118–19.

8. "Report on Canada," March 1, 1968, p. 39.

economies of scale. Though Canadian wages are below those in the United States, labor productivity, too, has been somewhat lower. High costs have been taken to justify tariff protection, which in turn has increased costs of production.

From this diagnosis a number of Canadian economists and officials and some businessmen have drawn a paradoxical conclusion. They believe that although an all-round cut of 50 per cent in tariffs was more than Canada could swallow in the mid-'60s, the country could cope with and benefit from the adoption of free trade with the United States or, as most of them would prefer, with a number of industrialized countries. To compete with tariff-free imports, much Canadian industry would have to be reorganized; but if free entry to other markets, and especially the United States, were assured, the reorganization would be worth carrying out. Instead of producing a wide range of things for the Canadian market alone, manufacturers would produce larger quantities of a smaller number of products for a market that was continent-wide or larger. The fact that much Canadian industry is carried on by subsidiaries of American companies would make this kind of adjustment easier; most firms would probably find it sensible to keep using their Canadian plants. Canadian costs would go down and the ability to export would increase. A further gain in competitive strength would come from importing machines and other producers' goods or components Canada now makes at higher costs at home. In the process Canada would become richer —but not every part of Canada, and therein lies a problem, since federalism remains a central issue of Canadian life. So runs the argument.

In short, an old idea has again come to life. In new circumstances, and with some different reasoning from that of the past, significant groups in Canada are again talking of free trade—perhaps with the world, certainly with the United States. And once again the idea is rejected by other Canadians as unrealistic, undesirable, or unacceptable. There is no need, for the purposes of this book, to work through the arguments in detail or to guess the outcome of the Canadian debate. But if the Canadians decide they want more free trade in one industry, in a few, or in all, questions will arise for American policy. The issues are not altogether hypothetical; some of the problems have already arisen, and some experience has already been gained.

The Automotive Agreement

If some day there is free trade between the United States and Canada, the automotive agreement of 1965 may look like the great first step toward it. It was not designed that way, however, nor intended as a trial run. It did not rise out of an atmosphere of great good will and the desire on both sides to get rid of trade barriers. Instead the origin of the agreement was an effort to avoid an imminent worsening of trade relations between the two countries. It eliminated tariffs but only freed trade in a rather special sense on conditions quite foreign to the usual idea of liberalization. But it was a major innovation in Canadian-American relations.

Almost all the automobiles, trucks, and buses produced behind Canada's 17.5 per cent tariff were manufactured by American-owned companies. Turning out a wide variety of vehicles for the limited Canadian market, these firms had higher costs than in the United States. They exported some cars and parts to the United States, but Canadian imports of these products, predominantly parts, were over nine times as great as exports in 1964.[9] In that year Canadian exports had already risen in response to an incentive scheme which to American eyes looked like a subsidization of exports. Under American law it seemed certain that the imposition of countervailing duties was only a matter of time. Canada, worried about its trade deficit and wishing to expand automobile production, could be expected to retaliate. While negotiators talked trade barrier reduction in the Kennedy Round at Geneva, Ottawa and Washington seemed on the verge of a North American trade war.

The two governments set about finding a better solution. After difficult negotiations they emerged with an agreement signed in January 1965 which, subject to certain conditions, removed tariffs on trade between them in new cars, buses, trucks, and most original but not replacement parts and accessories. On the American side the limiting provisions are simple, requiring only a provision to be sure that products of other countries do not come indirectly through Canada[10] and administrative agreements to be sure that parts were for original and not replacement use. The Canadian arrangements are more complex. The only ones who can take advantage of the duty-free entry are com-

9. There are some difficulties about the statistics for reasons well explained in an excellent study by Carl E. Beigie, *The Canada-U.S. Automotive Agreement: An Evaluation* (Montreal: Canadian-American Committee, sponsored by the National Planning Association [USA] and the Private Planning Association of Canada, 1970), Appendix E, pp. 157-64. Trade figures throughout this section are taken from the *Fourth Annual Report of the President to the Congress on the Operation of the Automotive Products Trade Act of 1965*, Committee on Finance, United States Senate, November 10, 1970 (Washington: GPO, 1970), which improve on those used earlier. Other figures come from this and earlier U.S. government reports and the Beigie study.

10. A product is eligible for free entry if less than half its value comes from materials imported into Canada from countries other than the United States.

panies producing automobiles, buses, and trucks in Canada, and they must satisfy two conditions. They must continue to produce in Canada enough vehicles to maintain the proportion to their sales of vehicles in Canada that existed just before the agreement came into effect. Moreover, this output must have "Canadian content" (i.e., value added by materials, parts, and labor) no lower in absolute value than the total amount in the base year.[11] These provisions of the agreement were augmented by commitments the Canadian government elicited from Ford, General Motors, Chrysler, and the other producers. In "letters of undertaking" the companies agreed that in each year they would increase the Canadian value added of their output by 60 per cent of the increase in the value of their sales of passenger cars in Canada (50 per cent in the case of commercial vehicles). They also promised that by mid–1968 they would increase their Canadian value added by another Can. $260 million.

It is easy to satirize the result as an agreement to free trade with the assurance that the consequences of free trade will not follow. But there is more to it than that. Two basic ideas are embodied in the agreement. For years Canadians had been studying and debating the possibility of integrating the North American automobile market so that Canadian plants could get the economies of scale by producing larger numbers of fewer models while importing others from the United States at lower cost than if they were produced in smaller quantities in Canada. The elimination of tariffs points in that direction. At the same time, the Canadians wanted to be sure that their country continued to have a significant place in producing for the integrated market. Most analysts thought they had little to worry about, and some suspected that in the natural course of events the Canadian share of the continental output would rise. But there could be no certainty and it was understandable that the Canadian government should insist on safeguards. Those written into the agreement amounted to an assurance that the assembly of vehicles in Canada would keep pace with sales in Canada and that the companies would not cut their expenditures in Canada below the 1964 level (which gave some assurance to the Canadian parts makers as well). But the letters went further. They made it certain that the companies' expenditures in Canada would increase faster than their sales there, at

11. This is a simplified statement which seems adequate for present purposes. A full appraisal of the agreement would require closer attention to such things as the methods of valuation, the application of the ratios to each category of vehicles separately, etc. References to automobiles throughout this section should be understood to apply in most cases to trucks and buses as well though the rules are sometimes slightly different.

least for the time being. This was a step toward another Canadian aspiration: a "fair share" of North American automobile production, usually thought of as a share equal to the Canadian market. Had permanent assurances of that sort been written into the agreement, real doubt would have been cast on whether it would in fact achieve its proclaimed objective of "the development of conditions in which market forces may operate effectively to attain the most economic pattern of investment, production, and trade." However, the letters focused on the three initial years, and, while they caused some resentment in the United States, they did not seem to vitiate the agreement for the long run. In the short run, there was certainly ample room for much rationalization of the industry within the limits set by the Canadian conditions.

The impact on trade was rapid and enormous. Exchange between the two countries of vehicles and parts tripled in two years and in 1969 came to over $6 billion, eight and one-half times the 1964 level of $731 million. The rise was not a balanced one. Though the export of American automobiles to Canada increased greatly, the movement in the opposite direction was much larger. By 1966, the United States was importing more cars (by value) from Canada than it was selling there and by 1969 the balance in favor of Canada was $800 million, even though American exports of cars amounted to sixteen times their 1964 levels.

The smaller trade in trucks and buses followed a similar pattern. Matters were different in parts and accessories, which made up 90 per cent of American automotive sales to Canada in 1964. The great expansion of assembling in Canada led to more than a tripling of imports from the United States and in 1969 the trade balance on these items (including repair parts that were not tariff-free) came to $1.2 billion in favor of the United States, in spite of a relatively more rapid growth of Canadian exports. The result was to give the United States an export surplus in all automotive trade of $96.7 million in 1969—a sharp drop from the $588.9 million of 1964. (A deficit was predicted for 1970.) No one had expected so large a shift or thought that the 1964 agreement would lead to a situation in which Canadian exports of automobile products "far exceeded the combined export values of wheat and newsprint."[12]

Behind these unexpected trade developments was just the kind of adaptation of production that was expected by proponents of the plan. The companies have been producing longer runs of models in Canadian plants, in some cases new ones, and exporting to the

12. In 1968. Bank of Montreal, *Business Review*, February 28, 1969.

United States while importing other models that were formerly produced in smaller numbers in Canada. The commitments made in the "letters of undertaking" were overfulfilled and the Canadian share of the North American market has risen. Employment has not risen as fast as output, which suggests a rise in productivity. These changes in Canada are clearly largely attributable to the agreement; it is hard to judge the impact of the reorganization on the much higher level of production and employment in the United States market.

In 1969 popular car prices were still 4 or 5 per cent higher in Canada than in the United States after allowing for differences in taxes. This was an improvement for the Canadian consumer over the 9 or 10 per cent difference that had been usual in 1964, but suggested that he was still not getting all the benefits of an integrated market. The Canadian automobile worker, however, gained more. The automotive agreement was a signal for the United Automobile Workers, the principal union in both countries, to press for the wage parity to which it had long aspired. It seemed only natural that men doing the same work for the same companies should be paid the same in Windsor as in Detroit, especially if Canadian productivity was about to rise. An agreement reached in 1967 provided for nominal wage parity by 1970, i.e., the same dollar pay, but in national currencies. At the time, the Canadian dollar was worth 92.5 American cents, but when it was allowed to float in June 1970 it soon appreciated to the point at which nominal wage equality became actual wage equality. In the parts industry, however, some wage differences continued.[13]

Formally, the automotive agreement is "open-ended." The access it provides to the American and Canadian markets "may by agreement be accorded on similar terms to other countries." It is hard to know how such language should be interpreted, given the special character of the U.S.-Canadian industry, but the provision is at least a form of insurance that neither party can claim an exclusive privilege by virtue of the agreement itself.[14] The American legislation giving the President power to put the Canadian agreement in effect also gives him power to make agreements with other countries mutually eliminating automotive tariffs (provided Congress does not

13. Labor worries about unemployment resulting from the reorganization of production were met by programs of adjustment assistance in both countries. Less than 0.3 per cent of American workers were declared eligible for adjustment assistance under the program; for Canada the figure was over 11 per cent and loans were approved to help several firms in the parts industry.
14. The suggestion has been made that Mexico, which has a fragmented, high cost automotive industry, might try to follow Canada's path, but the conditions are quite different.

overrule him by concurrent resolution). European and Japanese companies that establish automobile plants in Canada could send their products into the United States duty-free if the Canadian content was high enough. They could not, however, import parts into Canada duty-free unless the Canadian government added them to the list of companies eligible to do so under the agreement. The French, Swedish, and Japanese companies assembling cars in Canada had not qualified by the end of 1971.

The effect of the automotive agreement on third countries is not easy to discern and offers a little lesson in the dangers of looking at trade figures alone. Canada, formerly a modest exporter, leaps ahead of the Common Market countries and Britain to become the United States's principal supplier of automobile products. The United States, which already had the lion's share, moves ahead to provide 96 per cent of Canadian imports of trucks, buses, and parts in 1969. Instead of 32 per cent of the passenger cars in 1964, it provides 79 per cent of a much larger trade in 1969. "A massive trade diversion!" is the first reaction, but of course it is an illusion. The alternative to buying more from one another was not importing from a third country but producing at home. North American production has been rearranged while the old statistical boundary has been kept. European and Japanese cars continue to increase their shares of both markets, if not of "imports." No foreign government has complained of injury, though it would have a right to under the terms of a waiver the United States received from GATT of the rule requiring equal tariff treatment of imports from members.

Canada did not need a waiver because its provisions for free entry do not stipulate that the vehicles or parts must come from the United States so long as they are imported by eligible manufacturers. Although there is no evidence that the United States had any great difficulty in getting the GATT waiver or had to expend significant bargaining power to do so, there may have been hidden costs. Over the years, it has often seemed as if the United States was the country most interested in the principle of equal treatment and most anxious not to have the rules of GATT eroded by easy and frequent exceptions. To some observers it appeared that in the automobile case some countries were almost eager to give the United States its waiver, perhaps with the thought in mind that if they subsequently came forward requesting an exception for a "special" case of some other sort, it would be just a little harder than before for the United States to resist. The alternative course of not asking for a waiver and extending the benefits of the Canadian arrangement to other countries was not acceptable right in the middle of the Kennedy Round when the United States was already heavily engaged in using a reduction in its low automobile tariff as a means of getting a cut in the much higher European and Japanese duties. In many respects the largest question the automobile agreement posed for United States trade policy was whether it was worth the departure it required from the principle of equal treatment. The same question may rise again with regard to other products. The answer will depend in part on experience under the automotive agreement and its impact on relations between the two countries.

Not everything has gone smoothly. When the agreement came up for review in 1968, the Canadians resisted the American suggestion that the need had passed for special arrangements to insure that production in Canada would keep on growing. The targets set in the original letters of undertaking had been passed, but the American companies again gave assurances that they would increase output in Canada. No specific amounts were mentioned, but it appears that the commitment to an annual increase of Canadian value added in relation to sales remains valid.[15] The earlier American interest in expanding the agreement to cover replacement parts and perhaps other equipment does not seem to have been pressed, perhaps because the President did not want to raise new issues with Congress. A partial advance had been made in this matter during the Kennedy Round, when as a result of hard bargaining by the Americans, the Canadians reduced their duties on some replacement parts by 40 per cent and on others by 29 per cent; the lower American rates were cut in half.

In 1969 the State Department initiated further discussions that had produced no visible results by mid-1971. The atmosphere was not one in which farsighted, broad-gauged thinking about the future of the agreement was likely to flourish. The American automobile industry was in a slump. Foreign cars were increasing their inroads in the North American market. Both Canada and the United States suffered from a combination of unemployment and inflation. Disputes about oil and the arctic probably spilled over into the automobile case. The large shift in the trade balance was attracting some unfa-

15. Beigie, cited, p. 103, footnote 12. The parent companies assured the United States government that the new letters from their Canadian subsidiaries did "not constitute new undertakings to increase Canadian value added." *Special Report on the Joint Comprehensive Review of the U.S.-Canadian Automotive Products Agreement,* transmitted by a Message from the President, Document No. 379, House Ways and Means Committee, 90th Cong., 2d. sess., September 4, 1968 (Washington: GPO, 1968) p. 5. If the letters had been otherwise interpreted, the President would have had to make a special report to Congress, and the most vulnerable part of the agreement might have been called into question.

vorable notice in the United States. An intensification of nationalist sentiment in Canada made it difficult for Ottawa to make any concessions to the United States without receiving clear benefits in return, while the main thing the Americans wanted was to make the agreement more equitable by modifying the Canadian safeguards. In Canada, equity was seen rather differently, as requiring some insurance that the weak would not lose out to the strong.

Official statements about the disagreement were restrained. The Americans argued that Canada had come through the three years' transitional period superbly and could now discard its special insurance policies. At best they were no longer necessary; at worst they were unfair and incompatible with the idea that trade and investment should be guided by the market. The Canadians thought that the adjustment was not complete. There was as yet no hard proof of the long-run competitiveness of Canadian automobile production; the speed with which production and trade had increased was a reminder of how fast change might go if it moved in the other direction. Cast in these terms, the argument seemed to be only about the timing of the removal of the safeguards. Some informed Canadians thought their government was taking a much tougher position. While free trade was important to permit rationalization, the real Canadian objective, according to this view, was the assurance that Canada would continue to have a "fair share" of the total North American output. It was hardly meaningful to speak of "the market" determining what was done when the decisions were in fact made by a handful of American companies in an industry noted for oligopoly and administered prices and not immune to pressure from Washington, or from the UAW. There was no reference in the agreement to a transitional period and Ottawa was, in effect, looking for permanent safeguards.

Pushed far enough, such positions could only lead to an impasse and raise questions about whether the two governments realized what they were doing when they negotiated the agreement in the first place. If a breakdown is avoided by compromise, a question would remain about the standards by which the agreement should be judged. By traditional measures of the benefits of reciprocal trade—and certainly any mercantilist-flavored concern with exports—the United States made a bad bargain. It was not as bad as it looked in the automotive trade figures alone; much of the equipment for the expanded operations in Canada probably came from the United States and an increase in Canadian incomes and employment creates a demand for American goods. Since the expansion of Canadian production was largely in the hands of American-owned companies, their increased earnings would help the balance of payments. So far as the American consumer was concerned, it was hard to argue that he reaped important benefits of the sort usually attributed to removing tariffs. But there were clearly gains in efficiency and productivity in the automobile industry as a whole, and, while a good bit of the advantage must have gone to Canadians, it is to be presumed that in so integrated a pair of economies some of the gains would flow into American hands as well. Instead of a conventional trade analysis what is needed is an approach that looks at the agreement as a way of increasing the efficiency of a major industry and so improves the allocation of economic resources. In such terms there are no commonly accepted standards for saying how the national interest shall be defined, but it is increasingly in such terms that foreign economic policy issues may have to be judged in the future (as we shall see from other instances). To be sure the gain to the U.S. automotive industry might not be massive since Canada remains only a small part of its market and productive base. The gains to Canada are almost bound to be greater because it loses the disadvantages of its smallness and obtains the advantages of size. But this result flows from the relation of the two countries and will characterize most arrangements that move toward fuller integration of the two economies.

Americans should be able to accept this disparity, I believe, and refrain from the fruitless attempt to extract a neatly balanced, point-by-point set of advantages from every agreement, provided the direction in which it moves makes sense. What makes the automotive agreement hard to swallow is the belief that Canada has tilted the board by insisting on special conditions that seem to create a privileged position with few, if any, risks. Though political opposition to the agreement in the United States has not been very serious, a perpetuation of the appearance of one-sidedness in combination with a shift in trade that looks unfavorable to the United States could lead to difficulties. The executive branch is in a somewhat defensive position with regard to the agreement since there was a good bit of congressional resentment at having it presented as a *fait accompli* on which legislative action was then necessary. If the supposedly transitional arrangements become permanent, the opinion will grow that the State Department was guilty of either incompetence in its negotiations or bad faith in presenting its case for the agreement to Congress. Such a result could add to the fairly widespread feeling that past American policy has been too one-sided, too much a matter of Americans doing things for other people, which is already making it difficult to shape a sound and farsighted American policy (see chap. 11, pp. 397, 410). Canadians should understand that the effects would be felt not only in their own relations with the United States but in the willingness of the United States to pursue broader aims of liberalism and international economic cooperation.

Americans, for their part, should understand that the Canadian government also has a domestic problem. At a time when many Canadians complain about American investment and worry about the heavy weight of the United States in their lives, Ottawa, through the automobile agreement, is stimulating American investment and making Canada more dependent on the United States market. Though the agreement's short-run benefits to Canada are demonstrable, there can be no certainty that free trade with no other conditions will always work the same way. Consequently, the Canadian government must feel a real need to be able to show that the benefits will continue and that it has a way of influencing the actions of the American companies. Given the disparities in size of the two economies, the fact that the main companies are all American, and the natural nervousness of a small neighbor, Americans, who are not uncritical of the automobile industry, ought not to have too much trouble understanding the Canadian position.

A natural compromise would center on revision of the safeguarding arrangements. One part of the effort should be to reduce or eliminate the kinds of commitments that make the agreement look unfairly one-sided to Americans. At the same time, there should be a clear recognition of Canada's need for some sort of countervailing power that could be brought into play if there were a serious loss of benefits to Canada or if there were reason to believe that production and marketing decisions in the industry were being swayed by pressure from Washington more than from Ottawa. Several different formulas can be devised that would meet these two needs, probably without making heavy weather about the ultimate logical clash between market-sharing and free trade philosophies. Extension of the agreement to some other products might play a part in a compromise, just as one side's concessions in the automotive agreement might be affected by what the other did in some of the other matters under negotiation. That result seemed all the more likely when revision of the automotive agreement became one of the U.S. government's objectives in the trade and monetary negotiations that started in late 1971. From the American point of view, particular importance would attach to the monetary arrangements between the two countries, which, as is explained below, have an important bearing on how the trade balance between the two countries affects the American balance of payments. If no compromise were reached and either country denounced the agreement (as each is free to do with a year's notice), there would be not only a considerable dislocation of production but a serious setback to economic cooperation between the United States and Canada.

OTHER POSSIBILITIES OF FREE TRADE

Since the '40s, Canada and the United States have had free trade in agricultural machinery. One of the biggest producers on both sides of the border is a Canadian-owned company, Massey-Ferguson. Much of its production is in the United States and it exports from there to Canada. But there is also a large Canadian export of combines and other equipment to the United States. As in the automobile case, the arrangement seems good for Canadian productivity and trade. For example, in 1959 "while one-third of the supply of farm equipment produced in Canada was exported . . . , the share for all other machinery was well under ten per cent."[16] Naturally, there has been a demand for wage parity, which, Massey-Ferguson officials have argued, might lead to their building new, more highly mechanized plants in the United States to replace older, labor-intensive installations in Canadian towns more remote from the main markets. Worry about the wage issue in other industries will continue to be a factor in Canadian thinking about free trade and is likely to strengthen the argument for obtaining assurances, like those in the automotive agreement, about what producers (and perhaps unions?) will do, at least in the first few years after tariffs are removed.

At one time or another, Canadians have given thought to the possibilities of free trade in chemicals, electrical goods, tires and rubber products, paper and pulp, several kinds of machinery, aircraft, and the products of a number of smaller industries. All look as if they could benefit by reorganization to supply a larger tariff-free market; none matches the pattern of automobiles in the smallness of the number of producers on both sides of the border and the extent of American control. Consequently, an agreement would probably be harder to negotiate and might not provide such ironclad guarantees of the expansion of Canadian production. It might also do more damage to third countries, making it harder to get waivers of most-favored-nation commitments. A shaking of heads about the impossibility of applying anything like the automotive formula to other

16. H. Edward English, *Industrial Structure in Canada's International Competitive Position: A Study of the Factors Affecting Economies of Scale and Specialization in Canadian Manufacturing* (Montreal: Private Planning Association of Canada, 1964), p. 26. The "arrangement" is not a specific agreement; the two countries moved to free entry separately and at different times.

industries is a common enough reaction in circles where these matters are discussed. Nevertheless, the links between specialization of production, access to a large market, higher productivity, and lower costs are strong, and one day Canadians may propose to free trade in one or another of these industries. Then the United States will again have to face policy decisions comparable to those in the automobile case.

Of course, Canada is interested in other markets as well as that of the United States, and an arrangement that involves a number of countries has obvious attractions compared to one with the United States alone. Much of the Canadian export strength continues to be in products firmly based on raw materials, such as pulp, newsprint, nickel, copper, and aluminum. Canadian diplomats have made plain their government's interest in multilateral agreements to remove barriers to trade in these products, but specific proposals seem scarce. If products are dealt with separately, there may be some question about the *quid pro quo* Canada could offer other countries when its export position is strong and its import demand weak. If some reorganization of the Canadian industry were required to concentrate on exporting some items while importing others now produced at home, there might be a question whether other partners in a multilateral agreement would accept special provisions favoring Canada's adjustment as willingly as the United States did in the automotive case. There may be instances in which Canada would find it difficult to adjust to free trade with a number of competitors. For manufacturing industries, however, the United States is usually the crucial factor. A study of the pulp and paper industry, for example, suggests that while Canada would gain more from an arrangement that provides free access to both European and American markets than from one confined to North America alone, the reorganization of its paper industry to do without tariffs would be just about the same in either kind of agreement since the main competition would come from the United States.[17]

Increasingly, Canadians are coming to realize that the barriers to their exports include their own tariff and not just the tariffs of other countries. A number of studies have shown that Canadian manufacturing costs are high not just because firms produce a relatively small number of many items but because machinery, materials, and components often cost more than in the United States or in world markets as a result of the Canadian tariff. Studies of investment in Canada point to the same factors in explaining why foreign-owned plants

17. N. S. Takacsy, W. E. Haviland, and E. M. Cape, *Trade Liberalization and the Canadian Pulp and Paper Industry* (University of Toronto Press, for the Private Planning Association of Canada, 1968), p. 91.

in Canada are less efficient than the mother companies (and often no more efficient than Canadian companies that have none of the supposed advantages of being part of large enterprises). As a result, steps have been taken to modify the tariff on machinery. For years, it was possible to remit duties on some kinds of machinery if Canadian producers could not supply 10 per cent of the market or more. After the Kennedy Round, in which machinery duties were cut, that policy was simplified and made more flexible. Government officials retain much discretion—a tariff may be levied to protect a single order—but one result of the change is to increase the share of imports of a number of kinds of machinery that come in duty-free. In 1971 the Canadian government proposed a plan for the tariff-free entry of tires (up to a percentage of domestic production) partly to reduce costs and partly to put other domestic manufacturers on an equal footing with the Michelin company, which had been given the right to bring in some tires without paying duty when it agreed to establish plants producing other kinds of tires in Nova Scotia.

There is a good case for further selective unilateral tariff reduction as a means of strengthening the Canadian economy. Governments have a strong disposition, however, to want to bargain their tariff reductions against tariff cuts by other countries. It may be that concern about their economy will move Canadians to propose more selective trade liberalizing agreements to the United States or others. Such agreements may then increase the domestic pressure to reduce the tariff on still other products as Canadian producers find it hard to compete in free-trade items if their costs are kept high by the effect of tariffs on the prices of the things they use. The experience of Canadian parts manufacturers under the automotive agreement was one of the factors making for the speedier and broader remission of duties on machinery. The study of the pulp and paper industry already cited points out that since tariffs on machinery, chemicals, and other supplies used by the industry are mostly higher in Canada than in the United States, "liberalizing trade only in papers could worsen the competitiveness of the Canadian pulp and paper industry."[18]

Canadian economists increasingly emphasize the fact that theirs "is one of the few industrial countries without duty-free access to a large market for all of its manufactured products."[19] To the old consciousness of the importance of trade liberalization to a country whose exports equal a quarter of its GNP, they add the concern about the structural problems of Canadian industry. Though trade is

18. Same, p. 91.
19. Economic Council of Canada, *Patterns of Growth*, Seventh Annual Review (Ottawa: Queen's Printer, 1970), p. 84.

growing and the situation is in no sense desperate, the pressure is rising for Canada to make some serious choices in trade policy. Its natural preference, like that of the United States, is for continuous progress in trade liberalization on a global, multilateral basis—for more of the Bretton Woods–GATT world. But if cuts are too modest, they raise the same problems that worried Canadians in the Kennedy Round. So if progress in general liberalization does not promise to be rapid enough, more radical alternatives may seem worth exploring. The idea of a North Atlantic Free Trade Area of Canada, the United States, Britain, and the rest of EFTA has always attracted Canadians. But Ottawa cannot open that door if it is shut in London or Washington so the Canadian dilemmas—if multilateral trade liberalization seems inadequate—will be whether to move toward free trade unilaterally or with the United States alone, either for some industries or in a comprehensive free trade area.

The trouble with the unilateral course is that it does nothing to give Canadian industries access to a larger market (unless their costs fall so far as to permit them to scale foreign tariff walls more easily than in the past). The trouble with the American alternative is the old one, fear of the loss of national identity and autonomy.[20] Not all Canadians accept that view. "Free trade with the U.S. would be good for Canadian political unity," is the view of one Canadian businessman.[21] His argument is that provincial imbalance and regional unemployment put national unity "in grave peril" and could be reduced by eliminating a tariff which many people in the Maritimes and western Canada have long felt hurt them for the main benefit of Ontario, and which Quebeckers are coming to see the same way. Among French Canadians, one can hear the argument that their nationalism is political and only the English-speaking Canadians are economic nationalists; closer ties with the United States may be seen as a helpful counterweight to dependence on Ottawa and Toronto.

Some of those who remain uneasy about too close an association with the United States have, nevertheless, come to the conclusion that a properly safeguarded free trade arrangement is the best course for

20. Some fear that free trade would reduce the ability of Canadian managers to make "independent" decisions. They point out that when Ford of Canada produces for the whole North American market, its activities must be tightly integrated with plans laid down in Dearborn and cannot be shaped by a judgment about production and sales in the Canadian market alone. There may be more shadow than substance in this issue, since the hand of Dearborn was probably none too light before, but I have found Canadian managers in other industries who take the argument seriously and, in consequence, oppose free trade.

21. Wilfred N. Hall, former president of Domtar, Ltd., Montreal, *The Financial Post*, December 26, 1970.

Canada. But the opposite view remains very strong. Politicians clearly sense the danger. In spite of the fact that the Liberal Party Conference of 1966 supported a resolution for a North American Free Trade Area, key ministers of that party, under Pearson and under Trudeau, have been careful to say that they were not moving in that direction. Even if the proposal gained supporters, the old pattern might well reassert itself: a strong case for a free trade area with the United States overturned—possibly at a late stage of discussions—by a strong nationalist reaction. But one cannot rule out the possibility that this time the old drama may turn out to have a new ending. If that proves to be the case, what should the United States do?

A FREE TRADE AREA?

The best initial stance is easy to describe. The United States should stand still and wait. The initiative should be left to Canada. It is Canada that has most to gain, but also Canada that would have to make the greatest adjustments. The United States should remain willing to explore sympathetically any proposals the Canadians may make either for a North American free trade area or for industry-wide arrangements and not turn them down out of hand even if they present obvious difficulties. Any more negative policy would be hard to justify, while an American initiative could be distorted into a grab for power and domination. Moreover, the American interest in free trade with Canada is not so great that a special arrangement to make it possible should be a major objective of U.S. policy.

Of course, proposals do not become acceptable simply because the Canadians have overcome their own difficulties or hesitancies in making them. While Canada may well need more safeguards than the United States and perhaps a longer period of adjustment, arrangements cannot be too one-sided merely because the Canadian economy is so much smaller than the American. Experience with the automotive agreement will certainly make Washington wary—and should have a similar effect on Ottawa. A former Canadian Ambassador in Washington told his countrymen: "If you are going to get any concessions out of the United States you must expect to negotiate something that they will regard as reasonably balanced."[22] It is not likely that Canada would find it profitable to bring about a difficult situa-

22. Testimony of A. E. Ritchie, Undersecretary of State for External Affairs, to a House of Commons committee, May 5, 1970, quoted in *International Canada*, May 1970, p. 123. He went on to say that favors could be quickly withdrawn and that accepting them, even if they were obtainable, would be "risking our independence in a way that I think we do not risk it when we negotiate a pretty hard-headed bargain on a particular point."

tion in the expectation that it could always be resolved as constructively as in the automobile industry.

A quiescent stance in no way implies that American officials and experts should not discuss the problems of general free trade, or of specific industries, with Canadian officials. On the contrary, confidential conversations of this sort and extensive joint studies will be essential to avoid misunderstandings about what each government is able or willing to do and to find solutions for some of the more difficult problems. The impossible or unacceptable should be identified early to dispel illusion. Canadians should not have to be reminded that agreement by American negotiators is no assurance of congressional approval. In view of the reaction to the automative agreement, it might be wise to consult Congress at a fairly early date.

Proposals for free trade in a single industry (or in a few products) would raise some problems not posed by broader measures. The American economic advantages would have to be demonstrated in narrower terms than those suggested by the general promise of a free trade area. A balanced bargain might be hard to strike—the industries would have been chosen for Canadian reasons, after all—without bringing in other industries or products and so further complicating matters. For both Canada and the United States there are disadvantages in having to ask other countries to waive their rights to equal trade treatment in a whole series of cases, not least because this process might make it harder to resist the spread of preferential agreements in Europe.

The case for freeing trade in a single industry is summed up in such prudential phrases as "one step at a time," "walk before you run," "don't bite off more than you can chew." All these maxims are in good standing in international economic relations and can be made concrete in the Canadian-American case by arguing that the combination of political and economic considerations that shape Canadian policy may make a limited agreement acceptable where a broader one would not be. A second major industry agreement coming after the automotive one, even though both were labeled "no precedent," would certainly look like the continuation of a process of liberalization. The liberalizing effects of limited agreements would be cumulative—for example, in strengthening the pressures for tariff-free entry of machinery and supplies into Canada. But the further such arguments are pushed, the more they strengthen the case for dealing with the problem comprehensively and undertaking to proceed toward the removal of tariffs on substantially all trade between the two countries over some reasonable period of time (if necessary, at a different pace for different industries). That course would overcome the objection of having to ask other countries to waive their rights to most-favored-nation treatment, since GATT permits members to create free trade areas among themselves.

A Canadian proposal to this effect would, of course, also present some problems for the United States. Some American producers, especially of minerals, and perhaps the people who live in some areas close to the border, might strongly object to their loss of protection, but it is hard to believe that the possible dislocations would be great enough to justify a negative decision. In hard cases, not only adjustment assistance and a gradual reduction of tariffs but also understandings about how business and government would behave in a transitional period might be warranted. Agriculture might be something else again. In times past, one could put an end to most speculation on a North American free trade area by asking two questions: Could Canada accept one that left out agriculture? Could the United States accept one that included it?[23]

Time has made this rhetoric less formidable. Farm products are less important than they used to be in Canadian sales to the United States (falling from 15 per cent in the early '50s to less than 3 per cent in the late '60s). After the Kennedy Round cuts are fully in effect, 30 per cent of Canadian shipments of farm products will enter the U.S. duty-free and the remainder will pay duties averaging 6 per cent,[24] hardly an insurmountable obstacle when people are talking of free trade. Of course, quotas on cheese and other products are far more restrictive than the tariffs, and Canadians may have given up trying to sell some things to the United States which would flow in if there were really no barriers. However, the Canadian emphasis on exporting manufactured goods and highly processed raw materials helps to defuse the issue so far as Canadian feelings are concerned. There have been changes in American farm policy as well (see chap. 8, pp. 260, 292). Canadian complaints are fewer. Some Canadian economists, "heartened by the increasing proportion of American agriculture that has moved into a market context,"[25] see the possibilities of moving toward free trade as considerably greater than they used to be. They are not so sure that Canada has as great a comparative advantage in a number of farm products as before, and not all troubles are blamed

23. A third question was whether a free trade area that omitted agriculture would meet the GATT criterion of covering "substantially all" trade between the two countries. GATT did not disapprove EFTA which omitted farm products except for some special arrangements, and it is hard to see how a different standard for American-Canadian trade would be justified.

24. "Report on Canada," *The Financial Post*, March 1, 1968, p. 47.

25. Gerald I. Trant, David L. MacFarlane, and Lewis A. Fischer, *Trade Liberalization and Canadian Agriculture* (University of Toronto Press, for the Private Planning Association of Canada, 1968), p. 113.

on the United States. There is also Canadian protectionism to reckon with, especially in fruits and vegetables.

These facts do not add up to the conclusion that with a little determination Canada and the United States could simply remove all barriers to trade between them in farm products or else ignore those barriers when forming a free trade area. It appears, though, that the farm problem is not so massive or intractable as to be unmanageable. A compromise that removed some barriers and left others untouched would not ruin the larger bargain. In still other cases the two governments might go behind the trade barriers and reach understandings about national measures affecting prices, production, and marketing. Such a step would be quite in line with what both countries may have to do in trying to come to terms with the European Community, as we shall see in chapter 8.

When they discuss these matters, Canadians show a clear preference for a free trade area rather than a customs union with the United States. A customs union, they feel, has political overtones they want to avoid and would require more coordination of national policies than they would like to commit themselves to. Both arguments have some validity. Perhaps only Canadians can make useful judgments on the political issue. The second argument makes sense but is easily exaggerated, considering the extent to which Canada must constantly adjust its economic policies to what happens in the United States. A free trade area has the further advantage of avoiding the tedious and potentially very troublesome process of adopting a common tariff for both countries against imports from the rest of the world—the essence of a customs union. In such negotiations, Canada would inevitably be at a disadvantage. While some American duties are higher than Canadian ones, an average of the two tariffs would probably be below the present Canadian tariff. However, the gain in liberalization from that would be more than offset by increased protection of the larger American market. Naturally there would be some tendency to align rates to avoid the nuisance of making compensations at the border when goods were imported into one country and shipped to the other. It seems likely that if each country were free to reduce its tariffs without having to get the other's agreement, there would be more liberalization of international trade than otherwise since each will continue to have an interest in striking trade bargains with other countries.

If Canada proposed a free trade area, one of the key problems for the United States would be to decide whether a favorable response would be compatible with the proposition—for which there is a strong case—that the United States can work more effectively for the organization of a desirable world economy if it does not form part of an economic bloc. For the United States to cleave to either Europe or Japan in ways that put the other at a disadvantage would clearly be unwise. But the argument that Canada is a special case is strong. It rests largely on the size and interdependence of the two countries.

Trade between the two countries is exceptionally large, and much of it is already free. A substantial share of Canadian production is carried on by American-owned companies; reorganization of their operations rather than trade diversion in a classic sense is the likely result of creating a free trade area, at least for many products, as the automobile case shows. While some special arrangements might have to be made to avoid damaging outside suppliers of some products, a further freeing of trade between the United States and Canada does not seem likely to threaten many of their interests.[26] What is done or not done about the removal of tariffs can make the two countries, or either of them, richer or poorer but is not the decisive factor in relations between two economies that are already highly integrated by more than trade. While Canada's potential gains from freer access to the American market are great, it can obtain them only by adapting its economy to that of the United States more fully than any other major country is likely to. The economic advantages for the United States are modest though attractive.

This line of argument would be strengthened if it were clear to all that other industrial countries were not yet ready for free trade with the United States, so that the creation of a Canadian-American free trade area would be a greater step toward trade liberalization than was currently possible on a broader basis. If that were not clear, the need for a choice might never arise since both the United States and Canada (for somewhat different reasons) are more interested in trade liberalization with a larger number of countries than just between themselves.[27] Even if they formed a North American free trade area, both countries would continue to have a strong interest (enhanced

26. Perhaps the largest number of questions would concern Mexico, a country that can also lay claim to a special relationship with the United States—though one rather different from Canada's.

27. All this sounds a bit pious. Of course Canada would gain a privileged position in the rich American market by a free trade arrangement, and some of its benefits would probably be gained at the expense of third countries. The price in terms of the reorganization of the Canadian economy is about the same as in moving to free trade with a larger number of countries and might be less if the United States accepted thicker adjustment cushions for Canada than others would. It is conceivable that some day a Canadian government should make a decision based on this kind of reasoning. But the political and psychological preferences for the wider world would probably continue to exercise their pull—if that option seems open.

in Canada's case by its political preferences) in expanding their trade with the rest of the world and in supporting GATT principles.

OTHER SPECIAL RELATIONS

It has been convenient to concentrate on trade questions because they bring into focus many aspects of Canadian-American relations and throw light on attitudes that affect other issues as well. But the special economic relations between the United States and Canada are far wider than trade. A Canadian historian has sketched the broader scene:

> . . . the bilateral relationship works as well as it does only because an elaborate and complex machinery of commissions, committees, boards, and other joint bodies has been developed over the years to deal with the common concerns of the two countries. . . . There are permanently constituted joint entities concerned with defense, with the boundary, with international waterways, and with fisheries. There are agreements making it possible for agencies in the one country to deal directly with their opposite numbers in the other country on such subjects as atomic energy, taxation, securities, customs, aviation, weather information, crime, conservation and recreation, agriculture, labor, immigration and naturalization, and radio and television. At a higher political level there are joint cabinet committees on defense and trade and economic affairs, as well as a Canada-United States interparliamentary group. All this is in addition to the enormous volume of work done in the embassies and consulates which each country maintains in the other. There is a regularly constituted procedure or apparatus for the conduct of almost every conceivable kind of Canadian-American business, making possible the smooth and quiet adjustment of the thousands of questions of common concern. The level of cooperation is so efficient and so constant that the general public is scarcely aware of its existence.[28]

Much of this remarkable apparatus for close cooperation is the administrative equivalent of all the peace bridges and road and railroad border crossings which remind one of an invisible boundary that separates the two countries, but divides them much less than boundaries usually do. There are other major measures of economic cooperation that are rooted geographically as well. Contiguity and the fact that the two countries have a common northern defense make it logical that the line between "domestic" and "foreign" should be erased for military purposes. Since 1958 the United States has put Canadian producers on an equal footing with those in the United States in defense procurement of a wide range of goods. Canadian firms are

28. Gerald M. Craig, *The United States and Canada* (Cambridge: Harvard University Press, 1968), pp. 314-15.

offered the chance to bid on Pentagon contracts; the "Buy American" magic does not apply against them, and the goods they supply are brought into the United States duty-free; official and private efforts have been made to help them overcome disadvantages resulting from the heavy concentration of research and development in the United States. The results have come in for a good deal of criticism by Canadians who resented the idea that a war in Vietnam which they disapproved of was being fought in part with equipment made in Canada. There seems little disposition on the government's part, however, to drop an arrangement that clearly contributes both to the expansion of exports and technological advance in Canadian industry.[29] Outside the defense industry, "Buy American" restrictions put Canadian producers at the same disadvantage as other producers. Canadians, for their part, also give preference to domestic producers in public procurement by both national and provincial governments.

Geography, security, and economics combine to make oil and gas of increasing importance in U.S.-Canadian relations. When the United States first imposed voluntary oil quotas in 1955 on grounds of "security," Canada was put on a preferred list. Later the controls were tightened, but Canadian oil still moved freely into Pacific Coast markets. The mandatory controls introduced in 1959 were at first applied to oil from all sources, but in a few months an exception was made for Canada. There was, however, a "gentleman's agreement" about the amount of Canadian oil that could enter the U.S. market. Whatever its precise provisions may have been, the unpublished understanding permitted a growth of 8 to 15 per cent a year in Canadian sales to the United States, compared to a growth of total American oil imports of about 4 per cent. As Prime Minister Trudeau described the arrangement, "Canadian oil producers sell to Western Canada and sell to the United States an amount roughly equivalent to the amount of oil that Eastern Canada purchases overseas and notably from the Venezuelan producers." The arrangement, Trudeau said, was "a continental oil policy of sorts."[30]

29. Trade figures do not show the share of Canadian exports to the United States that move under this arrangement, but from 1959 to 1965 U.S. defense procurement *expenditures* in Canada ranged from 26 to 68 per cent of annual Canadian exports of "inedible products" to the United States. Bruce W. Wilkinson, *Canada's International Trade: An Analysis of Recent Trends and Patterns* (Montreal: Canadian Trade Committee, sponsored by the Private Planning Association of Canada, 1968), p. 72.

30. Press conference in Washington, *The New York Times*, March 26, 1969. Like Americans, Canadians have a habit of speaking as if the continent stopped at the Rio Grande. I shall accept this convention for the time being, with footnote 26 regarding Mexico in mind.

The Nixon Administration's re-examination of the control of oil imports raised questions about what this "sort of" policy might develop into; the reaffirmation of the system of quotas made clear that the first basic question was how much oil the United States would take from Canada in the years ahead. The Canadians were hopeful, and public opinion was shocked when in March 1970 the United States imposed new restrictions. These proved to be temporary, and arrangements were worked out that made it likely that in 1971 the United States would increase imports to the point of taking all the oil Canada could send through existing pipelines. The cabinet-level Joint Canada–United States Committee on Trade and Economic Affairs agreed that for future years "arrangements should be worked out quickly to permit . . . full and unimpeded access to United States markets of Canadian crude oil and petroleum products, surplus to Canadian commercial and security requirements."[31]

Canadian ministers assured Parliament that they had made no commitments to a continental energy policy and stressed the fact that it remained up to Canada to decide how much oil was "surplus." On the American side it was clear that long-run commitments to provide a free market for Canadian oil were linked to "arrangements . . . to assure continuity of supply in times of emergency."[32] Part of the problem, Americans noted, was that eastern Canada depended more heavily than the rest of the continent on overseas oil, some of it from North Africa and the Middle East. No doubt the future of Alaskan oil, its transportation and distribution, the possibilities of new finds on the Canadian part of the northern slope, the routes of new pipelines, and the way production is regulated in both countries would all come into consideration in future negotiation.

So would natural gas. This fuel has been the occasion for all manner of controversies and complex decisions on both sides of the border, involving such matters as the dependability of supply if a provincial government has the right to cut off exports, the powers of the regulatory agencies of both countries, the competition between far-off but domestic gas and nearby but foreign supplies, what routes are "safe" for Canadian pipelines and what competitive "threats" they pose for American producers.

Electricity, too, will have to be taken into account. The easy switching of power through the existing grid might grow more difficult if there were an uneven incidence of shortages while demand was rising on the two sides of the border. From the Bay of Fundy through Niag-

---

31. *The Department of State Bulletin*, December 14, 1970, p. 731.
32. U.S. Department of State, *U.S. Foreign Policy 1969–1970: A Report of the Secretary of State* (Washington: GPO, 1971), p. 24.

ara Falls to the Columbia River, the two countries share water power. Its development on the Canadian side has sometimes depended on having an American market for electricity, which raises questions as to how matters should be rearranged when Canadian demand increases. Geography again comes into play, making the northeast and the northwest (seen from the United States) look like natural regions of supply and demand for electricity regardless of boundary and emphasizing Quebec's and Labrador's connections with New England rather than with Puget Sound.

Other uses of water have always played a great part in Canadian-American relations, whether the issue was offshore fishing, navigation on the Lakes and the St. Lawrence, or, increasingly, pollution and the responsibility for abating it. Canada has much more pure water than the United States. When the possibility is suggested of diverting streams that now flow into Hudson Bay to the Great Lakes so as to help, indirectly, the expansion of irrigated farming in Arizona and New Mexico, Canadians begin to bristle. Always valuable, water has become an emotional subject as people have begun to realize how their ways of life have damaged the environment. In Canada, that reaction combines with other emotions to foster resistance to anything that suggests that the giant to the south might be given easy access to streams and lakes once thought of as inexhaustible.

Not only liquid raw materials but solid ones as well are increasingly preoccupying Canadians. The country's economic growth owed much to mining and forestry, and they remain vital in spite of the expansion of manufacturing and services. The value of raw materials has depended on world markets and foreign capital, and especially those of the United States. More than one Canadian has spoken to Americans in the same vein as the Secretary of State for External Affairs in 1964, Paul Martin, who then referred to North America's resources as "a common asset to be used for our common benefit."[33]

Forecasts would be risky, but some new notes are to be heard in what Canadians say about these matters. Even more than in the past, they are suspicious of the implication of expressions like "common asset" especially in the mouths of Americans. They intend to make the Canadian share of the "common benefit"—and of decisions as to how resources are to be used—as large as possible. There is an increasing awareness that Canada is richer in raw materials in relation to its current requirements than any other industrialized nation. In a world in which the rewards of international cooperation are great but are at least partly allocated by hard bargaining, Canadians see that their raw materials position may be an even greater asset in the

33. Quoted by Craig, cited, p. 318.

future than in the past. Just how they are to use this advantage is not always clear. Among the ideas that are discussed are limiting foreign ownership, stipulating the performance that is to be required of foreign developers, and linking access to Canadian raw materials with the opening of markets for Canadian exports of manufactures. There are other parts of the puzzle as well. However they are put together there is little doubt that thinking out a raw materials policy and developing a strategy to go with it will be significant factors shaping Canada's future relations with the United States and the rest of the world.

Pervading all the other interrelations of the Canadian and American economies are those of money and the governmental policies affecting its flow and use. The movement of capital between Canada and the United States has long been one of the biggest facts of Canadian economic life, whether the issue was the growth of American direct and portfolio investment, the financing of the trade balance, the transmission of American business cycles northward, the difficulty of holding down inflationary pressures when large volumes of funds flowed in, the need to raise interest rates to hold capital drawn to New York, or the potential strain on the balance of payments of an ultimate outflow of funds as interest, dividends, or the withdrawal of capital itself. Canadian banks operate in New York (but American banks are given few opportunities to function in Canada). Portfolio investment from the United States is often very large; the borrowings of Canadian municipalities and provinces usually exceed those of private companies. The money markets of the two countries are highly integrated. Whatever interest rate policies the Canadian authorities may be following for the moment, "Canadian expectations about future long-term rates in Canada are closely linked to long-term rates in the United States."[34]

One of the reasons Canada adopted a flexible exchange rate in 1950 was to gain a little more freedom of maneuver in domestic economic policy than was possible when the impact of changes in the United States was transmitted through a fixed rate for both dollars. The experiment worked quite well until late in the decade. When it broke down, the main source of the trouble was the Canadian government's domestic policy rather than any specific disadvantage of either the floating rate or the American tie. Canada returned to a fixed rate of 92.5 U.S. cents in 1962 and held it until June 1970 when the Canadian dollar was once again allowed to float in an effort to ease the

34. Richard E. Caves and Grant L. Reuber, *Canadian Economic Policy and the Impact of International Capital Flows* (University of Toronto Press, for the Private Planning Association of Canada, 1969), p. 75.

inflationary pressure of the strong balance of payments position that developed at the end of the '60s without formally revaluing. This step, like the first one, was not motivated primarily by a futile desire to escape from the influence of changes in the American economy, but flexibility was judged by many Canadians to provide more freedom of domestic action in adjusting to them. One result of the second float was that the Canadian dollar had already risen in value before the U.S. government made a realignment of exchange rates a major objective of its policy in the fall of 1971.

A test of what the close financial links of the two economies meant for American policy came in 1963. President Kennedy announced that he would ask for a tax on the issuance of foreign securities in the United States; before Congress acted, an exception was worked out for new Canadian issues. Without it, the Canadians thought, they would be seriously hampered in new development, would lose reserves, and would be constricted in normal financial operations, for example, the rolling-over of provincial, municipal, and company debts in the New York market. In return for the exemption, Canada agreed (either initially or when the legislation was extended in later years) to hold its borrowing in the United States to normal levels, prevent nationals of third countries from evading the American tax by borrowing through Canada, and not to increase its foreign exchange reserves.

Two years later, Washington issued guidelines to American-owned companies abroad, which Canadians thought would force the remittance of profits that would otherwise be reinvested in Canada. Though the U.S. government explained that it did not intend to alter the usual practices of American companies in Canada, Ottawa issued counterguidelines urging the investment of profits (and also calling for the purchase of goods in Canada that the American guidelines had recommended be bought in the United States whenever possible). The argument faded away, compromise presumably being helped by the fact that no formal action was necessary to reach an acceptable application of the guidelines.

The climax of this sequence came when the United States at the beginning of 1968 moved to mandatory controls on foreign investment. Again Canada was exempted, in return for an undertaking about preventing the leakage of funds through Canada and a commitment to hold all its U.S. dollars (apart from working balances) "in U.S. government securities which do not constitute a liquid claim on the United States."[35] The effect of these measures can be dramatized, without being greatly distorted, by saying that they bring Can-

---

35. Letter of Mitchell Sharp to Henry Fowler, March 7, 1968, reprinted in *Balance of Payments Reporter*, Commerce Clearing House, p. 1383, par. 1042.

ada almost within the United States balance of payments in several major respects. That such an agreement should be possible expresses the special economic relation between the two countries in a way that nothing else described in these pages does. The possibility also suggests itself that the recognition of common interests that made so comprehensive and fundamental an agreement possible may also make it easier than in the past to resolve other difficulties. There is, however, nothing inevitable about such a development, as was made evident when Canada was offered no exemption from the import surcharge imposed by the United States in August 1971. Moreover, it soon became evident that, so far as Washington was concerned, reducing the unfavorable trade balance with Canada was a significant objective.

DIRECT INVESTMENT

Sometimes arousing emotion, always good for stirring up suspicion, frequently the occasion for sharp differences between the governments, and a standing stimulus to Canadian nationalism, American direct investment in Canada epitomizes the characteristics of the economic relations of the two countries set out at the beginning of this chapter: closeness and size. A dozen ways of stating the facts and more than a dozen sets of figures all convey a few essentials. American investment in Canada is very large, in both American and Canadian terms. Much larger than any other foreign investment in Canada, the amount of capital controlled by American companies is greater than the investment of Canadians themselves in several sectors of mining, manufacturing, and the production of petroleum. Many of the largest Canadian companies are American-owned. Often the major producers on both sides of the border are the same firms. Though some of the American-owned companies confine themselves to the protected Canadian market, many export. Some, especially those producing or processing raw materials, are concerned primarily with the American market and are often vertically integrated with the rest of the enterprise in the United States. Many American companies handle their Canadian business as part of their domestic activities, not through their foreign departments.

The large American presence has naturally worried some Canadians. They ask themselves whether it contradicts their wish to have an independent place in the world with a foreign policy no longer linked to that of Britain and not necessarily aligned with that of the United States. In matters of economics they ask if decisions made in Wilmington or St. Louis can really take full account of the considerations that are most important to Quebec or Calgary. In one way or another there has been an almost constant search for ways of either holding down American investment or else making it somehow more Canadian in behavior or shared ownership. The former approach has never gone very far. Not enough capital was available from other sources, Canadian or foreign—or at least did not put in an appearance —and no Canadian government has been willing to forgo the financing of growth by effectively penalizing American investment. More than money was involved, as the American companies have brought technology, reputation, access to markets, and the supposed advantage of size. However, restrictions have been put on foreign ownership in banking, insurance, and communications, and in the exploitation of natural resources in federal territories. In 1970 the government prevented the sale of a uranium mine to American interests and laid down new restrictions for the future. Ottawa resisted the sale to American interests of the largest Canadian-owned oil company. During the same period, a sizable stock exchange firm and two major publishing houses—one the leading supplier of textbooks—were sold to Americans. The reaction of a number of Canadians was to urge that the list of activities in which foreign control should be banned be made longer.

There is a whole spectrum of less direct measures that have been discussed in Canada. Overt tax discrimination has been rejected in the past and would be hard to justify. Various fiscal devices have been suggested to encourage American firms to share the ownership of their northern affiliates with Canadians. While some American companies have done this, others have preferred to keep full ownership while putting shares in the American parent company on Canadian stock exchanges. So far as advancing Canadians in management, carrying on research in Canada, and otherwise responding to the Canadian environment, many companies think they have performed reasonably well, but their critics disagree. Many of these matters are not easily dealt with by law and regulation, and Canadians may get more of what they want by a combination of urging and pressure than by more formal action. Some improvements—for instance, providing fuller disclosure of the accounts of American-owned companies in Canada—are more matters of reforming Canadian law than of American resistance. Also in Canadian hands is the long-debated and finally created Canadian Development Corporation, to help mobilize domestic funds and provide more government financing, thereby offering an alternative to American takeovers when it seems in the public interest to do so.

Quite a different family of problems arises when the U.S. government lays down the law for American-owned companies in Canada in ways that appear to conflict with the policies of the Canadian government. The two most familiar examples are the application of American restrictions on trading with the Communist countries and the antitrust laws. Since the days of the Eisenhower Administration there have been arrangements for consultation on such issues. They do not work perfectly, nor is it clear that they ever could while the policies of the two governments differ. But so long as both sides recognize a common problem and do not try to insist on exclusive jurisdiction, there is room for compromise. Some Canadians believe that at least some of the United States antitrust activities improve competition in Canada more effectively than Canadian policies do. The United States has licensed sales to Communist countries by American-owned companies in Canada that would have been forbidden for the American parent. Nevertheless, a problem remains: there *is* a conflict of jurisdictions, and the weaker party is bound to feel at a disadvantage. American-owned companies in Canada sometimes stay away from Communist business instead of seeking the approval they might get from Washington. Patent pools and other measures the Canadian government wishes to encourage as steps in reorganizing industry can be handicapped by the inability of American companies to take part without violating the antitrust laws.

The problem is not confined to Canada, but it takes on a special character there because of the extent of American investment. Perhaps, as they continue to work at these problems, which they cannot escape, the two governments will break new ground and find ways either of aligning policies or of yielding, on the part of one or the other or both, some of the sovereignty (or at least the claim to it or conception of it) that makes the issue so troublesome in the first place. A far more serious conflict of jurisdiction—that of the American balance of payments controls—was resolved in a very fruitful manner. And perhaps U.S.-Canadian cooperation will break a path that can be followed in relations among other industrial countries as well (see chap. 6, pp. 195–96, 209–13).

When its own policies are involved, the U.S. government must be in the front line in dealing with Ottawa, but on many other investment issues its proper position is less easily defined. Canada's key problem in these matters is how to achieve its national political and economic aims without scaring off American investment. That should be principally an affair between the Canadian government and the U.S. businessman. No one can be sure in advance where a satisfactory line can be drawn. Businessmen naturally warn against the bad consequences of measures they later find they can live with quite happily.

But officials and politicians cannot assume that the wish of Americans to invest in Canada above all other places in the world is so great that they will accept any terms that are offered them to do so. While Washington should often be just an interested bystander, it is bound to become involved some of the time. Canadian regulatory action may skirt the edge of discrimination and inequity which it is proper to resist. But the right response is not always obvious. The law that prevents Canadian firms from deducting as business expenses the cost of advertising if it appears in non-Canadian publications and is directed to Canadians is certainly discriminatory. Whether the U.S. government should have exerted as much pressure as Canadians allege it did to secure an exception for the Canadian editions of *Time* and *The Reader's Digest* is not so clear.[36] Newspapers and magazines are politics and culture as well as business. When the question is not the treatment of established interests but of reserving some kinds of activities to Canadians, American forbearance seems in order. The Canadians may be wrong in thinking that an extension of American banking into their country would make it harder for them to manage their economy, but it does not seem of the first importance for the United States to persuade them to change their minds. Even if, for example, an established American company can make a convincing case for the view that it could bring certain Canadian raw materials to market faster and cheaper than a newly formed Canadian enterprise, it is best left to Canadians to choose the course they prefer.

There are conflicting forces at work in Canada. The rejection of past efforts to penalize American investment was not all the work of Washington. Somebody besides the publishers must have wanted to have Canadian editions of *Time* and *The Reader's Digest*. Culture is imported more than it is exported. Many Canadian investors act as if they prefer to own a share in the whole of Du Pont rather than just the part in Canada. The Prime Ministers of Newfoundland, Quebec, and some of the other provinces devote great effort to promoting American investment. Some French-speaking Canadians regard capital from Toronto as almost equally foreign and politically more objectionable than investment from New York. The motivation of those who talk of freedom of action for Canadian managers is not always shared by those whose main interest is in jobs for Canadian workers. Not all Canadian managers would prefer full authority over a smaller

36. The cancellation of defense contracts and a "revision" of oil quotas are said to have been threatened. "One senior Canadian civil servant reported privately to the Prime Minister that he had never seen the State Department so unyielding." Peter Newman, *The Distemper of Our Times* (Winnepeg: Graywood, 1968), p. 209.

domain to a place on a ladder to more power and higher income in New York or Chicago.

While much of the reaction against American investment focuses on its effect on domestic Canadian affairs, there is a growing awareness in at least some circles of the close connection between the investment issue and Canada's long-run place in the world economy. Does American ownership inhibit Canadian exports, keeping the Canadian subsidiary "in its place" while the United States company supplies both the American and foreign markets? Or does the link with American technology and capital make possible Canadian participation in the international division of labor in a better way than could have been achieved by a smaller Canadian enterprise operating alone. Would investment from Europe or Japan—when it was available—offer better prospects? (It at least provides some diversification and is welcomed for that reason.) Does the presence of one big foreign firm ruin the chances of its Canadian competitors? The answers to these questions are not the same in every instance; what thoughtful Canadians are trying to do is to discover ways of distinguishing cases and influencing the behavior of investors. The kinds of considerations involved are closely linked with those that helped shape the automotive agreement and affect calculations about the possibility of free trade in other sectors as well. As in so many other countries (see chap. 5, pp. 167–72), policies on trade and investment are increasingly being understood as dovetailing with "industry policy"—the shaping of the kind of economy that will most benefit the nation. For example, a government committee has been trying to decide what kind of computer industry will give Canada a strong position in the world through specialization in the production of relatively few items instead of the inevitably weak position that would result from attempting to produce a wide range of products on a small scale in the historical pattern of Canadian industry.

All these factors, some of them contradictory, will play a part in shaping the investment policy of the Trudeau government and its successors. What weight will be given to each element and what devices will be resorted to to achieve the multiple purposes is not predictable as this is written. It seems certain, though, that there will be more regulation than in the past and more arrangements intended to give the government power to influence the pattern of investment and development. When such a policy is put forward, three broad decisions will have to be made. Canadians, through their Parliament, will have to decide whether the measures go far enough to satisfy nationalist feelings while not going so far as to threaten Canada's economic interests. American businessmen will have to decide whether the new regime is one with which they can live if they must, or whether obstacles—or perhaps just uncertainties—have been created on a scale to make Canada a far less interesting place to invest in than in the past. That decision will undoubtedly differ according to industries and firms. The United States government will have to decide whether there are any parts of the Canadian program to which it ought to take exception as a matter of policy and what role, if any, it should play in the inevitable negotiations and disputes between American businessmen and the Canadian government over the new rules.

Only the last of these questions is central to the subject of this book. The answer cannot be given with any clarity in the face of largely hypothetical circumstances. A number of points made earlier in this chapter (in the discussion of trade and monetary matters as well as investment) suggest considerations that ought to be taken into account. It would be fortunate if the Canadian program were one about which Washington felt able to say, "It is up to the Canadians to decide how they want to treat foreign investment and up to American business to decide how it wants to react to that treatment" and stop at that. That view should be carried as far as is reasonable, but it seems almost certain that more will be required. Even if Washington takes its stand only on certain broad principles of equity and treaty commitments, it will almost certainly be drawn into the consideration of cases as well, not just initially but later on. The economies are too close, the interests too great, and the linkages between private activity and public policy too numerous to avoid that.

There is no special reason to suppose that the United States and Canada are on the verge of a creative new understanding about investment. Past and present differences are likely to be exacerbated by episodes, by charges of bad faith, by politics. Canada will continue to assert sovereignty, and Canadians will complain if American-owned firms behave differently from the way they think Canadian firms would behave. In Canada the complaints of consumers, labor, environmentalists, anticapitalists, or anyone else against one business or another seem somehow more pointed if the business is American. The United States will neither ignore the size of its stake north of the border nor permit Canada to become a large loophole for the evasion of American trade and financial laws. However, while a continuing series of problems is inevitable, they need not add up to a major clash of interests or policies. The sparring goes on in a ring which provides boundaries even if there are disputes about the rules and the referees sometimes join in the fighting. It may well be, as this section has suggested, that the boundaries are becoming firmer and the rules clearer because of a better understanding than in the past that the alternatives for Canada (and for that matter the United States) are fewer and less attractive than they once seemed. If that is so, American investment in Canada, one of the most obvious and troublesome of the old issues, may begin to look like one of the foundations of a new— or newly understood—relationship between the two countries. It is not likely, though, that this result will follow if American businessmen take the view that investing in Canada should be no different from investing in the United States.

Greater Interdependence?

The automotive agreement, the interest in more free trade, the balance of payments understandings, the arrangements on oil and defense production, the discussions of resources, and the possibilities in investment all seem to be part of a piece. Each involves the Canadian and the American governments in something more than "foreign economic policy." The problems are at once foreign and domestic, being in fact a facet of the complex task of operating, on one land mass, two highly interdependent economies through a combination of private activity and the working of two separate sovereignties. Each government must, therefore, continually act in a way that accommodates a mixture of common and divergent interests. Nothing either government is likely to do will really alter in a major way the basic circumstances in which they have to carry on their affairs. They can handle their problems much worse than they have been handled, and probably better, but they cannot escape having to deal with a basic set of problems. Interdependence, common interests, the wish for independence, and the implications of a special relationship all establish the boundaries. To operate successfully within them requires of each country a certain basic approach to the other that will shape the whole relationship, whatever is done about a specific issue. For the United States the keys to this approach lie in not forgetting the manifold implications of the disparity in size of the two economies and in responding sensitively to the Canadian understanding of what Canadian independence means.

For Canada the beginning of sound policy seems to lie in accepting the close relation with the United States as an inescapable fact of life and seeking policies that would permit Canada to get the greatest possible economic advantage out of the circumstances. That view is held by many Canadians but not by all. The Minister of Finance in the Trudeau government said, "if we are to seek out and develop a sophisticated manufacturing economy making a few products well and exporting them to world markets, we will have to rely on a liberal policy being maintained by the United States."[37] That even an American failure to follow a liberal policy might drive the two countries closer together is suggested by the Economic Council of Canada's comment that if the United States took "significantly more protective measures . . . it would be essential for Canada, in its own interests, to press for special exemption on the basis of the high degree of economic interdependence between the two countries."[38]

Roy Matthews, a Canadian economist of British origin, has put the basic issue more broadly. He predicts "a recognition of the very special relationship with the United States and a greater willingness to seek ways to exploit this unique position rather than worry and complain about it." Looking at the relationship, he says, will lead to

> the conclusion that Canada has little to fear, and a great deal to gain, from a closer interlocking of certain aspects of the two countries' economic systems, particularly as it can be achieved through elimination of trade barriers. Enhanced industrial effectiveness, gained through a continental rationalization of manufacturing operations on each side of the border, will come to appear irresistibly attractive, because of its potential for increasing Canada's wealth and thus lessening the real political restraints imposed by the difference in Canadian and U.S. living standards. Or, to put it another way, such an alignment will appear not only relatively free of adverse consequences for political sovereignty, but capable of permitting Canada to pay a higher price for independent policies desired in other sectors.[39]

THE ODD COUPLE: CANADA AND JAPAN

Thousands of miles of contiguity along a land frontier versus thousands of miles of separation by sea—two sets of relations to the United States could hardly contrast more. In their economies, too, Canada and Japan are very different. Politically and socially the one is marked by similarity to the United States, the other by differences from it. Nevertheless, the continental land mass that is larger than the United States and the chain of islands with an area less than California's share some characteristics in their place in American policy.

To start with, they are not Europe. Taken together, as the arithmetic at the beginning of chapter 3 showed, they have an importance in American trade and investment about equal to Europe's. To be sure, they cannot be "taken together" in anything like the sense Europe can; on no reasonable basis can they be thought of as a potential

37. Edgar Benson, quoted in *International Canada*, November 1970, p. 240.
38. *Patterns of Growth*, cited, p. 87.
39. "A New Atlantic Role for Canada," *Foreign Affairs*, January 1968, p. 343.

unit with the size and strength to "look the United States in the face" as Europe may come to do in political and economic matters. Nevertheless, as major portions of the rich industrialized non-Communist part of the world economy neither can be left aside in shaping the central features of American foreign economic policy.

American trade and capital are more important to Japan and Canada than to Western Europe. For each of the countries, economic relations with the United States have a special place. Something of that special character is indicated by the fact that for a long time the United States has had cabinet-level joint committees with Canada and Japan that are still only under consideration with the Europeans. Although there is an element of window dressing in these arrangements and the workaday channels of economic diplomacy are probably more important than the superstructures, nevertheless, there is a point to these formal arrangements which stress that in each set of relations more is involved than the traditional work of foreign offices.

Different as they are, Canada and Japan also have some similar interests in the way the world economy is organized. Heavily dependent on international trade and finance and not positioned for the kind of regional economic integration that has been so important to post-war Western Europe, they are in many ways just the kinds of countries for which the Bretton Woods world picture was drawn. Cooperation, multilateralism, and equal treatment are of great importance to them. Though Canada is inextricably intermixed with the American economy to a greater degree than any other country and may become more so, it prefers to maintain the broader framework as well. For Japan the wish to have the advantages of a Bretton Woods world entails a challenge to its willingness to conduct its own affairs somewhat differently than in the past. Neither country is free from qualms and questions about the alternatives it faces, and whatever choices they make will confront the United States with further decisions.

Their importance to the United States, its importance to them, and the common interest the three countries have in a cooperative, multilateral economy, covering as much of the world as possible, combine to give Canada and Japan a significant place in any attempt to think through the principles of American foreign economic policy. And the very different kinds of problems they present to the United States exemplify another important point: that along with firm adherence to principles and broad policies which is essential to the consistent pursuit of aims must go considerable flexibility in the application of rules to cases if a viable international economy is to be maintained and policy that is sound in principle is to be workable in practice.

PART II

The Future Coming in Sight

5

Trade Policies

Every author loves a turning point. In search of a little drama, some find one where other people see only a bump in the road or the turn-off to a dead end. But in the history of American foreign trade policy, there can be no doubt that the Trade Agreements Act of 1934 marked a real turning point. For a generation since, American trade policy has followed the main lines set then. Broadened at the end of World War II, the approach rather tentatively advanced in 1934 reached a culmination in the multilateral tariff negotiations of 1964–67 called the Kennedy Round. Are we now approaching another turning point? The burden of much of this chapter is that we are—because the nature of trade policy is changing radically. But change, while it brings new emphases, does not altogether eliminate old problems.

What Remains of the Tariff Problem

The change is partly the result of what was accomplished in the Kennedy Round, and in the years of tariff reduction leading up to it. The average tariffs on nonagricultural products other than mineral fuels coming into the great industrial nations will be 10 per cent or less after all the concessions made in the Kennedy Round are fully in effect: for the Common Market, 8.1 per cent; Japan, 9.5; the

United States, 9.6; and Britain, 10.6.[1] This is a far cry from 1935, 1945, or even 1955. What it means for the United States, as an importer, was summed up by Joseph A. Greenwald, U.S. Permanent Representative to the OECD, when he said that "the average level of American tariffs has been reduced by four-fifths from a 1930 peak of 50 percent to 9 percent when the Kennedy Round cuts are fully implemented in 1972."[2]

Of course, the 10 per cent average obscures some very high rates, occasionally over 100 per cent. While most of these touch only a little trade, some are important. Many are concentrated, as in textiles and watches. Though all major trading countries have some rates over 20 per cent on manufactured goods, few go beyond 30 per cent. The United States has more than most other industrialized countries but far fewer than before the Kennedy Round.

The real level of protection is often higher than these percentages suggest. If an article costing $1 has in it 50 cents' worth of raw materials that are duty-free, then a 10 per cent tariff on the finished product provides 20 per cent protection for the manufacturing process. Only when raw materials or other components carry the same duty as the finished product is the nominal tariff rate the same as the "effective" one, as it is called. If the inputs pay a higher rate of duty than the finished product, the effective rate is lower than the nominal one. Since most industrial countries levy lower duties on raw materials than on semifinished products and then still higher rates on finished products, nominal tariff rates on manufactured products usually understate the degree of protection. Two empirical studies[3] indicate the following spread between nominal and effective rates for goods as a whole at pre-Kennedy Round levels:

---

1. Ernest H. Preeg, *Traders and Diplomats: An Analysis of the Kennedy Round of Negotiations under the General Agreement on Tariffs and Trade* (Washington: Brookings Institution, 1970), Tables 13-1 through 13-4. The figures for "manufactures" alone, excluding unprocessed or slightly processed materials, are 0.2 percentage points higher in Britain, 0.3 for the United States, 0.5 for the Common Market, and 1.2 for Japan. The methods used in averaging are described in the source.

2. *The Department of State Bulletin*, December 14, 1970, p. 724.

3. Bela Balassa, *Trade Liberalization among Industrialized Countries: Objectives and Alternatives* (New York: McGraw-Hill, for the Council on Foreign Relations, 1967), Table 3.2, p. 56. See also pp. 44-59 and 178-84. James R. Melvin and Bruce W. Wilkinson, *Effective Protection in the Canadian Economy* (Ottawa: Queen's Printer, for the Economic Council of Canada, 1968), Table 2, p. 29. For Canada, 1963 figures for 133 industries were used to calculate an average effective rate that is 21 or 24.4 per cent, depending on method. For the other countries, pre-Kennedy Round 1962 figures were used.

	U.S.	U.K.	EEC	*Japan*	Sweden	*Canada*
Nominal rates	11.6	15.5	11.9	16.2	6.8	13.1
Effective rates	20.0	27.8	18.6	29.5	12.5	24.4

Immense statistical difficulties stand in the way of portraying the world tariff structure in meaningful, uniform, up-to-date figures giving effective tariff rates. Further scholarly work will help to clarify the picture, but it may never become possible to base general tariff negotiations on agreed measures of effective rates instead of economically crude but legally precise nominal rates. Awareness of the difference can, however, play a part in negotiations. The issue is not altogether new. Without the benefit of sophisticated techniques, businessmen and officials have long taken account of the difference between tariff rates on finished goods and on the things that go into producing them. From 1861 on the American tariff on woolens was geared to that on wool (except for two brief periods). A traditional Canadian complaint is that the United States makes it easier to import pulp than paper or lumber than wooden products and so discourages processing in Canada. The Canadian manufacturers' pressure for reduced duties on machinery discussed in the last chapter was concerned with effective protection even if the words were not used.

The Kennedy Round probably reduced over-all effective protection since duties on manufactured goods seem to have been cut more than those on raw materials and semifinished products. (Because the latter rates were generally lower, even equal percentage reductions would lower the margin of effective protection.) While the pattern of effective protection among countries and products may not be the same as that shown by comparison of nominal rates, it is on the latter that we must fall back while bearing in mind that the figures usually understate the degree of protection. Low by historical standards, a 10 per cent tariff is not negligible, any more than any 10 per cent tax would be. How burdensome to trade such a rate is (or one of 5 or 20 per cent) varies according to product, market, and competitive conditions. There is no reason, though, to reject common sense views that, by and large, high rates are more restrictive than low rates; many rates below 5 per cent are largely nuisances; and, while many other factors have contributed, the reduction of tariffs has played an important part in the expansion of international trade. It follows that the industrial countries cannot ignore the remaining tariffs.

Experience has been encouraging. The Kennedy Round was not an isolated phenomenon but the culmination of a long and deliberate process. The Common Market and EFTA have shown that it is possible to eliminate tariffs completely on large segments of world trade without bringing on major disturbances or forcing unacceptable adjustments in important industries. The idea that tariff levels spell life or death for great industries is less plausible than ever. Inevitably the question arises: If this far, why not all the way? Does the record of the last twenty-five years not suggest that in the next ten or fifteen years tariffs could be completely removed, perhaps by gentle stages, at least on most of the trade in manufactured goods among the industrialized countries?

Doubts spring to mind. The last quarter of some tariffs may be much harder to remove than the first three-quarters. Even the Kennedy Round failed to bring about a major reduction in duties on some important products. Every country has some hard cases which, for a long time, it will want to make exceptions of in any general freeing of trade. The wave of protectionism in the United States that followed the Kennedy Round raises doubts whether the wide support for the passage of the Trade Expansion Act in the early '60s could be mustered for a comparable effort ten years later. Proponents of European integration fear that global free trade would weaken the bonds of their Community. The accomplishments of the past twenty-five years have come in a period of great economic expansion in the industrial world, which made adjustment to tariff changes relatively easy. Reactions from government and industry might well be very different if growth were slower and there were periods of stagnation.

These doubts are well founded. At a minimum they suggest that the process of further tariff reduction may be slow and difficult. But that is nothing new; it is only when one's eye sweeps quickly across the terrain that the road from the Trade Agreements Act to the Kennedy Round seems straight and smooth. Decisions about how to treat imports of manufactured goods from less developed countries pose further difficulties which the advanced countries are only beginning to face. Preoccupation with this problem or with the increasingly complicated relations among themselves in matters other than trade may well cause the industrialized countries to postpone major decisions about what to do next in tariff policy. Nevertheless, there is no escaping the conclusion that free trade, so long an impossible ideal for some and a worrisome specter for others, has become, for the first time in nearly a century, something that can be seriously contemplated as a reasonable objective of policy.

Even without accepting so ambitious a goal, governments will have to decide how to go about the reduction of tariffs in the future, since they are sure to demand action of one another. Another, less elaborate Kennedy Round concentrating on trade in manufactured goods is one possibility. It would almost certainly have to deal with more than tariffs, for reasons which will become apparent later in the chapter. Another possibility would be to work out a formula for the gradual reduction of tariffs over a period of years. All duties might be reduced by a uniform amount every few years. Alternatively, some duties might be reduced faster than others because they were higher to start with, or more slowly because some countries needed longer to adjust than others. A country's obligation might be to reduce the average of its tariffs (or the average in each of several categories of tariffs) by a certain amount each year. This formula would permit each country some flexibility, going slowly on some duties if it went faster on others, while assuring the same results in the end. All sorts of variations and combinations can be imagined. The target can be free trade or an agreed common level of tariffs or simply a certain amount of reduction.

The idea of working to a formula is not unrealistic. The Common Market and EFTA have found a commitment to staged reductions a powerful instrument in insuring performance. The OEEC's code of trade liberalization successfully used a formula that gave countries some flexibility in the removal of quotas (but left a good bit of argument about some of the criteria and the meaning of the basic measurement). Changes in American policy—if they can be preserved—have weakened the objections that made tariff reduction by formula unacceptable to the United States when it was proposed in GATT in 1951.[4] The purpose of a formula is to provide simplicity and automaticity, the former to get out of the jungle of complex negotiations, the latter to insure results. Not all products would have to be included; but if governments are more anxious to protect than to liberalize, there is no point in considering this method.

With or without a formula, governments will have to consider the possibility of harmonizing tariff rates, eliminating disparities in tariff structure, and linking tariff reductions with the removal of other kinds of trade barriers.

In the Kennedy Round the Common Market made a great issue of the fact that the dispersion of rates in the American tariff was much greater than in its own external tariff, which had been smoothed by averaging the original national tariffs. A highly uneven tariff was inherently more protective, said the Europeans. Where major disparities existed between American and European rates, a smaller cut in

4. It seemed impossible to get such sweeping powers for the President (just as the powers granted under TEA were hardly conceivable at that time). A general reduction of all tariffs would have conflicted with the policy of selectivity to avoid injury to American producers but seems compatible with across-the-board cutting in the manner of the Kennedy Round.

the lower rate should be considered equal to a larger cut in the higher rate, in the Common Market view. While the United States resisted the proposal (as put forward it would have greatly limited reductions and made a one-sided bargain), the underlying idea had some merit and a rather wide appeal. It is also not new, having been long a standby of low-tariff countries, though in a relatively unsophisticated form. GATT rules recognize that a commitment not to increase a low tariff could be equated with a reduction in a high one. At the beginning of the trade agreements program, it was tacitly accepted that, because of the height of the Hawley-Smoot rates, the United States would have to make greater cuts than other countries.[5] While the average tariffs of the main trading countries are now fairly close together, disparities in individual rates will keep the issue alive.

Harmonization can mean many things: the same rates on the same products, rates on the range of products country A sends to B that are comparable to those of the quite different things B sends to A, an average according to some agreed-on standard, a ceiling on all tariff rates, etc. There are important differences among these definitions; some make more economic sense than others. But the fact that much of the trade among the industrialized countries is the exchange of similar items, or items within certain broad categories, such as machinery, electrical equipment, vehicles, and chemicals, suggests that the eventual aim—if it is not free trade—will have to be something like general tariff uniformity. It could be argued that the simplest thing to do would be to agree that all tariffs should be the same, say 10 per cent, or, at least, that they not be above that level. It is not true, as is sometimes said, that if this were done the effect would be the same as if there were free trade; international trade would be taxed in a way that domestic trade was not. Moreover, unless some tariffs were raised or new ones introduced, 10 per cent would not be a universal rate, just a general ceiling. Still it is probably true that for a wide range of manufactured goods a standard rate would tend to reduce the importance of tariffs in international competition and would be something to which businesses could fairly well accommodate themselves.

Harmonization, the elimination of disparities, and even the complete removal of tariffs will not be accepted as equitable if some countries rely almost entirely on tariffs to restrict imports while others use different kinds of barriers as well. (The reverse happened in the '50s when the low-tariff Scandinavian countries argued that under the OEEC's arrangements for the removal of quotas they were giving

5. John W. Evans, *The Kennedy Round in American Trade Policy: The Twilight of the GATT?* (Cambridge: Harvard University Press, 1971), p. 8.

up more protection than high-tariff countries like France and Italy.) It seems likely, then, that the reduction of tariffs by formula or efforts to find rules about harmonization will work only as part of a broader approach. The same conclusion is suggested by the need to find ways of dealing with products (or industries) which governments are not willing to subject fully to rules for tariff reduction. Not insurmountable obstacles, these considerations show that the use of even the simplest kind of formula for tariff reduction will prove more complex than it might seem.

Uncertainty about how to conduct future tariff negotiations and the importance of at least preserving past accomplishments suggest that a desirable step would be for the industrialized countries to declare a tariff truce among themselves. No new tariffs would be introduced; existing rates would not be raised. To a degree such a truce exists, in that the tariff reductions made in the Kennedy Round and other GATT negotiations are bound against increase except in accordance with certain rules. But there are many products not so covered, and a broader tariff truce would do much to reduce the risk of deterioration while the industrialized countries explore the best ways of negotiating about the increasingly complex economic relations among themselves, of which tariffs are only a part. No doubt such a truce would have to be accompanied by some kind of escape clause saying what should be done if a country found itself in difficulties because of a sudden flow of imports, or whether tariff surcharges might or might not be used by countries in balance of payments difficulties, and what the rights of countries would be if others violated the truce. But the very process of agreeing on such matters would force governments to face up to some of the issues that are otherwise likely to create future difficulties among them.

Nontariff Barriers

Historically, those opposed to tariffs have been called free traders, but now we see that even the complete elimination of tariffs would not bring free trade. Behind, alongside, and even within the tariff structures of the world are other kinds of measures, loosely and sometimes inaccurately called nontariff barriers. As a class, they are not new. Over thirty years ago Percy W. Bidwell wrote at length about *The Invisible Tariff*, "a comprehensive system of administrative controls over import trade."[6] Then and later, getting rid of quantitative restrictions was one of the great aims of American trade policy. As quotas and exchange controls were largely peeled away in the late

6. (New York: Council on Foreign Relations, 1939), p. 2.

'50s, tariffs once again resumed their importance; now major reductions in tariffs are making nontariff barriers more prominent.

To try to list nontariff barriers and then to consider what might be done about them is an eye-opening exercise. Their range and variety defy simple prescription as to either goals or methods. The future of international trade negotiations, it soon becomes apparent, will be far more complex than the past, involving an ever-widening range of issues.

Quotas and exchange controls present familiar problems. For the most part, the matter is one of enforcing the comprehensive rules in GATT and the IMF Agreement. The cases where something more is involved are referred to in other parts of the book, for example, cotton textiles, energy, Japan's export and import quotas, and the use of direct controls by countries in balance of payments difficulties. Agriculture, a prolific source of other nontariff barriers as well as quotas, presents special problems which are considered in chapter 8.

The Kennedy Round was not the first time that nontariff barriers had been dealt with in close conjunction with tariffs, but it was unusual that one device should play so prominent a part in the negotiations. American Selling Price (ASP) has emerged from the footnotes and stands, for many people, as an archetype of nontariff barrier. In fact, such usage is an example of mislabeling since ASP works through the tariff. Imported products are valued at a fictitious price higher than the real one at which the goods were bought abroad with the result that the tariff on them is increased. A whole host of other practices belong in this general category. Arbitrary or fantastic customs classifications put goods in high-tariff brackets; narrow customs definitions only slightly disguise discrimination; volume is calculated in a way that taxes water as if it were whisky; cumbersome formalities and burdensome procedures make the passage of goods through customs a costly and somewhat uncertain process. Such devices have long been the subject of international discussion. Some are covered by international agreements, but there is no end to them and no simple formula can deal with all. Their elimination or regulation is obviously part of the process of trade liberalization. If tariffs were eliminated, these irksome ancillaries would disappear, and in that respect they are different from most other nontariff barriers.

Another well-recognized kind of "nontariff barrier" dealt with in the Kennedy Round was antidumping duties. Here the paradox of the terminology is even more obvious since the barrier that is raised is precisely a tariff (or duty). What sets the process in motion is the practice of sellers charging lower prices in a foreign market than they do at home. Never enforced to the hilt, the principle is generally accepted, but there is constant suspicion that national antidumping rules and procedures are abused for protectionist purposes. The international standards set in the code agreed on in the Kennedy Round had three main targets: the uncertainty and delay of American procedures, Canada's failure to require a demonstration of injury to its producers, and the absence of publicly ascertainable standards in the practices of many countries. It is too soon to judge how well the new code will work, but it seems probable that antidumping measures will become lively subjects of international concern as the reduction of tariffs makes businessmen more sensitive to their foreign competitors' pricing arrangements.

Commonly linked with antidumping arrangements are countervailing duties, those imposed to offset subsidies paid by foreign governments. From the point of view of the producer in the importing country, antidumping and countervailing duties are indeed of a piece: he is looking for protection against unfair competition, regardless of its cause. For the study of nontariff barriers, however, the distinction between the two devices is important and interesting. The target of one is the pricing policy of private business and, of the other, government aid to business. These two large and complex fields are full of thickets of nontariff barriers and other trade-distorting measures that cannot be adequately dealt with by penalty tariffs of the sort imposed under antidumping and countervailing duty laws. Even within the range of issues that can be dealt with by these long-established practices, the issues are not simply those of "unfair competition" between businessmen in the exporting country and those in the importing one. There are also exporters in third countries, who may lose markets to dumping or subsidized competitors. How strongly the government of the importing country feels about what the foreigners are doing may depend on whether domestic prices are kept high by monopolies or restrictive practices. It may also take some account of the benefits its consumers get from being dumped on. "Injury" to domestic producers is not always clear-cut, even if the competition appears to be "unfair." Subsidy may simply compensate for a disadvantage placed on a producer by his own government.

Profusion and variety burst forth from any serious effort to list nontariff barriers. "Buy American" laws are only the best-known example of a cluster of widespread practices discriminating against foreign goods in government purchasing. Some European countries have "road taxes" that fall disproportionately on large (and therefore largely American) automobiles. Goods imported into the United States have to carry marks and labels showing their country of origin. While the labels *France* on women's gloves and *England* on men's overcoats may be worth a number of dollars on the retail price, *Belgium* on rolls of barbed wire and *Japan* on concealed components in radios do not by themselves make sales. *Hong Kong* on tiny paper parasols may neither entice nor repel buyers, but the cost of stamping it there must be high in relation to the value of the product. Other countries have other labeling laws with the common characteristic of subjecting foreign products to rules that do not apply to the same article when produced domestically.

Even if the same law applies to domestic and foreign products, it may affect them differently. Specifications on engineering equipment or on supplies for building are written, naturally enough, in terms of domestic habits and in the domestic system of measurement; to do the opposite would be absurd, but the fact remains that there is an impediment (sometimes a small one) to international trade that does not exist for domestic trade (in either country).[7] Standards imply inspection, and it is not surprising if new or unfamiliar products from abroad, whether household appliances, structural steel, or industrial machinery, are subjected to scrutiny different from that given the standard models put out by large domestic producers. Sometimes the inspection is carried out by a technical association with its inevitable connections with domestic producers; it is understandable then if German and French exporters of certain machines to Italy become suspicious when that association for months at a time does not provide examiners, and as a result delivery dates cannot be met.[8] In some parts of the United States boilers have to "be stamped with the seal of the American Society of Mechanical Engineers, which is not issued to manufacturers located outside the United States and Canada."[9]

Even when motives are above reasonable suspicion, separate sets of national standards, each designed with the domestic situation in mind, can hamper trade and reduce the advantages of serial production. European producers complain about some of the automobile safety devices required by the United States; even within the Euro-

7. An OECD study suggests that the need to produce for a number of foreign markets and to many different foreign specifications is one of the reasons efficiency in European engineering industries is lower than in the United States where the domestic market absorbs a much larger share of the output. Organization for Economic Co-operation and Development, *The Engineering Industries in North America—Europe—Japan, 1966–1967* (Paris: Author, 1967), pp. 108–109.
8. CEPES (Comité Européen pour le Progrès Économique et Social), *Die Befreiung des Welthandels von Nichttarifären Handelshemmnissen* (Frankfurt am Main: Deutsche Gruppe e.V., 1967), p. 36.
9. William B. Kelly, Jr., "Nontariff Barriers," in Bela Balassa, ed., *Studies in Trade Liberalization: Problems and Prospects for the Industrial Countries* (Baltimore: Johns Hopkins Press, 1967), p. 306.

pean Community national rules differ about brakes, headlights, and other equipment. Several years of work by the Community's Commission and the member governments have been necessary to get agreement on a limited amount of standardization. Tractor speed in Germany is limited to 20 kilometers an hour and in the Netherlands 16, while France permits 27; consequently the product best adapted for each home market is at a disadvantage abroad.[10]

Health and sanitary regulations, whether they concern fresh vegetables, dried figs, canned goods, or pharmaceutical products, create a maze through which, remarkably enough, billions of dollars' worth of goods find their way in international trade all the time. How much potential trade is lost and at whose expense is unknown. No doubt many, perhaps most, of the regulations are warranted; others are unnecessary and outmoded, the results of a process to which bureaucrats, technicians, businessmen, and reformers have contributed haphazardly for decades. Whatever the origins of the rules, changing them is made more difficult by the fact that they give domestic producers protection against foreign competitors. But cynicism is not always a sound guide to the true motives behind nontariff barriers. The American sanitary legislation forbidding entry of fresh or chilled meat from countries where hoof and mouth disease was endemic was for many years a favorite example of alleged hypocrisy. It was a source of trouble between the United States and Argentina, sometimes in periods when Washington worked hard to find ways of being nice to Buenos Aires. Arguments were developed to show that looser American regulations and improved practices in Argentina would be adequate to deal with the risk. The flavor of protectionism—never far away in American farm policy—was detected by many. Yet the Department of Agriculture made a strong case and carried weight in Washington on technical grounds and not just the political ones its critics suspected. To be overcautious in the face of danger can be a virtue even when it is also good politics. The seriousness with which the U.S. government took the matter was reflected in its contributions to wiping out the disease in Canada and Mexico. The damage resulting from an epidemic in England in 1967–68 that may have had its origin in Argentine meat lends strength to the case.

Nontariff barriers are used to help in arms control, drug control, and the preservation of threatened species of birds and animals. They affect exports as well as imports. Japan is asked to limit its sales of competitive products; the United States limited exports of copper to preserve domestic supplies and hold down the domestic price from 1965 to 1970, and refused to sell computers to be used in France's

10. CEPES, cited, p. 36.

nuclear bomb program. Import quotas are the natural reinforcements of many national farm policies. Even when no barrier is placed at the frontier, national policies may narrow the market for foreign goods and widen them for domestic output by, for example, subsidies, tax concessions, or preferential credit arrangements. Practices of this sort, which are growing in importance and are often more closely tied to the pursuit of major national economic aims than to the wish to restrict trade, make "nontariff barriers" a less accurate, though more convenient, label than the one Robert E. Baldwin used as the title for his excellent 1970 study for the Brookings Institution: nontariff distortions of international trade. The very breadth of that term and the glimpse of the panorama sketched in the last few pages point to a central problem that hardly existed when tariffs and quotas were the dominant instruments of trade policy: Where to begin?

The difficulty is not that of listing all the practices that ought to be considered, obscure and technical as some of them are. Governments made a good start during the Kennedy Round and have since carried their efforts further. GATT, the OECD, and UNCTAD have all been active, along with business groups and academic researchers. The offending practices can be classified in several different ways: by type, by intent (is the aim really to restrict trade or is that result incidental to something else?), by relation to provisions of GATT, by importance, and by the chances that governments will be willing to negotiate seriously about them. The last two criteria are clearly central to any decision as to how to proceed, but they are also not very easy to apply. Some practices are widespread and clearly important to international trade, such as discriminatory governmental purchasing, while other nontariff barriers affect only a small amount of trade or have only a minor effect on a large amount of trade. In a large number of cases, however, the real impact of trade-distorting practices is not at all clear, and informed individuals differ in their appraisals. So far as negotiability is concerned, there is much room for differences of opinion, and the right answer may depend less on dispassionate analysis than on how hard certain governments want to push a matter.

The difficulties that arise from lack of agreement on what to negotiate about are illustrated by the first major confrontation on nontariff barriers to follow the Kennedy Round. The episode also throws light on how far-reaching some of the ramifications of trade-distorting practices may be.

The Border Tax Issue

Taxes that have the same effect as tariffs are banned by GATT and so are export subsidies. But this prohibition does not apply to measures intended to equalize the domestic and foreign impact of what economists somewhat quaintly call "indirect taxes," such as excise, sales, and turnover taxes. To put foreign goods and domestic goods on the same basis, a levy equal to the domestic tax may be placed on imports while exports are exempted from the tax. In making this rule, the drafters of GATT were following long-established practice based on the belief that indirect taxes are largely passed on to the consumer whereas taxes on profits are largely paid by the producer. Nowadays economists have doubts about the incidence of direct and indirect taxes, but there is no consensus on the best way of handling the problem (especially since the distribution of the burden probably changes with market conditions). It is generally agreed, however, that if border taxes remain fixed long enough, their trade effects will be absorbed in exchange rates.

Indirect taxes are much more important in the Common Market countries than in the United States, which makes border adjustments primarily for a few excise taxes. After years of preparation, the Community was ready, by the late '60s, to move toward the harmonization of indirect taxes. The first step was for the other five countries to replace their separate systems with a value-added tax (VAT) resembling the one which had been in effect in France all along. Later, the six countries were to move toward uniform rates with the expectation that by some time in the '70s they would all have a VAT of somewhere around 15 or 16 per cent, representing a reduction in France's rates and an increase in everyone else's.

From 1916, Germany had used a turnover tax levied every time goods changed hands. The border adjustment for most products was 6 per cent on imports with a rebate on exports of 7 per cent. When the VAT system was introduced the adjustment was set at 11 per cent for most products and could be expected to rise later on.[11] The change did not result from an increase in the domestic impact of the new tax but from the fact that under the old system the border adjustment was set rather arbitrarily whereas the VAT permitted a precise adjustment; in short, there had been less than complete compensation under the old system, according to the German analysis.

In terms of American reaction, the timing was very bad. In the eyes of businessmen the tax increase nullified some of the tariff reductions agreed on in the Kennedy Round. Fuel was added to the rising

---

11. Other products paid half the rate, and there were some exceptions. Details, or indeed precision, about taxes and border adjustments, the methods by which they are collected, etc., are not important to the points made here so my whole account is oversimplified.

fire of protectionism. Officials in the executive branch found it hard
to resist protectionist moves by arguing that the United States must
do nothing to upset the bargain made at Geneva. The prospects of
the legislation to repeal American Selling Price—in which the Germans expressed a strong interest—were dimmed. Officials had, of
course, been aware for some time that the problem was going to
arise.[12] They based their objection to the German action on the
charge that the change in border tax adjustment was equivalent to a
devaluation of the mark by 2 or 3 per cent, a step hardly justified for
a country with a strong balance of payments surplus.

If the United States felt that something must be done and did not
wish to violate GATT, several courses were open to it. It might introduce border adjustments for a number of its own indirect taxes
(some state and local) that were traditionally ignored. The amounts
did not seem large, and it turned out that European countries could
build up the total on their side as well if they wanted to. (They
might have agreed to refrain from doing so as part of a broader arrangement by which foreign tariff cuts would be accelerated to help
the American balance of payments, but the proposal depended on
congressional action on ASP, which was not obtainable.) A more
radical alternative would have been for the United States to adopt a
value-added tax itself and then make suitable border adjustments.
Whatever the case might be on domestic grounds for making such a
change in the fiscal structure, to base a decision on the expected effect on imports or exports would be strange logic in a country where
foreign trade is so small a share of GNP. And the action could certainly not be taken quickly.

A third possibility was to change the rules. That seemed to be the
purpose of the United States's raising the issue in GATT. It would
be difficult, though, to find a set of rules that were economically and
administratively sensible and also acceptable to most countries. At
one extreme is the abolition of border adjustments, so that all products would bear only the taxes of their country of origin (with possible exceptions for selective excise taxes, measures intended to
restrict consumption of certain items, etc.). At the other extreme,
border adjustments could be permitted for taxes on corporate income as well as indirect taxes, if some good way could be found to

12. In 1965, before the Kennedy Round was over, the then Chief of the State
Department's Division of General Commercial Policy gave an unofficial analysis
of the issues to a business group. He said that while existing border tax arrangements posed no problem, "any correction for undercompensation . . . will have
a definite trade impact." Sidney Weintraub, "Border Tax Adjustments and the
GATT," *The Tax Executive*, July 1965, p. 311.

segregate the share of the former that was truly attributable to exports. Such proposals as have been advanced have not commanded much support and no major changes in the GATT rules are likely to be made, at least for a long time.

The Europeans, who deny there is a problem, are clearly not going to change their tax system because the United States does not like it. Counsels have been divided in Washington, but by mid-1971 the effort to get a change in the international rules seemed to have been dropped. As part of its trade program, the Nixon Administration proposed a device that would reduce direct taxation on American exports. The possibilities of an American value-added tax continued to be studied but with the emphasis on its domestic effects.

Several changes in Europe helped reduce American concern with the border tax issue. In the fall of 1968, as part of an effort to avoid raising the value of the mark, the German government reduced its border tax adjustments (for an announced period of eighteen months).[13] The revaluation of the mark in 1969 further eased the problem. Belgium and Italy, probably largely for domestic reasons, postponed their adoption of value-added taxes. When Belgium arranged to have the system come into effect at the beginning of 1971, it imposed a tax on exports equivalent to the border tax remission, thus neutralizing part of the stimulating effect on its balance of payments surplus.

A new possibility seems to have been opened, that of linking border taxes to a country's balance of payments position as well as the domestic rate of the VAT. One can think of the possibility that the practice will come to be accepted—even if there are no formal rules— that countries in strong surplus do not raise border taxes and perhaps lower them. Even if the domestic rate is changed, border adjustments should only be altered slowly so that the trade effects can be absorbed gradually. While countries will surely not surrender the freedom to decide how heavily they will rely on indirect taxes, awareness of international repercussions may come to have an influence on border adjustments and perhaps even on rates.[14] If exchange rates can

13. France at the same time raised its border adjustments but this corresponded to an increase in domestic VAT rates, whereas the Germans did not change the domestic rate.

14. There are other methods. Baldwin suggests specific changes in GATT rules; *Nontariff Distortions of International Trade* (Washington: Brookings Institution, 1970), pp. 99, 100. Weintraub mentions a proposal for a standstill agreement at existing rates of border adjustment, coupled with a provision that further adjustments (if they are not accompanied by changes in the domestic rates) should be compensated for in the same way as changes in tariff rates that have been bound in GATT agreements; cited, pp. 313-14.

be made somewhat more flexible as part of the process of improving the mechanics of adjustment to balance of payments changes (see chap. 7, pp. 222–25), the prospect of border tax changes will be reduced.

There can be no assurance of such happy results; renewed friction could flare up. In either case, we have a cautionary tale with at least three lessons relevant to the general problem of negotiating about nontariff barriers. The first lesson is how hard it may be to get agreement that a nontariff barrier really exists or is serious. Neither the initial reaction of American businessmen that border taxes are tariffs nor the Common Market contention that there is no problem at all stands up. The correct assessment seems to be the economists' view that there is a trade impact but only under certain conditions and that its scale is often smaller than the tax rate itself first suggests. The second lesson of the episode is that in an increasingly interdependent world even well-established rules may be called into question and become matters of international concern.

What the third lesson is depends on what happens. International friction leading to no improvement would show the risks a country runs when it makes a great issue of something without having thought through the kinds of corrections that would be both satisfactory to it and acceptable to others. If Washington faces the dilemma of admitting impotence or explaining that it had acted impetuously and now found that the issue was not as important as it had seemed to be, part of the price might be a loss of domestic support for future negotiations. A different lesson would be taught if the initial impasse gives way to some progress toward a modification of behavior in the use of border tax adjustments. Then it would appear that when national interests seem to be adversely affected, it is sound to take initiatives calling for change even if it is not very clear at the outset what the changes will be or how acceptable to others. It will not follow that impulse is the best guide to policy, but the clarification of the issue through international discussion will appear as more than a minor by-product.

Government Purchasing

Quite different lessons about nontariff barriers in general can be learned by looking at a quite different case. In contrast to the uncertainties about border taxes, no one doubts that government procurement that discriminates against foreigners is a trade barrier. The question is what can be done about it and by what group of countries. To date, progress has been very limited. EFTA has some rules cast in the general, rather loose terms common to that organization where informal cooperation is a major mode of work. The European Community has been discussing a code which would put enterprises of the member countries on a more or less equal footing and so, in effect, give them all preferential treatment over outsiders. The possibilities of reaching a more comprehensive and more detailed agreement have been explored in the OECD but not pressed to any conclusions.

One does not need to have sat in closed sessions to imagine the difficulties that have been encountered. Almost the first principle is that simple solutions are unacceptable and probably inequitable. A ban on national legislation giving preference to domestic suppliers would strike down the United States's Buy American rules but leave many other countries free to continue their discrimination since it rests on administrative order or unwritten established practice. Any effort to regulate practice immediately raises questions about how it is to be policed. For instance, to create effective international standards for competitive bidding—a common safeguard against discrimination among domestic suppliers—would be an ambitious undertaking. Moreover, governments do not subject all purchasing to competitive bidding for a number of reasons, many of them entirely defensible. In any case, governments are unlikely to accept the proposition that commercial considerations or administrative economy alone must be allowed to govern public procurement. Security considerations are a recognized exception to most trade agreements, and concepts of national security reach far when the survival of an industry may be at stake.

Security apart, government purchasing has to be looked at as a tool of national policy, not just a form of housekeeping. It may be used to favor small business or depressed areas or as a means of developing new industries. It may be used to check the growth of monopoly or resist restrictive practices or discipline those who try to raise prices. If the public sector is large enough, the difference between buying at home or abroad may have an important bearing on the level of activity in parts of the economy and on business cycle policy. The carrying out of national plans, the encouragement of investment in certain industries, and the pursuit of a number of other goals of public policy may depend in part on the direction of government purchasing. While it may well be argued that the shift in trade that might result from even extensive reduction of discrimination in procurement is not likely to nullify major policies, governments will want safeguards and some freedom of action in their use of procurement as an instrument of economic policy. Not all aims can be subordinated to the liberalization of international trade.

Another set of questions concerns the definition of government procurement. Cities, states, provinces are large purchasers. There are limits to the rules that the federal government in the United States or Canada can make about what cities, states, or provinces do. Public utilities may be privately or publicly owned. In Europe, public corporations run major industries; if the rules do not apply to them, would they apply to the body that runs the U.S. Postal Service? What reciprocal offer could the United States make if it asked for nondiscrimination in the purchasing practices of the British Steel Corporation, Charbonnages de France, and the Bundesbahn? Are government contracts for construction to go only to firms that do not discriminate in their procurement? Tied foreign aid, a special form of government purchasing, raises still different issues.

These questions, complications, and obstacles are not paraded to make the task look impossible or to suggest that no important progress can be made without solving all the problems. Quite clearly something useful can be done by a number of devices. A statement of principles would be an advance over the existing situation. A stronger effort than has been made in the past to enforce GATT rules on state trading would help with some points. An attack on the kind of national procurement practices that have no other justification than protection, even if it were confined to a limited range of activities, would by itself create a very different situation from what exists now. Discrimination to favor depressed areas could be permitted if it were no greater against foreigners than against domestic producers outside the area. Some rules could be agreed on even if they were subject to exception and the difficulties of uncertain implementation and policing. The very process of arguing about how internationally agreed principles or guidelines were to be applied might make a difference.

This quick survey is not intended to show how to reduce the nontariff barriers created by government purchasing but rather to show what a wide range of problems must be encountered whenever that effort is made. The conclusion applies to many other nontariff barriers as well. So does the suggestion of the last paragraph, that limited agreements may be the path of progress, however unsatisfactory their imperfections make them at the outset.

Multiple Approaches

The heterogeneity of nontariff barriers means that in dealing with them governments must have multiple aims and multiple approaches. In some cases the aim may be a flat ban on certain practices, but often what is called for is regulation, not outlawing. Quite different kinds of rules will be needed to deal with different barriers. If impediments to trade result from the fact that each country pursues the same objective in a different way, the difficulty could be reduced by harmonizing national measures. No great political hurdles might be thought to stand in the way of agreement on some fairly technical matters, such as the drafting of uniform rules on safety or specifications, but a moment's reflection on the history of the efforts to standardize screw threads or to adopt common weapons in NATO makes it clear that this may be an illusion.

At first sight, the logical response to heterogeneity appears to be a series of separate agreements. The antidumping code would be followed by one on customs procedure, an agreement on government purchasing, an understanding on road taxes, etc. Sometimes this will be the best course, but the separation of issues can also inhibit agreement. Countries are not equally interested in the removal of each type of barrier; in negotiations over road taxes alone, the United States would have had nothing to offer the Europeans to persuade them to end their discriminatory practices, but a bargain was struck when road taxes were linked to ASP. Formally or not, it may be necessary to balance agreements on quite disparate nontariff barriers. And as we saw in a preceding section, arrangements on nontariff barriers cannot be totally separated from tariff bargaining.

In many cases the natural objective will seem to be agreement on a set of rules about a certain type of nontariff barrier (or a group of related practices). Sometimes, though, a more modest aim may have to be accepted. Country A may be willing to stop doing something that damages country B's sales of widgets but not be willing to promise to refrain from ever engaging in the same kind of practice with regard to any product. A commitment to hold a consumption tax on one product to a certain level for a period of time might seem reasonable even if it were impossible to agree on a set of general rules with the same immediate effect. No doubt some progress in the removal of nontariff barriers could be made in this way. But compared to the acceptance of general rules, there are disadvantages in a discrete series of understandings. Such a system seems less stable and offers a weak foundation for building lasting agreements. It also falls easily into a pattern of bilateral deals or arrangements among a few countries that exchange favors not extended to others and so introduce new elements of discrimination into international trade.

One of the problems posed by the heterogeneity of nontariff barriers is where to start in dealing with them. The most clearly identifiable and those that lend themselves best to regulation by some kind of international code may not be the most important. Should the emphasis be on steps that will quickly find wide acceptance or on getting started on the hardest problems which will undoubtedly take years to solve? One guideline is a pragmatic one: Who feels badly enough hurt by another country's practices to make a major effort to change them? But complaints alone are not enough, as the border tax episode shows; there has to be some prospect of working out mutually advantageous agreements. Another need is some clear evidence that governments are really interested in doing something about nontariff barriers. Everyone complains about everyone else's nontariff barriers, but a complaints procedure set up in the OECD is rarely used. Businessmen, who are best placed to judge the effects of many barriers, have made few specific proposals. Some seem to concentrate on adapting themselves to the status quo. Others may wonder whether they would be helped or hurt by a general attack on nontariff barriers. Some may be aware of the ramifications of the problem and fear that it will lead to not just governmental but intergovernmental interference in their activities.

It is, however, a business group that has provided the most comprehensive suggestion for dealing with nontariff barriers. Guided by Jean Royer, a former Assistant Secretary General of GATT, the International Chamber of Commerce (ICC) in 1969 recommended that each government formally declare its intent to remove or reduce nontariff barriers, to refrain from introducing new ones or making those in existence more restrictive, and to accept the obligation to consult with those who feel seriously affected by its practices and to move toward the acceptance of rules governing the use of nontariff barriers.[15] Easily given and as easily made meaningless, a declaration of intent to reduce nontariff barriers could, nevertheless, be an important benchmark. The obligation to consult would be the vital *modus operandi* of the proposal. As a continuing arrangement it would provide assurance that any matter of importance would come under international scrutiny (the proposal suggests procedures and emphasizes the role of the GATT secretariat and committees of experts). Its ultimate value, however, would depend on the kind of criteria adopted to judge what is acceptable or not. These might be built up on something like a common law basis or might be written into codes or other forms of agreement.

15. *Non-tariff Obstacles to Trade*, report prepared by the Joint Committee on Non-tariff Obstacles to Trade (Meeting on April 28, 1969). For present purposes I have singled out the key features of a proposal that is more elaborately worked out than my summary indicates and that suggests what might be done about a number of different barriers.

Almost any workable agreement, whether arrived at by the method recommended by the ICC or otherwise, would have to provide procedures for complaint, consultation, negotiation, and settlement of disputes. A general agreement leaves room for dispute as to how it is being applied; a detailed agreement requires rulings; a series of specific commitments will give rise to violations and exceptions. Moreover, these processes may not be confined to the limited purposes for which they are originally set up. It is in the nature of nontariff barriers that the removal (or limitation) of one is likely to reveal (or lead to the creation of) another, so that a complaints procedure may turn out to be the principal means of dealing with nontariff barriers, specifically and in general. What is not in an agreement at the outset may well find its way there as time goes on.

A general commitment to consult or negotiate could be enhanced by some broad pledges, such as not "unnecessarily" to impede or distort international trade and to negotiate to minimize the damage to others from any "necessary" actions. If they are honest, governments will not go beyond such loose commitments concerning trade-distorting practices as a whole (i.e., those not covered by specific agreements). The reasons are simple. Many important trade-distorting practices are closely linked with the kinds of measures governments must continually take to manage their economies. Too much is at stake to believe that trade liberalization should always be regarded as the most important objective. Moreover, the interpenetration of the industrialized economies and their openness to one another increase the number of measures that come to be thought of as damaging other countries' interests, so that a pledge made today about nontariff barriers in general will be discovered five years from now to cover unthought-of activities. No government can make so open-ended a commitment except in a highly qualified form.

An illustration of the uncertain future is provided by the surge of concern with pollution. The governments of most industrialized countries feel the need—but in different degrees—to improve the environment in which their people live. National control over pollutants will become stricter and more elaborate. What may not be produced or used domestically cannot reasonably be imported, whether it be automobile engines, industrial and agricultural chemicals, or household detergents and garden sprays. Packaging and containers, long the subjects of international scrutiny, will be looked at in new ways. What airplanes can fly over what areas and what kinds of ships may enter harbors will be subject to new rules. In one sense merely an extension of what is already done about health and safety, regulation to protect the environment may grow astronomically. And if governments apply different standards, nontariff barriers will multiply. Products that are not themselves capable of polluting will also be affected since restrictions on the use of fuel and more stringent requirements about the disposal of wastes and exhausts will impose new costs. How the costs are paid for will affect the competitive position of producers, and countries will follow different practices. Taxes may be used to regulate as well as to distribute burdens among producers, users, and the general public. Sometimes there will be a good case for border adjustments. Even when this is not so, producers will press for matching taxes on imports or trade restrictions and measures to avoid penalizing exports.

Many problems could be avoided if governments adopted uniform standards and arranged financing so that it did not distort competitiveness. Because concern with the environment is general in industrialized societies, a good basis for cooperation exists. Perhaps much will be accomplished, but it is unlikely that governments would agree on all standards even if they responded only to scientific advice without the admixture of commercial pressure. Priorities and possibilities differ from country to country, and to let the need for international agreement slow an already complicated task will often seem unacceptable. At least initially, then, there is likely to be a growth of nontariff barriers and trade-distorting practices as a by-product of meritorious effort throughout the industrialized world. There is also an opportunity, because the problem is foreseeable, to reduce the difficulties by consultation and cooperation.[16] A step in this direction is an OECD procedure for notification and consultation inaugurated in 1971.

Even where there are no major changes in the range of government activities, new questions will arise about nontariff barriers and trade-distorting practices. Because of their increased exposure to foreign competition as a result of the lowering of tariffs, businessmen will think more often of the possibilities of antidumping duties. The resulting arguments about the justification of pricing practices, the difficulty of getting acceptable data, and the attempt to apply uniform standards to antidumping rules will suggest the possibility of international rules about price discrimination. Foreign subsidies will be scru-

16. Interesting additional possibilities arise. Should trade policy be used to exert pressure on laggard governments whose failure to raise standards is regarded either as an effort to get an unfair trade advantage or as a hazard because their pollution affects others? Will proximity, shared water courses, ocean currents, and the patterns of prevailing winds become reasons for trade discrimination not applied against more distant countries? Will common standards among a small group come to resemble preferential arrangements directed against outsiders? The question will arise whether it is right to sell to foreigners pollutants that are banned at home but not abroad.

tinized and countervailing duties invoked. Questions will arise. Are tax exemptions, investment allowances, accelerated depreciation, government-financed research, and low-cost government loans to be regarded as subsidies? Are subsidies that help an industry adjust to new competitive conditions or offset the disadvantages of responding to a national policy of providing employment in a depressed area subject to the same strictures as other kinds of subsidy? How are subsidies to be compared with other practices that give domestic producers an advantage over foreigners? What start out as discussions of nontariff barriers will more and more become considerations of "the conditions of competition," and then private business practices will be drawn into the picture.

Not only trade in goods will be affected. Sensitivity to price changes will raise questions about national shipping laws, rate discrimination, and subsidies; domestic transportation rates, too, are likely to come under closer scrutiny because they affect foreign trade. Other services are growing in importance in international economic relations as a result of improved transportation and communication and the interpenetration of economies. Films and film-making, records and tapes, computer software, industrial and fashion design, architectural and industrial drafting, book production, and a number of professional services are becoming more and more internationalized. The regulations and taxes to which these activities are subjected, though only partly analogous to nontariff barriers, seem likely to become more frequent objects of international negotiation.

The prospect begins to sound alarming. Trade policy no longer appears to be just a matter of removing obstacles which primarily benefit special interests but of finding means of either coordinating the ways governments manage their economies or of rendering their uncoordinated efforts less harmful to one another. Who believes that governments are prepared to agree, or even negotiate internationally, about all these things? Or that the results of their doing so would always be good? If the removal of nontariff barriers means that the governments are going to have to negotiate with foreigners about matters which are already infinitely troublesome to deal with within the bounds of national sovereignty, why start? The vision induces paralysis.

Things are not quite that bad. The process I have sketched is a dynamic one, involving a kind of dialectic in which each step leads to, or at least makes more logical, another step; the solution of one problem, if it does not create another problem, at least makes one more manifest. That is quite different from saying that, because all these things are interrelated, you cannot reasonably act on one without acting on the others. Though it may seem illogical to draw a line separating one kind of behavior from another with which it is linked, a line can be drawn. It was drawn around tariffs and quotas without great regard to the effects of nontariff barriers; it can be drawn around a practice on which international agreement can be reached to separate it from those which cannot, or cannot yet, be regulated. The identifiable creates its own boundaries, and the manageable as well.

We appear to have come far from the consideration of such humdrum matters as fictitious prices for customs valuation, road taxes, labeling requirements, and safety regulations for automobiles. The effort to look ahead and apply a bit of imagination has produced a kind of soaring leap into unfamiliar territory; much of it is beyond the horizon, but that does not mean it is not there. How long it will take to get there is not clear, but at each step the horizon recedes and the terrain in between changes at least a little. It is, as we shall see, a region to which other lines of policy also lead.

An Industry-by-Industry Approach?

Nontariff barriers and trade-distorting practices are often linked very closely with a government's policy toward a specific industry. One of the obstacles to further tariff reduction is the reluctance found in every country to expose certain industries to international competition. These two facts suggest that future trade negotiations might well deal first with one industry and then another instead of trying to deal with a wide range of trade barriers all at once. The idea has a short history and an uncertain future.

In the course of the Kennedy Round it became clear that it was going to be especially difficult to get agreement on the removal of tariffs in several important industries. Early in 1965, groups with limited terms of reference were set up on chemicals, cotton textiles, iron and steel, pulp and paper, and nonferrous metals, principally aluminum. What they achieved varied in scope and quality.[17]

Looking ahead, Sir Eric Wyndham White, then Director General of GATT, gave the term a different connotation. Without being specific—the Kennedy Round was not yet over—he spoke of some major industries "characterized by modern equipment, high technology, and large-scale production, and by the international character of their operations and markets." By treating these industries separately, he suggested, it might be possible to negotiate arrangements leading to

17. The results are assessed in Preeg, cited, chap. 6, which also gives an account of their work, but their origin is explained in his chap. 5, pp. 89 and 90.

free trade "within a defined period."[18] It is typical of the genial magic of Sir Eric that he should somehow turn a procedure for dealing with hard cases inside out and offer the prospect of free trade at salient points in the world's industrial economy. He did not subsequently elaborate on his plans, and his main concern may have been to find a fresh focus of attention for negotiations after the Kennedy Round. In any case, the idea is worth examination because it might provide a way of dealing with the more-than-tariff problems that confront trade policymakers.[19]

Concentration is the key advantage of the industry-by-industry (or sector) approach. By focusing on all the barriers to trade in a given industry, it gives an opportunity to take full account of relations that are not usually dealt with in depth in trade negotiations. Tariffs and nontariff barriers can be looked at together, along with other kinds of governmental measures that help domestic producers and hurt foreigners and also private business practices. Judgment about effective protection can replace emphasis on nominal tariff rates. By looking at an industry in depth, negotiators would make realistic judgments about the effects of existing barriers and practices and the results of removing or altering them. Other forces bringing about change in the industry could be taken into account to see if they helped or hindered adaptation to new conditions. Understandings might be reached on the pace of adjustment instead of leaving this crucial matter to each government's politically colored view of what was possible. Any results achieved could be expressed in terms of the advantage each country would get in the future instead of being justified as a formal balancing of tariff concessions on past trade, the traditional way of measuring "reciprocity" (see chap. 10, pp. 364–70).

Whether an industry would lend itself to this kind of negotiation would depend on its organization and character. In complex multiproduct industries, major countries are apt to import as well as export, and so the chances are improved of finding a basis for balanced advantage in trade. When a significant part of each country's industry is foreign-owned, some firms are, in a sense, on both sides of the negotiation and can probably adjust more easily than producers with only

18. Speech to the Deutsche Gesellschaft für Auswärtige Politik, October 27, 1966, "Perspektiven des Welthandels nach der Kennedy-Runde," *Europa-Archiv*, Folge 22, 1966, pp. 793-802. Quoted from mimeographed English text distributed by GATT.

19. There are, to be sure, already some industry agreements: the European Coal and Steel Community, the international cotton textile arrangement, and the automotive agreement between the United States and Canada. It would be misleading to examine the approach just sketched in the light of these three cases which are grouped by hindsight, not by their common characteristics.

one base. The sector approach may also be promising in new industries where barriers are minor and in rapidly growing industries where barriers are mainly nuisances to many producers. The less important the trade barriers, the smaller the gains from abolishing them, but there may be value in insuring against new ones and perhaps even in setting a good example for other industries.

When technology is rapidly changing, invention, innovation, and the diffusion of control over know-how by patent licenses and other means may do far more than trade barriers to shape world trade. Governments that fear that their countries may not share adequately in technological progress may find in the sector approach a basis for agreements that help them keep abreast of change better than the often futile method of restricting imports.

It seems obvious that the industry approach is more likely to work when there are relatively few producers, as in the cases Wyndham White seemed to have in mind. Not only is agreement easier among fewer people, but such producers are likely to be relatively strong and able to cope with change. In contrast, in an industry with a large number of producers, the gamut from the strongest to the weakest will be great and radical liberalization of trade may mark quite a few for sacrifice. Wide geographical distribution within a country, as in the American textile industry, may inhibit agreement, while in other industries concentration of production in a few hands makes it possible to judge with some accuracy what will happen if trade barriers are removed. Therein lies a danger; a few producers can agree more easily than a large number that no big changes will be allowed to follow from the removal of trade barriers.

Worry about this point has made some people reject the industry approach. Strong producers seem certain to have a major influence, not only on what arrangements are made but on how they are carried out. It is easy to believe that they will try to decide among themselves what the pattern of world trade should be. To reach agreement, the strongest firms may have to agree to stay their competitive hand and guarantee weaker ones against serious damage. A "balanced bargain" may easily mean the freezing of past shares of the market. The same kind of approach may be taken by governments; it was, after all, the Canadian government that insisted on assurances from the American automobile companies before agreeing to "free trade."

There is no doubt that this sort of thing might happen under the industry approach, but it is not entirely clear that the risks are greater than under a different approach. After all, governmental trade barriers have often been essential props for private agreements. If what a government really wants is restriction, it is not likely to think that the way to maintain it is through an industry agreement that removes trade barriers. The failure of cartels in the past has resulted less from what governments have done than from the outbreak of competition among the cartel members or between them and outsiders. What begins as an understanding may become a misunderstanding when incentives grow great enough. The chances of competition are greater when trade·barriers are fewer, and for that reason governments may see the industry approach as a way of increasing the likelihood that public decisions, not oligopolistic private ones, will dominate.

The chances of the industry approach's becoming a vehicle for liberalization depends on the strength of conflicting forces. How great is the desire of producers to be free of past impediments? How strong are those who will accept liberalization only if they are shielded from its results? Where will governments put their weight if there are serious conflicts of view in the industry? Will the combination of restriction-minded businessmen and some governments block the increased competition that should result from the removal of trade barriers? Can drastic trade liberalization be achieved if transitional arrangements are made to cushion the results of removing trade barriers? How can such arrangements be kept temporary and made to exert pressure for the rationalization of production and trade instead of becoming a new form of protection?

Quite different doubts arise as to whether the industry approach, narrowing the range of products eligible for negotiation, would reduce the chances of removing tariffs by ruling out the traditional practice of exchanging concessions on completely different products. To strike a balance entirely within a single industry may prove quite difficult. Experienced negotiators have told me that they are skeptical of what could be achieved in so narrow a framework. They believe that the industry approach would put less pressure, not more, on governments to reduce their duties.

There are related questions about how one should define an industry for the purpose of liberalizing trade in it. The automobile industry seems a reasonably clear case, but the Kennedy Round showed the concern of some participants to treat trucks differently from passenger cars and the Canadian-American agreement makes distinctions between original and replacement parts. It is stretching a point to call the chemical industry one industry. Producers are concerned about tariffs and import restrictions on the things they use as well as on those they sell, so that one industry agreement may depend on action in other industries. Such problems present important practical difficulties and make it clear that the "industry-by-industry approach" is not as neat and simple as it sounds. They show that it may well be necessary to negotiate about what to negotiate about and suggest that sometimes a bargain will be possible only if several industry negotiations are going on at the same time.

The problems inherent in the sector approach do not, however, constitute grounds for rejecting the idea altogether. "Not proven—but possible" seems a better verdict if the objective is liberalization. But the reasons for doubt suggest another possibility. Perhaps the industry-by-industry approach has something to offer in the case of those industries that governments regard as so important to the national interest that they will not take the risk of removing trade barriers unless they are sure that the result will not mean the elimination or serious deterioration of national capacity in that kind of production. Another possibility is that the industry approach might prove useful in cases in which extensive liberalization is only a remote possibility until major adjustments have been made in national economies. By their nature these cases do not easily lend themselves to international agreement, but it is not impossible that an open international examination of the sources of resistance to liberalization would suggest the possibility of limited arrangements that would reduce some of the conflicts between national practices and even make some governments' policies more effective than they could be when they were based on national action alone. A far cry from the idea of moving to free trade, industry by industry, these possibilities are worth keeping in mind as we probe still further into the complex interplay of external and internal factors that now characterize the economic relations of the industrialized countries.

BUSINESS PRACTICES

Sometimes in rough country one finds ponds or tiny waterfalls that call attention to an underground stream. So it is with the references here and there in this chapter to private business practices that affect international trade. Antidumping rules are concerned with foreign pricing practices; other trade distortions are rooted in understandings among domestic producers; restrictions, whatever their purpose, may protect market-sharing or price-fixing arrangements or even monopolies; the allocation of quotas for exports or imports tends to perpetuate a division of the market among certain sellers or buyers; patents, hardly mentioned so far in this book, have long been objects of international concern because of the restrictions they may impose on trade and competition. The stream will come to the surface again in the next chapter, since government policy toward investment can have an important bearing on the state of competition, and the rise of the multinational enterprise raises new questions about the regulation of business in the public interest.

Like real underground streams, this one is sometimes hard to follow and always hard to channel. The postwar record of seeking international agreement on private business practices is not a distinguished one. The difficulties of the past seem bound to persist, but the widening scope of foreign economic policy seems equally bound to lead to new attacks on the problem.

The designers of the Bretton Woods world picture, it will be recalled, looked backward as well as forward. One of the things they saw was that in the interwar period

> there were few industrialized countries, outside of the United States, in which the production and sale of manufactured goods were effectively competitive. . . . Giant combines and . . . powerful cartels . . . fixed prices and terms of sale, divided productive activities, markets, and customers, limited production, assigned quotas in output and sales, and enforced . . . regulations by the imposition of penalties.[20]

Perhaps the description of the past was a little too vivid but there was no doubt about the validity of the conclusion for the future: "The effort to expand trade by reducing tariffs and eliminating quotas might well be defeated if no action were taken to prevent the erection of private tariff and quota systems by international cartels." It was also logical to conclude that "if action against restrictive business practices in international trade is to be effective, it must be taken by many states in accordance with a common understanding as to policy."

Consequently, the Charter of the International Trade Organization (ITO) had a chapter on restrictive business practices. It was difficult to negotiate and showed it. Few if any countries were willing to go anything like as far as the United States with its antitrust laws. A deep-grained European attitude that one should distinguish between "good" and "bad" cartels made it impossible to rule out any restrictive practices as such. The criteria by which results were to be condemned necessarily remained general. Differences limited the area of agreement; enforcement had to be left almost entirely in national hands. The result was a set of ambiguous rules and complicated procedures. From the beginning, objective observers had honest doubts about how they would work. But the Charter pointed a direction, provided a forum for complaints, and gave any government that wanted it a chance to

20. Clair Wilcox, *A Charter for World Trade* (New York: Macmillan, 1949), p. 103. The next quotation is from p. 105.

push for international action. And there was little doubt that the alternative was, from the American point of view, "not a better agreement, but a looser one, or perhaps no agreement at all."[21]

In the end there *was* no agreement at all—but not to any important degree because of the deficiencies of the business practice rules. Even before the ITO Charter was certifiably dead, but when its end was in sight, the United States proposed that the U.N. Economic and Social Council try to work out an international agreement dealing with business practices. A committee was appointed which soon found how much disagreement there was, and nothing came of the effort. GATT did not inherit the ITO provisions about business practices. From 1955 to 1960 there were discussions about adding something along these lines, but they bore little fruit (a study and affirmation of the fact that complaints about restrictive practices might be in order under some GATT provisions). As part of its work on European productivity in the '50s, the OEEC had some experts look into business practices. In the '60s, its successor, the OECD, continued to explore the subject, slowly and quietly published texts and studies, and in late 1967 established a loose arrangement for government consultation and the exchange of information. Like so many other subjects, restrictive business practices appear on the agenda of UNCTAD,[22] but nowhere, as the '70s open, is there any broad intergovernmental arrangement for effective action in these matters.

Something more has been accomplished on some narrower bases. The European Coal and Steel Community is, among other things, a device for the international public control of heavy industry. Its High Authority was given powers—not always effectively exercised—over mergers, cartels, prices, and restrictive practices. The Common Market Treaty has more comprehensive, but in some ways weaker, rules. Though the process is slow and uncertain, a body of Community law is being built up and a number of private efforts at restriction have been checked. EFTA, too, made rules about restrictive practices. They depended largely on intergovernmental cooperation, and only a few cases were formally dealt with. One of the reasons these trading

21. "A Cartel Policy for the United States," Report of the Committee on Cartels and Monopoly, in George W. Stocking and Myron W. Watkins, *Cartels or Competition?* (New York: Twentieth Century Fund, 1948), p. 424.
22. In the ITO negotiations, as now, the less developed countries saw themselves "as consumers of cartelized goods and services," in Wilcox's phrase, and wanted something done (cited, p. 107). They are apt to want to exempt from any rules that might be made their numerous state enterprises and sometimes monopolies in infant industries as well. Commodity agreements, which look like government cartels to some people, are generally favored by less developed countries, at least in principle. About this subject I shall have more to say in another book.

groups felt the need to concern themselves with business practices was that they were freeing trade among themselves; one of the reasons they were able to agree on at least modest steps was that their commitments to economic interdependence among themselves were comprehensive. Both conditions are becoming more and more true of the industrial nations as a whole, which suggests that the time may be approaching when governments will once again turn their attention to the international regulation of business practices.

One reason the problem has not seemed pressing is that the postwar period has been one of great expansion. There has been less incentive to take restrictive action than if times had been bad, and also fewer chances for outsiders to detect any secret agreements that might have been made. But the impulses are not dead. As the expansion of world steel capacity appeared to outrun demand in the latter part of the '60s, some familiar reactions showed themselves. The German industry organized a series of sales agencies to reduce competition. The Chambre Syndicale de la Sidérurgie in France put forth plans to avoid what is usually called, in those circles, "destructive" or "cutthroat" competition. Even the dynamic newcomers in Japan spoke of their willingness "to promote harmonious and mutually satisfactory relations with the steel industries and other industries of the world."[23] American steelmen found in the State Department a surrogate who did not have to fear the antitrust laws when it asked foreigners to restrict their shipments. Other industries have not been immune to similar reactions.

Even if economic growth in the '70s should be slower than in the '50s and '60s, the conditions would not be altogether propitious for restrictive tendencies. The greatest threat to international cartels has not been government action but competition, either from outsiders or from members of the cartel who saw the opportunity to gain something for themselves while others held up prices or confined their selling efforts. The same bad times that stimulate restrictive agreements spur the parties to them to press their own advantages in this way. The removal of trade barriers makes international competition easier and deprives governments of weapons they have traditionally used to support the market-sharing arrangements made by producers. Increased international investment, too, has put more sellers in more markets. Widespread awareness of the gains to be had from being the first to exploit a technological advance may make it harder than be-

23. Yoshihiro Inayama, President of Yawata Iron and Steel Co., Ltd., "A Challenge to the Steelmakers of the World," *Report of Proceedings*, First Annual Conference, International Iron and Steel Institute, Brussels, November 11–12, 1967, p. 55.

fore to persuade some firms that their interests are best served by preserving the status quo.

Not all the problems arise from simple restriction or the possibility of suppression of technological progress. In the late '60s and early '70s, the United States underwent one of its greatest merger movements, marked this time by the construction of conglomerates; the full implications have still to be worked out. There is a marked foreign spillover, but in Europe the increase in mergers mostly created larger non-conglomerate units, partly to meet the needs of the modern world for size and partly to cope with the challenge of American giants. While European governments may object to one merger or another, they and the Commission of the European Community support and sometimes foment this development. Investment policies, whether national or those the Community is trying to work out, are much concerned with competition and the structure of industry. In the United States, too, questions are being raised about industrial structure and foreign trade. For example, should those who administer the antitrust laws take more account than in the past of world markets in judging the maximum permissible size of American companies? Would certain mergers enhance the ability of some industries to meet import competition without trade restriction? Whether the target is limiting restrictive practices or something else, governments are increasingly concerned with influencing business behavior; their efforts are often directly concerned with foreign trade and investment, and sooner or later, by one route or another, they will find themselves dealing with some of these problems internationally.

The difficulties that made it so hard to draft satisfactory provisions for the ITO would again beset any comprehensive endeavor to regulate restrictive business practices. However, one gap between the United States and Europe has been partly closed. During the postwar period Britain, Germany, and to a lesser extent several other countries have adopted stronger laws to check monopoly and restriction than they had in the past. Like the European Community's laws, they differ significantly from American antitrust measures, but they differ even more strikingly from the prewar European practices. The similarity of texts alone can be misleading. As the history of antitrust in the United States has shown, administration, enforcement, and the government's attitude largely determine how business is regulated. European views differ greatly as to whether it is wise to try to "legislate competition." A rapid convergence of policies on both sides of the Atlantic is unlikely, and an even greater gap separates these countries from Japan. On key issues, domestic economic and political considerations remain dominant and sometimes delicate. But if the governments feel they have reason to try, the gap that still exists might be easier to bridge than it was twenty-five years ago.

To go through the travail that will be needed to remove some of the remaining governmental barriers to trade and ignore those imposed by private business would indeed be "high-level shadow-boxing," as a State Department commentary on the ITO Charter put it. And yet it may well seem neither necessary nor wise to make a new effort to reach a comprehensive international agreement governing private business practices. Specific needs will become clear, probably with increasing frequency as economic relations among the industrial countries become more complex. In dealing with problems as they arise, governments may put together, piecemeal, a set of arrangements without a superstructure that will begin to look like international cooperation about business practices. The trouble with such a course is that it is likely to produce a certain amount of confusion and inconsistency and may add to the conflicts between national policy and the pursuit of broad economic advantage that already characterize international economic relations. As in the case of nontariff barriers —which themselves raise questions about business practices—a process of consultation and complaint that leads to increased discussion of basic issues and the possible formulation of rules may both clarify the seriousness of the problems and provide some means of solving them.

NATIONAL INDUSTRIAL ADJUSTMENT

The unprecedented freeing of trade among the industrialized countries in the postwar period has not been accompanied by economic dislocation, massive unemployment, or the decline and fall of major industries. General, sometimes very rapid, economic expansion—some of it traceable to the removal of trade barriers—has, in the aggregate, more than offset the contraction that has taken place in certain lines and certain places. Nevertheless, one of the reasons some trade barriers have been reduced less than others is fear that the resulting imports would, by their volume or price, destroy or seriously damage a domestic industry. Even if they one day accept the idea of free trade, governments will insist on retaining the right to limit imports in some circumstances so that domestic producers are not driven to the wall at a pace that is politically unacceptable, socially damaging, or economically wasteful. Such fears may not be justified; the whole of postwar history suggests that they are at least exaggerated. Nevertheless, it seems prudent to be prepared for the possibility that further trade barrier reduction or, indeed, sharper foreign competition resulting from other causes may call for greater adjustment in the future than in the past. The existence of a set of policies for coping with this problem might in itself improve the chances of making trade barrier reduction possible even if general economic expansion is slower in the '70s than in the '50s and '60s. Not only progress, but even the preservation of the liberalization already achieved may depend on the ability to bring about adjustment as an alternative to restoring old trade barriers.

Adjustment, as the word is used here, refers to the national economy as a whole, but the initial focus is, of course, on the industry or industries directly affected by import competition. There may be some, probably rather small, American industries that would be all but wiped out if they lost their protection against imports. For the most part, though, it is as Percy Bidwell once said: ". . . tariff changes usually . . . determine only the dimensions of the industry."[24] Though some firms may go out of business, others will be able to cope with foreign competition. Within many American industries the range of productivity, profitability, financial strength, and other factors is very great between the strongest and the weakest firms. Even the variation in technology is wide, as in the textile industry where some plants are highly capital-intensive and others follow traditional methods in which labor costs are probably crucial. Whether the best adjustment is to increase productivity, to diversify product lines, to concentrate on certain kinds of activity, or to close up shop and get out of the industry altogether is a matter that will differ with the plant, the firm, the industry, the region, the investor, and the workers. Sometimes new competitive pressure will bring out the best in an industry so that it becomes far more competitive in domestic and even export markets than was believed possible. Where protection has long been a way of life, the relatively weak part of an industry may be larger and the problems of adjustment greater than elsewhere in the economy.

A protected industry, including the strongest firms in it, can be expected to resist the idea that it should have to adjust to import competition. Shifts in domestic competitive pressure—new firms, new plants, new techniques, new capital, new substitute materials—have to be accepted as inherent in the American economy; but imports can be checked by government action, and foreign competition offers a highly visible target. Indeed, if domestic pressures are already strong, imports are likely to be singled out as the straw that is breaking the camel's back. Whether this judgment is correct or not, it

24. *What the Tariff Means to American Industries* (New York: Harper, for the Council on Foreign Relations, 1956), p. 289.

does not follow that the public interest coincides with that of the industry. On the contrary, unless the circumstances are quite exceptional, the long-run public interest is best served by insuring that American resources—materials, capital, labor, and management—are used as efficiently as possible. Ability to meet foreign competition is, as a rule, a significant test of efficient allocation. There is, however, a public interest in seeing to it that adjustment to new competitive conditions be made as humanely and with as little waste as possible. The least apt, whether as workers, managers, or entrepreneurs, will usually be among the hardest hit. Often weak spots are regionally concentrated, sometimes in places where alternative employment is not easily found. It is a proper matter of public concern both to ease the impact of adjustment and to facilitate the shift to alternative employment of human and other resources.

The first requirement is time. That is one of the easiest things for policy to provide. The heart of the problem is the use to which time is put. In the past the United States government has not done much to insure that time was well used. Whether it could do more is the first question to be considered in discussing future adjustment policy. The thought that the answer is affirmative already has a place in American history—but a rather peculiar one.

Adjustment Assistance

Raised in discussions of postwar trade problems during World War II, the idea of governmental adjustment assistance played almost no part in public debate about trade policy for some years afterwards.[25] A few rather tentative suggestions met with sharp rebuffs from both business and government. Part of the negativism seems to have stemmed from a certain confusion of purpose. The idea of compensating people for a change in government policy—though it has an honorable but rather sparse history—was rejected with a good bit of suspicion, probably wisely. Doubts about the feasibility of establishing

25. The first clear proposal for adjustment assistance linked to American trade liberalization that I know of is Eugene Staley and Winfield Riefler, "Two Proposals for Tariff Reduction," No. 17, in *American Interests in the War and Peace* (New York: Council on Foreign Relations, 1945), mimeographed. In a report for the International Labor Office a year earlier, Staley had advocated industrial adjustment policies for all countries to meet changes in world production and trade and gave special attention to the need for industrialized countries to open markets for products of the less developed countries by moving out of certain lines of production. A skeptical analysis of the whole problem, including the case against compensation, was provided by Clair Wilcox, a leading advocate of trade liberalization, in "Relief for Victims of Tariff Cuts," *The American Economic Review*, December 1950, pp. 884-89.

sound criteria for "injury" were coupled with fears of creating a new kind of pork barrel. Advocates of greater trade liberalization worried about the effect of directing attention to the "damage" it would bring and doubted that the promise of aid would win many supporters to their cause. Subsequent discussion mostly rejected the idea of compensation and put the main emphasis on adaptation, making clear that measures that simply bolstered up a weak industry indefinitely were not contemplated.

In 1953, the Public Advisory Board for Mutual Security (the Bell committee) suggested tax adjustments, federal loans to firms, government aid in retraining workers, and a number of other devices to help cope with the increase in imports that could be expected from measures of trade liberalization it was proposing. Like most reports sponsored by an outgoing administration, this one had little impact; but then the Commission on Foreign Economic Policy (the Randall Commission), appointed by the Eisenhower Administration to look into a whole range of questions about foreign economic policy, provided the launching pad from which the idea of adjustment assistance moved into the orbit of serious possibilities. Organized labor provided the fuel. David McDonald, head of the steelworkers, attached to the Commission's report a statement (not endorsed by the other members) advocating a fairly detailed program of adjustment assistance. From then on Congress was never without one or more bills on the subject, none of which passed. By the end of the '50s, the idea of adjustment assistance was a staple of trade policy discussions and then became a major feature of the Trade Expansion Act of 1962. With strong labor support, moderate opposition from business, and a good deal of skepticism in Congress, an elaborate program was enacted into law and then became a dead letter.

The tests of injury required to trigger adjustment assistance and some other procedural provisions were so tightly drawn that the law proved inoperable during the Kennedy Round and its immediate aftermath. When legislation was needed to put the 1965 automotive agreement with Canada into effect, adjustment assistance was provided on somewhat easier terms, which were made use of by a number of groups of workers in the years that followed. This law became the model for a revision of the more general adjustment assistance rules proposed to Congress by the Johnson Administration and then taken up again in the Nixon Administration's proposed trade legislation of 1969. In that year the Tariff Commission for the first time made use of the TEA's adjustment provisions; a new interpretation of the law that ascribed current injury to tariff cuts made well in the past made certain steelworkers eligible for governmental aid. Early in 1970

President Nixon, acting on the basis of the Commission's finding of injury, invited the piano and glass industries to apply for adjustment assistance at the same time that he granted the one partial tariff relief and refused it to the other. A task force from the executive branch studied the shoe industry, and the President initiated adjustment measures before using his authority (for the first time) to ask the Tariff Commission to make an escape clause investigation.[26]

Other cases have followed, making clear the Nixon Administration's belief that adjustment assistance is a good alternative to import restriction. The request for new legislation was not acted on and meanwhile efforts were continued to make the old law work. How well this can be done and how effective the assistance being given will prove to be are matters about which it is too early to form a judgment as I write. There are, however, some broader issues that need to be considered about the purpose of adjustment assistance, the use of import restraints to gain time, and the relation between these measures and other government economic policies.

The availability of governmental adjustment assistance is not likely to persuade people in protected industries to become free traders. It could, however, influence the judgment of people whose interests are broader. For instance, a Congressman with both protected and export industries in his district could reasonably make a different calculation as to how he should vote on a tariff measure if he knew that adjustment assistance was available than if his choice seemed to be one of turning his back on one segment of his constituency to favor the more general interest of the rest. Similarly, the leadership of the AFL-CIO could point to adjustment assistance in justifying its support of trade liberalization in the '60s in spite of the fact that some unions in protected industries opposed the removal of barriers. How much the failure of adjustment assistance to work may have influenced the shift in emphasis in organized labor's position on trade policy at the beginning of the '70s is hard to say, but the problem of a divided interest will persist for labor as well as for business, as a section below makes clear. Communities, too, have an interest in knowing that, if local plants are shut, workers' incomes will be to some degree sustained and help provided to retrain them for other jobs. The dominant community interest, however, is likely to be in the possibility of bringing in new industry; this is one of the reasons why, as will be argued later, adjustment assistance must be thought of more broadly than in the past.

The possible influence on attitudes toward trade liberalization pro-

26. *Report of the Task Force on Nonrubber Footwear* (Washington: GPO, 1970); White House Press Release, June 24, 1970.

vides too thin a basis to justify adjustment assistance. The more fundamental political significance of the approach lies in two implied principles. On the one hand, adjustment assistance recognizes a public interest in helping achieve the best possible adaptation to changes brought about by measures of public policy, whether the help is given to private people or communities. On the other hand, adjustment assistance recognizes the principle that the preservation of a certain pattern of private interest should not be allowed to block change that is in the public interest. No producer (employer or labor) has a just claim that the continuation of his existing activities should be paid for by the rest of the country simply because he cannot compete with imports.

These principles were absent from American trade policy before 1962. The doctrine of "no injury" through selective tariff reduction made them illogical. When it was decided to cut tariffs across the board instead of item by item, the possibility of injury had to be accepted. But then the TEA's adjustment assistance provision proved inadequate. This book is not the place to discuss precisely what kind of legislation would be best or which kinds of assistance are superior to others, important as these matters are. The fundamental point is that unless it is accepted that private interests may be hurt by measures taken in the public interest, future American trade policy (and indeed other elements of foreign economic policy as well) will be seriously circumscribed. If this fact is accepted, it makes sense to discuss adjustment assistance as a way to bridge the gap between general and particular interests in a manner that promotes justice, human values, and efficiency.[27]

The Escape Clause

An approach of the sort just sketched has implications for international agreement on the temporary use of trade restrictions to pave the way for greater liberalization. The idea is already accepted in such arrangements as the practice of spreading tariff reductions over a period of years. In hard cases, the period could be made longer, without losing the prime virtue of establishing a clear-cut time limit. GATT rules that permit the temporary raising, or restoration, of barriers to help meet a difficult problem and the resort to foreign export restraints to get breathing space also have the advantage of incorporating some external pressure for adjustment. In the case of purely

27. The general interest does not have to be calculated in terms of the specific barrier; it can reside in the interest in trade barrier reduction generally or the link between the reduction of a specific American barrier and the reduction by other countries of barriers to American exports.

national measures, it is harder to be sure that barriers are in fact removed when they are supposed to be. The tendency for the supposedly temporary to endure is proverbial; the aim of policy should be to reverse the presumption.

One way of doing this is to treat the escape clause not as a protectionist measure but as a tool to help bring about the adaptation of American industry to freer trade. It could serve at once as a support and a goad. To achieve this requires, once more, an abandonment of old concepts of injury.

It is on these old ideas that the origin of the escape clause rests. It was introduced at an early stage of the trade agreements program to assure domestic producers that if the government's negotiators miscalculated and a tariff reduction permitted an unexpectedly heavy flow of imports, the promise of "no injury" could be redeemed by restoring the original tariff, or part of it, or even imposing higher barriers than before. How injury was to be defined, whether plants, firms, or industries were to be taken into account, what causal link had to be established between tariff concessions, imports, and injury engendered much debate in the '40s and '50s and a number of changes in the law. Though industry frequently called for the use of the escape clause, successive Presidents—who had a good bit of discretion in the matter—invoked it rather sparingly.[28] Nevertheless, it was correctly viewed, at home and abroad, as a protective device that set limits to how much trade liberalization could be expected of the United States.

Though many escape clause cases dealt with minor products (such as straight pins, clothespins, and thermometer blanks) several were quite important, notably those concerning Swiss watches, lead and zinc, and bicycles. When the escape clause was used, the repercussions were often greater than the trade involved seemed to justify, as when President Kennedy raised the duty on window glass and woven carpets just after the Dillon Round of tariff negotiations had ended in 1961 and thus set off a major dispute with the Common Market. Even though most applications for relief under the escape clause were denied, the uncertainty about what might happen in any case was regarded by foreign producers as in itself an obstacle to making a major selling effort in the United States. ("If you succeed, you fail," they said, "and lose the investment of several years' work in sales efforts.") The threat of escape clause action was a key weapon in persuading the Japanese to limit their exports to the United States. And

28. From April 1948 through October 11, 1962, there were 169 applications under the escape clause. In 41 cases the Tariff Commission found that the complaining industry had suffered injury. The President accepted the Commission's findings in whole or in part and took protective action in 15 of the cases.

underlying all these concrete factors was the fact that the theory or philosophy of the escape clause (insofar as specific devices of American government policy can be said to have a theory or philosophy) was that trade liberalization should not be carried to the point of so dislocating American industries that they could be said to be "injured."

By emphasizing adjustment and tightening criteria the Trade Expansion Act of 1962 opened the way to a reinterpretation of the escape clause, but instead made it a dead letter. In sharp contrast to the '50s there were, between July 1962 and the summer of 1969, only thirteen new escape clause applications, all of which failed. Moreover, between 1965 and 1967, the higher tariff rates or quotas imposed under earlier escape clause actions were removed in six cases, including lead and zinc, watches, and stainless steel flatware. One result was that industries interested in checking imports abandoned the escape clause route and sought either legislation or the executive branch's help in getting other countries to curtail exports.

At the beginning of the '70s, the Tariff Commission found injury in several cases and the Nixon Administration broke new ground by making use of adjustment assistance without imposing trade restrictions (except for postponing cuts on piano duties negotiated in the Kennedy Round). It also made clear that if any restrictions were introduced under the escape clause, they would be frequently reviewed to be sure the industries in question were making efforts to adjust. One need not go into the merits of these cases to see that they move in the right direction. They also bring out a fundamental point often obscured in general discussion. Import barriers benefit a whole industry, whereas adjustment assistance is geared to the needs of specific firms, plants, and groups of workers.[29] This distinction opens the way to adjustment without restriction of trade if the "injury" is not general.

Too sharp a separation of the two methods may not always be practicable. Ascertaining the best way of aiding a large number of firms or workers to adjust is likely to take time; if there is widespread dislocation, temporary restraint of imports may seem necessary to let the administrative machinery and then the adjustment programs work efficiently. The risk of having to resort to this method can be reduced by more frequent and flexible uses of adjustment assistance and even by anticipating problems before they become acute. This may prove difficult, however, as long as adjustment assistance can only be acti-

29. The steel cases mentioned earlier were not escape clause actions, having been brought by workers who can claim adjustment assistance but not ask for the imposition of barriers.

vated by demonstrations of damage from imports, a point to which I return later.

It is also conceivable that the escape clause could be used constructively without a program of adjustment assistance. For example, an industry might be making a reasonable adjustment to rising imports without government help under the adjustment assistance program, but might require a little more time to bring the process to a satisfactory point. Some significant reorganization of the industry might be under way that seemed likely to increase its competitive strength. In such cases, temporary protection might be justified so long as there was assurance (through a firm time limit or frequent review) that the protection would not become an excuse to slow up the adjustment. Or a "flood of imports"—to use the cliché—may be the product of exceptional circumstances (domestic or foreign; for example, an unexpected surplus) that can be expected to pass, or be brought to an end, in a reasonable period of time and that does not reflect the long-run inability of the domestic industry to cope with foreign competition.

The principles suggested in the last few paragraphs, though finding support in the Nixon Administration's handling of its first escape clause cases, are not yet generally accepted as lasting features of American policy. Congressional support for a change in the escape clause in 1970 was clearly motivated by concern for protection, not adjustment. The bill that then passed the House would have moved the country back toward the pre-1962 position by making it easier for industries to claim injury without proving that the main cause was an increase in imports resulting from past tariff concessions. In some cases, quotas would have been called for and the President's ability to overrule the Tariff Commission reduced. While a strong administration that gave high priority to trade liberalization and emphasized adjustment might administer such legislation in a constructive way, its ability to resist protectionist pressures would be weakened. Indeed, one of the main purposes of this sort of legislation is to limit the President's freedom of action and strengthen congressional control in trade matters without going so far as to restore the pre-1934 position when Congress itself handled all tariff matters in detail.

The past and future administration of the escape clause presents far more intricate problems than these few paragraphs may suggest. Fine changes in legal language, differences in interpretation by shifting majorities in the Tariff Commission, voluminous facts about the condition of an industry (and sometimes great gaps in the facts), controversy about their meaning, and the President's need to take account of a wide range of considerations in acting on the Commission's recommendation—the whole process shot through with political considerations—make for difficult, tedious, and often unsatisfactory analysis. Yet in these complex, technical issues which sometimes seem trivial lie important determinants of the character of American trade policy.[30] On the one hand, frequent resort to the escape clause with no objective other than to stop imports can seriously undermine a policy of trade liberalization. On the other hand, to think of abolishing the escape clause or rendering it totally inoperative is neither realistic nor sensible; other countries as well as the United States require means of dealing with difficult problems of adjustment by the occasional, temporary interruption of trade. Intricacies apart, the choice lies in the approach. One can understand that the escape clause's enemies regard it as a barbarous relic of the bad old days, while its friends see it as the last recourse against free trade run wild. Perhaps a sounder view would be to regard the escape clause as a potentially troublesome but also controllable emergency device which is to be resorted to only in exceptional circumstances as a temporary support for measures of adjustment that will work better with than without it and which might—like so many other things in national policies in the future—be subjected to some degree of international surveillance.

Pseudoadjustment Through Market Sharing

In the eyes of some people, the inadequacy of the escape clause lies in its uncertainty. Ideas of "injury" vary. While the long process of proving it goes on, the injury grows worse. If the injury is proved, the President may still not raise import barriers. If he does, foreign goods may continue to come in in disturbingly large quantities and at troublesomely low prices. It would be far better, say some of these people, if everyone knew exactly where he stood. Both the domestic producer and the foreign supplier could plan more sensibly if they knew what share of the American market they would be permitted to supply. Formulas for achieving that result differ but their essence is that the level of future imports would be related to the current or recent shares of domestic production and imports in meeting Ameri-

30. A good demonstration of the far-reaching implications of apparently limited technical changes is provided by an analysis of the relation among the bills before Congress, the proposals of the Nixon and Johnson Administrations, and Tariff Commission interpretations of the pre- and post-1962 laws by a former chairman of the Commission, Stanley Metzger, in "The Escape Clause and Adjustment Assistance: Proposals and Assessments," *Law and Policy in International Business*, Summer 1970, pp. 352-401.

can demand. Under most formulas imports would increase if demand grew, but usually only in a fixed proportion. The domestic industry would be assured either an absolute volume of sales or a certain proportion of the market.

"Fair shares" is the rallying cry of this approach and its proponents usually contrast themselves favorably with those who would restrict imports even more tightly (and, of course, with those who are said to be ready to sacrifice domestic jobs and profits for the interest of foreigners). No legislation of this kind has been enacted but there are some similarities in the law that establishes quotas if meat imports rise above a certain level and in the arrangements under the international cotton textile agreement that permit imports to rise by 5 per cent a year (regardless of what happens to domestic consumption).

If imports were permitted to rise faster than domestic demand, market-sharing arrangements could be regarded as instruments of adjustment. Considerably cruder than adjustment assistance that was directed only to the weakest spots, they would have some advantage in avoiding complicated government intervention and—if they were allowed to work—in putting an industry on notice that unless it improved its competitive performance it would have to expect an increasing volume of imports in the future. Circumstances might arise in which some such formula, based perhaps on international agreement, would seem to be a reasonable way of permitting adjustment without disruption. Even then the market-sharing approach might give more protection than was really necessary, entailing a greater economic burden for all but the protected industries. The basic difficulty, however, is that the aim of most market-sharing proposals is not in fact adjustment but resistance to it. In a purely national measure, that animus is almost sure to be strengthened. Like increased use of the escape clause by the United States, the introduction of any significant number of market-sharing laws would almost certainly encourage resort to measures of similar effect abroad, thus intensifying the device's inherent bias toward perpetuating past patterns of trade and production rather than encouraging the flexibility and adaptation that are among the rewards of trade liberalization.

Labor's Resistance to Change

It is nothing new for workers as well as employers to ask: "How can we compete against foreigners who pay wages only half, or a third, or a tenth of ours?" Economists have a set of clear answers, made familiar by frequent use. Not wages but labor costs are the issue. Americans, with their skills and machines, can often produce several times as much per man hour as foreign workers and so more than offset wage differentials. When foreign productivity rises, wages will rise also, narrowing the difference. It is natural for labor to be cheaper in some countries than others; economies will founder if they cannot make use of their assets. To single out wages instead of some other cost, say that of fuel, raw materials, or capital, as the source of unfair competition is unreasonable; to offset all differences in costs by tariffs (a theory once embedded in American law but not, fortunately, in practice) would eliminate the possibility of trade. It is true that low labor costs give foreigners a competitive advantage in producing some things, but Americans have other competitive advantages. By concentrating on them the economy gains and with it labor as a whole, though some workers, like some employers, may lose when the pattern of international advantages shifts against them. To those who found such reasoning somewhat abstract, the clincher in the economists' argument was the plain fact that the United States, which had long paid the highest wages in the world, successfully sold its products in foreign markets and usually exported a good deal more than it imported. Moreover, export industries for the most part paid higher wages than those that required protection.

All this remains true. It is possible, though, that some new factors add weight to labor's case. The increased ease with which American or American-style management can be combined in a low-wage country with the identical technology used in the United States may make the wage gap more important than it used to be. Though foreign wages may rise more rapidly than before, they are not likely to keep pace with the increase in productivity. Even if the process described by economists eventually works itself out, there will be a longer period in which the difference in labor costs explains the advantage of producing abroad. Certainly many American businessmen seem to believe this.

Such an analysis, if it is correct, does not invalidate the fundamentals of the argument for trade liberalization. It is certainly true, though, that an increase in the speed with which technology spreads accelerates changes in trade patterns and so exerts pressure on the United States for a more rapid adjustment than has been usual in the past. This is particularly burdensome for labor. The electronics industry provides a striking illustration. Radios, TV sets, and other equipment that only a few years ago were strong American exports are now net import items; processes developed in the United States and only recently cited as examples of technological lead are now carried on in Taiwan and Hong Kong to take advantage of lower labor costs. The American electronics industry can continue to thrive; even exports can grow; but the industry's demand for labor changes. Different skills are required to produce aerospace guidance systems, semiconductors, and other advanced products. The people who have made radios may not be able to fill the new demand. The opening of a new plant in California is of limited help to those thrown out of work by the shutting of one in Pennsylvania. There may be a permanent shift in an industry's labor needs that can only be offset by the rise of new demands in another part of the economy.

It would require much empirical research to discover just how great the problem of labor dislocation from changes in foreign trade is or is likely to become in the United States. While magnitudes alter cases, it is possible, without that knowledge, to suggest how what has already been said in this section about the problems of trade and adjustment applies to labor's situation. In one respect the analogy with the position of the employer is clear: the interest of workers in an established pattern of employment and income should not be allowed to outweigh a public interest in import liberalization. At most, the labor case, like that of the employers, justifies temporary restriction to provide time to make a satisfactory adjustment to changing circumstances. Where labor's case differs from the case for a protected industry as a whole is in the nature of the public interest in the welfare of the people affected. The brunt of adjustment falls on workers. Unemployment, dislocation, loss of a market for skills based on training and experience, uncertainty as to the future, and readjustment of ways of life at what may be a fairly advanced age create human problems that are properly matters of public concern. Labor usually lacks the mobility and resources of management and capital; it is less able to cope with accelerated change. Therefore, the case for adequate government help to cushion the impact of change is strong, and while the emphasis should be on measures that improve a worker's productivity through the creation of new jobs with retraining and relocation if necessary, there should not be too strong an objection to the inclusion in such a program of an element of compensation for the effects of public policy, especially for workers who are unable to find jobs as good as those they have lost or who have to retire early.

The labor interest in protection and adjustment is not uniform. Workers in industries that suffer from foreign competition may lose by trade liberalization even if they benefit from adjustment assistance. Those in expanding industries, especially export industries, gain from freer trade. Large segments of labor are not directly involved in foreign trade; construction workers and those in most service industries, for example, ought to weigh their consumer interests heavily, especially if they are engaged in occupations in which production per man hour can probably not reach the heights that justify the highest industrial wages. The workers of the future will be better off in an economy that is flexible and allocates its resources well than in one that has preserved inefficiency and lost adaptability by protection. While it is understandable that the AFL-CIO should try to submerge these internal conflicts of interest in the spirit of labor solidarity, it does not follow that support for protection in fact reflects the best interest of the majority of workers even in the short run and almost certainly not in the long run. A strong, even generous, program of adjustment assistance would help to clarify the issues.

To the extent that the problem of import competition is really one of foreign wage rates, labor has another possible approach, but it is not very promising. A long-standing labor proposal has been that goods should be barred from international trade or penalized if they are not produced in conformity with fair wage standards. The principle is well established in some marginal cases, such as the products of prison labor or forced labor. To achieve the broader purpose, several international labor bodies have proposed an amendment to GATT defining fair standards. It has never been accepted and, if it were, might not go very far toward meeting American labor's complaints.

Two standards are proposed which would justify corrective action. The first is whether an exporting firm is paying wages that fall below some national standard. The second is a much looser international comparison asking whether an exporting firm's "hourly and unit labor cost" is "unjustifiably below those of the same industry in the complaining country."[31] There are obvious difficulties in applying such standards, particularly the second, and it is unlikely that action of this sort will receive strong international support for some time to come. On a less formal basis, it is possible that as governments more and more discuss conditions of fair competition, labor practices, like pricing and subsidy arrangements, will be drawn into the negotiations, but hardly in terms that would go far to alter the problems now faced by American labor. Leveling up of labor costs among the industrialized countries is more likely to come from the play of internal forces in Europe and Japan than through international trade pressure (though it may be hastened by some international cooperation among countries; see chapter 6, p. 188). So far as the less developed coun-

31. Karl Casserini, Chief Economist of the International Metalworkers Federation, in *A Foreign Economic Policy for the 1970s,* Hearings before the Subcommittee on Foreign Economic Policy of the Joint Economic Committee, 91st Cong., 2d sess. (Washington: GPO, 1970), p. 230.

tries are concerned—where more and more of the problem originates, as American labor sees it—trade barriers that penalize wages below those of rich countries are more likely to diminish social welfare than increase it.

If international action is likely to be a blind alley and protectionism is to be resisted as burdensome to the public interest, how is labor's real, if sometimes short-run, interest in coping with the problems of import competition to be met? To answer, "by adjustment assistance" sounds hollow after past American failure to meet labor's expectations on that score. And yet, it is a better answer than the others, though only a partial one. To make it an adequate answer, adjustment assistance must not only work better than before but be conceived more broadly. It must be informed by an awareness of the human problems that may result from making the economy more adaptable and by a determination to alleviate the private burden that is the price of public benefit. Assistance to workers should be a part of a broader policy of facilitating adjustment by national and international measures. Adjustment to import competition should be seen as part of a wide process of adjustment to change in the economy. The success of all these endeavors depends on making the American economy a milieu in which adaptation and flexibility are the natural order of things, and that in turn requires policies making for full employment, economic growth, and the equitable distribution of burdens and benefits.

Adjustment in a Broader Setting

The burdens of economic change are not very different whether change stems from increased imports or some other cause. When change has a domestic source, the American tradition is that adaptation to it is mostly left to private activities within a framework provided by the antitrust laws, the interstate commerce clause, the bankruptcy laws, and a fairly long list of other measures. When special problems are felt to exist, government intervention may take the form of support (as in past silver purchasing), or regulation (as in natural gas pricing), or both (as in the prorationing of oil and in agricultural policy generally). Often the government's aim is to help the industry resist the pressures of the market, sometimes on grounds of national security, but there are also measures aimed mostly at meeting the problems that come from accepting change, not resisting it. The government could be said to provide adjustment assistance to business in the form of investment credits and small business loans, to localities through grants for urban rehabilitation and measures to encourage employment in depressed areas and attract industries to them, and to workers (especially for minorities and those having below-average education or skills) in the form of education and training programs. Sometimes one or another of these measures can properly be used separately because it seems adequate to deal with a specific problem. But often the success of one depends on its being used in conjunction with others; for example, to be sure that there are jobs for people trained in certain skills. And when problems are more general, involving stagnant or declining industries and several depressed areas, only a combination of programs offers much promise of success.

It is to this family of measures that adjustment assistance focused on import competition belongs. To recognize import competition as a source of dislocation is reasonable enough and may help in directing attention to needs. But to treat import competition as something quite different from other sources of difficulty is not wise policy. For one thing, it is often difficult, if not impossible, to say how much of an industry's problem—or, more realistically, of the problems of workers and individual firms in the industry—really stems from import competition: industries that have difficulty adjusting to import competition usually suffer from other troubles as well. For another, the source of the pressures for adjustment is a secondary matter compared to finding the best way of making the American economy function well. That requires a response to total circumstances more than to specific factors. When imports play an important part in creating a problem, the government has a weapon it otherwise lacks because imports can be curbed. But unless the curb is temporary, it cannot contribute to adjustment. It is beyond the scope of this book to try to determine when adjustment is best left to the unaided efforts of producers and when some form of public assistance would make for a better transition. But it is clear that the emphasis should be on change; the American economy would function badly if, for example, the assurance of government aid shielded enterprises from bankruptcy as a general thing. Measures to encourage adaptation and change may go well beyond adjustment assistance in the narrow sense; they may involve wages, prices, taxes, the administration of the antitrust laws, and anything else that bears on the competitive strength of American business. To judge what is tenable, the problem must be viewed broadly, not as one of import competition alone.

Action taken to help smooth a transition should be more concerned with the results to be achieved than with the source of the pressures that make change necessary. If good results require a transfer of resources from some industries to other kinds of activities, government help must bear some relation to what these new activities are. It is foolish simply to shift the problem of adjustment from one group or place to others that will then need help. Sensible policy will have higher aims, trying to insure that the new activities will be self-sustaining for as far ahead as one can reasonably see. It follows that if the government has to concern itself with adjustment on a greater scale than in the past, the government will have to formulate views about the desirable structure of American industry. In Europe, Canada, and Japan "industrial policy" is coming to be a central feature of national economic policy, often for quite different reasons. May not the same thing be happening, though a good bit more slowly, in the United States?

At any rate, there can be no doubt that the United States will take measures that influence the structure of domestic industry and that in doing so it should look at the national economy in an international setting and not in isolation. This means, for example, that the horizon of government policy-makers should include the possibilities that imports will grow, and they should neither ignore the impact of what they do on foreign trade nor tacitly assume that imports can be checked if they become troublesome. If measures are taken to bring new industries into depressed areas, they should not be industries that are likely soon to call for protection. Financial aid to small business should not encourage activities that depend on the tariff's being above a certain level. Schemes for training and employment should draw people into strong industries not weak ones. Urban minorities may be a good source of labor for the clothing industry but, if the reason is that the wages of these people are exceptionally low, the future is not promising. If the United States is going to justify quotas on the grounds that an industry "has been of particular importance in providing employment opportunities for those . . . who are relatively disadvantaged" (as the American representative did at the Sixth Annual Review of the Cotton Textile Arrangement),[32] it should also have some idea of how to improve the situation so that after a reasonable period the protection will no longer be needed. To protect people from hardship is an important function of government, and sound industrial policy will concern itself with welfare, equity, and the social cost of change; but to encourage people to move into areas of the economy that are already in difficulties is not economical, statesmanlike, or kind.

Even if anything like a comprehensive industrial policy is a long way off in the United States, a primary objective of whatever partial

32. *The Department of State Bulletin,* December 2, 1968, p. 581.

measures the government takes (including decisions not to intervene in certain situations) should be to make the American economy as competitive and efficient as possible. For the economy to be as productive as possible, all resources have to be used where they are most efficient and not sheltered in less productive uses. It can no longer be assumed that American exports will somehow take care of themselves. To be as competitive as possible in world markets, American producers should not have to carry the burden of protection for the less efficient segments of the economy either by an increase in the price of things they use or in money wages higher than they would need to be if living costs were allowed to benefit from cheaper imports. Moreover, import competition is itself a force making for efficiency and a useful factor in the constantly changing process of securing the right allocation of American resources.

INTERNATIONAL INDUSTRIAL ADJUSTMENT

Whether the United States has good or bad adjustment policies is a matter of concern to other countries. Up to a point they can make their views felt sufficiently to have them taken into account in Washington. If the escape clause is used, for example, countries from which past tariff concessions are withdrawn are entitled to compensation under GATT rules. Either the United States must reduce tariffs on other products, or the country affected will withdraw concessions it gave the United States. This arrangement has a bearing on how the use of the escape clause affects the broad national interest (which the law says the President is to take into account), which may lead to a different conclusion from one based only on the interests of the industry affected by imports (which is all that concerns the Tariff Commission in its investigation and recommendations). It is also the rudimentary, but well-established, beginning of what might become a more international approach to industrial adjustment.

If escape clause actions were sure to be short-lived, compensation by temporarily changing tariffs on other products might seem arbitrary, sometimes disturbing, and on the whole not worth the effort.[33] A commitment to a time limit for the escape clause action could be accepted as a reason not to ask for compensation, particularly if evidence were offered that real adjustment was under way. The threat that others would eventually strike back if the limit were not kept might then help speed the adjustment. Out of such an arrangement

33. But it might have a certain surreptitious advantage if ways were found of making compensatory reductions permanent, presumably by asking for matching concessions once the escape clause action was over.

could develop international standards permitting the temporary erection of trade barriers and international surveillance of the adjustment process. GATT already has a procedure concerned with some of these situations. The fact that it has not been extensively used suggests both a preference for national action and the difficulty of agreeing on meaningful common standards when cases vary so greatly. Still the preservation of liberalization depends on departures from it being limited to what others will tolerate, so the need for at least acceptable procedure is clear, even if standards remain general. An agreement to eliminate tariffs on a substantial part of the trade among the industrialized countries would itself both stress the need for a method of dealing with emergencies and make compensatory tariff adjustment a less attractive tool than it has been.

The adjustment problem involves more than tariff removal. Negotiations about nontariff barriers, trade-distorting practices, fair competition generally, and the difficulties of particular industries will confront the industrialized countries with a series of adjustment problems. What they decide to do in concrete cases, gradually eliminating some practices, permitting others to continue subject to certain rules, and providing ways to consult about still other issues, will all rest on some implicit understanding of the kind of adjustment each country will have to make. The hard cases—the sectors in which governments have allowed relatively little liberalization—are to be explained largely by unwillingness to accept the kind of adjustment that it is thought would result from removing trade barriers. As the discussions of the industry-by-industry approach showed, the chances of overcoming past difficulties may depend on international understandings about more than the removal of trade barriers. In effect, such understandings would combine the willingness of each country to make certain adjustments in its industrial pattern and the acceptance by others of restraints on trade so that the requirements of adjustment should not go too far.

Sometimes adjustment can take place within an industry, but it may also involve the transfer of resources to other lines of activity. To avoid creating new difficulties, the focus of national adjustment policy must broaden, and so may the foreign interest in what each country does. The most obvious rule, as the discussion of American adjustment policy suggested, should be to avoid simply shifting the burden of adjustment to another protected industry. But more ideas than this are required if adjustment is to be undertaken on any scale as a conscious process subject to a certain amount of government guidance. One needs, quite clearly, some view of the kind of national economy that would be desirable. It is not only trade policy that poses this question, as we shall see in the discussion of investment issues in the next chapter. But no matter what the motives, the measures governments take—or fail to take—to shape and then carry out an "industrial policy" have a great bearing on the future of international trade.

As·a perceptive French analyst has pointed out, "a collection of interventions by the state does not necessarily add up to an industrial policy."[34] And in most countries a collection of interventions is what we commonly find: regional policy to build up underdeveloped or depressed areas; encouragement of investment in one industry or another; government prodding on the reorganization of industry (most recently to build units capable of competing with American giants); the placing of government contracts to create a domestic capacity for computers or something else; maintenance of certain trade barriers while others are removed; and a host of other measures. Often government intervention has come rather late in an effort to shore up established industries that are suffering from new competition, low profits, or the difficulties of adapting to changing circumstances. Rarely, as Stoleru points out, can one say that the interventions are part of a general strategy; and when there is one, "it is not in general based on the search for competitiveness."

Much of "industrial policy" ignores international factors. The bias is inherent in the fact that governments are dealing as best they can with national problems and responding to domestic political and social needs. If the foreign dimension cannot be ignored, it is apt to be seen as a disturbing element, especially if it takes the form of import competition which, for example, increases the pressure on weak industries or makes it harder for new ones to get started. A series of clashes between measures of industrial policy and the opening of frontiers which the industrial nations have undertaken is unavoidable. If an industrial policy that concentrates on sheltering the weak or preserving existing structures is allowed to dominate, it will become a new source of substitutes for outlawed trade barriers. If industrial policy emphasizes adaptation and has as one of its objectives the competitiveness Stoleru calls for, then clashes between national measures and open frontiers can be limited and treated as aspects of national and international adjustment. Whichever alternative is followed, there are international repercussions. The industrialized countries are so much exposed to one another that what any one of them does about its own industrial policy will influence and be influenced by the action of others. Though they may not agree or even negotiate

34. Lionel Stoleru, *L'Impératif Industriel* (Paris: Editions du Seuil, 1969), p. 151; the next quotation comes from p. 149.

about any given matter, each has to take account of what the others do and how they will react to what it does.

At a time when national industrial policies are so fragmentary, it may seem laughable to speak of international industrial policies, and yet there are some measures that can be looked at in that way. The preamble of the Long-Term Cotton Textile Arrangement, which foreshadows a gradual shift of the industry toward the less developed countries, is a kind of declaration of industrial policy—though not one voiced or carried out with great conviction. The search for a formula to insure that European countries, Japan, Canada, and the United States will all grant "equivalent" tariff preferences to LDC exports is a kind of burden-sharing with implications for industrial structure and adaptation. European cooperation in research and development usually involves a distribution of activities and an allocation of contracts among participants; a general aim is to share the benefits, but another consideration that is often present is the fostering of certain industries in each country. The same is true of "co-production" arrangements for NATO procurement.

In the aircraft industry, the life and death of firms and whole segments of national production may depend on getting or missing a very small number of contracts. Major balance of payments effects are common; security considerations are obvious. Governments have a great influence on international trade and the pattern of national production through their purchases, the direction of policies of government-owned or subsidized airlines, the licensing of aircraft, the financing of research and development costs, and informal indications of their interest in certain transactions. The failure of Rolls Royce in 1971, the consequent threat to Lockheed, and the steps taken by the British and American governments provided an unusually dramatic demonstration of interdependence; but the fact that every industrial country has been involved in shaping a policy toward the aircraft industry that was both national and international was there for all to see all along. It seems inevitable that future developments will move in the same directions and that in all probability government decisions will be provided with a more fully worked out underpinning of long-run policy (even if that policy includes the view that companies should be allowed to fail in some circumstances).

Steel presents a different case. Though governments have never been indifferent to what happened to their steel industries, there was a fairly high degree of trade liberalization even before the Kennedy Round. At Geneva the governments haggled hard over a few percentage points on moderate tariffs and in the end most cuts were modest, leading to a rough "harmonization" of duties at around 8 per cent. Almost immediately afterwards the American industry strongly demanded quotas against rapidly increasing imports. Within the nominally free market of the European Coal and Steel Community, a series of steps were taken to reduce competition. The formation in 1967 of an International Iron and Steel Institute with headquarters in Brussels, no matter what its founders said, inevitably raised echoes in an industry with a history of international cartels (though not very successful ones).

A whole series of problems gave rise to these events. They concerned a rapid expansion of steel-making capacity in the world, the growth of Japanese exports, the uneven adaptation of new technology, and a variety of circumstances that made government and producers unwilling to accept the free play of competition (which in steel is not like competition among grocery stores). Insofar as the American steel producers had a case for protection based on the public interest, it rested largely on the need for time to adapt itself to changing conditions (unless one believed that in the long run the level of steel production required for American security could only be maintained by protection). In agreeing to restrain shipments to the United States, Japanese and European producers were tacitly accepting the idea that this form of adjustment was better, at least for the time being, than pressing a competitive advantage that might lead to American restrictions. A rapid turnaround in the world steel market by mid-1969 provided a warning about the limited validity of forecasts and the dangers of shaping long-run policy in response to immediate pressures. Nevertheless, it seems clear that trade liberalization alone—even the maintenance of what has already been achieved —will not be allowed to determine the future of the steel industry. Governments will not keep their hands off if national capacity is threatened with a serious decline. A process of adjustment—however temporary, however good or bad—is taking place by a combination of private and public measures, some agreed on, some unilateral, and some that can best be described as parallel. It is not likely that there will soon be an international steel agreement comparable to an agreement on wheat or some other commodity or even one confined to the process of adjustment. But what is happening in steel is different from the unaided adjustment that has taken place in other industries and also from government-aided adjustment on a purely national basis. It is taking place not because someone selected a certain method of dealing with the steel problem, but because the problem imposed the approach. And unless efforts to solve the problems are abandoned and governments resort to national trade barriers, something like an international industrial policy for steel will be working itself out.

Something similar can be said about energy where the problems of adaptation are far greater than in steel. Technological and economic changes alter the relations of coal, oil, gas, and nuclear power. Reduction of high-cost domestic production of coal in Europe is painful. Dependence on imported oil, which is inescapable for most countries, creates trepidation. Europe and Japan try to circumvent the dominant position of American and British oil companies in the world market. Nuclear energy grows in importance, promising a new degree of national self-sufficiency but only if certain supply problems can be met. The almost incredible possibility of a power shortage in the United States was a sharp reminder in 1971 that even in an industry where long-range forecasting, advanced planning for production, and lengthy lead times are taken for granted, results are not always what they are expected to be.

Trade liberalization, even if it were attainable, would not solve the industrial world's energy problems. The prospects of any kind of general international understanding on energy are remote, and it is far from clear what kind of arrangement, if any, would be desirable. Few countries have a coherent national energy policy; they take a combination of measures to deal with, or mitigate, the "coal problem," "the oil problem," "foreign dominance of the industry," and so on. National needs and possibilities keep changing. Years of work have not produced agreement on a common energy policy for the European Community. There is no doubt the public interest is involved, but there are many publics.

And yet some accommodation of interests has to take place, and does. There may be understandings or there may be interrelated sets of actions and reactions, involving governments and companies, producers and consumers, rich and poor, those blessed with multiple choices and those faced with either/or. Some results are mutually beneficial; others involve a zero-sum game in which one's gain is the other's loss. The conflicts of interest are domestic as well as international. Though it seems most unlikely that there will be an international industrial policy for energy in any clear-cut sense among all the advanced nations (there may be in Europe and between the United States and Canada), it is also unlikely that there can be a constructive and continuing accommodation of interests in a changing situation unless the protagonists guide their actions, whether they act separately or in agreement, by some conception of what could properly be called international adjustment and so, by implication, an international industrial policy.

My argument may seem strained, my terminology too strong. But, as Plato may have said of a myth, "possibly, nay certainly, this is not true, but there is something more or less like it which is true." This chapter, not just its last section, traces a sequence that seems hard to deny: trade liberalization requires adjustment; adjustment implies some view of an acceptable structure for the national economy; the steps taken—or allowed to be taken—to attain that structure may affect other countries; if each country ignores what the others do, it will not achieve its own aims; if it confines itself to resisting the effect of what others do, a new set of international distortions will be erected that will deprive the countries of at least some of the fruits of their trade liberalization. In other segments of policy, as we shall see in subsequent chapters, there are analogous sequences. It is, of course, quite possible that people will not be willing to move further toward accepting that adjustment must be, to a degree, assented to internationally as well as nationally, but then they will be changing the direction in which they have advantageously moved for twenty-five years. And if they persist in the direction they are going, they will move, or perhaps stagger, toward a set of policies that will give an agreed-on shape to the industrial structure of the free world.

A Clear Direction?

A chapter that started as a discussion of trade liberalization has ended with a discussion of adjustment—some of it to changes in trade and some as part of a larger process of constant economic adaptation that is an essential attribute of growing, modern industrial economies. The transition is sound. Trade barriers are removed not to increase the volume of trade but to improve the use of resources, a purpose served by many other policies as well.

The avenues of approach to the trade policy issues of the '70s all intersect. The Kennedy Round carried the process of postwar trade liberalization to a point at which it is reasonable to think seriously about the elimination of tariffs on trade in manufactured goods among the industrialized countries. But the tariffs that remain are not unimportant and their removal, whether by past methods or by new devices, will not be possible without more attention than has been given in the past to a whole array of government measures that are only inaccurately described as nontariff barriers. An effective attack on nontariff barriers, which almost everyone approves in principle, will require many different kinds of approaches and a wide variety of new kinds of international agreements. Codes, formulas, and rules will all have their place, but none of them is likely to be comprehensive enough to deal with the many different kinds of impediments to international trade that are imposed by governments, either deliberately or as by-products of their other activities. Every step forward will reveal new problems or make old ones seem more serious. Guidelines as simple as reducing duties and removing quotas will no longer suffice. An increasing number of governmental, and private, practices will be called into question because of their effect on other countries. Even to defend them will require the discussion with foreigners of a wide range of matters usually thought of as strictly national affairs. The line between "foreign" and "domestic" will become blurred; what was once internal will become increasingly external.

Trade liberalization is not a goal in itself nor is the improvement of the conditions of international trade to which it can contribute the sole aim of governments. They are bound, then, to weigh what can be accomplished by freer international trade against other kinds of action, as they have always done; but it seems likely that in the future more of this weighing will have to be done internationally, or at least discussed with other governments, than in the past. Even when the resistance to liberalization in anything like its traditional sense is great, there is scope, perhaps need, for international negotiation, to reduce the burden of acting alone, to make policies more effective, or to meet the complaints of others. More is involved than trade policy, however broadly conceived, as the next few chapters will show.

The old trade policy questions have not disappeared but new ones have come crowding onto the scene. Unless the governments of the industrialized countries abandon the course they have followed with great success in the postwar period—that of economic cooperation for mutual benefit through the more efficient use of the world economy—they will be led into new fields. In either case, the turning point in trade policy will be a real one.

6

International Business
and National Governments

To bring the traditionally domestic into the international arena may be something new in trade policy, but it is familiar enough in matters of foreign investment. When nationals of one country invest in another, the distinction between what is foreign and what is domestic becomes blurred. An American-owned company in Germany is part of the German economy, but not in precisely the same sense as a German-owned company. It is also an American company, but not in the same sense that an American-owned company working entirely within the boundaries of the United States is. Direct investment results in an activity in one country that is, in some degree, controlled or directed in another and may depend for its existence on markets and sources of supply in still other countries. This kind of "international production," as Judd Polk has called it, has become a major link between the economies of the industrialized countries.

Good global statistics are lacking, but the facts for the United States, the biggest of the investors, are striking. While exports more than quadrupled between 1950 and 1970, the value of American private direct investment abroad increased nearly sevenfold. Its fastest growth was in manufacturing, which rose from one-third to two-fifths of the whole. Geographically, the great emphasis was on Europe which doubled its share, coming abreast of Canada's more or less steady 30 per cent. Investment in Japan has also grown rapidly, but restrictions keep it a small part of the total. In short, the thrust of the growth of American direct investment in the postwar period has been toward intensifying the interconnections of the advanced industrial economies of the free world.

The $80 billion of American private direct investment abroad—actually worth more than this figure for book value suggests—is in a real sense part of the American economy though it does not fall within the traditional bounds of customs barriers, the area where the dollar is legal tender, or the geographical-statistical unit that is the usual definition of a country in international economic relations. It follows that a conception of national economic interest based only on the geographical unit is inadequate. When a foreign government lowers its tariffs, it affects not only exports from the United States but the position of American companies inside its boundaries. "Foreign" goods coming into the United States may be produced by companies whose profits also flow into American hands. Transactions that are treated alike for balance of payments purposes are significantly different if Americans are at both ends rather than only one.

The magnitudes involved are impressive. Judd Polk estimates sales by American-owned companies abroad in 1968 at $128 billion, compared to direct investment of $64 billion and exports of $34.6 billion. He would add another $69 billion for the U.S. "share" in foreign sales represented by other kinds of American investment abroad.[1] Obviously such sales are not the same as exports, but they have a relation to the American economy—and so to the national economic interest —that is not taken into account in traditional trade policy. Polk interprets his estimates to mean that the "United States' main linkage with other markets is clearly through production facilities there, not through trade."[2] One need not go quite so far to agree that a view

---

1. *The Economic Implications of the Multinational Corporation* (New York: United States Council of the International Chamber of Commerce, 1969, mimeographed), p. 14.
2. Same, p. 3. Perhaps the situation is not as fundamentally different from the past as the large figures suggest. In a pioneer study, Frank A. Southard, Jr., stressed the "astounding" growth of American investment in Europe in the 1920s, but cautioned his readers not to forget that "other American companies sell directly to European buyers . . . goods that . . . far exceed in value those sold by the European organizations of American companies." *American Industry in Europe* (Boston and New York: Houghton Mifflin, 1931), p. 16. If, however, Polk's 2 : 1 ratio of sales to investment is applied to the Department of Commerce's figure of $1.35 billion of U.S. direct investment in Europe at the end of 1929, sales by American-owned companies would be estimated at $2.7 billion, well above the $1.36 billion of manufactured and semimanufactured goods the United States exported to Europe in 1929, but only a little higher than total exports to

limited to exports and imports would give a grossly inadequate picture of American involvement in other economies. The point is widely accepted and so is the corollary stated by William M. Roth, President Johnson's Special Representative for Trade Negotiations, that it is "clearly necessary for the United States to achieve a more effective coordination of trade and investment policies and a greater understanding of the specific effects of foreign investment."[3]

But how this is to be done is far from clear. Does the growth of "international production" require a change in American trade policy? Are past policies aimed at promoting and protecting American investment abroad no longer adequate? Does the rise of what is often called "the multinational corporation" radically change the framework of American policy? The rather different perspectives suggested by these questions are examined separately in the three sections that follow, and then an attempt is made to put things back together again. While the balance of payments aspects of direct investment cannot be entirely excluded, their proper place is in the next chapter with the discussion of other capital movements.

Links Between Investment and Trade

Barriers to international trade have generally been regarded as major stimuli to foreign investment. The United States in the nineteenth century, Canada in the twentieth, dollar-short Europe at the end of World War II, and the creation of the Common Market provide familiar examples of the process of how businessmen have felt compelled to invest behind a tariff wall that threatened their exports. It might seem to follow that the reduction of trade barriers would curtail investment. But recent history belies that idea. Free trade removes the incentive for establishing some plants abroad, but other factors sustain the surge of investment. Lower costs, the location of raw materials, and the wish to be close to customers all play a part. The speed of transport and communications makes it easier than ever before to carry on business in several parts of the world. There is a new awareness of foreign possibilities and something of a vogue

---

Europe of $2.34 billion. In 1968, sales of American firms in Europe were 3.5 times total U.S. exports to that area. Mira Wilkins has pointed out that the $2.65 billion of U.S. direct investment abroad in 1914 and the $54.6 billion of 1966 each equaled 7 per cent of the GNP. *The Emergence of Multinational Enterprise: American Business Abroad from the Colonial Era to 1914* (Cambridge: Harvard University Press, 1970), pp. 201-202.

3. *Future United States Foreign Trade Policy*, Report to the President submitted by the Special Representative for Trade Negotiations (Washington: GPO, 1969), p. 70.

for "going international." Raymond Vernon has traced a "product cycle" which makes it economic to move production abroad at a certain stage in technology while producing newer goods at home.[4] When a competitor invests in a foreign market, many businessmen feel they must follow suit or risk losing ground. If a company is big enough, fear of the antitrust laws may make investment abroad look like a better path to growth than expansion at home. Still other motives could be added to the list, but they would only strengthen the conclusion that investment among the industrial economies is stimulated by far more than trade barriers.

Like trade liberalization, the removal of barriers to investment widens the businessman's choice of ways of meeting demand and reduces impediments to the better allocation of world resources. Though the objectives are complementary, they have to be pursued by rather different kinds of governmental policies which, while they may only rarely conflict with one another, may impose a choice of priorities. By the end of the '60s, many American observers had come to feel that more needed to be done than in the past to take account of foreign restrictions on investment when negotiating about trade barriers. Not many, however, have gone on to explain just how this is to be done.

When the focus is narrow, the case is clear and strong. Restrictions on investment may impair the value of a tariff reduction by preventing businessmen from setting up marketing, servicing, or assembling installations they judge necessary to export efficiently. Agreements about government procurement are likely to involve both trade and an understanding about the status of foreign-owned firms. Negotiations about other nontariff barriers, taxes, subsidies, and the problems of individual industries may all require understandings about both trade and investment to produce meaningful results.

Quite different kinds of links between trade and investment have been illustrated in the automobile industry. Starting in 1968, the United States has pressed Japan both to remove its quotas on imports and to ease the restrictions that kept American firms from establishing plants in Japan. In place of the traditional aim of removing trade barriers, Washington had put the up-to-date aim of providing effective entry into the Japanese market. In the Canadian-American automotive agreement, the Canadian government made the removal of trade barriers conditional on assurances about the investment by American automobile firms in Canada. In the first case, the would-be investor and exporter in a sense doubles his request. In the second,

4. "International Investment and International Trade in the Product Cycle," *The Quarterly Journal of Economics*, May 1966, pp. 190-207.

the weaker party imposes conditions to insure that free trade will
not reduce investment.

Other examples would pose still other issues. If all the American
companies interested in a certain foreign market were already established there, should the United States make it its business to try to
have the foreign country's tariff on the products of these companies
lowered? Would giving a reciprocal concession in the American tariff simply pay the entrance fee for companies in third countries? The
American interest might be judged differently if third-country suppliers were at least in part American-owned firms or if the removal of
trade barriers would stimulate additional American firms to become
exporters. Governments sometimes permit American investment only
if they are assured that the mother company will permit the new
plant to export; might they not ask the United States to reduce its
tariffs so that the new enterprise (and others) could compete better
in the American market? If a foreign country's output of certain
products came entirely from American-owned plants, might it not
urge the United States to join with it in trying to persuade third countries to reduce their barriers on these products?

The threads of possibility could be twisted into more and more
intricate patterns to show what may result from linking trade and
investment in international negotiation. The reasonableness of that
linkage seems clear, but to suppose it leads always to the conclusion
that restrictions should be removed on both investment and trade
would be misleading. Matters will look different according to
whether a country sees itself as receiving or providing investment
and whether its emphasis is on the balance of trade, the balance of
payments, the allocation of resources, the expansion of production,
or some other objective of national policy. Even for the United
States the choice of the right emphasis for policy is complicated by
some uncertainty as to when investment displaces trade and when
it encourages trade. Stimulated in part by the dispute about the
American government's imposition of controls on direct investment,
a number of studies were made during the '60s to clarify the relations
of investment and exports. The results throw light on the question
but are not altogether conclusive. The most comprehensive statistical studies depend to some degree on unprovable assumptions about
what might happen in different circumstances. Studies that emphasize motivation are open to other questions. Persuasive evidence
about a selected number of instances leaves doubt as to whether the
results can be applied more generally.

Even clear facts are open to different interpretations. One-quarter
or more of U.S. exports go to American-owned firms abroad. Accord-

ing to some, this shows that direct investment is a major element in promoting exports. But to the extent that the subsidiaries are sales agencies, it may be that trade has induced the investment rather than vice versa. It is clear that American-owned firms abroad often get capital equipment from the United States, but they do not buy there regardless of cost and may be under foreign pressure to develop local sources. Even if an American company establishes itself in a foreign market specifically to produce something it formerly exported, the result may also be to increase sales of other items that it produces in the United States.

While the reasons for supposing that investment stimulates trade are clear, the difficulties of making confident generalizations are neatly indicated by a few of the findings of a Department of Commerce study of "reasonably representative" data about the trade of a number of American companies and their foreign affiliates in 1965. Half the exports by the parent companies went through the affiliates, which "indicates the importance of the foreign affiliates in the export business . . . but . . . also shows that some of these companies succeeded in exporting very large amounts of goods without the help of their foreign affiliates." The largest exporters included some with very small sales to affiliates—as in the steel and aircraft industries— and others that sold much through their affiliates, notably automobiles, machinery, and chemicals. In all the totals, trade with Canadian affiliates bulked very large, especially in the automobile industry. Half the sales through the foreign affiliates were of goods not further processed abroad. Often affiliates bought nothing from the parent.[5]

The difficulty of coming to precise conclusions is not new. When American investment in Europe expanded rapidly in the '20s, the American Federation of Labor was disturbed by the thought that production abroad was displacing sales from the United States. In response to a Senate resolution, the Department of Commerce said in 1929 that "it would be impossible to measure the actual loss to American export trade involved in the establishment of an American branch plant in a foreign country."[6] At about the same time the International Telephone and Telegraph company told an enquiring economist, "It is not possible for any American manufacturer to compete in the foreign markets in the field of telephone equipment with

5. Marie T. Bradshaw, "U.S. Exports to Foreign Affiliates of U.S. Firms," *Survey of Current Business* (Department of Commerce), May 1969, pp. 36, 41, 44.
6. *American Branch Factories Abroad*, Senate Document No. 258, 71st Cong., 3rd sess., quoted in Herbert Marshall, Frank A. Southard, Jr., and Kenneth W. Taylor, *Canadian-American Industry: A Study in International Investment* (New Haven: Yale University Press, 1936), p. 268.

the same article made in foreign countries." To close factories abroad
would give the business to foreign competitors and "no more American communication equipment would go from this country than
goes at the present time."[7]

Similar statements are made today. When businessmen expand
production abroad, they explain that they could not hold certain
markets or even get into others by exporting. If they did not get inside a foreign tariff wall or take advantage of lower costs or locate
nearer their customers, someone else would and American exports
would be displaced. Sometimes there is clear-cut evidence that this
view is correct; at other times it is hard to say how much of the foreign market could have been held by exporting and for how long and
at what profit. American-owned firms abroad may sell to third countries and displace still other exports from the United States, or they
may open new markets which will be supplied from several sources,
including the United States. In either case, the direct export displacement that may result from a decision to invest abroad is only part of
a much more complicated process. For example, if the result of
American investment is to increase the general level of demand in a
foreign country, there is a chance to sell more American goods
(though perhaps not those formerly exported). The same result
might be achieved if the investment came from some other source,
but in either case the effect on American trade depends on the competitiveness of American exports and the import policy of the other
country. To the extent that the movement of American enterprise
abroad improves the allocation of world resources, it has a diffuse as
well as direct effect in increasing trade.

The answer to the question whether American direct investment
abroad helps or hinders American exports (or has no effect on them)
seems to be, "sometimes one and sometimes the other." More precise
answers can be given about some parts of the process, but flat generalizations depend on intuition or bias, not evidence. While stimulating to intellectual curiosity and research, such uncertainty would not
make much difference to American policy if there were no departure
from the traditional position of favoring freedom for both trade and
investment. But the latter objective has been called into question.
The implications of restrictions on investment imposed by the United
States government for balance of payments reasons are discussed in
the next chapter. Potentially more important is the challenge posed
by organized labor at the beginning of the '70s. The rise in investment
abroad, it was said with increasing frequency, meant that business was

7. Southard, *American Industry in Europe*, cited, p. 199.

depriving American labor of work and income at home. Business was exporting jobs instead of goods, as the slogan had it.

Part of labor's concern was with those investments abroad that led to increased competitive imports into the United States. The share of U.S. imports from American-owned plants abroad increased from about 5 per cent in the '50s to something between 10 and 15 per cent at the end of the '60s; but of course not all of this competed with domestic production, and a very large part of it was accounted for by automobile imports from Canada. Not statistical measurement but observation of cases provided labor's best evidence. Firms were named which had closed plants in the United States and opened new ones abroad. Some of the most disturbing facts came from the electronics industry, long a standard example of American export strength based on technological advantages. Increasingly, American firms produced components in Taiwan or Korea for incorporation in finished equipment produced in the United States. Often, as a logical next step, they shifted the production of whole lines of equipment to the foreign plants. Even in protected industries, one form of adaptation was to combine domestic production of some items with the import of others from plants established abroad; long the practice of some watch companies, the same step was considered by producers of textiles and steel. Businessmen pointed out that labor was not necessarily the loser from such activity. The United Automobile Workers certainly had a stake in strengthening the ability of American companies to compete against small foreign cars. If Detroit's method was to design compacts that used gearboxes and other items produced in American-owned factories abroad, labor had at least to reserve judgment as to where the balance of its interests lay.

Labor found a more clear-cut target in Items 806.30 and 807 of the U.S. tariff code, which made it possible to export things produced in the United States, assemble or process them further abroad, and then re-import the finished product while paying duty only on the foreign value added. Though the largest imports under those provisions in 1969 came from Europe and Canada, what the arrangement meant for labor was symbolized by factories just south of the border in Mexico. Businessmen could always give the hard-to-check-on answer that without Item 807 higher domestic costs would force them to locate the whole operation abroad.

Even if an American-owned plant abroad does not ship to the United States, labor sees an export of jobs if the plant produces goods that might have been exported from the United States. Naturally enough, labor spokesmen have stressed low foreign wages as a factor inducing American business to go abroad, and the old cry of "unfair competition" is strong. It has been easy, too, to evoke memories of the "runaway plants" of the '30s when producers of textiles and other consumer goods sought to escape unionization in New York and New England by setting up shop in the south or the Pennsylvania hills. If the labor case is valid, though, it should apply whether low labor costs or something else was the main inducement for going abroad. Old investment as well as recent investment might be cast as a villain. But even the immediate thrust of the labor charge is hard to analyze because the case against exporting jobs is usually mixed with the case against importing foreign goods (especially from low-wage sources) that would threaten to displace American labor. So far as the two aspects can be separated, the latter has been dealt with in chapter 5. For the rest, the labor charge rests on the presumption that American investment abroad displaces American exports, at least much of the time. As we have seen, this view cannot be accepted in any simple or sweeping sense though it is almost certainly true in some instances. The issue here, however, is what could be done to act on labor's complaint—and what would be the consequences?

Labor spokesmen have proposed changes in the tax laws so that it should not be more attractive for businessmen to invest abroad than to export. While such comparisons may prove difficult to make, the principle seems reasonable, subject to one important qualification. While there would be little justification for the United States government to give American businessmen special advantages if they invested in Western Europe, Canada, and Japan, inducements to invest in the less developed countries have to be seriously considered as a way of helping their development.

A step beyond governmental neutrality is the idea that direct investment should be penalized or controlled so as to slow down "the export of jobs." On this basis, labor appears to favor continuation of the restrictions on direct investment imposed for balance of payments reasons. Logically anomalous, it is not politically unheard of to support something that has a different purpose and different rationale from one's own aims. In this case, though, such a course might not be very promising for labor since the balance of payments controls do not seem to have checked the growth of American-owned production abroad but only altered the way this investment is financed. Presumably for this reason, the AFL-CIO Executive Council in May 1971 spoke of the need to take into consideration "the kind of investment that would be made abroad, the product involved, the country where the investment would be made, the linkage of the investment to the flow of trade and its effect on U.S. employment and the national economy."[8] The "legislative direction" called for in the statement would apparently give the President power "to regulate, supervise and curb" not only the outflow of capital but also the export of technology. Exactly how this turn of the screw is to be applied is not clear, but such controls would certainly have to be selective, forbidding, or perhaps penalizing, some investments and not others.

The prospect is not an attractive one. Apart from the large matter of principle whether a potential government veto over foreign investment would be a desirable innovation, there are very practical questions. In circumstances which will rarely be crystal clear, should the judgment of government officials about the effect of an investment on exports overrule that of businessmen? What other things than exports should be taken into account? Would today's negative decision have to be reversed tomorrow if a foreign competitor entered a certain market? Should exporting be favored over investing if it were half as profitable? Should investments be permitted if the entrepreneurs promise not to sell back to the United States? These questions correctly make the task of regulating investment to check the "export of jobs" look formidable, but there are some arguments on the other side. While a businessman may be the best judge of how to hold a foreign market, he is also an interested party. The high level of expertise that can be developed in bureaucrats is well exemplified by the history of securities and exchange regulation. In enforcing the antitrust laws, whether through judicial determination or consent decrees, the government alters business behavior in detailed and precise ways. Nevertheless, the road of government regulation of private foreign investment is not one on which it would be reasonable to embark without the demonstration of very compelling need in serving the public interest. Milder measures—such as some sort of screening process or informal consultation through which the government might advise against certain investments—would raise doubts about effectiveness and equity and still pose the same fundamental questions: Would the economy benefit from putting a brake on foreign investment? If not, should something be done to alleviate any burden that investment puts on labor?

A debate would help put the labor case in proper perspective. Some probable results can be anticipated. It would become clear, for instance, that even if the fostering of exports were a dominant aim of national policy, it would not always be certain what policy should

8. "Statement by the AFL-CIO Executive Council on the Critical Need for New International Trade and Investment Legislation," reprinted in *Foreign Trade*, Hearings before the Subcomittee on International Trade of the Senate Finance Committee, 92d Cong., 1st sess. (Washington: GPO, 1971), p. 184.

be followed toward investments. Second, it would have to be acknowledged that the promotion of trade is not the sole or dominant aim of policy; the advantages of trade lie primarily in improving the use of American and world resources, a process to which investment and other forms of activity can also contribute. Third, the very considerable difficulties of government control over investment and the risks of producing undesirable results would become clear. All these considerations militate against pursuing the kind of policy that seems implicit in the positions advocated by labor in the early '70s. At the same time, two other points would emerge that would lend support to labor's worries. First, it is undoubtedly true that while an American businessman can sometimes maximize his profits or better pursue his other objectives by investing abroad than at home, American labor gets its jobs and incomes as a direct result of the one transaction and not the other. Second, even if there are benefits to American labor, for example, through a subsequent increase in demand for exports and an expansionary effect on the economy from the return of profits, the immediate effect of export displacement—whether caused by an American investment abroad or something else—may be quite disruptive to employment, at least temporarily.

If a diagnosis somewhat like this were borne out, it would suggest several possible lines of policy. The disadvantages of detailed government regulation and the inability to know in advance all the export effects of American investment abroad make control over investments intended to curtail "the export of jobs" an undesirable alternative. The question of the different return to labor from investments at home and abroad should be treated not by policies that try to pinpoint the effects of specific foreign investment decisions but as part of the general problem of managing the American economy, which requires attention to welfare and equity as well as to aggregate demand, growth, etc. To the extent that there are problems of unemployment—including inadequate growth of employment—resulting from the loss of export markets (whether associated with American investment abroad or not), these should be regarded as matters connected with the adjustment of the American economy to change. The perspective, in short, should be comparable to that suggested in chapter 5 for adjustment to import competition; the aim should be flexibility, not the perpetuation of a given pattern of employment. It must be recognized, though, that the burden of a change in the structure of production, whether within an industry or between industries, often falls more heavily on workers than on managers or investors. The human capital of skills and experience is usually less transferable than financial capital and does not benefit from the depreciation that eases the disposal of machines and buildings. It is to the human problem of cushioning the impact of change, the social problem of insuring that people and communities have the chance to make the most of their ability and resources, and the economic problem of keeping manpower flexible enough to optimize its use that policy should be directed.

What kind of government intervention might be required for these purposes is a subject beyond the bounds of this book. Ideally, policies would exist to deal with such problems whether they were caused by the export of jobs, import competition, domestic competition, or technological progress. In practice it might prove helpful to design special programs to deal with cases arising from the "export of jobs"—if such cases are detectable. The analogy with adjustment assistance for import competition is closest if an American firm is shutting down or curtailing domestic operations because it has expanded production abroad. But if, as is often the case with large enterprises, the expansion abroad means only a slower potential growth in certain domestic plants or a shift in the kinds of activity, there are far better chances for smooth adjustment; cooperation between enlightened management and enlightened labor can do much without the need for government assistance. The pressure on management to be "enlightened" would include the wish to reduce the risk that labor discontent would reach the point of forcing the government to some kind of action, through taxation if not by direct control.

If labor continues to feel that the "export of jobs" is a serious problem and that government measures to reduce it are not likely to be taken, it would seem natural for unions to see what they can do about the matter by themselves. An obvious first line is to put greater emphasis on job security, possibly with special arrangements pertaining to any effects on American employment that can reasonably be linked with a company's expansion of production abroad. Contracts that guard against unemployment resulting from automation and other kinds of technological innovation provide something of a precedent. The success of such an approach may well depend on the willingness of workers to change the kind of work they do— though without loss of pay—as often happens when new equipment is installed. Neither labor nor management in the United States is likely to go so far as to accept the arrangement in some Japanese enterprises—by custom more than contract—whereby the worker has something like lifetime job security but in return must stand ready to change the nature of his work when management so decrees. Such an arrangement does not fit well with the American ethos and risks introducing costly rigidities into the economy; to escape them, alternatives will have to be sought as unemployment becomes less and less acceptable as a form of economic adjustment.

A second line of approach for labor is to try, in some fashion, to follow the company abroad. Only very limited possibilities exist to do this directly. Canada is a special case, where most unions are affiliates of much larger American unions. In a few countries where local unions are weak or nonexistent, representatives of American labor may be able to help organize, especially if the company agrees that they should; the United Steelworkers have accompanied American firms to a few less developed areas. More often, however, the question is one of cooperation with established foreign unions. Often the American union can provide information on the financial condition of the company, its competitive position, and other factors relevant to the kind of local wage it could pay. It may also enhance the bargaining position of the local union by showing what kinds of arrangements have proved possible in the United States and suggesting innovations in employment practices and the scope of labor-management contracts. There are, of course, innumerable obstacles in the way of American unions' pursuing this course: language, differences in circumstances and approach, resistance by foreign unions and foreign governments (some of whom do not want their unions strengthened), reluctance of the American firms to carry their domestic labor problems with them, the scarcity in the unions of people with the necessary skills, and the limited return that can be expected from a slow and somewhat costly operation. But even if international trade union cooperation reached new heights in the future, its effect on foreign labor costs might not seriously reduce the incentive of American companies to invest abroad.

The possibility of increased activity by American unions abroad is related to an emerging international labor response to the growth of the multinational corporation, about which more will be said later. As a defense against the "export of jobs" as diagnosed by AFL-CIO spokesmen at the beginning of the '70s, this line of action promises only marginal advantages, at least in the short run. More negative policies, such as strikes and boycotts of companies that transfer production from the United States abroad, are also not promising except in relatively minor instances. It is hard to find any satisfactory course of action which focuses on the investment process unless labor could exert pressure on management to introduce new technology that would make exporting more profitable. (Incidentally, organized labor should be found in the forefront of efforts to encourage foreign investment in the United States—the "import of jobs.") The most constructive solutions seem to depend on seeing to it that there is no net "export of jobs" by insuring the continuing adaptability of the American economy to a changing world economy. Perhaps labor is bound to be more often a reactive rather than an initiating factor in this process, but its response is vital to the success of public policies. Somehow the objective of maximizing labor's share of currently produced national income must be combined with the avoidance of measures that may reduce the income to be shared in the future. High real wages for American labor depend to an important degree on the ability of the American economy to expand, which in turn requires adaptability that can be enhanced by investing (or buying) abroad.

The government's principal task in this matter should be to manage the economy so as to assure growth and a high level of employment and thus reduce the risk that jobs will be, in any meaningful sense, "exported." Second, it should stand ready to help to smooth transitions, cushion the impact of change on workers, and try to minimize friction from the apparent (or real) conflict of interest between labor and management arising out of foreign investment. Third, if the evolution of the American economy should take such form as to shift the distribution of benefits away from wage earners (organized and unorganized) and toward investors and management, that fact would have to be taken into account in the shaping of the great host of government activities that bear on the distribution of welfare in the society, not least taxation. Finally, if the growing complexity of international economic relations should result in the government's continuing in one way or another to exert some influence on the process of international investment, then it should take into account the effect of investment on employment in shaping whatever policies it follows, nationally or internationally.

As this last paragraph suggests, the examination of labor complaints about American foreign investment proves to be not a digression from the topic of the links between investment and trade but an evidence of the convergence of policies in the two fields which must in the end be judged by common standards about their effect on the American economy.

FOREIGN INVESTMENT POLICIES

Not American controls over investment but foreign controls of American investment have provided the central problems of past policy. While the theme of freedom versus regulation dominated much past discussion and is far from dead, many of the major questions about the present and future concern the kinds of regulation that may be practiced and what their results will be.

Though the freeing of current payments was one of the goals of the Bretton Woods efforts, governments retained the right to control capital movements. Otherwise, it was feared, short-term capital could be a serious source of instability; the aim was not to limit direct investment as such. In the immediate postwar years, the European countries restricted the export of capital and encouraged, at least in principle, investment by Americans, since the dollar shortage was also a capital shortage. Washington, for its part, also tried to stimulate the flow of capital abroad, to the less developed countries as well as to Europe. After a slow start, American investment in Europe began to build up fairly rapidly in the second half of the '50s, though less in response to government encouragement than to other factors. In the first postwar decade, some American companies, holding substantial sums in blocked currencies, had an inducement to find uses for the funds by investing in Europe. Then the surge of European recovery opened new opportunities which looked especially attractive when the rate of economic growth was higher in Europe than at home. Since 1964 the annual increase in American direct investment in Europe (including funds raised abroad) has never been less than $1 billion and often much more.

Generally favorable to American investment, especially when the flow was rather modest, European governments were also rather wary, for understandable reasons. One of the first to limit the activities of American businessmen was the military governor of the American occupation zone in Germany, General Lucius D. Clay, who was said to want no carpetbaggers following the troops and buying up assets at bargain rates while the country's economy was flat on its back. In somewhat the same vein, European governments were apt to prefer investment that established new enterprises to having Americans take over existing firms. They liked to keep some kinds of activity in national hands and were sometimes responsive to their own producers' wish to be shielded from American competition. Concern for the balance of payments made them happy to see dollars flowing in but a bit worried about what the outflow of profits would be in later years. The balance between welcome and resistance varied considerably from country to country. Few governments did much that greatly discouraged American investment in general, though there were cases in which it was stopped or made difficult and some sectors, such as the oil industry in France, where it was closely regulated.

As the European economy got stronger, American investment increased and so did the worries. Although Americans owned a relatively small share of Europe's industrial plant as a whole, they played a major and sometimes dominant part in the most advanced industries, such as electronics and computers, in some of the great areas of growth, notably automobiles, and also in oil.[9] Far from the kind of dependence that bothered the Canadians, many Europeans felt that they faced a dilemma between permitting the American share to grow and forgoing the technological and managerial advantages the Americans brought. To have up-to-date "national" industries in some fields seemed, ironically, to require accepting foreign ownership and control. By the late '60s a few wistful glances were being cast at Japan, which had modernized with great rapidity while sharply restricting foreign investment.

Not all Europeans believe they have a problem worth worrying about, and it is far from clear that advocates of restriction will win out. For the countries in the Common Market, where so much of the investment is taking place, there is a special problem, as the French discovered when their resistance to the establishment of a General Motors plant resulted in the American firm's investing in Belgium and exporting its cars to the French market. The obvious response, a Community policy toward foreign investment, has been impeded by disagreement about what the policy should be and a certain rivalry for American installations. There may come to be a common policy, or elements of one may emerge as part of the effort to reach agreement on the encouragement of international mergers within the Common Market, the creation of Community corporations and a Community-wide patent system, and the negotiation of common energy and transportation policies. To the minds of some Europeans, the proper response to *le défi américain* is not restriction but competition through the creation of European enterprises on a scale to match the market the Europeans have created.

In the mid-'60s, Washington changed one of the terms of the problem the Europeans faced. Where once there had been only encouragement and support for American investment in Europe and a call for the freeing of capital movements, restriction appeared. Looking for ways to reduce the balance of payments deficit that had become uncomfortably large, the Kennedy Administration in 1963 introduced an interest equalization tax intended to deter foreign borrowing in the American market. This was followed in a few years

9. The situation was not altogether new; a careful, heavily documented study published in 1931 concluded that as a result of the "Europeward movement of American industrial enterprise," American interests "have gained a dominant position in the European electrical, telephone manufacturing, automobile and motion picture industries, a powerful position in the petroleum industry, and a foothold in the metal industry." Southard, cited, p. 111.

by a series of measures limiting American bank lending abroad and also the export of funds for direct investment. Never as voluntary as it was originally proclaimed to be, this program became less so as time passed. It also became more elaborate; "balance of payments guidelines" were set down which required the remittance of earnings from overseas activities as well as stemming the flow of funds abroad. Although government statements emphasized the temporary character of the controls and proclaimed the wish to remove them "as soon as possible," they persisted into the '70s, though with some easing.

In spite of the restrictions, Americans continued to build up their investment in Europe. They found some of the money they needed in Europe, especially in the Eurodollar market. Often it cost more than it would have in the United States, but there is little evidence that any major activities were deterred by that fact. While such financing was not entirely new, the shift in emphasis was significant for American-European investment relations in at least three ways. First, it underlined the basic fact that "international production" is created by more than a flow of funds from the investing country. Management, technology, patents, know-how, and other elements of the entrepreneurial act are the essentials; being part of a broader enterprise is often vital; ownership and control, themselves not identical, need not correspond to the amount of money provided by one party rather than another. Second, the American companies have shown that the potentialities for raising industrial capital in Europe are greater than was previously realized; they have introduced new techniques into that capital market and to some extent have unified and expanded it. Third, as a consequence of the new pattern of financing, new issues have arisen between the United States and Europe. The feeling behind the remark, "It is bad enough for the Americans to be buying up our industries, but to have them do it with our own money. . ." is likely to be stronger than any gratitude for the benefits the new financing techniques may provide for Europeans with money to invest or for the improved functioning of European capital markets. The Americans are seen as competing for European funds and disrupting a system in which European companies often had preferred positions in their national capital markets, sometimes even monopolistic positions. Some governments are uneasy about American financing by methods that escape their control. In some countries, banks see their traditional influence on industry being weakened by the development of new sources of financing. Whether American funds flow freely or are checked, it seems clear that the issues with which governments will be concerned in the future will be even broader and more complex than in the past.

Plainly, the '70s will differ from the two preceding decades. The United States remains, as it has long been, an advocate of the free movement of private capital, but it professes its faith less often and less loudly, perhaps because it has demonstrated that when the balance of payments is involved, principles may give way to *raison d'état* on the western as well as the eastern shore of the Atlantic. Europe feels less need of American investment now than in the ten years after 1945 but is getting more of it; though strong, Europe remains a bit nervous. Disposed to be choosy about what it gets, it has not found an altogether satisfactory technique that combines both promotion and control. The financial balance between the two sides of the Atlantic has altered, and, quite apart from whatever may be the future of American financing abroad, Europe has again become an important capital exporter with a significant share of its new investment going to the United States. Less obvious than the differences is one important similarity between the '70s and the '40s and '50s: A sound American policy should be concerned not only with what happens, or might happen, to the American stake abroad represented by direct investment in Europe (or any place else) but with the way what is done about international production will shape the world economy in the long run. How the combination of old and new forces will play itself out is impossible to foresee, but it is not hard to identify the main issues with which American policy toward investment in Europe will have to deal in the '70s.

Two old stand-bys remain central: getting access and discrimination. Neither is as clear-cut as it sounds, except in principle and at the extremes. The extremes will not often be reached; it is hard to imagine a European government putting a flat ban on all American investment or formally and systematically discriminating against all American-owned firms in a thorough-going way. The principles (which would bar the extremes) are easily enunciated and have been widely accepted, but their application is imperfect and is likely to become more so. No matter what rules or principles they accept about equal treatment and the right of establishment in their territories by American firms, few European governments are likely to follow a practice of unqualifiedly welcoming any and all American entrepreneurs and of overlooking the difference between foreign- and domestically-owned business in the conduct of national policy. Instead, they will continue to try to steer a course that garners the benefits of foreign investment while still quieting some of the worries about it. What this means will be different in different countries and at different times, but a certain number of common factors will be at work.

As in the past there will be concern, at least sometimes, about whether the future outflow of funds linked to present investment may not prove a burden on the balance of payments. Washington's rules about the remittance of profits will be scrutinized and perhaps some day resisted. Europeans suspect that American firms producing abroad are sometimes prevented by their parents from exporting their goods as vigorously as they should. A new emphasis may be put on joint ventures aimed at introducing American management and technology but increasing the European share of profits and control. Buying technology—or an exchange of licenses as Europe's own research and development expand—will seem more attractive and feasible than before. For a mixture of political, security, cultural, social, and generally nationalist reasons, there will be fairly widespread resistance to "too much" foreign investment—though the idea of what is "too much" may change. Foreign domination of certain sectors of the economy, or even any foreign participation at all in some activities, will be resisted. Objection to close-in American competition may manifest itself in any place where domestic interests are strong enough. In guiding their national economies, whether by means of general plans, regional policies, specific campaigns to emphasize one kind of development or slow another, or otherwise, governments will pay special attention to foreign investment. They may be as interested in encouraging as restricting it, but they will want it to perform according to their lights.

None of these factors is new, but it seems likely that reactions to the increase of American investment will grow. There is no single way for the United States to cope with all these pressures. Issues will frequently arise in the form of cases, and what can or cannot be easily, properly, or effectively done by the U.S. government will depend to an important degree on circumstances rather than general ideas of policy. Often, the investment issue will be part of a broader problem. To the extent that European governments have a justified concern about the effects of investment on their balance of payments, much of the remedy lies in the general improvement of the international monetary system and its adjustment process. Where restriction results from the resistance of domestic producers to foreign competition, it has to be regarded as a form of protectionism comparable to that which produces trade barriers. Against restriction based on strong political or cultural forces, it is unlikely that American policies will avail very much; it will be for the Europeans, nudged sometimes by example or perhaps even a bit of preaching, to decide when the material costs of restrictions outweigh their less tangible benefits. When we come to questions connected with governmental direction of the economy, the terrain changes; the key question is how to work toward a situation in which there is no excuse for discriminating against foreign investors so long as they follow the same rules that apply to domestic companies. Both American policies and those of foreign governments are involved.

At the end of World War II, the United States modernized its long-established Treaties of Friendship, Commerce, and Navigation to cover investment more clearly and fully. One major objective that was largely achieved so far as Western Europe was concerned was to secure "national treatment"—the assurance that an American-owned company, properly constituted under the laws of another country, should be treated equally with the truly national firms of that country. The treaties provide fairly good insurance against overt discrimination over a wide range of issues. There is little doubt, however, that in most countries there is some degree of discrimination in practice if not in law.[10] Permission to invest often depends on a company's undertaking certain commitments. Though American subsidiaries in Europe are major suppliers to European governments, contracts are sometimes not awarded to them because they are foreign-owned. Though subsidiaries of American firms get from European governments export credits for sales to Communist countries that the parent companies could not get from their own government, they may well be discriminated against in the receipt of government capital on favorable terms for other purposes. Few subsidies to foster research are likely to go to American companies.

How serious this kind of discrimination is, is hard to judge. Most American firms seem resigned to a certain amount of it and believe that nothing is to be gained by making complaints that raise issues between governments. Quite often they feel that the long-run advantages of establishing themselves as "good citizens" can be gained only if they take care of these problems by themselves as much as possible. Washington has taken few initiatives in these matters. Nevertheless, the subject is one on which American policy should remain clear-cut in principle so that it can be invoked when suitable. In many matters there is a link between national treatment, or the lack of it, in investment and the kind of practices that will be negotiated about when governments come to deal seriously with nontariff barriers and trade distortion.

As the Europeans react to the growth of American investment by forming larger entities to compete more effectively with foreign-owned firms, the question of national treatment takes on a new edge.

10. The treaties do not prevent some activities from being closed entirely to foreigners nor do they prevent nationalization or state monopolies.

Efforts to develop a national computer industry or preserve an aircraft industry or balance energy sources in a politically and socially acceptable way are almost bound to put the foreigner at a disadvantage. He will certainly not get the same help or privileges given to domestic competitors, through government purchasing, subsidies, and other devices. As Europeans see it, they have infant industries which their governments must shelter to turn them into infant prodigies. "Science policy," an increasingly popular field of government activity, is likely to add to the nationalist bias of policy toward foreign investment. Even when the government's role is primarily to encourage mergers, it will favor those among national producers and may resist the entry of new American competitors until the enlarged domestic company finds its feet. Or it may prevent an American takeover of a company earmarked for a part in a merger that is to produce a stronger national enterprise.

What is happening on a national basis may also take place among the Common Market countries on a Community-wide basis. Some of the proposals for creating Community-franchised corporations to eliminate obstacles to international mergers among the Six would reserve this status to enterprises beneficially owned by Common Market interests. Such a rule would seem to Americans a step back from the principle of "national treatment." Europeans are apt to regard it as a natural evolution of the process of integration, which inevitably distinguishes between members and nonmembers just as the common tariff does. In such fields as patents, transport, and energy policy, the combination of less-than-national treatment with development of Community policies is likely to give rise to a continuing series of differences about the treatment of American investment.

The United States government complicates the claim of national treatment for American-owned firms abroad by applying to them some parts of American law. The most familiar instances concern trade with the Communist countries and antitrust, which raise issues of the sort already discussed in the chapter on Canada. The substantive effect of these actions is easily exaggerated; some American antitrust actions may actually help foreign governments regulate domestic business or benefit foreign consumers. Nevertheless, to treat American-owned companies abroad as, for certain purposes, part of the American economy and not the economy in which they operate lends color to the view that when American investment comes in a certain amount of national sovereignty goes out. Reactions are exacerbated when American investment appears to sharpen the impact on Europe of the dollar's difficulties. It is annoying, on the one hand, if, in defense of its balance of payments, the United States requires companies to remit to the United States profits that they might otherwise have chosen to reinvest in Europe. On the other hand, if Europe is fighting off a wave of dollars it feels to be inflationary, part of the recrimination is apt to focus on direct investment and its close links with the Eurodollar market. More, not less, government concern with these issues is likely to be the order of the day in the '70s.

It is easy to invent "scenarios" about how disagreements will lead to even sharper disputes between the United States and other governments about investment; but they can be misleading. There is room for agreement as well as unending dispute. Although there is no neat symmetry of common interests like that in trade, with each country interested in a reduction of the other's barriers, the issue is not simply that the United States is trying to promote the freedom of investment while the Europeans are resisting it. Interests in Europe are divided. The competition the European businessman wants to keep out may bring welcome relief to the European consumer in new products, lower prices, and perhaps even a new spirit of competition in the local supplier. European governments have been happy to give tax concessions to American firms that bring jobs to depressed areas. The man responsible for running a nationalized industry may accept the principle that he should buy his computers domestically—but not if they do not work well. It is not only American companies that are discriminated against: De Gaulle resisted a Fiat investment in Citroën, the German government kept French interests out of its energy industry, and the British blocked an expansion of the Swedish share in the production of bearings.

A good bit of what is old about foreign investment policy is taking on increased importance as a result of the growth of "international production." But some of the old formulas do not work; it is hard to claim national treatment for an American company abroad if it is not free to act as a national. As they develop "industrial policies," national governments make even greater efforts than before to influence the investment activity of business, national and international. Through this process, as in trade, the growing complexity of international economic relations is forcing governments into new areas of policy and negotiation. Before going farther in trying to map the new terrain, we need to add one more set of complications, those connected with the rise of "the multinational corporation."

The Multinational Corporation

Rocketing into popularity, the term "multinational corporation" has become a modish label to be pasted on discussion of almost any aspect of foreign investment or international business. Used that way, the term obscures instead of illuminates an important phenomenon which, as Raymond Vernon, one of its principal students, once said is indubitably "there," however much people may disagree as to just how it should be defined.

One does not have to be a European—or Asian or Latin American —to feel that in quite a few cases the words "multinational corporation" have become a slightly mealy-mouthed euphemism for "big American company with large overseas interests." For it is plain that a company that is "multinational" by most of the definitions in use may still be clearly American; and most of them are. Yet to ignore Unilever, Shell, Philips, Nestlé, Alcan Aluminium, Ltd., and Massey-Ferguson would be to miss an important point. At the same time, to insist on a definition so rigorous that it denied the label of multinational to any enterprise that could also be identified as predominantly of one nationality would so narrow the field that the topic would be marginal to the concerns of this book except in its longest looks ahead. What we are talking about is a form of international business that in part exists and in part has to be imagined. What is beyond doubt is that it is rapidly growing in size and becoming more "multinational."

As their foreign business spreads among a number of countries and grows in volume relative to domestic business—and certainly when more income is generated abroad than at home—an increasing number of American companies can properly be called multinational. Not only do they have to be "good citizens" of more different countries, which is the way businessmen like to describe themselves, but as they decide what it is in their interests to do, "foreign" considerations become more important than "American." While governments are not of equal weight, the number to whose pressures the company must respond grows. It can only be a matter of time before some of the companies ask themselves whether a headquarters in Switzerland, or Luxembourg, or perhaps even Singapore would make more sense than one in New York. Increased employment of foreigners, more access to the top management in New York for people whose highest aspiration in the past might have been to head a foreign affiliate, more employment of Europeans to run Latin American subsidiaries and Latin Americans in countries other than their own, representation of foreign affiliates on the boards of the parent—these are symptoms of multinationalism rather than its essence, which lies in the spreading of company interests over a number of countries.

Although it may be a long time before there are many important corporations which are so multinational in their interests, ownership, management, and behavior that they are not in some meaningful sense American (or of some other nationality) as well, there is little doubt of the trend of the '70s. This trend creates new policy issues, not just those of old foreign investment writ large. Like the growth of "international production," the multinational corporation has the potential of raising issues that traditional policy does not adequately deal with. The United States is concerned not just because American business is involved but because the new issues reflect broad changes in economic relations among the industrial countries.

The more truly multinational the enterprises get, the more problems will arise simply because policy remains largely national. It is, or becomes, of the essence of the multinational enterprise to pursue a strategy which will be as global as circumstances, its interests, and its structure permit. In pursuit of its corporate aims—profit maximization, growth, or whatever intermediate goal attracts it—the multinational enterprise will try to build whatever structure of production, distribution, and financing seems to make sense. To get the benefits of specialization and size, it may concentrate certain kinds of production in certain countries for sale all over the world; it may produce parts in three countries and assemble them in the fourth for sale in all four and beyond. It can build plants of an optimum size before local demand would justify that course, knowing that it can use the output in some other part of the world. It can integrate its raw materials production, processing, manufacturing, and selling as it wishes —provided governments let it.[11] Much of the international trade in which a multinational enterprise engages may also be intracorporate trade, the exchange of goods among its affiliates; and its "internal" corporate financing includes a large number of international financial transactions.

Consequently, questions of two quite different sorts arise. Will the multinational enterprise largely escape national controls and so frustrate national economic policies? Will the fact that the policies governing international trade and investment are national policies impair the operation of multinational corporations and prevent them from contributing as much as they could to world income and productivity?

A huge corporation (or, more exactly, complex of corporations) with a world-wide credit standing and access to many capital markets

---

11. Its operations are not confined to industrialized countries, of course, and may well be a significant factor in future industrialization of less developed countries as multinational corporations find it desirable to establish manufacturing facilities there with pre-established customers in the form of affiliates in industrial countries. To maintain the focus of this section the discussion of these matters—which, of course, raise questions about trade policy—is omitted.

can finance in one place what it is forbidden to finance in another. It can adjust its affairs so that profits are taken where taxes are lowest. If permitted, it can price goods that move among affiliates higher or lower than comparable transactions among independent buyers and sellers. It can absorb tariffs that bear more heavily on smaller, nationally based companies. Often it can, if it wishes, be less responsive than such companies to the governmental pressures that do much to make "indicative planning" work or that make "voluntary" controls effective. In a set-to with one of the governments within whose jurisdiction it operates, its bargaining power is enhanced by the ability to accept losses in one place while expanding operations in another—or simply by its mobility. When considering investments, the widely dispersed multinational enterprise has a greater choice of where to put its efforts than the smaller company for whom the desirability of getting into a specific market is more likely to be dominant, leaving it less able than the multinational corporation to bargain for terms or resist the demands of the government. Small countries may find themselves outclassed financially by the biggest multinational corporations.

How often the multinational entrepreneur is really free to make all these choices is not altogether clear. It is easy to exaggerate his immunity to national pressures and regulations. An official sitting in Washington sees the problem very differently from one in the capital of a small or weak country. Businessmen are apt to regard references to their relative invulnerability to national pressures and controls as at best rather poor jokes. For them a good part of the daily grind consists of dealing with action or threatened action by several governments that would reduce the efficiency of the multinational operation or even destroy its rationale. Resistance and compromise, appeasement and avoidance, education and counterpressure all play their parts. In the process a certain confusion develops between what it means to be a corporate good citizen of each country in which the enterprise operates and to be a good citizen of the world, where there is neither sovereign nor constituency, a role which a free-ranging entrepreneur might feel he was playing if he believed in the identity of the common interest and his own (or at least their substantial overlapping).

There is a good case for the view that the hallmark of the multinational corporation is the "shift from autonomy of affiliates to centralized control and integration."[12] Therein is a direct challenge to one

12. Jack N. Behrman, *Some Patterns in the Rise of the Multinational Enterprise*, Research Paper 18 (Chapel Hill: Graduate School of Business Administration, University of North Carolina, 1969), p. xiv.

or more national governments—and a contradiction of the business-man who sincerely argues that his national companies behave like true nationals. Apart from whatever wish it may have to escape, or offset, measures taken by one government or another, the multina-tional corporation following a global strategy decides what each of its constituent parts should do on the basis of the needs of the enter-prise as a whole. Hence the fear of those responsible for a national economy that the decisions to export or not, to import instead of buy-ing locally, to expand or contract or even to shut down, to lay off men or add to the demand for local capital will all be made in re-sponse to different stimuli from those that would move a local entre-preneur and by people whose concern with the impact of what they do on the national economy is secondary. The local managers of the affiliate will try hard to fit into the national pattern and sometimes that will be the best tactic. If their unit's function is primarily to pro-duce and sell in the home market, their difficulties may not be too great. But when they are truly multinational and pursuing a global strategy designed to maximize their own interests, companies increase the differences between themselves and domestic companies and, in-deed, between their behavior and that of foreign-owned companies that have greater local autonomy.

The factors that help the multinational entrepreneur to escape na-tional jurisdiction, the contrary pressures that make him responsive to the wishes of governments, the dynamics of investment and interna-tional production, ideas about national interests and the ways of translating them into policy, all keep changing. Many issues that be-gin as familiar problems of foreign investment are transformed as time goes on into new kinds of problems. It takes only a little imagi-nation to start thinking about the possibility of intergovernmental action that would reduce conflicts of jurisdiction over multinational enterprises and at the same time prevent their getting around national policies by, in effect, playing one sovereignty off against another.

The most far-reaching proposals of this sort call for the creation of an international body that would provide the kind of public oversight of multinational corporations that governments normally provide at home. There might be an international incorporation procedure; there would almost certainly have to be agreement on rules and prin-ciples to apply to multinational corporations in general or to some key features of their behavior; these standards would have to be enforced by some kind of intergovernmental action. Somewhat more modest proposals call for international agreements to deal with generally recognized issues, such as taxation, which national laws are to apply to what kinds of activities, and what is to be expected of corporations subjected to conflicting national policies. Where firm commitments to precise rules are not acceptable, provision would be made for consultation, a complaints procedure, and international studies and recommendations aimed at slowly widening the area of agreement. Still other proposals concentrate on specific trouble spots and suggest bilateral agreements in which, for example, the United States would give up some of its claims for extraterritorial jurisdiction in return for assurances that American-owned firms would be treated as truly "national." A series of bilateral agreements might well develop into multilateral arrangements. From the initially limited and specific, they would probably tend to grow in scope (if they worked). Sometimes the emphasis would be on the common interest of governments in keeping business behavior in agreed channels, while at other times the governments would be divided about their own interests, as in the allocation of revenue.

Few businessmen would welcome these prospects. They would be happy, of course, for any reduction in double taxation but might find some tax havens closed. They would be attracted by a limited agreement that reconciled the conflict between national jurisdiction and multinational fact if its gist was to let sovereignty (but not business) end at the water's edge. There would be few complaints, for example, if the United States agreed to stop trying to apply antitrust laws or rules for trading with Communist countries to American-owned firms abroad. More ambitious efforts would seem to businessmen to foreshadow something as bad as national controls and probably worse. One can sympathize. It is easy to imagine an international bureaucracy far more cumbersome than national ones which, whatever their faults, are at least familiar to the businessmen who have to deal with them. When it comes to dealing with the governments of other industrial countries, many American businessmen prefer handling their own affairs to asking Washington's help with the attendant risk that politicizing the dispute will make it worse. Some will go very far to avoid a situation in which foreign policy issues may continually insert themselves in business affairs, but few have yet shown themselves prepared to give up altogether the right to call on their government for help.

It is not likely that any comprehensive intergovernmental regulation of multinational enterprises will be undertaken soon. Governments lack the common ground, or impetus, to come to an agreement on anything as complex as the international franchise and regulation of corporations. They will continue to lack it at least until the belief that multinational enterprises are strong enough to defy, or undermine, national controls is more fully borne out, or until conflicts of national jurisdictions become more general and serious than they have been. Even then conflicts of interest and differences in views about what should be done will make general agreement on common rules difficult. But it is also unlikely that nothing will be done. It is in the nature of society that the growth of power sooner or later calls forth resistance to it. And when new forms of private power in some degree challenge such strong and numerous centers of established power as national governments, the reaction is not likely to be long delayed. The future will see a continuation of past and present efforts of national authorities to shape the behavior of multinational corporations. But the setting is changing. While "multinational" will more often than not continue to mean "American," the number of multinational enterprises which are non-American is growing. By almost any definition, multinational corporations are becoming more numerous and more multinational. The incentives for governments to move toward various kinds of international action to deal with them are clear and can hardly fail to produce results.

It is an interesting question whether there will be another kind of response as well, from labor. Some years before the AFL-CIO became seriously concerned about the "export of jobs" resulting from foreign investment, several American labor leaders had interested themselves in the possibility of working out cooperative arrangements with unions in other countries so that international companies would, to some extent at least, confront international labor. Sometimes the targets were simply competing firms in the same industry. There were comparable efforts by unions in the Common Market countries from the early days of the European Coal and Steel Community. Several of the international trade secretariats in which unions in related fields cooperate for a number of purposes have made moves in the same direction, notably the International Metalworkers Federation which deals with steel, automobiles, shipbuilding, machinery, and some electrical industries. During the latter '60s, these efforts produced modest but rather interesting results. There were cooperative studies of the global industry, exchanges of information about companies and their labor practices, several kinds of technical assistance in collective bargaining, and some mutual support, such as the refusal of Ford's German employees to handle work transferred from its Belgian plant that was on strike. In 1969 the International Federation of Chemical and General Workers' Unions took the lead in a fairly successful coordination of bargaining by Italian, French, German, and American unions against the St. Gobain glass company.

There are great difficulties in the way of this kind of effort. Though the unions have some internationalist traditions, they are essentially national organizations, each in a quite different political and social setting from the others. Political and ideological divisions within and between countries, differences in standards, strength, and independence, and sometimes conflicts of interest make the task of coordinating action formidable. Together the unions face a company that wants to preserve its freedom of action; separately they face governments that will differ from one another in the intensity with which they oppose inflationary wage settlements, want to avoid strikes, and worry about the impact of what happens in one industry on others or about how the experience of one foreign investor will affect another's decision about where to invest. When plants are located in less developed countries as well as in Europe and the United States, matters are further confounded, as they are when Japan's rather special labor-management relations are involved.

The potential of international labor as a countervailing force to international business will not remotely approach the power of governments for a long time. Nevertheless, there is an inherent logic in the proposition that the internationalization of production should include labor as well as management and finance. The multinational corporation may not beget the multinational union, but it will certainly stimulate international cooperation among unions as it does cooperation among governments. There are some fairly close analogies. A government's concern that a many-faceted business can elude its jurisdiction is matched by a union's concern that its "social partner"—as the Europeans like to call labor and capital—will bargain by invoking its foreign capabilities, if it does not slip away to another country altogether. It is as reasonable for workers to say that their employer's ability to pay wages should be judged by the profitability of his whole global enterprise as it is for governments to concern themselves with the tax loss that might result from looking at the books of only one national slice of the enterprise. Those who are divided know what they have to do if they do not want to be ruled, difficult as they may find the process.

Whether its opponent is labor or government, the multinational corporation is often seen as the vehicle of international integration whose progress is checked by essentially disintegrative, national forces that are trying to exact a price that will be paid in terms of global, and sometimes national, welfare. Something approaching an ideology is building up on this point. The multinational corporation, bringing together capital, labor, management and other skills, raw materials, and marketing in whatever combinations and whatever places prove most productive, is seen as a factor working for integration of the world economy, while the national government appears as the parochial blocker of integration. This view has some validity but suffers from too narrow a conception of integration, probably exaggerates the potential of the multinational corporation, and implies an oversimplified view of the interests of nation states and the powers that drive them. Still, the contrast is suggestive and can be seen as a facet of a problem endemic to foreign economic policy and encountered more than once in these pages: How to reconcile national policies with the advantages of unimpeded economic activity on a global basis.

Though we credit the multinational entrepreneur with a global viewpoint (or at least a more international one than governments ordinarily have), he is pursuing a particular interest, in a given competitive situation, and the international integration that serves his purpose is not necessarily identical with the integration that would maximize world welfare. If there were enough of him—if all entrepreneurs were capable of functioning globally should that seem the best course —the chances of approximating that kind of integration would be improved. The analogy popular with some commentators between the potential of the multinational corporation and the part big corporations played in the late nineteenth century in making the American economy truly nation-wide (integrating it) is suggestive. It is important, though, to remember two things: in the United States the result was achieved by a blend of freedom and regulation, not simply setting business free; the problem of regulation in the present case is complicated by the lack of a single sovereign serving a single public interest (however defined).

The problem arising from national attempts to regulate the multinational corporation is familiar. In acting against a practice that seems damaging to its national interest, a government may be interpreting that interest too narrowly. Its own people may stand to benefit in the long run (or even in the short) from the broader international division of labor the multinational corporation might achieve, even if existing patterns of trade and production were for a time disturbed. But even if the government were correct in judging that there would be some long-run damage to its national interest, the alternative might well be damage to the interests of another country. In a world of separate sovereignties such conflicts can be resolved only by compromise. But a compromise quite acceptable to a multinational corporation would not necessarily do anything to promote the interests of others and might considerably reduce the validity of the claim that global business is an integrative force.

If, for instance, the multinational corporation set up a plant in a certain country because otherwise it could not get around a trade barrier (or other kind of restriction), its activities would not be integrative. Such a step might even intensify the bad use of resources if it enlarged the protected market for domestic suppliers who used resources inefficiently. Of course, these things are equally true of any company. The case for the multinational corporation as integrator must rest, in such a situation, on one or both of two lines of argument: first, that because of its character the multinational corporation can perform behind the barriers in a more economic way than another firm (perhaps by minimizing the importance of the barrier); second, that once established behind the barrier the multinational corporation will have less interest than another company would have in continuing protection (perhaps because it wishes to integrate the new plant into its global operations). It might then become a source of pressure for liberal trade and investment policies in more than one country at once, provided its positions were secure enough.

Only time will tell how strong multinational corporations are as integrators in this rather different sense. It is probably fair to say, though, that, more than most businessmen, multinational corporations have an interest in both freer investment and freer trade. Whether the public interest would also be served by that course and whether it is a realistic goal are matters that take us back to the questions that have been dealt with piecemeal throughout this chapter.

INCOMPLETE CONCLUSIONS

Three cuts into the complex issues surrounding investment policy have left us with a few fairly definite conclusions, some probabilities, and some fairly large questions. Not surprisingly, certainty decreases as the issues become broader and more basic.

The growing importance of international investment is clear, along with the increasing complexity of the issues it raises. At a time when the economies of the industrial countries are becoming more open to one another than ever before, direct investment and the "international production" associated with it are proving to be major vehicles for interpenetration. It follows that investment policy (a term that covers many things) is becoming more important than ever before and that the number of issues in which more than one government finds itself interested is increasing.

The link between trade and investment is real but not simple. Sometimes the significance of what can be achieved by a further reduction of trade barriers will depend on what is done about investment (or perhaps vice versa), and sometimes nothing that can be done in trade policy will begin to equal in importance what is done or not done about investment. For the most part, however, the relation between the two will differ according to circumstances and no precise guideline can be laid down as to how national policies toward trade and investment can be harmonized.

While there is a common interest among developed countries in the removal of trade barriers, the freeing of investment is not so clearly an objective all will agree on so long as such a high proportion of international investment is American. In these circumstances, it may be an illusion to suppose that the formula "link negotiations about trade and investment" will improve the American bargaining position. While there is a common interest in reducing trade barriers, the bargaining position of the United States in trade is no stronger than that of the European countries. If the United States is the sole *demandeur* in matters of investment, its position is somewhat weaker. With regard to Japan, matters are different; the American market is so much more important to Japan than Japan's to the United States (important as that is) that to link improving access by trade and improving access by investment seems a natural American strategy. Canada's position is different again; it needs both American capital and American markets to a greater degree than the other industrialized countries but most resents its dependency. Obviously, these different balances will affect the number of instances in which the United States will have to consider such questions as whether it is wise to ask for the improvement of foreign treatment of American investment in return for a lowering of American trade barriers or to avoid the mingling of these issues which is otherwise likely to develop. In either case, broader concepts of "reciprocity" are needed than the traditional ones of trade bargaining with its mercantilist bias that exports are always better than imports. (See chap. 10, pp. 364–70.)

The issue is not, however, just one of the United States as investor versus other countries in which American companies invest. The recipients of investment have divided interests. Against their uneasiness at the growth of alien ownership of parts of the economy must be set the benefits to growth and employment. Against the wish to develop national capacities in science and technology must be set the possibility that American firms will do more to enlarge a country's resources in those fields than could be achieved by purely domestic efforts over a long period. The foreign competition resisted by some domestic producers would bring benefits to domestic consumers. And so on. More and more the problem may come to be seen not as whether or not to keep out the foreigner, but on what terms to let him in. To that problem there can be no single solution. No formula can have predictable results since the approach of both parties will be that of bargainers, and what each will settle for depends more on circumstances than general principles. Europe's objective, according to a French official of the Community, should be "to hasten the development of large American firms to see to it that they have as strong an interest in Europe as in the United States and that they pay as much attention to the point of view of European governments as to that of their own."[13]

A new dimension to international investment will be added in the '70s. Foreign direct investment in the United States, which amounted to $3.4 billion in 1950 rose to $6.9 billion in 1960, and to $13.2 billion by the end of 1970. By then new money was coming in at a rate of over a billion dollars a year compared to less than a third of that a few years earlier. Canadian holdings came to $3.1 billion by the end of 1970 and most of the rest was European. The investments have been spread over manufacturing, distribution, finance, oil, mining, and smelting. Among a large number of relatively small transactions there have been several very large ones and others that are undoubtedly intended to provide the basis for later expansion. Quite often European investors have acquired existing American companies (as Olivetti did Underwood in 1960) while others have started new enterprises, expanded existing ones, or formed joint ventures with Americans.

The reasons for European investment in the United States are not very different from those for American investment abroad: better access to an important market, an improved competitive position, sometimes the acquisition of raw materials. No doubt some European firms have wanted to challenge on his home grounds a competitor who had already invaded their markets. The rapid increase is probably explained more by new capabilities than new motives. Growth, mergers, profits, better access to credit, and the improved balance of payments position of their governments made companies able and willing to mobilize and risk the large resources that are often required to lay an adequate basis for American operations. Another new factor, which may be more important in the future than in the past, is the growing belief that one of the best ways of keeping in touch with American research and innovation is to have a place in the American

13. René Foch, *Europe and Technology: A Political View* (Paris: Atlantic Institute, 1970), p. 53. To achieve this, Foch recommends that Europe systematically prefer investment by multinational firms to imports from the United States, insist that companies establish research laboratories in Europe partly to employ "scientists who would otherwise be tempted to emigrate to the U.S. There seems no reason why European governments should not entrust research contracts to such laboratories, if a suitable patents policy can be worked out." There should, however, be a common Community policy so that European governments would not compete against one another for American investment.

economy instead of waiting to see what American companies are willing to bring to Europe or license there.

There is every reason to suppose that foreign investment in the United States will continue to grow. Interesting results should follow. "International investment" will no longer be predominantly a matter of what Americans do abroad. The investor's approach and psychology will become more influential in Europe while the common reaction of those who are "invested upon" will become more noticeable in the United States.

American policy toward foreign investment is generally liberal, but there are restricted areas and some problems arising from federalism, since certain business activities are regulated by the states. For a number of years the federal government has actively encouraged foreign investment in the United States, and a number of states and municipalities have offered tax and other concessions to foreigners as freely as to Americans. These policies are likely to continue and may even become more important if the increase in foreign investment reveals obstacles that governmental action might help remove. But it is also likely that a sizable increase in foreign investment will show that Americans are not immune to the reactions that create problems for American industry in other parts of the world. Not so many years ago a Senator expressed concern that Swiss investments in American industry might cloak Russian interests. In 1969 a Congressman raised questions "on foreign policy grounds" about a proposed arrangement that would eventually give British Petroleum a majority of the shares in the Standard Oil Company of Ohio. It was hardly surprising when Europeans then became suspicious about the motives of a subsequent antitrust action, though in the end there appeared to be no real grounds for suspicion. (The uncertainty of where antitrust will strike, disconcerting enough to American businessmen, is regarded as a special hazard by European investors, but it is one they will have to live with just as American firms abroad become used to different methods of government regulation.) Some American banks have been unhappy about the incursion of foreign banks into the United States. The growth of Japanese investment in Alaska and the West has stimulated some complaints about displacing local activity and gaining control of mineral resources.

Complaints and restlessness may amount to little more than pinpricks, but they will do something to change the atmosphere. At the same time, there will be a subtle shift in bargaining power. As the foreign "stake" in the United States grows, foreign governments will have to take it into account in shaping their policies toward American investment. If an American company were denied the right to establish itself in France, it would be only human if its officials were tempted to urge the United States government to frown on a French competitor's plan to invest in the United States. If Japan does not ease its restrictions on foreign investment, Americans will begin to ask whether Japanese should remain free to invest as they choose. The results may be good. One need not imagine the United States changing to a policy of restriction; the others may make concessions to reduce that risk. But more and more occasions are bound to arise on which governments have to negotiate about investment questions and make decisions that clarify policy. Problems of investment may come to be seen more clearly as common problems resulting from the interpenetration of the industrialized economies, not as something that concerns only the position of American business in the rest of the world.

There is no need to wait for the future to see that the industrialized countries share a problem in satisfying themselves that international production serves their several conceptions of the public interest. By Judd Polk's calculation, the value of international production by the late '60s was greater than that of the gross national product of any country except the United States and the U.S.S.R.[14] Governments were far from powerless to cope with the resulting problems, but their power was divided among many national sovereignties. The aims of one sometimes conflicted with those of another. For most governments, though, there was the common underlying problem that the already great difficulty of managing a national economy is increased if important elements in it respond at least in part to a different music, played in a foreign capital or company headquarters. For all, there was the additional fact that there is an inescapable—but not total or necessarily disastrous—conflict between multilateral enterprises with global horizons and national governments responsible to domestic constituencies.

Three broad lines of evolution are possible: a weakening of national controls as corporations find more ways of getting around them, a tightening of national controls, and the development of more intergovernmental methods of dealing with the problem. The first generates its own opposition; the second can be checked either by the op-

14. And by the end of the century would equal the GNP of all countries combined if the growth rates of the '50s and '60s continued. "The New World Economy," *Columbia Journal of World Business*, January-February 1968, p. 9. The statement in the text comes from *The American Role in the New World Economy* (New York: United States Council of the International Chamber of Commerce, 1970, mimeographed), p. 2, where it applies to the American-owned share of international production alone.

position of other governments or by the conclusion that the economic price of too much nationalism is too high; the third suffers from all the difficulties of devising new methods of international cooperation and persuading governments, whose interests at any given moment are quite disparate and whose constituencies are national, to adopt them. No doubt something will be done along all three lines, though only the third has the potentiality of coping constructively with the problem in the long run. It would be too much, though, to expect rapid progress in cooperation when there is as yet so little agreement about the objectives to be sought.

A prudent analyst might stop at this point; having portrayed the forces at work, one could leave the future to the future. But those who try to look ahead in policy have to try to do a bit better than that. Without claiming certainty for either prediction or prescription, one can discern some of the problems that will arise as governments try to cooperate.

Some difficulties could be removed by universalizing national treatment, regarding every corporation as equal with every other one carrying on the same kind of activity in the same jurisdiction. There are, however, limits to what can be achieved in this way. National treatment will not be attractive to business if it simply admits companies to the privileges of a very restrictive system. Governments will not be satisfied if by conferring national treatment on multinational enterprises they in fact put the latter in a freer position than their truly national enterprises. Both concerns point to the need for more international understandings, the first stressing the establishment of minimum standards of freedom, the second encouraging joint action by governments. The logical counterpart of making truly national treatment a standard would be for governments to give up their claim to control the behavior of their companies abroad, either by law or influence. If so sweeping an abandonment is not acceptable (or not believed), a more modest formula might call for restraint plus a willingness to discuss the issue when important objectives of policy are thought to be involved in either country.

With or without true national treatment, investment issues will arise in negotiations about trade, nontariff barriers, the conditions of competition, and national industrial policies. The results might take the form of international agreement, but they might also become apparent in national behavior consistent with informal understandings.

Often disputes will be about cases more than principles. That is apt to be so even if the question is whether broad rules already agreed on apply in a certain instance or whether the settlement of a specific issue is likely to become a precedent and to that degree a new rule. The parts of national policies that are absolute (for example, a ban on certain types of foreign investment) are usually secondary to the wish to insure that there is not "too much" investment of a certain sort, or in a specific place, or at one time, or that the investor accepts certain obligations, or—even more important—that he in fact behaves in a certain way. In dealing with such issues, compromises are always possible that permit this, but not that, that give some of what was asked for, but not all. The step from the discussion of principles to decisions on cases can hardly be avoided and neither can the linking of one case with another to make a balanced bargain. If, for example, the United States continued to follow a double policy of favoring American investment abroad but restraining the amount of capital that could be exported while France followed a policy of welcoming, or at least accepting, American investment in general but resisting the expansion of American ownership of some parts of the economy, or requiring certain safeguards, then sooner or later Paris and Washington might well find themselves agreeing that one transaction should be allowed to go forward while another was blocked and a third permitted if the terms were somewhat altered.

That is not a very attractive prospect. While such case-by-case negotiation would make possible some useful investment that would be prevented by purely national regulation, it is hard to avoid the conclusion that, if a large part of international investment depended on the consent of two governments with power to alter details as well, the results would be highly unsatisfactory. The juxtaposition of two sets of governmental policies, with different aims and different priorities relevant to the matter in hand, is not too likely to double the benefits or halve the difficulties of strictly national regulation. It is at least in part the foreshadowing of this possibility that encourages many businessmen to believe that they are best off dealing with their investment problems themselves, concentrating on relations with host governments and minimizing the requests they make of the government of their own country. But the combination of controls over the export and import of capital closes them in, and an objective view of the kind of world economy that is evolving suggests that better means should be found of insuring that the impressive economic potential of international production serves as wide a public interest as possible. That it needs freedom is clear, but it will not be given complete freedom. Societies are not prepared to let private enterprise function entirely without supervision internationally any more than domestically.

To the minds of many, the free movement of investment capital is the natural counterpart of free trade; if one is a goal, the other should be as well. If the market is the best guide to how resources should be used, ought it not to apply to capital as well as goods? There is much to be said for this view, but the analogy is not as clear as it seems when one begins to probe the theoretical basis of the two statements. We clearly need some new theory that takes more account of the mobility of factors of production than does classical trade theory and that somehow comes to terms with the mixture of national sovereignty and economic interpenetration with which the industrial world seems likely to live for a long time to come. The chances are that the theory will show that the freer movement of capital (or enterprise) will maximize world output when certain conditions are met and that to optimize welfare (according to some standard) still another set of conditions will have to be satisfied, mostly affecting distribution of benefits. How closely either set of conditions is achieved will depend largely on whether governmental policies conform to certain standards. Since in the real world these policies will be shaped in large part by separate constellations of national aims and pressures, they will diverge from the pattern prescribed by the theory and so weaken the argument that capital moving "freely" in response to them will produce the best results. Consequently, progress toward the best investment policies that are realistically possible for the industrialized countries will involve not just removal of national controls but some degree of international understanding about the criteria by which measures influencing investment should be guided and as much harmonization as possible in the application of these measures.

Not surprisingly, the problem is in many respects analogous to that of the future of trade policy with its new emphasis on trade-distorting practices and the impact of national industrial policies. In dealing with the movement of enterprise and technology (and the capital that goes with them), the industrialized countries have a range of possibilities, as they do in dealing with the exchange of goods. Unless they reverse the course they have been following and deny themselves the benefits of interpenetration and openness in their economies, they will have to find new ways of combining the removal of some restrictions with the use and constant adaptation of measures intended to guide and influence what happens. They may take a series of national actions that to some degree parallel or complement one another and to some degree conflict. Out of conflicts and retaliation may come agreements that eliminate or moderate conflicts. They may approach the problems of harmonizing policies directly by seeking agreements that accommodate some national controls, forbid others, and regulate still a third category. They may do this on a broad basis or a narrow one, by trying to draft codes of detailed rules or agreeing on procedures for applying general principles to cases.[15] They may pursue several courses at once for different purposes. But whatever they do, they cannot escape increased consultation and negotiation over a wider range of issues.

The result may be to widen the range of freedom for investment but, if so, that will be the result of something different from just applying more wholeheartedly than before the Bretton Woods formula favoring the free flow of capital but permitting national controls over it. That formula is no longer adequate, but the substitute for it is neither simple nor clear. Policies that were capable of embodying national interests when countries were separate economic units do not suffice to express the extended conception of national interest required by international production. The production, trade, profits, employment, and growth of companies engaged in international production are of concern to more than a single country, yet no one government can deal altogether satisfactorily with the problems that result. In trying, it can reduce the benefits (to itself and others) that international business is capable of offering. Freedom is desirable in order to let enterprise function as it should, but the businessman will not, and should not, be allowed absolute freedom internationally any more than he is domestically. However, the drawing of boundaries to his freedom and the continuing surveillance (in many forms) that is the essence of the regulation of business in the public interest cannot be achieved internationally in the same way that they are within any one country. The striving to find a right relation between international business and national governments promises to be the greatest generator of new elements in foreign economic policy we have yet come on in this book.

15. To this line of approach belongs the suggestion of a GATT-like arrangement to deal with a wide range of problems concerning investment and the multinational corporation. Paul M. Goldberg and Charles P. Kindleberger, "Toward a GATT for Investment: A Proposal for Supervision of the International Corporation," *Law and Policy in International Business*, Summer 1970.

7

World Money and National Balance

That the International Monetary Fund and the International Bank for Reconstruction and Development—literally Bretton Woods institutions—were agreed on before trade arrangements were worked out in detail was partly an accident and partly a reflection of priorities. To provide a financial system where otherwise there might be chaos seemed more urgent than getting down to the removal of specific trade barriers. The experience of the '30s was vivid in the minds of those who planned for the postwar world; they knew that if the international monetary system did not work well, the chances of liberalizing world trade would be just about nil. At the same time, the trading arrangements were often spoken of as the keystone of the system. It seems remarkable, then, that the failure to create an International Trade Organization did not greatly damage the Bretton Woods arch. That fortunate outcome was largely the result of the "interim" establishment of GATT and of the way the Marshall Plan laid the groundwork, in Europe and the United States, for genuine liberalization when the dollar shortage waned. Dynamic forces—sometimes helped and sometimes hindered by government policies—produced great growth in the industrial world and an interpenetration of national economies that to a degree leaped over trade barriers. Most important of all, the world stayed well clear of the kind of depression that had haunted the minds of those who in the '40s shaped the institutions and agreements that were tested in the '50s and '60s. Because of these happy results, the Managing Director of the Fund in 1969 could say without irony that the "difficulties of these latter years" which the Bretton Woods system had encountered "have mercifully been still financial in character."[1]

The difficulties Pierre-Paul Schweitzer was talking about concerned exchange rates, the adequacy of reserves, and the adjustment of national economies to changes in their international payments position. A situation had developed in which, he said, "financial crises seem almost to have become a regular feature" of the international monetary scene. That scene was only in part the one for which the sets had been designed at Bretton Woods; other features were shaped by the changing positions of the dollar in the postwar world economy and the strains and challenges which had resulted in significant changes in the international monetary system during the late 1960s.

For much of the first postwar decade, the International Monetary Fund did not function as it was expected to; in fact, so far as some of the most important activities of the period were concerned, it hardly functioned at all. As a source of funds for Europe it was largely displaced by the Marshall Plan, the credits that preceded it, and the American balance of payments deficits that helped put dollars and gold in other people's reserves. The Fund's "scarce currency" clause, intended to put pressure on the extreme and chronic creditor, was not applied to the indubitably scarce dollar, and that was probably just as well. The exchange rates established in the immediate postwar years proved to be in many respects unrealistic, and, when changes were made, the Fund had only a secondary part in the process. It was some years after the end of the Marshall Plan before most European countries got rid of the balance of payments restrictions on current account that the Bretton Woods agreements aimed at eliminating.

The further realignment of exchange rates, the end of the dollar shortage, and the assumption by most European countries of full obligations under the Fund's Articles of Agreement combined to create in the late '50s and early '60s conditions much closer to those envisioned at Bretton Woods than had existed at any time since the end of the war. The Fund became more important. But soon the international payments system was plagued by a new set of difficulties arising from persistent large deficits in the United States balance of payments, and the related tendency of foreign countries to turn their dollars into gold. Matters were further aggravated by the recurrent

1. Address of Pierre-Paul Schweitzer at Queens University, Kingston, Ontario, June 2, 1969, reprinted as a supplement to *International Financial News Survey*, June 6, 1969, p. 180.

difficulties of the pound sterling and the sometimes unsettling effects of enlarged and speeded-up flows of short-term capital.

In the '6os, American initiative elicited a rising degree of international cooperation, much of it focused on innovations and *ad hoc* measures to meet repeated crises. Worry about the long-run adequacy of these measures, doubts about the validity of the modified Bretton Woods system that had grown up around the dollar, and differences over the proper place of gold reinforced the fear of a liquidity crisis that had been voiced by some observers. How could international trade and payments continue to expand rapidly when the production of gold could not keep pace while the acceptability of the dollar was jeopardized by the very deficits that made the dollar available? Long and difficult negotiations to find ways of allaying these fears were made no easier by the fact that international monetary reform and the management of the U.S. balance of payments deficit, though in principle distinguishable, were in fact inevitably intermixed. The result was the creation, just in time for the '7os, of a system of Special Drawing Rights (SDRs) for members of the International Monetary Fund and a change in the role of gold.

A major amendment of the Bretton Woods system, SDRs were intended in the first instance to meet the need for liquidity, but their creation could lead to other things as well. In a world in which most international finance is largely a matter of bookkeeping, it seems ludicrous to adopt such newspaper terms as "paper gold" or "international paper money" to distinguish the SDRs. The labels have some validity, though, in underlining the analogy between the new international step and the way governments regulate domestic money supply to meet the needs of the national economy. In certain circumstances, by agreed procedures and in limited amounts, money was to be created by intergovernmental action.

The SDR agreement was only one step. There was no doubt about its direction, but there was doubt about how far the world would go on the new path. Like most major international agreements, this one compromised national disagreements by resolving some in a balanced bargain, papering over others (for how long no one knew), and leaving still others to be dealt with later. Similarly, the 1968 agreement that separated the private and official markets for gold was not guaranteed to limit the place of gold in the monetary system forever—but that might be its result. It might even lead eventually to the complete demonetization of gold; if not, old arguments about the gold price would sooner or later unsettle the international monetary system once again.

In key places throughout the world there are people who would gladly move further in the direction pointed by the decisions on gold and SDRs. But there are others who only acquiesced in what they hoped would be a limited amendment of the old system for fear that the alternative would be collapse. They would not make another major move unless the brink came in sight once more. Just that seemed to happen when in August 1971 the United States suspended the convertibility of the dollar into gold and called on other countries to raise their exchange rates. This crisis, like others before it, may well be the prelude to further important changes in the monetary system. How this might come about is examined in the epilogue to this book, but the fundamental alternatives and the major long-run possibilities are those discussed in this chapter and arising from the whole postwar experience.

There is, for example, the basic problem of what countries in balance of payments difficulties ought to do. Insofar as there are "normal" rules, they can hardly be applied to the United States so long as the dollar is not only a national currency but an international one. But what other rules should apply? Would it be preferable to circumscribe the dollar's role and create more truly international money in the management of which other voices will count for as much as those in Washington and New York? The issues are more than technical; they affect both the character of the international economic system and the freedom of action of the United States not only to manage its economic affairs but to pursue a foreign policy that calls for aiding developing countries and financing an American military establishment abroad. As Henry Aubrey put it, "the so-called defense of the dollar is not . . . a separate policy objective to be tackled by specific measures when crises loom. It is part and parcel of the entire complex of the American international position."[2]

A sharp division between the United States and other major countries on monetary issues could lead to a division in the Western world between countries willing to tie themselves to the dollar in some sense and those abjuring the "dollar area" for another system (possibly one making more use of gold). A sundering of the international payments system, which for all its difficulties and weaknesses has retained its essential unity, would create new risks and dangers. The terms of reference for the formulation of national policies would be changed in far more than monetary matters. While a dual system might be made to work well, its existence would call into question much that has been said in past pages about the probable course of

2. *Behind the Veil of International Money*, No. 71 of *Essays in International Finance*, January 1969, Princeton University, pp. 15-16.

future events and the kind of American foreign economic policy that seems to make sense.

These vital monetary matters have been much written about in recent years; little would be gained by summarizing the whole monetary debate. We can return to the essential issues after examining two areas where the interrelation of monetary issues and the other aspects of foreign economic policy discussed in the rest of this book are particularly marked: the international adjustment process and the constraints that balance of payments problems put on American policy.

THE ADJUSTMENT PROCESS

The separation of subjects that should be treated together is a common characteristic of foreign economic policy. National bureaucracies are in this respect like books, different parts deal with trade, investment, and monetary matters in spite of their close connections. Policy in each field acquires a certain rhythm or momentum so that what is done, or attempted, at any given moment is determined more by what has been done so far and what is aspired to next than by a fresh assessment of the whole range of policy options at each moment. Every government has its GATT people and its Fund people; and while those international organizations, and others, work together on some occasions, it is more common to find each looking after its own affairs. The tendency to separate trade and financial policy was strengthened for the United States by the fact that for much of the postwar period financial policy was mostly a matter of dealing with the rest of the world's problems while the tariff was in part, as a famous phrase has it, a local issue, involving compromises with American private interests as well as foreign governments. The long-standing distinction became blurred when, over the protests of American businessmen, Washington began controlling the flow of capital as a way of dealing with balance of payments deficits in the mid-'60s. The separation of trade and financial policy will be less tolerable in the future than in the past thanks to the combination of openness and interpenetration of economies that has made it necessary to link trade and investment in the formation of policy. Nowhere is that more evident than in the heightened concern about the adjustment process.

Back in the days when half the world was in balance of payments trouble, it was taken for granted that countries with foreign exchange difficulties would restrict imports and discriminate between hard and soft currencies; eventually they might also have to devalue their currencies. As their payments positions improved, the European countries imported more freely but restraints on the export of capital remained common. Even after most currencies became convertible and other kinds of measures were relied on to deal with most problems, trade restriction as a last resort remained an accepted part of the process of adjusting to temporary balance of payments difficulties for most countries—but not for the United States. It had come by a different road. Its trade adjustment had been that of the good creditor, reducing tariffs and providing equal treatment to other countries even when their reciprocity was more formal than real.

When the Kennedy Administration decided that the deficit in the American balance of payments would not go away by itself, it specifically rejected any restriction of imports as unwise and unnecessary. To have done otherwise would have made it all but impossible to launch and then carry through the Kennedy Round. Some steps were taken, however, that affected trade, such as the tying of foreign aid to the purchase of American goods, tightening Buy American rules, and concentrating procurement for troops abroad on American sources. The Johnson Administration held to this line, but in 1967 and after there was serious discussion of the possibility of levying some kind of charge on imports (and perhaps providing a matching encouragement to exports). The idea was dropped, but it remained not far below the surface and played a part in discussions of a value-added tax.[3]

In 1969 President Nixon rejected the argument that because of "the disappearance of the [trade] surplus . . . we should abandon our traditional approach toward freer trade."[4] Nevertheless, his efforts to improve the balance of payments in August 1971 included an import surcharge.

The issues will rise again whenever the United States has to examine the range of measures it might take to deal with balance of payments deficits. Businessmen resent capital export controls. There are strong resistances to the idea of curtailing foreign travel. Cuts in military expenditure are limited by political and strategic considerations. Trade

3. See chapter 5, pp. 128–31. Some of the reasoning summarized there played a part in the decision not to introduce a border tax for balance of payments purposes, though there were those who were attracted to the idea as a way of offsetting the European action. There was doubt, however, whether a border tax would do much to change the American trade balance. There was also a risk that if modest rates were proposed, Congress would greatly raise them for protectionist purposes (though some argued that the chances of blunting the protectionist drive would be improved by placing a limited general tax on imports).
4. U.S. House of Representatives Committee on Ways and Means, *Proposed "Trade Act of 1969": Message of the President, Draft Bill*, 91st Cong., 1st sess. (Washington: GPO, 1969), p. 1.

is, after all, the biggest item in the balance of payments; should it be left untouched if, in fact, the United States has a troublesome balance of payments deficit? If it is not necessary or wise to control the import of goods, is it sound to restrict the export of capital, a policy which three administrations followed?

Before these questions can be answered, a broader one must be posed: In terms of the organization of the free world economy as a whole, what kinds of rules or practices about international adjustment are desirable? Then we ask how these arrangements apply to the United States and, finally, whether the United States is likely to be in serious balance of payments difficulties in the '70s—or, indeed, was in the '60s.

Adjustment Without Restriction

If there is sufficient liquidity in the international monetary system and a deficit country can take the right domestic measures quickly enough to rectify its balance of payments problem, there is no international issue. But if the deficit persists, then sooner or later the country's access to credit is made conditional on its pursuit of policies that others judge likely to restore balance. The policies may be those prescribed by creditor governments or an international organization or those previously agreed on as part of the rules of adjustment. There may be a clear-cut disagreement between the government of the deficit country and the foreign prescribers; more often the external pressure will mainly strengthen the hand of those inside the deficit country who hold certain views about what should be done. Even if there is no disagreement about the main objectives of policy, there can be serious differences of view about the proper mix of fiscal and monetary policy, tolerable levels of unemployment, the effectiveness of incomes policies, price guidelines, "jawbone control," and the like. More fundamental conflicts arise if a choice seems needed between contradictory courses, for example, contracting demand to reduce imports and encourage exports or increasing demand so as to reduce unemployment and avoid the waste of leaving productive capacity idle. Sometimes what is at stake is not only equilibrium in the balance of payments but also a country's long-run economic health and perhaps political stability as well.

While the discipline of balance of payments pressure may help a government take necessary but politically unpopular steps, it may also impose choices too difficult to be made on grounds of financial rectitude alone. Those who press a country hard to improve its balance of payments have a responsibility to help it avoid serious damage in the effort—and partly in their own interests. A good adjustment system is one that satisfactorily combines outside pressure and help with a certain freedom of national action.

When economies are as closely linked as those of the industrial countries, a high degree of coordination of national policies must be a continuing objective. But the desideratum is extremely difficult to achieve. Often it takes a crisis to move very far along these lines, and then much of the "coordination" consists of some governments doing two things: tolerating distasteful actions by those that are in difficulties, and making an effort to refrain from offsetting the results. Preventive coordination to avoid difficulties is rare, even in a group as small as the European Community. But the price of failing to find some way of harmonizing policies is high. A great reduction of economic relations with the rest of the world is not acceptable, but at the same time close links make it hard for a country to carry out a satisfactory adjustment unilaterally. Only if the others assent to what it is doing—and sometimes not even then—will they refrain from trying to protect themselves from the results of what it has done. The rocky road through these dilemmas is the one the industrial world has to follow, not least because readjustment is a never-ending process in which the main burden moves from one country to another.

A classic method of adjustment is to alter a currency's exchange rate. Often disturbing, as all big changes in an interconnected system are likely to be, it is also a remedy for disturbances resulting from the effort to sustain a rate much higher or lower than what the market will bear. Its beauty lies in the fact that the change of one thing brings about changes in many. By bringing a national economy into a better relation with the international economy, it grants a degree of freedom to reconcile domestic and foreign aims and, if successful, reduces the pressure on foreign authorities or national policy decisions.

The architects of Bretton Woods provided ways of altering exchange rates. But with the chaos of competitive devaluation in the '30s on their minds, and the vision of a well-ordered world economy before them, they limited the conditions in which changes were permitted and set out procedures intended to assure an orderly process. Though there were a number of important devaluations in the '40s and '50s, opinion was growing by the late '60s that the system was in a certain amount of difficulty because rates had become too fixed. Quite apart from the special problem of the dollar, one of the difficulties was that the decision whether to devalue (or even to appreciate) a major currency had become heavily weighted with political implications and ideas of prestige.[5] The liberalization of trade and payments, the growth of investment, and the interpenetration of economies increased the mass of credits or debits that might pile up against a given country. By the same process, the combined stake that traders, bankers, and investors had in anticipating changes in the value of a currency grew. The world became fuller than ever before of sophisticated money managers whose efforts to move ahead of events created pressures that helped bring some of the events about. To discourage or punish speculators governments proclaimed their intention of not changing the value of their money; sometimes they were successful, but in the process made "firm pronouncements on the fixity of their exchange rates" which, as Pierre-Paul Schweitzer pointed out, "inevitably made it more difficult for policy to respond to changed economic conditions."[6] Consequently, instead of exchange rates being adjusted, other things were adjusted to the exchange rates.

The natural reaction to this development was increased interest in the possibility of making exchange rates more flexible, or at least easier to change. Long a favorite among academic economists, the idea that the price of a currency should be allowed to respond to supply and demand in international markets more fully than by moving the 1 per cent above or below parity permitted by the Bretton Woods system began to be looked at seriously by governmental and banking circles during the late '60s. While a completely free market in currencies was fairly easily ruled out, proposals were made for a whole array of devices that would permit wider fluctuation around official exchange rates or a change in rates by relatively small steps. Proponents argued that innovations of this sort would avoid the accumulation of resistance that made change difficult under the old system. Temporary pressures could be more easily absorbed; gradual adjustment to persistent pressures would be less disruptive (and politically easier) than waiting until a big change was necessary. The strength of conflicting forces could be judged better by observing their performance in a freer but still limited market than by trying to guess how much pressure they were exerting on an ostensibly im-

5. The attitude is not new. In the streets of Pesaro in August 1926 Mussolini said: "I will defend the lira to the last breath, to the last drop of blood. I will never inflict on this marvelous Italian people, who for four years have worked like heroes and suffered like saints, the moral shame and the economic catastrophe of a collapse of the lira. . . . Our lira, the symbol of the Nation, the mark of our wealth, the fruit of our exertions, of our strength, of our sacrifices, of our tears, of our blood, must be defended and will be defended." B. Mussolini, *Scritti e Discorsi* (Milan: Hoepli, 1934), Vol. V, pp. 386-87.

6. Cited, p. 178.

movable object. Governments would gain time for other measures to take effect and would add one more tool to their kit for the management of adjustment.

The case against greater flexibility has several main elements. One is the fear of instability and confusion arising from uncertainty about the value of a currency. "Practical men" in business and government who once held this view nearly unanimously are now divided in their opinions, perhaps because fixed rates have turned out also to have large elements of uncertainty. A second argument is that limited flexibility cannot do the trick because pressures weak enough for it to absorb are not the real source of difficulty. Businessmen and bankers will continue to shy away from the weak currency and favor the strong and are adept at finding ways of pursuing their interests even if the rules are changed. In the opinion of some, limited flexibility would in fact provide a set of signals that would induce speculation. Some people oppose flexibility for fear that it would reduce the pressures on governments to take the stringent measures required to improve their basic situation and now forced on them by aversion to devaluation. This last view often reflects the businessman's suspicion that if devaluation is made easy, politicians will use it to escape the need to take a firm stand against inflationary forces, especially wage increases and government spending. On quite a different plane is Charles Kindleberger's trenchant argument that the industrial nations would be taking a step backward if they adopted a system of fluctuating rates which would "break up the world market for goods and factors, in contrast with the fixed-exchange-rate system which operates on the principle of one market, one price, and one money."[7]

There is a separate argument against fluctuating rates among the six countries of the European Community. Further progress in economic integration (and even the protection of what has been achieved) may well depend on more coordination of national policies, not less, and fixed rates will add to the pressures for moving in that direction. But unless the coordination is achieved, it is hard to keep the rates fixed. Community relations were upset in 1968 and 1969 when the French and German governments first resisted and then gave in to pressures to devalue the franc and raise the mark's exchange value. That experience stimulated efforts to move toward closer monetary cooperation. But in May 1971, not long after an agreement had been reached to narrow the margins within which Community currencies could fluctuate, disagreement on how to cope with

7. Charles P. Kindleberger, "The Euro-Dollar and the Internationalization of United States Monetary Policy," *Banca Nazionale del Lavoro Quarterly Review,* March 1969, p. 10.

a heavy inflow of dollars led to a floating of the mark and the guilder while the lira and the French franc remained fixed and the Belgian franc kept a foot in each camp by using two rates for different purposes. The failure of the Community countries to give a common response when Washington called for realignment of exchange rates a few months later threw further doubt on their ability to maintain fixed rates among themselves. A case can be made for the view that until better means of coordinating policy are established, some flexibility would help make necessary accommodations, especially as new members enter the Community. But alterations of exchange rates are also disturbing, especially as they upset the calculations on which the Common Agricultural Policy is based. Sooner or later the member countries will probably try again to move toward unifying their currencies. If they succeed, the flexibility issue will look different, since it will have become a matter of the relation of Europe's single currency to those of the rest of the world.

The idea of introducing some degree of flexibility into exchange rates has gained some notable converts. The widening of the margins in which currencies could move around the new parities established at the end of 1971 was a compromise but reflected a shift in sentiment. There are, however, many people who still resist the uncertainty and automaticity of formulas for flexibility. Some recommend instead an easier and more frequent resort to small exchange rate adjustments within the International Monetary Fund's existing framework of rules. Some combination of the two approaches may well appear in the international monetary system of the '70s. No revolutionary results should be expected, but the step would probably make a useful contribution to the adjustment process. Much of its significance might lie in a shift away from treating international monetary problems as matters of national prestige, hard to resolve without crises, and toward a more functional approach to money (which would not be less "political" in a fundamental sense).

Adjustment with Restriction

Faced with problems of balance of payments adjustment, governments frequently reach for the levers of control over the flow of goods and money across their borders. Though capital movements may be restricted first, trade, the largest element in international payments, is often the main target. Import restrictions offer quicker results than measures that affect trade only by contracting domestic demand. They invite less political resistance at home than deflation and in some circumstances may be less costly in terms of growth and employment. By combining domestic measures with import restrictions, governments increase the number of tools with which they can manage the difficult and complex process of achieving adjustment at acceptable costs and may be able to avoid carrying any single measure to extremes.

There is, of course, another side to the story. The apparent gains from cutting imports by quotas, exchange controls, or surcharges may be illusory—and are almost sure to be if there is no contraction of domestic demand. By encouraging domestic production of competitive items, import controls can divert goods from export and in time lead to a shift in resources from more to less efficient uses. This danger can be reduced by aid to exports, such as subsidies or tax exemptions that make it more profitable to sell abroad than at home. (But export subsidies raise their own problems in the form of foreign reactions; the Common Market countries put strict conditions on their acceptance of French export subsidies in the fall of 1968, and the United States imposed countervailing duties.) Even though the professed purpose is adjustment, import restriction can hardly avoid being tinged with protectionism. Germans, Belgians, and Italians were quick to point out that France's measures to "save the franc" in the fall of 1968 included restrictions on imports that French producers of steel, refrigerators, household equipment, and some other products had wanted for some time. The heaviest criticism of the American measures of 1971 was directed against the import surcharge precisely because it was regarded as a response to protectionist pressures. In that case, as in others, the fear was strong that import restrictions would prove more durable than the balance of payments crisis itself.

As in the case of export subsidies, one of the main safeguards against the abuse of import restriction is suspicious scrutiny by other countries that may retaliate. But retaliation could frustrate a reasonable adjustment program as well as one that concealed ulterior motives. Forbearance by other countries as well as a careful selection of measures by the one in difficulties is an essential ingredient of the adjustment process. With a good bit of success, this balance has been struck in most cases by *ad hoc* understandings, sometimes more or less tacit and sometimes quite specific and linked to credits. A natural question is whether the whole process might not better be regularized, perhaps by drawing up rules, perhaps by establishing a procedure for dealing with each case as it arises, more likely by a combination of the two. In a sense something like this already exists. GATT and the IMF often play a part in adjustment arrangements. Waivers of their rules are required in many cases; at least this is nominally so, but sometimes a temporary closing of the eyes to technical violations or a formal approval of what has already been done takes the place of more active involvement.[8] The OECD, too, has taken part both by studying the adjustment process and recommending ways of improving it and by providing the necessary escape clauses in its codes for the liberalization of current transactions and capital movements. The case for doing something more rests largely on the increasing complexity of relations among the industrialized countries and the frequency with which governments might usefully resort to adjustment measures of one sort or another. Preventing crises is, after all, better than having to deal with them and if more frequent use is to be made of exchange rate changes, it would be sensible to link them with an understanding about other measures of adjustment as well.

An international understanding about adjustment would have to take account of more than tariffs, quotas, and exchange rates. Other kinds of trade-restricting measures come into consideration, for instance, the tightening of government procurement practices, pressures on private firms to buy domestically whenever possible, and the tying of foreign aid. For the most part more modest in their impact than broader controls, these devices are often easier to apply without generating strong foreign opposition. They are also easy to abuse for protectionist purposes if only because they are selective. We have seen that international agreements on barriers of this sort are likely to be less clear-cut and harder to police than those on tariffs or quotas. To permit departures from the normal rules for balance of payments purposes will further complicate a difficult task, but the logic will be hard to resist. An adjustment code would also have to take account of a wide range of financial controls, such as those intended to influence the leads and lags in payments for imports and exports, curb spending on foreign travel, and temporarily limit other kinds of outflow. Border taxes, though their main function is different, can also sometimes be dealt with as part of the adjustment process and might, as was suggested earlier, be subjected to rules that would reduce the risk of their generating international friction.

The kind of adjustment measures just sketched focus on current transactions. International agreement about them is largely a matter

8. One of the anomalies of the adjustment arrangements is that GATT permits countries in balance of payments difficulties to use quotas but not milder measures, such as tariff increases or surcharges. There are understandable historical reasons for this distinction connected with the wish to avoid interfering with the reduction of tariffs, but in present circumstances it would seem sensible to change the rule and permit the use of import surcharges for adjustment, subject to comparable rules and international surveillance.

of accepting departures from a supposedly "normal" state of relations among the industrialized countries in which trade and payments move quite freely. Matters are somewhat different when capital movements are concerned. The Bretton Woods agreements left them under national control, and there is only a limited range of international agreement on how the controls should be used. Most European countries have limited the access of foreigners to their capital markets and the freedom of their nationals to send money abroad. The United States joined the parade in the mid-'6os. Though the American steps were taken specifically for balance of payments purposes, other governments have often been concerned primarily with the use of controls for the guidance of domestic investment. Money has a penchant for fluidity, however, and by the end of the '6os short-term capital movements had reached such a size that a key problem in balance of payments management for most industrial countries was to find ways of countering, manipulating, or compensating for their ebb and flow. Much of the large reversal in the U.S. balance of payments between 1969 and 1970 was the result of short-term capital movements.[9] The outflow to Europe continued in 1971, largely in response to differences in national interest rates and credit conditions, but then grew as people began to speculate in the spring on the rise in the value of the mark and afterwards on the fall of the dollar.

The largest single element making short-term capital movements so central to the adjustment problems of the '70s is the Eurodollar market (or, more exactly, Eurocurrency market, though dollars remain dominant). In part a response of international business and banking to national efforts to limit capital movements and hold down interest rates, this recent creation—invention is too deliberate and mechanical a word—grew to something over $50 billion in about a decade. Mobility and versatility have made it and the related Eurobond market useful for many purposes: for the placing of liquid funds for very short periods and the issuance of relatively long-term bonds to finance American investment abroad, for speculation, and as a source of funds for banks of one country or another, including the United States, when national credit was tight. It has been employed by banks, business, investors, speculators, central banks, the Bank for International Settlements, and the foreign trade banks of Communist countries. Efforts by governments and central banks to influence the operation of the Eurodollar market or offset its effects have had only limited success. The very qualities of size, mobility, sensitivity, and versatility

9. A sober statistical report by the OECD Secretariat speaks of "an almost tidal wave of short-term funds." OECD, *Economic Outlook*, December 1970, p. 22.

that have made the Eurodollar market so useful have made it hard to reach by national controls and created a major new difficulty in the way of improving the international adjustment mechanism.

Robert Roosa, whose acquaintance with these matters is intimate, has concluded that

> . . . a long and painstaking review and appraisal of the place of capital transfers and investment in the adjustment process . . . should begin now. . . . The starting point . . . must be a recognition that the world now has an extraterritorial market in dollars (and on a lesser scale in some other currencies). That market, along with the great enlargement of direct and portfolio investment on the part of most of the leading industrial countries, calls for a fresh look at the meaning of capital flows across the exchanges, as well as those across the frontiers, of countries whose currencies are in use internationally.[10]

More than any of the other issues discussed in this section, this one shows that the adjustment problems of the future go well beyond those conventionally associated with a country's balance of payments difficulties. The issues concern "normal" as well as abnormal circumstances and go to the heart of what is meant by the "coordination of national policies" that is so often prescribed—correctly but with deceptive ease—as the solution to so many problems.

Adjustment by Countries in Surplus

One of the main "lessons of last time" in the minds of those at Bretton Woods was that it had been inconsistent for the United States in the '20s and '30s to expect Europe to pay its war debts if the United States refused to lower its tariffs on imports from Europe. In the future, it would be recognized that the creditor had some responsibility to help to make the international economic system work (i.e., for adjustment). At the same time, part of the American resistance to Keynes's proposals for an international clearing union was based on the view that they put too much of the onus on the creditor, even to the point of eventually extinguishing debts that were not repaid. In the '60s, Americans once again found themselves in the pre-Bretton Woods frame of mind of emphasizing the creditor's obligations—but they had different "creditors" in mind: the European countries with strong balance of payments surpluses, Japan, and Canada. Not surprisingly, officials of some of those countries saw the situation differently and stressed the responsibilities of the

10. *The United States Balance of Payments and the Dollar,* remarks at the International Conference on Financial Outlook of the National Industrial Conference Board in Geneva, Switzerland, May 19, 1970, p. 13.

country with the deficit, especially when that country was the United States.

There are a number of ways in which a country with a strong balance of payments can contribute to the adjustment process. The most sweeping is to reduce its own surplus by raising the value of its currency. There is usually much resistance to such a course, and other methods will probably be tried first. Credit to those in deficit can make a big contribution, and in this respect the postwar record is quite good. A country persistently running large surpluses can also contribute to the adjustment of others by increasing imports and investing more abroad. Here matters become more complex. Direct investment is a process with its own determinants. Portfolio investment responds to interest rates and possibilities of growth that only sometimes draw funds to deficit countries. The best prescription for importing more is to stimulate domestic demand. But a country fearing inflation will be chary of that course. Import liberalization can have only a limited effect if it is regarded as temporary; if it is to be permanent, governments used to reciprocal tariff bargaining will be reluctant to go as far unilaterally as a strong payments position might warrant. For a member of the Common Market, there is the added difficulty that it cannot reduce import barriers unless the group acts as a whole, but the other members may not be in as strong a balance of payments position.

If there are only one or two deficit countries, trade measures are still harder to use. Unless new discriminations are to be introduced into world trade, surplus countries can treat imports from those in deficit more liberally only if they are willing to liberalize trade in the same products among themselves, a decision that is not likely to be made simply for the sake of easing another country's adjustment problem. Government purchasing measures and *ad hoc* transactions may help, but usually only on a limited scale.

One of the major contributions that countries with balance of payments surpluses can make to the adjustment process is to refrain from retaliation for the damage done to their trade or financial interests by the adjustment measures taken by deficit countries. This seems a minimal contribution, but it is an essential one since even with the provisions of financial aid to countries in deficit in return for understandings about the policies deficit countries will follow, it is unlikely that the need for direct restrictions on trade and payments can always be avoided.

Next Steps

The key to a constructive handling of balance of payments difficulties is the acceptance by the industrial countries of the idea that the adjustment process is a cooperative one. This is already implicit in the practices that have grown up. With it goes the idea of international surveillance which has to rest on some kind of agreement about what measures are suitable and how they should be used. While no generalization will cover all these cases, certain presumptions can be made. For instance, it might be accepted that if import controls are to be used, they should for the most part be general in order to reduce the risk of their abuse for protectionist purposes and of their distorting domestic production. Much the same might be said of subsidies or other forms of assistance to exports. While any country in deficit needs a certain amount of autonomy in deciding how to meet its problems, compromises that depart from this pattern ought to be worked out, so far as possible, by international agreement. Since the controls are to be firmly labeled "temporary," a key element of international surveillance may well be a schedule for their removal which may be cast in terms of dates, or the achievement of certain conditions. There can be agreement, too, on such things as the maximum rates of import surcharge or export subsidy.

Something like this now happens in many cases. The pound, the franc, the lira, and many other currencies (including once upon a time the mark and, in a somewhat different fashion, the dollar) have been the beneficiaries of an international mobilization of credit intended to make adjustment easier, less costly, and less disturbing than if it had to be carried out on a purely national basis. Pressure and surveillance, in varying proportions, have accompanied the help. Whether the industrial countries should try to reach more formal agreement on rules for adjustment is a matter for argument, the lines of which have been sketched above. If there are agreements, they should not be so tight that they prevent flexibility in handling quite different kinds of cases; rules on some points, guidelines on others, and an agreed statement of objectives might be the right formula.

Because so many different kinds of measures are involved, moves toward more formal understandings might prove easiest if they dealt with parts of the problem separately, building on existing agreements.[11] It is essential, however, that the parts be treated more or less consistently and that as wide a range of measures as necessary be applied to every case. Moreover, an approach that deals only with crises when they arise will fall short of the best that the industrialized

11. For example, one possibility would be to revive interest in the OECD's Codes of Liberalization which cover a surprising range of matters; the approach there might be to define more precisely the terms on which the rather sweeping escape clauses are to be applied.

countries are capable of. There will continue to be emergencies but one of the objectives of an up-to-date adjustment policy will be to limit their number. One of the most useful contributions that even a moderate increase in the flexibility of exchange rates can make is to improve the warning system to facilitate preventive action, and, in a sense, help spread the process of adjusting over a longer period. To deal with short-term capital movements and the Eurodollar market will require day-to-day actions by governments even when difficulties are not pressing or apparent.

In an interdependent world, with the processes of change accelerated in many fields and with large and volatile supplies of short-term capital, adjustment has to be seen as a continuing part of the fitting of economies together, not just an emergency effort reserved for extreme cases. Whether they go at the matter formally or not, how the industrial countries deal with adjustment is a matter of major importance to the whole future character of their relations. Why this is so is underlined by Richard Cooper in the conclusion of one of the most seminal studies of those relations. Interdependent countries, he points out, have three alternatives. One is the coordination of their policies, but they are not prepared to carry that process very far. They will not finance deficits indefinitely, the course that would assure the maximum national autonomy. To impose controls over trade and payments is the third course, but if the practice is too extensive it destroys the advantages of international exchange and specialization. To keep the benefits of interdependence and the freedom to pursue national objectives required by the existence of separate nations, governments must combine elements of the three courses. The price of a failure to do so is high.

> Failure to accept consciously some combination of these alternatives and to work toward its efficient operation would seem at first an apparent acceptance of increasing economic integration. But it would have all the weaknesses of high, uncoordinated interdependence, including competition in national policy analogous to, but more subtle than, the competitive depreciations of the 1930s. Ultimately it would probably result in an indiscriminate rejection of international economic integration, involving uncoordinated and unsystematic use of restrictions on international transactions. This would be politically corrosive as well as economically costly.[12]

12. *The Economics of Interdependence: Economic Policy in the Atlantic Community* (New York: McGraw Hill, for the Council on Foreign Relations, 1968), p. 263.

THE AMERICAN BALANCE OF PAYMENTS

Because the adjustment process is so central to the international economy, the United States would have a strong interest in improving that process even if its own international accounts were a model of stability and showed no signs of ever causing any trouble. Instead, the American balancing act has not gone very smoothly and has sent repeated shudders through the audience. But this does not lead to the conclusion that conformity to an adjustment process improved along the lines sketched in the last few pages would establish the right relation between the American economy and the rest of the world. That is so in large part because the dollar is different; an adjustment system that was far better suited than the one we have to the needs of most of the economies of the industrialized world would not by itself perform the same function for the American economy —and, therefore, not for the international economy as a whole.

At least, this seemed to be the case up to August 1971. The drastic steps taken then set in motion a process which may change the position of the dollar in the world (in ways explored in the epilogue). But even if the international monetary system changes more rapidly than might be expected, there will be little if any alteration in some other factors that make adjustment different for the United States from what it is for the other industrialized countries. As always, there is the intractable matter of size: whether the American accounts are in surplus, deficit, or balance makes more difference to the rest of the world than if any other country is in or out of equilibrium; if the United States has to take measures to adjust, the impact on the rest of the world may be great; if others have to finance an American "deficit," the sums required are large. At the same time, foreign transactions make up a relatively small part of American economic activity. Foreign trade is smaller compared to domestic production for the United States than for any other industrial country of the free world. Consequently, Henry Aubrey estimated, "in normal times . . . to reduce American imports by a sizable amount, say $1 billion, GNP may have to be reduced by perhaps as much as $20 to $30 billion, a drop much more severe than in any postwar recession."[13]

Another respect in which there is unlikely to be rapid change is that several major elements in the outflow of payments from the United States would not respond to ordinary economic measures of adjustment—whether at home or abroad—because they are determined

13. Cited, p. 6.

principally by political and military judgments, notably those concerning military aid and the maintenance of American troops abroad. It is in the monetary measures applicable to the dollar that the middle and late '70s may be unlike the preceding decade. In the '60s, the dollar could not be devalued by national action except by raising the price of gold, which would have undone one of the major monetary reforms of the period. A kind of devaluation could be achieved if other countries appreciated their currencies in relation to the dollar either specifically or as a result of introducing more flexibility into the international system. To float the dollar itself, the United States would have had to sever the link with gold as it did unilaterally on August 15, 1971, with resulting disturbances considerably greater than if it had acted in agreement with others. Even if the monetary system is changed in other respects, so long as the dollar is the main reserve currency and the vehicle of the largest share of international transactions, the criteria for judging whether an American balance of payments deficit is desirable or troublesome will continue to be different from those which apply to other currencies. The fact that too few people understood this point contributed to the difficulties of the past.

Past Troubles

During the '60s the world economy and American foreign economic policy were plagued by a general concern about the persistent, though fluctuating deficit in the United States's balance of payments (according to the method of accounting long used by Washington). The deficit was not new, but in the '50s it helped solve problems instead of creating them. At that time it contributed much to the re-entry of Europe and Japan into the world economy; it was the main vehicle for the creation of liquidity in the expanding world monetary system; it had a central role in the redistribution of reserves which improved the balance of that system. The larger deficit of the '60s continued to be the main source of liquidity, but as their reserves grew a number of European governments turned dollars into gold on a scale that raised questions in some minds as to what would happen when the United States could no longer meet such claims. Even those who regarded the gold problem as secondary sometimes began to wonder about the future place of the dollar in the international monetary system. The failure of Washington's efforts to eliminate the deficit, or at least keep it at a low level, for more than a year or two at a time, added to the concern.

This concern was based on a traditional view. Deficits were bad; they could not be endured indefinitely and would have to be corrected or the strength of the dollar would remain in doubt. To others the United States had preached fiscal prudence, balance, and the dangers of living beyond one's means; its homilies were now to be applied to itself. It seemed reasonable, at first, to suppose the problem was a temporary one and could be dealt with by moderate measures and patience. Through a process that has been touched on piecemeal in earlier pages, other countries were asked to help and the United States took a series of measures, first mild and then stricter, to curb the deficits. There was progress. In some years the deficit was cut to what seemed quite tolerable levels, but in others it grew again. By almost any method of accounting (and there were several), 1970 was one of the worst years on record. If the standards of 1960 were still valid, one would have to forecast a period of considerable disturbance in international economic affairs and an indefinite continuation and intensification of American restrictions on trade and payments.

To be sure, the difficulties of the '60s had some good effects. It was probably healthy for Americans to discover that they were not immune to the disease that had so troubled other major countries; some experience of the difficulties of making adjustments could contribute to better understanding and cooperation. Empathy is more enlightening than sympathy. The balance of payments helped make Americans aware of the nature of their involvement in the world economy. International monetary cooperation broke new ground not only technically but in its demonstration of the degree of interdependence that existed among the industrialized countries. The fact that other countries could significantly help the United States and do it in their own interest proved that "cooperation" was no longer a one-sided affair. As the first measures of cooperation proved inadequate, the persistence of the balance of payments deficit helped persuade Washington that international monetary reform, long deprecated as unnecessary and disturbing, should be seriously undertaken. A larger European (especially German) contribution to defense costs and what will probably be lasting improvements in European capital markets were by-products of the effort to deal with the American balance of payments problem. Perhaps the most significant result of all has been an educational one to which I shall return later. Americans and foreigners alike see more clearly than before the implications of the fact that "the dollar is different."

In its direct impact on American foreign economic policy, however, worry about the balance of payments has been bad. The tying of foreign aid, the widening of Buy American margins, and the imposition of controls over the export of capital are all backward steps.

New problems were created in dealing with foreign governments by subjecting American companies abroad to balance of payments guidelines. Though the trade barrier reductions of the Kennedy Round were shielded from bad effects, balance of payments deficits made the subsequent wave of protectionism somewhat harder to resist and caused some hesitation in Washington about pressing for such measures as an international agreement limiting "buy national" practices. The prospects of new trade initiatives were put in jeopardy.

One reason the United States was able to push so far along the Bretton Woods road in the '40s and '50s was that it had no need to worry about its balance of payments. If, however, the United States lives in a constant state of worry about balance of payments deficits, then restrictions, perhaps temporary and perhaps permanent, will become part of the regular arsenal of American policy. At best, any new measure, any proposed initiative, would have to be judged not only by whether it contributed to the removal of barriers, the liberalization of international trade and payments, and the better use of world resources, but also whether it was likely to improve, or at least not hurt, the United States balance of payments. This is often an extremely difficult calculation to make and not one in which there can be much confidence in any but the shortest term. The natural result would be great caution and little initiative. In terms used earlier in this book, the emphasis of American thinking would shift toward a narrower conception of national interests and away from the broad concern with the shape of the international economy as a whole that has been so important an element in American postwar policy.[14] A poignant question would arise: The problem of dollar shortage was overcome in ways that greatly liberalized international economic life; has that success created a dollar plenty that will mark an era of restriction?

That the balance of payments should become so negative a factor in American policy in the '70s seems almost inevitable if deficits persist and the fear of their consequences that was shown in the '60s is sound. There is, however, another point of view or, rather, several which open some other possibilities. Before the crisis of 1971, a number of different arguments had been mobilized to show that the dollar

14. Preoccupation with the balance of payments is bound to affect other aspects of foreign policy. While the results of looking at foreign aid, military deployment (bases as well as troops), political commitments, and the assumption of responsibility in cooperative endeavors in terms of the balance of payments may not always be bad, there is a confusion of standards involved. Balance of payments arithmetic does not measure real costs in the sense that should be relevant for a rich country. And while restraint in overseas activities may often be a virtue, it should be undertaken for the right reasons, not factitious ones.

was not weak, or at least that its position was not very alarming. For example, Professor Kindleberger said that when the United States exports long-term capital while Europe holds liquid dollar assets, the result "is not a deficit in any meaningful sense but international financial intermediation, a useful economic function which supplies liquidity to the world when and as needed."[15] In a slightly different vein, Professor Mundell, viewing the United States as "the world supplier of reserves," likened the balance of payments situation to that of the Federal Reserve System, which "is in perpetual deficit because it pays out more dollars than it takes in."[16] Employing a quite different approach, Professor Vernon added up American claims on foreigners, gold reserves, and U.S. direct investment abroad to reach a total that at the end of 1967 exceeded foreigners' claims on the United States by much more than at the end of 1958 in spite of the gold losses and foreign dollar accumulations in between. He concluded that "there need not have been the self-diagnosis of weakness and the occasional manifestations of panic that have been seen over the past decade."[17] These concepts, and others that could be added to the list, are not academic toys, patriotic window dressing, or efforts to define away the problem; they are part of the clarification of issues that has resulted from the effort to shape a sensible American policy toward the balance of payments. In the course of a decade quite a few American businessmen whose first reactions to the enlargement of deficits was rather conventional and negative began stoutly to contend that the dollar was strong by any relevant test. The record deficits of mid-1971 shook the views of some; the actions of August of that year were clearly based on a different reading of the situation. Nevertheless, the approach is not irrelevant to judgment about what American balance of payments deficits may mean in the future.

So long as the dollar is the main reserve and vehicular currency in the world, deficits in the American balance of payments are rational and needed (though they may not be necessary in every year). No dollar deficit, no international liquidity. The growth of SDRs or other kinds of monetary reforms could change this rule, but the process may be slow. Even a deficit larger than the amount the world needs for current working purposes may be no cause for alarm if it reflects the per-

15. Cited, p. 5.
16. Robert A. Mundell, "Real Gold, Dollars, and Paper Gold," *The American Economic Review: Papers and Proceedings of the Eighty-first Annual Meeting of the American Economic Association,* May 1969, p. 329. He goes on to say, "Words are harmless; it is the action taken on misinterpretation of the meaning of concepts that do [sic] the damage."
17. Raymond Vernon, *U.S. Controls on Foreign Direct Investment—A Reevaluation* (New York: Financial Executive Research Foundation, 1969), p. 17.

formance by Americans of some useful function, such as intermediation between those who wish liquid assets and those making long-term
investments. Very large movements of short-term funds, while they
may be awkward, reflect temporary conditions, not underlying factors.
But the elements in the deficit caused by bad management of the
American economy, such as inflation, should be eliminated.

The question really is what should be measured to determine how
strong or weak the dollar is. The gist of much of the case for what may
be called the optimistic view is that the manifold interconnections of
the economies of the industrial countries, and the key place of the
dollar in them, make traditional accounting misleading if not altogether irrelevant. For example, a flow of nearly $7 billion of "foreign"
funds into the U.S. money market in 1969 was made up principally
of transfers of Eurodollars to American banks from their branches
abroad. The point is akin to one made at the beginning of chapter 6
about the inadequacy of old concepts of national interest when an
important part of the national economy can be said to be abroad.
In a book like this, it seems wise not to be drawn into a close analysis of the differences between the different ways of keeping balance
of payments accounts—liquidity, official settlements, basic, "adjusted over-all," etc. The suspicion grows that it is more than a joke
to say that the reason the British were not aware of balance of payments problems in the nineteenth century when sterling had a position
similar to the one the dollar has now is that they lacked the statistics that would show them they should be worried. Perhaps the American prescription for peace of mind will be to produce so many figures
that none will seem as alarming as the single figure which stood alone
at the bottom of government tables in the early '60s. A judgment about
what ought to be done about the balance of payments should be the result of a realistic assessment of alternatives, not a response to a cate-
gorical imperative that deficits are to be eliminated regardless of
consequences. This may be thought obvious, and yet it registers a
different spirit from that in which these issues have sometimes been
approached.

The Policy Issues

Long-run forecasts of the balance of payments can be suggestive as
to trends—for example, the increasing importance of foreign investment income to the United States. They can hardly be expected, however, to give more than a gambler's estimate of how the accounts are
likely to balance in any given year or block of years. After all, the
balance of payments is a thing of margins, a place where a fringe of

the American economy converges with the marginal transactions of dozens of other economies. The balance of the balance—the "deficit" or "surplus" by one system of reckoning or another—is a tiny sum resulting from the interplay of an almost infinite number of lines of force, political, psychological, and military as well as economic. Some are temporary and some are lasting.

Short-term forecasts of the balance of payments, though subject to wide margins of error, can be useful in judging whether the time is propitious for one sort of action or another, but do not help much in providing assumptions for shaping foreign economic policies that can be pursued over a decade. Large and rapid capital movements, the speed with which trade flows can change, and the probable pressures for accelerated adjustment in the American economy all make the '70s a period of uncertainty.

Many problems would disappear if the balance of payments improved sufficiently, and stayed that way. Good luck is a great aid to policy, but statesmanship must allow for the luck's being bad. The sizable adjustments in exchange rates that followed the floating of the dollar in 1971 improved the chances of reducing or eliminating the American deficit. But one cannot really tell whether the U.S. balance of payments in the '70s is going to be better, worse, or not very different from that of the '60s. If the same arithmetic produced the same reactions and led to the same policies as in the early and middle '60s, then the prospects would be poor for the United States's taking any major initiatives for further liberalization of world trade and payments (or even for its going along with the initiatives of others). The problem would be how to conduct a mercantilist policy in the least harmful way.

Given uncertainty, one might conclude that the only reasonable approach to balance of payments policy is to "play it by ear," hoping for the best, moving as far as circumstances permit, but being prepared for the worst. Something like that is inevitable in the conduct of any policy, but it gives little to build on and may inhibit the pursuit of liberalizing policies that take a long time to carry out. If one of the aims of American policy is, as I believe it should be, to open the economies of the industrialized countries further to one another, then a major element in that policy should be an approach to balance of payments problems that avoids new restrictions as much as possible. Such an approach would have three parts: a different assessment of the balance of payments problem from that of the '60s, further pursuit of international monetary reform, and domestic policies that eliminate some of the pressures on the balance of payments by measures that do not imperil other objectives.

The key to the reassessment lies in the views of the balance of payments labeled above as "optimistic." While they may not contain the whole truth, the arguments sketched there are clearly very weighty. In addition to their analytical validity, they have pragmatic support that has been underestimated. The "realism" of the opposite approach which stresses the weakness of the dollar and the need for disciplining the American economy was less impressive at the end of the '60s than it had seemed a decade ago. The predictions of disaster if the deficit were not eliminated had not been fulfilled. The very difficulty of eliminating it suggests that its causes were not fully understood. Whether the 1970–71 deficits undermine this argument is a matter on which I find it impossible to form a judgment at the time this book goes to press. But even in the face of such uncertainty, the perspective that gains strength is one that views as ludicrous the idea that the position of the United States in the world economy depends on whether one puts a plus or a minus sign in front of a sum of, say, $3 billion, less than one-half of 1 per cent of the gross national product. It is true that the combination of national monies and an international economy produces monstrosities, but there is much to be said for the common sense view that this only proves there is something wrong with the system. To argue otherwise is like saying that pyramids are not well built if they cannot stand on their apexes.

It would be meretricious to argue that analysis should be determined by policy. Facts are facts, not matters of taste, and one's preference for liberal policies is no justification for taking what I have called an optimistic view of the balance of payments. But that is not the purport of what I am saying. In blunt summary, the argument runs this way:

If deficits in the United States's balance of payments are regarded as dangerous and their elimination is a matter of first priority, then the animus of American policy will be toward restriction and contraction as long as the deficits persist. An extended period of American restrictions on trade and payments would deprive the United States and other countries of the solid advantages of freer economic intercourse and might well lead to a good deal of disintegration in the relations of the industrialized countries.

An alternative course would give much weight to the analytical and historical evidence for believing that the conventional narrow view of balance of payments deficits, their dangers, and their causes is not correct when applied to the United States. This does not mean that nothing needs to be done about the American balance of payments. It does, however, lead to the conclusion that it is not desirable to subordinate all other objectives to correcting the balance of payments position because

(a) some of the supposed corrections would in fact be harmful, and (b) when corrections are desirable, the measures needed to make them can be designed to exact the minimum price in the sacrifice of other goals.

We are not dealing with absolutes. The range of informed, cogent opinion, scholarly and practical, is wide enough to make a dogmatic or unqualified conclusion suspect. The analysis that leads to the more restrictive course exacts a price that the other avoids. Pursuit of the more optimistic line of approach does not prevent reversion to the more restrictive if that proves warranted; the opposite switch is more difficult. Consequently, there is no intellectual dishonesty in the argument that wise policy for the United States is to act as if the more optimistic diagnosis were correct until proved wrong.

Whether a successful policy can be built on this approach depends in part on the reactions of people in the rest of the world. They cannot be expected to make reassessments in quite the same way as Americans do, especially if they suspect a form of intellectual window dressing. It is naturally hard for them to apply different standards to the American position from those they would apply to their own, or to that of England or France, for example. But the case is not hopeless. The arguments have objective cogency, not just an appeal to Americans. When central bankers refrained from changing dollars for gold in spite of what their inner voices may have counseled, they recognized the common stake of all in an international monetary system which gave a special place to the dollar. Europeans know that drastic adjustments by the United States could hurt them. Germans, and others, do not want to see the dollar "strengthened" by a general withdrawal of American troops from Europe (a course that might well weaken the dollar in the long run). Sound bankers of any nationality know that the real value of the dollar rests on the strength of the American economy, not the exact balancing of accounts, and that great deflation would be too high a price to pay for balance.

In spite of these facts, the dollar deficits of 1970 and 1971 were accompanied by a crescendo of European voices calling on the United States to "do something" about its economy, to "put its house in order," in the classic phrase. Perhaps the advice was sound. Maybe the loss of faith in the dollar was an epiphenomenon of the failure of American domestic economic policy to deal with unemployment and price inflation. The argument for an optimistic view of the balance of payments does not deny the need for sound domestic economic management. In any case, the European pressure played a part in bringing a major shift in American policy in August 1971. To the extent that the domestic program succeeds, and the realignment of exchange rates as well, there will probably be an improvement in the balance of payments. But as there can be no guarantee against deficits, a proper perspective on the American balance of payments remains important to the shaping of the rest of American foreign economic policy as well.

There is much contagion in these matters. To carry conviction in the long run, argument and verbal exposition will have to be supported by the demonstration that by putting balance of payments issues in a new perspective it is possible to manage the domestic economy effectively and to pursue a constructive foreign economic policy as well.

More Reform?

Inheriting a bad situation, the Nixon Administration had its troubles with the domestic economy, but mostly struck the right note so far as the balance of payments was concerned. In part that was a matter of not striking quite so many notes as in the past. There were far fewer remarks by officials about the bad state of the balance of payments and no suggestion that eliminating the deficit was one of the principal aims of the President. Though no great trade initiatives were taken, this was clearly not for fear of the effect on the balance of payments. Several steps were taken toward the untying of foreign aid which had been imposed originally on balance of payments grounds. The approach seemed to be working well, as even the serious deterioration of the 1970 accounts did not become a focus of official concern in public, and the picture of American monetary officials in international meetings was not that of harassed men.

But as Eurodollars and other short-term funds flowed to Europe in large amounts during the spring of 1971, Washington's aplomb was met by growing irritation and discontent on the other side of the Atlantic. The reaction was hardly surprising. The situation was full of frustration. The Americans appeared to be acting as if record deficits in the balance of payments were nothing to them, while leaving it to other, smaller countries to cope with the resulting disturbances. Part of the reason the dollars were flowing to Europe was that the Americans had lowered interest rates to help cut unemployment. The result was that Europeans got dollar reserves they did not want, while the related expansion of domestic credit increased the already troubling inflationary pressures. The impact differed from country to country, so it was not surprising that governments chose different ways of dealing with the problem; nevertheless, the inability of the Six to agree was embarrassing since they had only recently registered their resolve to move toward a monetary union. French annoyance at the German handling of a difficult situation underlined the close psychological connection between money and power.

Precisely those connections, often exaggerated and sometimes imaginary, made the place of the dollar in the international monetary system galling to many people in other countries. The domestic political compulsions of the United States produced results in the international monetary system to which other countries had to adapt themselves while the American government retained a higher degree of freedom from balance of payments pressures than any other country. Few influential Europeans can actually have thought it sensible for the United States to increase unemployment by deflation in the spring of 1971. Though there were those who thought that higher interest rates and expansionary fiscal measures would be more desirable, there was no broad consensus about an alternative American policy that would have dumped fewer problems on the rest of the world. Indeed, one could draw added frustration from the fact that some of the funds coming into Europe did not reflect a deterioration of the basic balance of payments of the United States. As a German banker pointed out, they were "not new dollars but dollar assets that European commercial banks acquired in the past years from American balance of payments deficits and held onto because they earned high interest in the Eurodollar market."[18]

While a different tone or style of American monetary diplomacy in early 1971 might have made some difference (a certain number of officials appeared to think so as they quickly sounded notes of concern), the basic source of frustration was a recognition of the facts of the international monetary system of the early '70s. The industrial world was indeed on what could fairly be called "a dollar standard," which had been shaped partly by the monetary reforms of the '60s to which other countries had agreed because there was no alternative commanding wide enough acceptance that would preserve unity of the monetary system. The American authorities were dollar-makers to the world and the world had only a limited choice as to how it would treat the product. How uncomfortable the position was, was made manifest when later in 1971 the United States moved to the offensive in balance of payments matters—with the result that even more problems of adjustment were thrust on the rest of the world than before.

Whether past problems can be avoided in the future depends in part

18. Kurt Richebächer, "Unverstandene US-Politik," *Wirtschaftswoche* (formerly *Der Volkswirt*), May 1971, p. 44.

on the answers one gives to three basic questions: Can the system be changed so as to reduce other countries' dependence on the dollar? Can the Europeans, or any others, strengthen their influence either for change or in the operation of the existing system? What should be American balance of payments policy in the face of uncertain alternatives? These questions are discussed here in fairly general, but fundamental, terms. How the events of late 1971 and early 1972 may affect these issues is examined in the epilogue to the book.

Alternative Paths of Reform

It would be natural for the Europeans and others to try to find a way of subjecting the United States to the same kind of balance of payments pressure they have to submit to (with due allowance for the smaller share of foreign transactions in the American economy). One way of doing this would be to restore the discipline of gold. Any such step should be firmly resisted by the United States (and would be opposed by many Europeans). To make such a system workable, the price of gold would have to be doubled or tripled at least. That step would ease the problem for a time but would only give a new lease on life to the system that led to the present difficulty and that has more than its share of irrational elements. If the world split between gold-area and dollar-area countries, quite a bit of repair work would become necessary to find a new way of conducting affairs.

Though the hankering after gold dies hard, European authorities would probably refrain from trying to make it the future arbiter of the international monetary system if the United States refused to agree. Quite a different way of reducing the disadvantages of having the dollar as both a national and an international currency would be to expand greatly the use of SDRs. Another possibility would be to create a reserve unit that combined SDRs, gold, and some dollars. Just as the Community already has a veto power over the issuance of SDRs (if it acts as a unit), so Europeans and Japanese could expect to have a stronger voice in the management of the man-made international currency than they have in decisions about the dollar.

The United States should wholeheartedly welcome steps in this direction. Although there are some significant advantages to the United States from having the dollar used as a reserve currency, it would not be sensible to try to retain this position against serious opposition, provided that agreement can be reached on a system that both functions adequately and gives all countries a reasonable share in its management. To explore the range of possibilities that would meet these two alternatives goes beyond the scope of this book. The issues are not simple. Honest disputes will mingle with the efforts of one country or another to get special privileges. The division of opinion about what is desirable will not always be between the United States and the rest of the world. How difficult it can be to clarify the choices is suggested by the fact that within days of the floating of the mark in May 1971 one monetary authority suggested that the moment had come to displace the dollar with SDRs, while another, of equal eminence, said that by putting an end to the creation of SDRs Europe could force a decision on the place of the dollar in the world.

Even if radical changes are made in the international monetary system, questions will remain about the future place of the dollar. If a new reserve unit provided monetary reserves, would the dollar still be the most convenient medium for transactions? How much freedom of action would the United States lose as it became subject to balance of payments pressures similar to those of other countries but kept the weight in the world that goes with its size and power? Would the dollar lose the advantages (and disadvantages) of what Susan Strange calls a "top currency"? Might it be joined in the position by a new European currency? Can an international unit, created according to formula, perform a function which historically "derives . . . from the issuing state's position of economic leadership which inspires monetary confidence even among political opponents"?[19] Such questions will remain speculative until (or unless) both the place of the dollar and the influence of Europe in international monetary relations change substantially.

A Stronger Voice for Europe

The monetary dilemma in which the governments of Europe found themselves in the '60s was that in spite of their great gains in economic power they must either accept the greenbacks produced by the American printing press or, by refusing to do so, jeopardize the whole international economy. They can avoid the same dilemma in the '70s only if the international monetary system is changed. Even if they are not fully agreed on what change should be made, the Europeans have reason to try to increase their influence. Their chances of succeeding will be improved if they can speak either with one voice or at least in sufficient harmony so as not to cancel out one another's influence. To that end two courses are open to them; both may be taken.

19. Susan Strange, *Sterling and British Policy: A Political Study of an International Currency in Decline* (New York: Oxford University Press, for the Royal Institute of International Affairs, 1971), p. 5.

The first is simply a matter of agreeing on a common stand or plan of action on whatever issues arise, such as the creation of SDRs. The basis for agreement would be the common interest in escaping the burdens of dollar-domination. How far that common interest stretches is not always easy to say. So long as each government has to think in terms of a national balance of payments, there may be significant divergences of views and interests, as the episodes involving the Deutschemark and the French franc in 1968, 1969, and 1971 emphasize. This difficulty would be overcome by the second course, the creation of a monetary union for the European Community. To have a common front against the United States is not, of course, the sole reason for embarking on this course (though it is not the least of its attractions). The difficulty is that to move very far in the direction of a monetary union requires acceptance by each of some share of the others' burdens of inflation and deflation, a high degree of coordination of national economic policies, and the exposure of each economy to potential disturbance from that of a partner. Although the Europeans have several times professed their will to proceed in this direction and each time gone a little further than before, they have each time also failed to generate enough momentum to make one certain that sooner or later they will complete the process. They well may, but progress will be slow. Nevertheless, a sense of forward motion may stimulate the will to agree sooner on common positions on major issues in the management of the international monetary system.

Progress toward a Western European monetary union would foreshadow a change in the monetary structure of the world. A European currency—the term is shorthand for a number of possible arrangements—rooted in a continent-sized economy that was also a major participant in the whole range of international economic transactions would have the potential of becoming an international currency in much the same sense as the dollar is and the pound sterling has been. Repeatedly, European spokesmen have said that they did not want their national or Community currencies to become reserve currencies, but that status is not always a matter of choice. If London with its remarkable equipment for international banking is part of a European monetary union, the prospects of the European currency's becoming a vehicle for international transactions would be good. Such a currency would offer an alternative to the dollar for some purposes and could be said, in a sense, to "rival" it.

Such a development should not by itself be distressing to the United States. But such financial power could be put to distressing uses. If a European bloc were dedicated to the proposition that gold should be restored to a larger place in the international monetary system' it would present a greater challenge than if the same view were held by a series of national monetary authorities. An aggressive beggar-my-neighbor policy that sought to shake world confidence in the dollar would have a better chance of success if its instrument were a single European currency rather than separate national currencies. But nightmares do not make good policy. For the same general reasons that the United States should welcome the drawing together of Europe (see chap. 9, pp. 304–11), it should be happy to see that area's monetary integration. But the achievement of such a goal should be left to the Europeans and not actively promoted by the United States. The American aim should be to minimize the risks that such power will be misused or that European monetary unification would produce a sharp cleavage. Before those problems become acute, quite a few others will probably have to be faced.

A Long Interim

Whether a European monetary union is eventually created, and even if the 1971 crisis hastens reform, there is almost certain to be a long period when the dollar will continue to have a central role in the monetary system. This is a fact the United States will have to take into account in shaping a balance of payments policy. Enough has been said about what is acceptable and unacceptable concerning the place of gold and of internationally managed international money in the system as well as the improvement of the international adjustment mechanism, perhaps partly by introducing some greater freedom in altering exchange rates. There is no doubt, too, that new efforts will have to be made to reduce the unsettling impact of massive short-term capital movements. But that is easier said than done.

Size, mobility, and versatility have made the Eurodollar market a magnet for money. Thanks to the same characteristics, the Eurodollar market has, in the words of one of those who know most about it, "not only made the pursuit of monetary-policy objectives more difficult but also exacerbated the familiar conflicts between domestic and international policy considerations."[20] Separately and together, national central banks have intervened in the market to improve its operation; through the recycling of funds they have tried to offset some of its movements. Some governments have agreed not to enlarge the market by putting dollar reserves in it. In a somewhat opaque situation where results are hard to judge, it appears that in some countries measures limiting the borrowing of Eurodollars by

20. Fred H. Klopstock, *The Euro-Dollar Market: Some Unresolved Issues*, No. 65 of *Essays in International Finance*, March 1968, Princeton University, p. 20.

banks and businesses are fairly effective, but not all governments have been willing to impose restrictions of this kind and some could probably not enforce them. To establish one kind of limitation on access to the Eurodollar market is to provide an incentive to find another way of achieving the same purpose; while a good bit of international cooperation would seem necessary to establish a reasonable degree of public control over this creation of private ingenuity, a series of national restrictions may be tried first simply because national controls are easier to impose. How successful they may be is another matter. Washington should take a cooperative attitude toward efforts to control the Eurodollar market without assuming any disproportionate responsibility simply because dollars are involved.

The calmness of the late '6os about balance of payments deficits was a great improvement over the worried (and largely futile) rhetoric of an earlier period. Whether the excitement of late 1971 will lead to progress or retrogression is not clear. Unless the terms of the problem are changed by major monetary reform, a basic condition for doing better in the future is that all concerned remain conscious of what has been learned about why American balance of payments deficits are different from those of other countries. The limits of unilateral adjustment by the United States should be kept in full view. There is nothing wrong with American officials' reminding the world that there is a connection between American security expenditures and the strain on the dollar. They must, however, abide by three rules: not to exaggerate; not to threaten (at least beyond the point at which the United States might actually jeopardize its own security by cutting expenditures); and not to assume that others will always approve of what the United States does in these matters. The general American posture on monetary affairs should be to stress the fact that they are an international responsibility. Because so many of them concern the dollar does not mean that the United States can deal with them by itself; but its inability to do so does not justify an appearance of leaving the problem to others. This sounds obvious, and basically it is, but a certain confusion about these simple propositions has been troublesome in the past and could become dangerously so in the future.

So long as the dollar remains "different"—in the sense explained earlier—there is a good case for something approaching a "passive" balance of payments strategy for the United States. That is to say, full employment, growth, stability, and other desiderata would not be subordinated to measures intended to eliminate balance of payments deficits, if only because a healthy American economy contributes more to world welfare than a weak or distorted one. But it does not follow that Americans should take the view that all the adjustments must fall on countries with balance of payments surpluses, any more than it makes sense for people in that fortunate position to use old-fashioned language about the debtor's obligation to make the whole adjustment (a principle that would have greatly hampered the world economy in the '40s and '50s). Precisely because other, smaller countries are stuck with a system in which they are greatly affected by what the United States does while the United States cannot be subjected to the same kind of balance of payments discipline that is applied to them, the United States should be sensitive to their right to a hearing. One of the original expositors of the "passive" strategy stressed the importance of recognizing its implication for others and of welcoming "the advice of other countries both in public and in private."[21] (It is at least partly because of a failure to dramatize this point that the policies of the early Nixon years became so vulnerable.)

In short, to put the balance of payments in a reasonable relation to the U.S. economy as a whole is not the same as ignoring its international implications and the consequent concern of others. On the contrary, this perspective underlines a point about the nature of relations among the industrialized countries that has already emerged in other parts of this book, that "domestic" affairs are more than ever before matters of international concern and will increasingly have to be treated that way. Of course, there already is a good deal of consultation in these matters. The OECD issues annual reports criticizing each member's economic situation in terms that are usually rather discreet. Far franker exchanges (one hopes) take place in OECD committee meetings, the Group of Ten, and the monthly sessions of the central bankers at Basle. The Joint Economic Committee of Congress has for some years invited foreign witnesses to talk about American policy. Perhaps the United States should take the lead in making a more dramatic gesture, just because the dollar is everyone's problem. Charles Kindleberger once suggested having a European representative in the Federal Reserve System's Open Market Committee; a panel of foreign economists attached to the Council of Economic Advisers would add to the interest of the Washington scene.

The question is not so much one of getting more advice as of knowing when to follow it. It took no aliens to point out that the United States ought to have taxed itself more heavily during the height of the Vietnam War. It was clear then that less inflation would have helped both the balance of payments and the domestic economy as

21. Lawrence B. Krause, A *Passive Balance-of-Payments Strategy for the United States* in *Brookings Papers on Economic Activity*, 3 (Washington: Brookings Institution, 1970), p. 350.

a whole. When there is a conflict between external and internal equilibrium, it is far from clear that the basic division of opinion about what to do would follow national lines. From the point of view of other countries, a monetary system that put real pressure on the United States would be worth far more than any arrangements for advice and consultation (unless, of course, the result of that pressure were to spread trouble throughout the world economy). In the absence of a good regulating system, the value of giving foreigners a voice would be to make plain that, although it is right not to subordinate sound domestic policies to balance of payments considerations, the United States should not completely ignore the balance of payments in the management of its domestic economy. There is enough uncertainty in the latter activity, enough balancing off of sometimes conflicting factors, to make it unreasonable to exclude balance of payments considerations entirely even though they are given a lower priority than would be possible in many other countries.

IMPORT RESTRICTIONS, EXPORT PROMOTION, AND INVESTMENT CONTROLS

Equal emphasis should not, in all probability, be given to such different ways of dealing with balance of payment problems as trade restrictions, controls on the export of capital, and measures to foster exports. But certainly the case for not restricting imports for balance of payments reasons is strong. Though small in relation to the domestic economy, American foreign trade is very large in the world economy. To cut American imports heavily would considerably damage some countries; to use selective controls to favor nations in weak balance of payments positions would generate many difficulties. The suspicion would be strong that the balance of payments was being used to cloak concessions to protectionist sentiment. From the Kennedy to the Nixon Administrations, the argument has been made that to restrict imports on balance of payments grounds would impair the chance of getting other countries to reduce their trade barriers. The point remains valid; if the United States cannot quite be Caesar's wife, it must at least shun trade restrictions until a compelling case can be made to show that something must be done and that other measures will have a worse effect on international trade and payments. Precisely this argument was used to justify the import surcharge imposed in August 1971. The skepticism with which this argument was greeted emphasizes the underlying problem.

The other side of the trade account, exports, presents a somewhat different picture. Like the encouragement of foreign travel and investment in the United States, the expansion of exports offers a constructive response to balance of payments concerns. Although the fostering of exports has long been an objective of government policy, it was unimportant through the '50s. The results of the increased attention given the task in the '60s are hard to judge. Direct promotional efforts such as trade fairs, trade missions, information, awards, etc., are not to be sneezed at, but, except for alterations in exchange rates, the most important measures probably concern export credit.

Rooted in rivalry, national export credit policies are always the subject of much argument. Every businessman thinks his foreign competitor benefits from government help that is denied him. Americans point to the export credit guarantees provided by most European governments and are told in return, "We have no Export-Import Bank." How far the programs that have been worked out in cooperation with private banks in the last decade have improved the position of American exporters and what they would gain from still more ambitious measures that have been proposed (such as a general Federal Reserve discounting of export paper) are matters that require a more detailed inquiry than is possible in this book. But the subject is closely related to issues already raised in chapter 5. The rates and terms of export credit and guarantees are near neighbors to the questions of taxation, subsidies, and the conditions of fair competition. A proposal of the Nixon Administration to permit the deferral of corporate income tax on exports, which may have been conceived as an American equivalent of border tax adjustments, raises questions of legality, retaliation, and the difficulty of justifying its ultimate net effect on the competitive position of this and other countries. As the example suggests, export promotion can lead to trade-distorting practices, foreign retaliation, or a race to subsidize competitive activity by measures that go far beyond export credit guarantees. (When the president of General Electric complained that his competitor in the bid for the Lockheed engine contract was the British government and not Rolls Royce, he was talking of a production loan and not an export credit guarantee, but the results were much the same.)

Clearly, export credits cannot be thought of only as balance of payments measures. What they and their like can achieve depends on what other countries do, as well as on American action. To take account of these facts, American policy on export promotion should be broadly conceived with the possibility in mind of negotiating at some future time about the standards, rules, and perhaps even specific features of national programs. One way of getting the process started would be to challenge foreign practices that appear to put American goods at unfair disadvantage in third markets (in much the same way as agricultural subsidies may have to be challenged). Finally, if export promotion becomes a major element of American policy, it should be undertaken with the clear understanding that the greatest obstacles to export expansion are foreign trade barriers and whatever lack of competitiveness there may be in the American economy. While there cannot be any certainty that the removal of trade barriers will lead to a greater expansion of exports than imports, trade liberalization contributes to the flexibility and ultimate competitiveness of the American economy and, consequently, to the long-run strength of the dollar.

A potentially more important stimulus to exports might come from governmental measures intended to encourage research and innovation that would help American industry to keep its traditional technological lead over other countries. Some people thought of these measures as filling a gap created by the decline of defense spending in the late '60s and early '70s. A more sophisticated line of reasoning stressed the need for purposive efforts moving toward an industrial policy of the sort discussed in chap. 5 (pp. 163–66) instead of relying on spill-over, tradition, and whatever built-in forces had looked after American interests in these matters in the past. Though thought by some people as a matter of domestic policy rather than export promotion, this kind of activity—which will be more and more important to the industrial countries—falls directly into the range of issues affecting the conditions of competition that cannot long be kept out of international negotiations.

While eschewing import restrictions on goods, the United States moved quite early to put a brake on exports of capital which were thought to be a clearly identifiable constituent of the balance of payments deficit in the early '60s. Whether control over one item in the balance of payments can long endure without stimulating an offsetting reaction in other items is a major problem in judging the interest equalization tax, the limitations on bank lending, and the restraints on direct investment imposed in the mid-'60s. Some associate the cut in capital exports with the decline of the export surplus in trade. Those who stress the growing importance of investment income to the United States argue that for the sake of relatively minor short-run gains the authorities risk killing a goose that will in the long run lay many golden eggs. Supporters of the controls say that the immediate gains are valuable and that a few years of control will not in the long run weaken the American investment position abroad. American direct investment has kept growing, with a much higher proportion of its financing coming from outside the United States. Presumably payment for that capital will over time reduce the funds that would be available for remittance to the United States, but so long as the financing takes the form of debt this may be temporary. American income from foreign investment has increased greatly during the period of the controls, partly as the result of the regulations but to a considerable extent because of the past growth of investment.

For present purposes, it is unnecessary to disentangle all the elements that go into the short-run effect of the controls. But when three Presidents call the controls temporary measures that will be removed "as soon as possible," one has to consider that they may prove lasting. To try to judge their probable long-run effects is awkward since no one has ever made a case for them as continuing instruments of policy. Are they to be judged in principle or in terms of specific rules, amounts, and effects? Are they to be considered a way to regulate direct investment or only to hold down the balance of payments deficit? Their effects might be altered greatly if attention were paid to labor's wishes to check the export of jobs or if the application of the American measures was determined in part by negotiations with other governments. On the one hand, these controls do not fit well with the open economic relations the industrial nations have developed over such a wide range of their activities. On the other hand, as national controls that do not so much restrict investment as alter its financing, the American restrictions are typical of the devices that are necessary to work out balance of payments adjustments under the existing inadequate system. But if it makes sense for the United States to follow a more or less "passive" balance of payments strategy based on the "optimistic" reading of the American position sketched above, what justification would there be for capital controls, especially if it is argued that trade controls are neither necessary nor wise?

The answer quite a few people give to this last question is that if something has to be controlled, better capital movements than trade because less damage results. However, after reviewing the arguments, Fritz Machlup expressed "grave doubts about any cost-benefit analysis which came to the conclusion that capital controls are less harmful than trade controls, because the allocation of capital among the countries of the world has an enormous bearing on the growth of the world economy and on the efficiency in the use of capital in the world at large." He went on to say, though, that "the most persuasive argument" that trade restrictions did more harm than restrictions on capital "is that capital movements are sometimes diverted in odd ways by existing government measures . . . so that new restrictions . . . need not always lead away from the optimum allocation of resources.[22] Here we have, I think, one clue to the way the capital export controls may be thought about in the future, i.e., as part of a complex of national controls, any one part of which cannot be judged in isolation.

A second clue, of a quite different order, points in the same direction. In Richard Cooper's judgment, the American choice of capital controls instead of trade controls "has been dominated, not by judgments of economic efficiency, but by considerations of political acceptability and the fear of retaliation."[23] In other words, the United States was simply imposing controls of the sort others already used; the Bretton Woods rules permitted such action; no odor of protectionism arose from it, and there would not be the foreign resentment that import restrictions would have evoked. Though some foreigners disliked the withdrawal of dollars, others probably harbored the illusion that the controls would slow the growth of American investment in their countries. Furthermore, the controls set well with the foreign view that the United States should "do something" about its balance of payments deficit. In the light of this history, proposals that the United States should remove the investment and lending controls must take into account probable foreign reactions. Until there is a fairly general acceptance of the kind of balance of payments approach sketched earlier in this chapter, it is understandable that Washington should move slowly (if at all).

The tenor of these last two paragraphs is not new to this book. American controls on the export of capital, it seems clear, have to be thought of not only in terms of their actual immediate effects but in relation to several other factors, not least the policies of other governments toward investment and its financing. Even a purely economic judgment about the effects of removing the controls depends on assumptions about what other countries do. Increasingly, as we have seen in other chapters, such matters are coming into international discussion. And even in their origins the capital export controls were parts of the adjustment process, which can no longer be thought of without giving attention to international cooperation concerning capital movements. So it is not altogether surprising to find Robert Roosa, no friend of controls, concluding that "Until norms are generally agreed upon, the likelihood is that controls of some form,

22. From the proceedings of the Claremont International Monetary Conference, Randall Hinshaw, ed., *The Economics of International Adjustment* (Baltimore: Johns Hopkins Press, 1971), pp. 151, 152. Machlup thought it possible, however, that the amount of trade restriction needed to obtain a given balance of payments effect would do more injury to economic welfare than the comparable restrictions on capital.

23. Same, p. 117.

blunt, imprecise and costly, will have to be maintained by the United States over most flows of capital across its frontiers most of the time."[24]

Seen in this perspective, the problem of what the United States should do about controls over capital exports looks different from the way it does when the controls are denounced because they are contrary to long-run American aims, dismissed as ineffective, or assessed in terms of a close study of their supposed immediate effect on the balance of payments. Each of these familiar approaches has a place in shaping policy. Some judgment of the effect of removing the controls is essential, though too much weight should not be put on the certainty of its conclusions. A demonstration that great damage flows from the controls would make it far more urgent to do something about them than most observers have thought was the case for some time—but the demonstration has not appeared. The question about ineffectiveness can probably be translated into one about the financial consequences of the controls. The conflict between the controls and the broad objectives of American policy is apparent. What is called into question by putting the issue in a wider setting is not the direction in which policy should move, but the terms on which it can reasonably proceed.

BACK TO ADJUSTMENT

The examination of the American balance of payments is easily recognized as a discussion of a particular manifestation of the adjustment process. Though the United States is a very special case, the questions that have to be asked are variants of those applied to other countries: How serious is a given deficit? How is it to be financed? Are restrictions necessary? What form of help are other countries to give? Where is the balance to be struck between leaving a nation free to choose its own way and forcing it to conform to the views of others? The fact that the answers are not the same for the United States as for other countries does not mean that the United States can go its way, handling its economy and foreign policy as it wishes with no regard for the rest of the world. The freedom from constraint conferred by the past place of the dollar was not freedom to isolate the United States from the international economy. The pain inflicted by the jolting efforts at adjustment made in the late summer of 1971 accentuates the point. For the United States there is no extrication, even if the dollar's position in the world monetary system is altered.

Whether such changes take place or not, there are beneath all the

24. Cited, p. 14.

intricacies two major truths: In today's interpenetrated international economy no nation, not even the United States, can cope satisfactorily with the problems of adjustment if it stands alone. The process must be a cooperative one if it is to work satisfactorily, whether the cooperation is expressed in agreed rules, boundaries around the freedom of national action, mutual assistance, or looser accommodations of uncertain durability.

The second basic fact is that the term "adjustment process" is only a kind of shorthand for the whole process of fitting national economies into an international economy, much as "the dollar shortage" was shorthand for the whole set of problems concerned with the external aspects of Europe's recovery and the American relation to it. A national balance of payments is only a nexus—or a *trait d'union* as the French graphically call a hyphen—which exists not in and of itself but only in relation to the difficult task of combining internal and external balance that every country faces. The balance of payments is the route by which each country affects all the others. The holistic metaphor of the bowl of balls, no one of which can be moved without the others moving, is nowhere more apposite than in relation to the adjustment process. Adjustment involves not just deficits but inflation, not just trade but free-flowing capital, not just surpluses but growth. To talk of the increasing need for some kind of coordination of national economic policies in an interdependent world in spite of the great difficulties any significant degree of coordination presents is to talk about the adjustment process.

It is no wonder then that there are few rules and no formulas and only a limited number of general principles to guide adjustment. It is a process that, properly understood, tears through what Irving Fisher liked to call "the veil of money" to the "real" economy, national and international, behind it. It may not be true, as a seventeenth century pamphleteer put it, that "those that have most gold have least grace," but there can be no doubt that "he that hath no credit shall have less commodity."[25]

25. *The Pennyless Parliament of Thread-bare Poets* . . . London, 1608, in *The Harleian Miscellany* (London, Robert Dutton, 1810), Vol. III, p. 72. I have altered the punctuation.

8

Agriculture: Stagnation or Change?

Not all the postwar policies pursued by the United States were consistent with the Bretton Woods principles, as quotations from two American agricultural economists make plain.

> Since 1934 the United States has been evolving a foreign trade and economic policy based on the merits of expanding world trade through friendly and cooperative action by nations. . . . During the same period of time, numerous farm programs were developed that required restrictions upon trade and other forms of protection for American agriculture as a means of implementing the programs. . . . Consequently, one branch of policy was interfering quite directly with the presumed needs of another.[1]

> There is likely to be serious conflict between a farm policy that is preoccupied with prices as supreme goals and a trade policy aiming at expanded world trade, for when prices *as such* are the goals, market intervention is inevitable.[2]

Gale Johnson's book, which had its origin in work he did for the State Department, and Addison Hickman's, which grew out of the concern and study of private people in New York and Des Moines, reinforced one another. Their policy prescriptions were much alike.

1. D. Gale Johnson, *Trade and Agriculture: A Study of Inconsistent Policies* (New York: John Wiley, 1950), p. v.
2. C. Addison Hickman, *Our Farm Program and Foreign Trade: A Conflict of National Policies* (New York: Council on Foreign Relations, 1949), p. 102.

The two books could have been written five years earlier or later and said much the same thing. A good bit of it is still true today, though some progress has been made in reconciling American farm policy and trade policy.

The conflict between them was not a postwar development. It stemmed directly from the contrast between the principles of the Trade Agreements Act adopted in 1934 and the agricultural policies adopted about the same time to cope with the depression and the "farm problem" that had plagued the United States even in prosperity. The trade policy sought to lower tariffs and remove quotas, while the farm policy aimed at raising farm prices in ways that virtually required the imposition of new restrictions on imports. The problem was not uniquely American. Over much of the world, governments were in one way or another trying to assure their farmers of prices higher than they could command in an unrestricted world market. Thus encouraged, domestic production expanded and governments had to find ways of disposing of surpluses or restricting output. To protect the high prices, high tariffs were needed, and, as these often seemed inadequate, agricultural trade was studded with restrictions on the quantities of goods that could be imported and sometimes flat prohibitions on trade. To enable their farmers to export or dispose of surpluses that accumulated as a result of encouraging domestic production, governments paid export subsidies or found other devices for bridging the gap they had purposely created between domestic and world prices. The net effect was to raise taxes and the cost of living for people who did not live on farms and to transfer income from industry and the services to agriculture.

Agricultural protectionism had other sources as well. An old rhetoric reflects deeply rooted notions about the sturdy virtues of farm folk, the desirability of social balance in a nation, and the need for some degree of national self-sufficiency in food. As in industry, mining, and everything else, protectionism in agriculture is also the result of the producer's wish to exclude competition multiplied by his political power. And farmers, though a minority in the industrialized countries, and sometimes a very small one, have long managed to make their power count. These factors combine differently from country to country, but the general effect has been to make agricultural trade barriers peculiarly obdurate and adamantine.

Growth and prosperity after World War II brought no great changes in the depression-spawned practices of subsidy, price supports, and quotas and did not divert the old currents of agricultural protectionism. In many countries balance of payments difficulties increased the pressure for fostering domestic agricultural production and holding down imports. Though the United States was under no such compulsion and had a strong interest in export markets since it was one of the world's major suppliers of farm products, it was in the vanguard of protection as it added import restrictions to shield domestic support programs. Britain, the world's largest farm importer, had, since the repeal of the Corn Laws, acted as if cheap food served the national interest. Without altogether abandoning that view, Britain increased its self-sufficiency to save foreign exchange. Much of the support its farmers received was in the form of direct payments so the consumer could still benefit from world prices. But by the '60s the strain those methods put on the budget led the British government, too, to move toward arrangements under which citizens paid farm subsidies as consumers rather than as taxpayers, and to more restrictions on imports.

GATT rules about tariffs, quotas, and nondiscrimination apply to farm products as well as to manufactured goods and raw materials. Only two exceptions are made for agriculture: (1) A country with a domestic program that restricts production has the right to limit imports to protect these measures or to help remove a temporary surplus. (2) Under an international commodity agreement that meets certain standards, a country may be permitted to impose import controls.

The first of these exceptions, which turned out to be by far the more important, seemed made to order for the United States. Yet it did not suffice, and in 1951 the United States was given a waiver permitting it to control imports of dairy products even though domestic output was not limited. The European countries did not need special arrangements since they had the right to limit imports for balance of payments reasons, so that "only the end of exchange control at the end of the fifties brought out the real nature of agricultural protectionism."[3] Not surprisingly, especially when one considers the American example, restrictions on farm imports survived the return to convertibility. While the barriers to trade in manufactured goods were coming down, slight, if any, progress was made in liberalizing trade in farm products. Efforts to attack the problem through commodity agreements came to little. A series of consultations about national farm policies in GATT and the OEEC helped illuminate the problem and may have led to some improvement here or there but did not alter the general picture.

The difficulty, not to say impossibility, of making any appreciable progress became so notorious that the mere mention of the subject

3. Gerard Curzon, *Multilateral Commercial Diplomacy* (New York: Praeger, 1966), p. 205.

in discussions among economists or bureaucrats was apt to produce laughter, sardonic or relaxed according to mood. State Department officials were heard to say that their hardest negotiations were those with the Department of Agriculture. Other reactions were despair, frustration, or a sense of futility, leading those concerned with trade liberalization to leave agricultural trade out of account, except for the necessary political gestures. Agriculture was, everyone agreed, "a special case"—so special that while everyone thought he knew what to do about it, hardly anyone believed anything could be done. Pretty soon it hardly seemed worth thinking about as an international problem.

Then, rather unexpectedly, the situation began to change. Of Europe's great part, more will be said later. It would be a mistake, though, to overlook the signs of change in the United States that manifested themselves by the early '6os. Farmers as well as town dwellers began to be uneasy about farm policy. Several factors helped shape the mood: a sense that some farmers were living well at some-one else's expense; the discovery that little farmers got much less benefit from public funds than great commercial farm producers; a belief that agriculture was dependent on government help to a degree incompatible with American traditions of enterprise and with many farmers' own feelings of what was proper; a growing awareness that much of American agriculture was highly productive, capital-intensive, and generally strong, not a weak spot in the economy that would collapse without help. Furthermore, it was disturbing to find that re-peated changes in farm legislation and its administration did not produce the results expected; land was taken out of production, but output increased as the remaining acres produced more than before. Technological progress during and after the war has made American agriculture immensely more productive than ever, but the result of efficiency was surpluses which accumulated at record rates in the '5os.

Absurdities developed. The government had long seen to it that cotton farmers were paid high prices, with the result that the govern-ment had to pay subsidies to exporters of the same cotton to permit them to compete with foreign producers. At the same time, foreign production of cotton was expanding, at least partly because the American program helped keep up world prices. Because of the dif-ferences between domestic and world prices, American textile pro-ducers had to pay more for their raw material than foreign manu-facturers did, and an already difficult competitive situation was made worse. Tightening of controls over textile imports would risk reducing the demand for cotton in Japan, the biggest customer. So still another subsidy was introduced, to lower the price of cotton to domestic textile producers. Such contradictions were not new. Under the Marshall Plan Denmark had been encouraged to export cheese and even given help in packaging and sales promotion for the American market where it then encountered new import quotas. But the cotton story with one payment or control leading to another was a particularly fine example of proliferation plus contradictory results. It was, eventually, set right by instituting direct payments to cotton growers instead of holding up the price. Something along the same lines had been done for wool in the '50s, but it was rare to find an agricultural anomaly dealt with so constructively.

The Rube Goldberg devices to which farm policy was driven helped bring it into disrepute. A shift in political balance also played a part—though it is hard to be sure just how great. The farm population was shrinking. The traditional over-representation of rural areas in voting arrangements was becoming more apparent and so more vulnerable. Probably the biggest single factor that helped change the atmosphere was cost. In 1965, a farm economist who played an important part in Washington during the Kennedy Administration said:

> For 10 years the urban voter has been beating a Fabian retreat with regard to farm program costs. But I for one believe that the retreat is about over. Thus, I believe that farmers will be forced, in the next 3 to 10 years, to accept some major changes in the present policy of price and income protection.
>   This is the really big lesson that I learned in the past four years.[4]

All these factors created a more fluid situation in American agriculture than had existed for years. Farm groups were willing to suggest changes in policy—perhaps for fear of having more drastic ones thrust on them. Ideas that were well known but politically taboo were more actively explored, but real changes in practice came slowly and mostly piecemeal. In all this, the conflict with foreign trade policy was usually a very secondary matter. The aim was to get a better, cheaper, and politically sounder farm policy. Then came a prod from Europe that hit trade policy.

Europe's New Means to Old Ends

How Europe prodded America and helped open the possibility of a new approach to international trade in farm products is a strange story. It was, of course, the new Europe, and we have come to understand how great a force for change that new Europe can be. But in

4. Willard W. Cochrane, "Some Observations of an Ex Economic Advisor: Or What I Learned in Washington," *Journal of Farm Economics*, May 1965, p. 461.

the matter of agriculture, it was at least as much the old Europe as well—the Europe of agrarian protectionism, governmental concern for peasants, and the insulation of the domestic market. The blend of old and new took the form of applying to a new, wider unit, the Common Market, the old principles of agrarian protection buttressed by some novel and ingenious devices.

It was surprising that the partially new Europe could do even this. Far more likely, one would have thought, would have been a different blend, much closer to the old. Lip service to Community aims might have gone along with maintaining the main elements of established national policies. New measures might have been designed so that they did not greatly unsettle things. Some steps might have been taken to favor intra-European trade at the expense of overseas supplies. Skepticism was strengthened by the postwar record. Great and largely successful efforts had been made to revive and improve European agriculture, but the progress was mostly within national markets. The removal of quotas on intra-European trade in farm products lagged behind the liberalization of other trade. Nothing serious came of proposals to do more: long-term contracts to stabilize production and intra-European trade; a Dutch plan for merging national markets; a French plan for a "green pool" in which markets would be "organized" to provide "security"; governmental support of arrangements among producers' organizations. Why should the Common Market be different?

The Treaty of Rome itself seemed to support doubt. Though it said that "The Common Market shall extend to agriculture and trade in agricultural products," it exempted these products from the precise schedule set up for the removal of tariffs on manufactured goods and raw materials. The signatories were to establish a "common agricultural policy" before the end of the transitional period, which would be 1970 at the earliest. One did not have to be a cynic to suppose that the effective unification of national farm markets and policies would be one of the last things the European Community would accomplish, not one of the first. A few people expected more and the common agricultural policy had its champions, some moved by interest, some by the wish to improve and rationalize European agriculture, and some whose main aim was to strengthen the ties that held the new Community together. The most important supporter, as it turned out, was France.

History is distorted whenever we are told that the basic equation in the creation of the Common Market was between the advantages Germany was to get for its industry and France for its agriculture. Nevertheless, it was true that French farmers would gain most from opening up the markets of the other five, and especially Germany, on a privileged basis and also from any redistribution of income from consumers or taxpayers of the Community as a whole to the Community's farmers. Once this was widely enough understood, Paris became the great ally of the Commission in Brussels in pushing for a real common agricultural policy, at least for those products of special interest to French farmers, notably wheat. Thus the acceleration of accomplishments over expectations that marked the Community's tariff reductions in its early years came to apply to agriculture as well. Instead of being the laggard many people expected when the Treaty of Rome was signed, France, with its currency devalued, its domestic finances in unprecedented order, a strong government, and an industrial output beginning to reap the benefits of ten years of planning and heavy investment, became a force for moving ahead with the Common Market, not a drag.

Ironically, it was by using a provision designed for its anticipated weakness that France, by threatening to delay the passage of the Community into its second phase, forced agreement on the basic formula for a Common Agricultural Policy (CAP) at the beginning of 1962. That was the watershed, but the remaining action on agriculture did not flow smoothly from it. Long, hard bargaining preceded a crucial decision about price levels for grain and then another about the division of financial burdens and benefits. The Community's performance in the Kennedy Round and negotiations between France and Germany about the CAP were intimately linked and shaped one another. A dispute over agriculture (and who was to make crucial decisions about it) was one of the factors that triggered the Community's greatest crises in 1965 and 1966. By the end of the '60s, the common policy applied not only to wheat and coarse grains but also to dairy products, eggs, poultry, beef, veal, pork, sugar, wine, fruit, vegetables, tobacco, rice, olive oil, and some oil seeds.

The structure that resulted has been called "one of the most esoteric, not to say tortuous, applications of marketing management that even the twentieth century has seen."[5] Facts, figures, calculations, advice, instructions, and, of course, funds flow through numerous interlocking circuits. Officials of the six governments and of the Commission, farmers, and the officers of farm organizations are all involved. More pages of the Community's *Journal Officiel* are devoted to agriculture than to any other subject; hundreds of decisions are issued in the name of the Commission or the Council of Ministers dealing with matters ranging from the charges to be imposed on

5. "A Guide through Mansholt's Maze," *The Economist*, March 13, 1965, p. 1164.

wheat imports to the kinds of warehouses in which surplus Parmesan cheese may be stored. Some decisions establish prices; others react to price changes. The word "price" itself has many meanings in the CAP, which is concerned with intervention prices, guide prices, target prices, support prices, threshold prices, farmgate prices, sluicegate prices, and a collection of foreign, or offer, or import prices calculated differently for different purposes. In spite of it all, crops and animals are raised, products are bought and sold, food is imported, exported, and consumed, or piled up in surplus storage or diverted to secondary uses and sometimes destroyed.

Fortunately, it is not necessary for the purpose of this book to examine the CAP in any detail. We are concerned with its salient characteristics, the general outline of how it works, and especially its relation to foreign trade. Its tendency is more important than any measurement of its performance as of a certain date. The step-by-step process by which the CAP has been put into effect and the transitional arrangements concerning trade within the Community can be left aside. As there are many differences in the way the CAP applies to one product or another, almost every statement in the next few pages is subject to some exception or qualification that is not explored. Grateful to be spared so much detail, the reader should also be alert to the dangers of oversimplification.

We are concerned with four central features of the CAP. (1) Farmers within the Community are to be assured that their products will sell at or near agreed-on prices, which are in all cases above world prices, often very far above.[6] (2) Barriers to trade within the Community will be removed but not those on imports from outside; consequently, producers within the Community will be in a preferred position in meeting Community demand. (3) The cost of this policy will be shared by the members. (National governments continue to provide some forms of aid to farmers but supposedly under conditions that do not affect prices, trade, or production unless the rest of the Community agrees.) (4) The CAP is supposed to improve the efficiency of Community agriculture and reform its structure. This has been only a subordinate theme so far; the importance it may have in the future will be discussed later.

6. For example, according to figures published by the Director-General for Agriculture of the Commission, the price Community producers received for wheat in 1967–68 was 85 to 100 per cent above world prices. For poultry and eggs the margin was 30 per cent; for pork 47, beef and veal 75, oil seeds 100, butter 297, and sugar 338 per cent. *Memorandum on the Reform of Agriculture in the European Economic Community*, Secretariat of the Commission, Supplement to Bulletin No. 1–1969 of the European Communities, p. 64.

In general outline, the CAP is not very different from the protectionist policies many countries have followed in the past. However, to treat six countries as one makes a difference. And the application of the CAP has been carried out with extraordinary thoroughness and great ingenuity. Nowhere is this more apparent than in the treatment of imports. No matter what device is used internally to support prices, the success of the CAP depends on shielding the Community market from foreign competition at lower prices. In this respect it is no different from many national policies. By that analogy we might expect to find the Community ringed about with quotas. But in fact the CAP makes no use of quotas or other direct import controls. It does not, however, rely on simple tariffs. Instead it uses for some major products a variable import levy that in effect closes the gap between the prices of domestic and foreign supplies. The cheaper the foreign product, the higher the levy; the higher the domestic target price, the higher the levy again. This self-sealing mechanism is applied in its pristine form only to grain and rice. For poultry, eggs, and pork the system is buttressed by an extra charge to offset the higher cost of feed grain in the Common Market (resulting in part from the CAP). In addition, if the foreign price for these products is below one arbitrarily set for the Community, there is an additional charge to make up the difference.[7] In the case of beef and veal, variable levies are used to supplement the regular tariff only if internal prices fall below a certain level. Other combinations are used for other products.

Whatever combination is used, it is clear that the aim of the import policy is to eliminate foreign price competition. If the machine worked perfectly, foreign producers would become residual suppliers who could sell only what the Community did not produce for itself at target prices. The choice of the support level is crucial to the effect of these measures. Because the CAP is shaped by bargaining among six governments, each with its own political problems and protected farmers, prices are often set higher than those which would satisfy the most efficient producers in the Community. In the same way, the need to satisfy one country or another increases the number of products brought under the CAP on terms imposing barriers to imports from the rest of the world.

Produced at high prices, most European farm products can be sold

7. "From the start of the CAP regulations, this 'gate' price was set high above the unsubsidized c.i.f. price of U.S. poultry." Oscar Zaglits, "Agricultural Trade and Trade Policy," in *Foreign Trade and Agricultural Policy*, Vol. VI, Technical Papers, National Advisory Commission on Food and Fiber (Washington: GPO, 1967), p. 177.

on world markets only at a loss. Here, too, the CAP plays an important role by providing Community financing for export subsidies. The money comes partly from the import levies (90 per cent of which the governments turn over to a common fund) and partly from contributions from national budgets according to an agreed-on (with difficulty) scale. Thus, from the point of view of outsiders who export farm products, the CAP not only extends European agrarian protectionism but sharpens competition in the rest of the world. Heavily subsidized international competition adds to the costs and burdens of agricultural policies for industrialized countries as a whole and is potentially highly disruptive. It brings out the worst in everybody.

When the six countries of the European Community formed their Common Market, it presented a challenge to American trade policy but there was promise and excitement about the challenge; it was plainly part of something big that was happening in the world, something that called for men to show their mettle in living with change and making the most of new opportunities. The CAP is a sorry contrast. This is not a challenge of shiny sword and shield; it is more a grubby cattle goad. A natural reaction is to draw back to the muddy wallow of past agricultural policy. There is some risk that that is what the United States will do. And yet, the CAP might, just possibly, serve as a prod to do something better. To assess that possibility we need to consider three questions: How important is the CAP to the United States? Is it likely to prove durable? What kind of negotiations can there be with a CAP Europe?

THE AMERICAN INTEREST IN FARM EXPORTS

Industrial leader of the world, the United States is also the largest exporter of agricultural products. Its farm exports in 1966–70 averaged about $6.5 billion a year, nearly one-fifth of total U.S. exports. Fluctuating from year to year as agricultural figures will, both the volume and the value of American farm exports have shown a strongly rising trend throughout the postwar period, with each cyclical peak higher than the last. Though aid programs account for a significant part of the total, the relative importance of "giveaways" has declined since the middle '60s. Though commercial sales have often been aided by export subsidies, most of these payments compensated for domestic price supports rather than real production costs above those of foreign producers. Though the shipment of farm products has not kept pace with the growth of other exports, it is no waning relic of an agrarian past.

Government policies have inhibited some kinds of change, but American agriculture is not stagnant. Although the traditional staple exports of wheat, flour, cotton, and tobacco are still important, their relative position has slipped badly as sales of rice, feed grains, and soybeans have risen, the last being now the leading U.S. agricultural export by far. The decline in agriculture's percentage contribution to the gross national product and the fall in the number of people who live on the land have been accompanied by major rises in productivity. While there is certainly some misallocation of resources in American agriculture, few experts doubt that the United States is one of the world's most efficient producers of a number of major farm products. As one drives or flies over the broad American farmlands, it is hard to believe that their direct contribution to the gross national product is only 3 per cent and that only 5 per cent of the American people live on farms. However, in a trillion dollar economy, agriculture's share of output is $30 billion, not a small sum in world terms.

While some major farm products are consumed almost entirely at home, such as meat and dairy products, much of American agriculture counts heavily on foreign markets. In the late '60s, exports took over one-third the production of cotton, tobacco, and tallow, over 40 per cent of the output of wheat, soybeans, and hides and skins, and more than half the production of rice. Western Europe is a major market for these products, taking nearly 40 per cent of American agricultural exports in the five-year period, 1966–70. Of the annual average of $2.4 billion of farm products sold to Western Europe in those years, $1.4 billion went to the Common Market, $400 million to Britain, $290 million to the rest of EFTA, and $160 million to Spain (all countries that may some day come under the CAP). If only "commercial" exports are counted (to exclude government aid programs), Western Europe's share is nearly 46 per cent and the Common Market's alone 28 per cent. The average annual sales of $4 billion to Japan, Canada, and Western Europe together amounted to 76 per cent of the farm exports for which the United States was paid in hard, usable currency in the years 1966–70.

The strong American interest in Europe's agricultural protectionism was clearly recognized in the Trade Expansion Act of 1962 and the Kennedy Round. Great emphasis was put on the need to get concessions from Europe on agricultural products if the results of the tariff bargains were to be satisfactory to the United States. Though not negligible, Kennedy Round tariff reductions and bindings on farm products of interest to the United States came nowhere near approaching in importance those for manufactured goods. Better results were obtained from Japan and Canada than from Europe, where the introduction of the CAP compounded difficulties that would have been great enough if the only obstacle had been traditional agrarian protectionism. The Kennedy Round was only the start of the trouble. Then the CAP was just being shaped and put into effect; by mid-1970 variable levies applied to products which, in the early '60s, had made up between 35 and 40 per cent of American farm exports to the European Community. Feed grains (especially corn), wheat and flour, rice, poultry and eggs, and in some years dairy products were the most important products affected.

During the early years of the CAP, American farm exports to the Community continued to rise, reaching a peak of nearly $1.6 billion in 1966. Over the next three years, they fell by about one-fifth, but in 1970 returned almost to the level of 1966. The products subject to the variable levy shared the initial growth but then declined more sharply than the rest, falling from 41 per cent of the total in 1966 to 27 per cent in 1969 when, at $340 million, they were below the level of 1961. Feed grains and wheat played an important part in the 1970 trade rise, but, even so, total exports of variable levy items stayed below the 1968 level.[8]

This simple picture, which conforms so clearly to one's expectations, naturally conceals a good bit of variation. The decline of shipments of dairy products from the unprecedented heights of 1963–65 was due not just to the CAP but also to the elimination of American surpluses and export subsidies. The "chicken war," precipitated when the CAP restrictions were imposed, concerned not a long-established trade but the skyrocketing sales of frozen poultry of the late '50s and early '60s. American sales of feed grains held up better than most variable levy products because Europe's production of poultry and cattle expanded faster than that of coarse grains; but, even so, the feeding of soft wheat and other surpluses at subsidized prices and increased use of oilcake made from American soybeans cut into the market. Rice, though subject to a variable levy, was sold in ever-increasing amounts before 1970, apparently in response to the European consumer's preference for the long-grained over the short-grained variety grown in France and Italy.

Exports do not necessarily expand because they are not subject to variable levies. Cotton, long on Europe's free list, made up nearly a quarter of American exports to the Community in the late '50s and only about 3 per cent a decade later. A decline in American supplies, cheaper

8. The figures in these and the following paragraphs are taken or calculated from *Foreign Agricultural Trade of the United States* (U.S. Department of Agriculture), March 1971, pp. 6-15.

sources in other countries, and the increased use of artificial fibers combine to explain the change. Nevertheless, although one cannot explain all agricultural trade movements in terms of the variable levy, the evidence is strong that this feature of the CAP is working the way it was expected to. Europe is not, after all, doing without the food and feed it used to buy from the United States; it is, for the most part, producing them—or their substitutes—at home. It was largely bad fodder crops in the Community that accounted for the rise in American sales in 1970.

It is not only the variable levy that Americans have to worry about. When tobacco was brought under the CAP in 1970, tariffs were left as they had been agreed on in the Kennedy Round; but a subsidy was offered to those who bought tobacco produced inside the Community and a promise given that what was not sold in this fashion would be bought by the authorities. Considerably less of a threat to American sales than a variable levy would be, this arrangement does, however, add to the disadvantages already created by the tariff-free entry accorded Greek, Turkish, and some African tobaccos.

It cannot be assumed that the CAP is static. Like any protective system, it generates pressures to fill its own gaps. To help dispose of surpluses of butter, wheat, and milk, the European Commission in 1969 considered a tax that would have struck hard at soybeans. American exports of this product (in the form of meal, cake, seeds, and oil), which came to some $83 million in 1956, had doubled by the early '60s, and amounted to $630 million in 1970, over 40 per cent of all U.S. farm sales to the Community. (The gain in soybean sales is greater than the total increase in U.S. exports of nonvariable levy products to the Community between 1956 and 1970.) The Commission's proposed tax was intended to encourage the consumption of butter instead of margarine and make it more costly to use oilcake for animal feed instead of surplus wheat and dried milk. The United States naturally objected and threatened to retaliate against imports of European automobiles and other products. The tax proposal was dropped but it seems likely that the issue will rise again in some form. The free entry of soybeans is, after all, a sizable loophole in the CAP's system of protection and, indeed, an illogicality.[9] The

9. A critic of the CAP who would like the general level of protection lowered argues that the distortions resulting from the free entry of soybeans are more costly than giving it the same protection as competing products would be. His case is not quantitatively demonstrated, but he shows vividly how the soybean "incoherence" helps generate a need for export subsidies for butter, milk, and wheat and discourages production of traditional foodstuffs. Adrien Zeller in collaboration with Jean-Louis Giraudy, *L'imbroglio agricole du Marché commun* (Paris: Calmann-Levy, 1970), pp. 64-70.

threat it offers works both ways, as the Europeans demonstrated a few years later when they let it be known that if the American Congress passed strongly protectionist legislation, they would quickly turn their attention to the soybean issue.

If the CAP is left unchanged as the Community is enlarged, the impact on the United States will increase. Britain in 1966–70 took nearly 30 per cent as much American farm produce as the six countries in the Common Market, and the rest of EFTA plus Spain took a slightly larger share. While the markets of these countries would not be "lost" any more than those of the Six have been, their disappearance behind "the iron curtain of the CAP," as someone has called it, would add substantially to the difficulties for American farm exports.

Many other countries besides the United States suffer from the CAP and have similar concerns about the enlargement of the Community; for example, Canada, Argentina, New Zealand, Australia, and several countries of Eastern Europe. The welfare of these countries is a matter of general interest to the United States, and, furthermore, a decline in their prosperity may affect American exports. When the CAP shuts farm products out of Europe, competition intensifies in the remaining world markets and prices fall. To this worsening of the position of more efficient producers than itself the Community adds further pressure by heavily subsidizing exports of its own surpluses. Some of the largest expenditures under the CAP are for this purpose, and sometimes the amount of the subsidy is several times the price at which the surpluses are sold.

There can be no doubt, then, that an important objective of American foreign economic policy should be a modification of the European Community's common agricultural policy. What is wrong with it is not that it is common but that it is so highly restrictive. In addition to its direct impact on American exports, the CAP adds severely to obstacles already in the way of agricultural trade liberalization and the more efficient use of world farm resources.

The Durability of the CAP

To cope with the problems posed by the CAP will not be easy for the United States. If new approaches have to be found that may be hard to fashion and slow to execute, it is only prudent to ask if the problem is likely to change significantly in some foreseeable period. If, for example, the chances were good that the CAP would be radically altered by the mid-'70s, some sort of holding operation aimed at minimizing damage might make sense. After all, the progress of trade liberalization in agriculture has been so slow that further delay, though undesirable, would not be a major setback. A look at the forces of change suggests, however, that waiting is unlikely to be enough.

It is quite clear, to start with, that American dislike for the CAP will neither kill nor seriously maim it. Nor should it be taken for granted that if the United States had the power to undo the CAP, it would or should be used. When the policy was first being formulated, Americans who warned that the only kinds of farm policies the Europeans would find it possible to agree on would be ones the United States would not like were told that even if this were true a common agricultural policy was necessary for the kind of European integration Washington wanted to see develop. The issues might be weighed somewhat differently nowadays. It is certainly true, however, that an integrated Western Europe requires some kind of common agricultural policy, and it would be shortsighted of the United States simply to try to block or subvert the effort—as distinguished from trying to alter its characteristics. Moreover, the alternative to the CAP is less likely to be liberalized trade than a series of protectionist national policies, and it would take some study to decide whether they were likely to be less damaging to American exports than the CAP. In any case, the question is not real; the United States cannot greatly change what the Europeans do in these matters by raising its voice or stamping its foot. An economic policy with the primary aim of forcing the Europeans to drop the CAP would sacrifice too many other American interests to be seriously contemplated.

It would be pleasant to think that British entry into the Community would lead to important changes in the CAP. Britain's long-standing concern with cheap food, its Commonwealth ties, and the small size of its agricultural population all lend support to the hope. But nothing major is likely to happen soon. A basic condition for British entry into the Community has been acceptance of the CAP pretty much as it exists, with time to make adjustments and special arrangements for New Zealand and some other Commonwealth countries. Some British farmers will become supporters of the CAP, taking advantage of its protection and high prices to expand their output. The fact that much of British farming is highly efficient by European standards may help to hold down costs and possibly bring down prices. Perhaps in the long run the addition of Britain will add enough to the Community's already strong urban and industrial interest to make an economical farm policy possible. (Britain and Germany have more real interests in common in these matters than is generally realized—except perhaps by Frenchmen—even though the German government has usually pressed for higher prices than the French wanted.) But in the short run, and perhaps for some time, one of the main effects of British entry will probably be to strengthen the CAP by providing new sources of funds and a sheltered market for what would otherwise be surpluses requiring export subsidies.

Though there are serious internal strains in the CAP, a whole set of basic political factors works to preserve it. One is support by people more interested in promoting integration than protecting agriculture; when progress in other fields is slow, the CAP becomes more precious. The wish to resist any dilution of Community ties following the addition of new members will buttress this attitude. Although struggles over the CAP have been major sources of strain in the Community, the fact that each dispute has been settled (at least for a time) because all the governments were in the end willing to compromise is probably a source of strength for the Community; agriculture is a rather good example of Monnet's maxim that integration thrives on crises. The French interest in the CAP—which explains much of its history—is very strong; it made France integrationist in a serious sense even during the height of President de Gaulle's anti-integration policies; at the same time it gives the other countries a major hold on France. The broadening of CAP has given farmers in other countries a stake in the Community program which their governments have to take into account even when they feel that the whole system is biased in France's direction. Being human, the leaders of the Community will not easily sacrifice all the hard work that has gone into creating and shaping the CAP; being politicians, they will be sensitive to the way a threat to the CAP would imperil a whole network of other understandings within the Community.

Time might weaken some of these factors. If the force of integration appeared to be spent, the CAP might be pulled apart as its supposed political value fell while discontent with its costs or inequities rose. There is, too, a possibility that the CAP will collapse of its own accord. The whole wondrous machine with its intricacies, internal balances, and multiple moving pieces might fall apart. Efficient administration of intricate policies is always hard; on a ten-country basis it might well prove impossible. Frustrated expectations multiply disputes; compromises are likely to be found by permitting new exceptions to general rules, perhaps on a national basis. One government or another may feel less pressure to carry out its obligations or be less willing to do something that is primarily of immediate benefit to the farmers of another Community country. The process of unifying national markets has run into many difficulties. As the value and workability of the CAP are called into question, the attraction of cheap overseas supplies may grow, so that governments ask for exemptions from the variable levy system, making the whole apparatus leakier than it was intended to be. The CAP has been jarred by currency changes in the Community: the revaluation of the Deutschemark followed by the devaluation of the French franc in 1969, the floating of the mark in 1971, and the realignment of rates that followed. Part of the disturbance was psychological; many people had harbored the illusion that the commitment to uniform farm prices stated in "units of account" (equal to the dollar) would prevent alterations in exchange rates. On a more mundane level, financial adjustments were introduced at the intra-Community frontiers, which to some degree separated markets that were supposed to be joined. Moreover, the German government introduced new subsidies to keep the returns to farmers in marks at their old levels. This step worried those who saw it as strengthening the "national" elements of the CAP at the expense of the "communitarian" ones, but it could also be looked at as a step toward the desirable practice of helping farmers through income subsidies rather than price support. None of these measures represented any liberalization of the CAP so far as outsiders were concerned.

Contemplating the CAP as it took shape, an observer might well have suspected that difficulties would come not from its failure to function but from its working well and rapidly. From the beginning it was plain that to pay farmers well above the world level, while shutting out imports and putting no limits on production (except in the case of sugar and potentially on tobacco), was a prescription for surpluses. Though European farmers have been leaving the land rather rapidly, the productivity (and production) of those that remain is growing. The same technological revolution that made it possible for one American farmer to produce as much in 1968 as three did in 1950 is under way in Europe, but with a lag. While eventually the need for protection and subsidies might fall, surpluses and subsidies would rise first unless the Europeans showed unparalleled flexibility, wisdom, and courage in their farm policies. Costs would rise and with them discontent. The CAP was more vulnerable on this count than national farm programs, since in each country the taxpayers and consumers were paying to support foreign farmers as well as their compatriots. (France receives much more than it pays; for Germany the situation is reversed. The relationship is one of the central political equations of the Community.)

By the end of 1968 it looked as if the rapid development that has so often characterized the European Community in other fields was bringing the potential difficulties of the CAP to a head much sooner than might have been expected. Production had so quickly outrun consumption that the Community found itself "saddled in the case of many products, with surpluses of which some cannot even be disposed of on the saturated world market. Even when there are outlets, the surpluses bear on the market so heavily that they can be disposed of only at a price which is very costly for the Community."[10] Wheat, milk, sugar, and butter were the main culprits; apples, peaches, tomatoes, and other fruits and vegetables were following in time; the list might well lengthen if the process that had brought self-sufficiency in pigs, eggs, and poultry did not stop there.

To get into these difficulties had been expensive; trying to get out promised to be more so. In 1960, before the CAP, the six governments spent just under $500 million for "market support." In 1967, together and through the Community, they spent $1.5 billion and in 1969 about $2.4 billion. With the expenditures called "structural" in Community jargon added, the cost came to $4.5 billion in 1969 compared to $1.35 billion in 1960. Some estimates reach a total of $7 billion by 1970, but this includes social security payments and some government activities not covered in the earlier figures.

In addition to the sums they provided as taxpayers, citizens of the Community were contributing to the agricultural policies as consumers by paying higher prices for almost all farm products. The Commission, however, was mainly concerned with the cost of market support, which had become "so astronomical as to threaten the whole existing system." In language that might well have been used by people who had always been skeptical of the CAP, its founding father, Sicco Mansholt, to whom the Commission memorandum can safely be ascribed, said: "The cost of intervention and refunds in an agriculture producing surpluses is a burden which is becoming intolerable for our Member States, and their economies are in consequence being deprived of resources which could be used to better advantage in improving the competitive strength of other economic sectors."

What governments will find "intolerable" in agricultural policy is not easily foreseen. In spite of the difficulties they faced, the Six were not ready to accept the long-term (and expensive) programs of structural reform that Mansholt proposed, and they were certainly not ready to cut the prices paid to farmers. In the next two

10. *Memorandum on the Reform of Agriculture in the European Economic Community*, cited, p. 25. The next two quotations come from pp. 45 and 25, respectively, and the cost figures from pp. 11, 45, 84, 85. The 1969 and 1970 figures come from Pierre Uri, *rapporteur*, *A Future for European Agriculture* (Paris: Atlantic Institute, 1970), p. 57.

years, they took a number of immediate measures to deal with surpluses, including paying for the slaughter of cows and the uprooting
of fruit trees and finding ways to dispose of butter, wheat, dried
milk, and some other products at a loss within the Community.
The sense of urgency decreased as the level of surpluses fell (in part
because of bad weather in 1970, an aid nature has given to more
than one bad farm policy). But action could not be postponed forever. Farmers increased their pressure for higher prices as inflation
raised their costs. The imminent negotiations over British entry
spurred the Six to work out a firm formula for future financing, and
that process sharpened the need to do something about both prices
and reform.

In March 1971, in one of the all-night sessions that have become
the ensigns of significant Community decisions, the Council of
Ministers steered a course between their clamant farmers and Mansholt and the Commission, who had revised their proposals. The
price increases for the year to come were on the modest side compared to the rise in other prices in the Community: 1 to 3 per cent
for wheat, rice, and coarse grains; 3 to 6 per cent for beef, veal,
sugar, and some dairy products.[11] In the matter of reform, a number
of steps Mansholt had long advocated were set forth in a series of
programs to be financed partly by Community funds but mostly by
the governments. If they worked, these measures would encourage
older farmers to retire early, speed up the shift of people from farming to other activities, favor the creation of larger enterprises, gear
production more closely to marketing, and offer incentives to lasting
programs of modernization.

None of the changes would make it possible for imports to come
into the Community more freely, though some possible long-run
changes in the structure of European agriculture—such as a shift
toward livestock production—would increase the demand for certain
foreign supplies. Improved productivity in Community farming may
well mean increased production as well, further narrowing the market
for imports. Though self-sufficiency has never been explicitly set out
as a Community objective, one gets a sense that the idea of it is regarded
as an acceptable, in fact rather comfortable and thus desirable, state of
affairs, at least for many products. The fact that prices are so far above
world levels does not seem to worry people, though it may some day
come to do so. In all the discussion, no word is said suggesting that
competition from abroad would be a useful instrument for bringing

11. Barley was raised a bit more than other coarse grains, and the skimmed milk
intervention price by 14 per cent, presumably to encourage the processing of milk
surpluses.

about efficiency in European agriculture or lowering prices. It is surpluses, and the cost of financing their export, that are the rub.

There are, then, no sudden vistas of freer farm trade to be discerned in the Community's difficulties with its CAP. There are, however, some possibilities for change that did not exist at the time of the Kennedy Round. A reduction of surpluses would itself help by reducing the volume of subsidized competition in foreign markets. Though price cuts may be politically impossible, governments have resisted farmers' demands to let farm prices keep pace with other prices in an inflationary situation. The idea seems to be gaining force that differential price increases can be used to shape European agriculture so as to discourage surpluses and stimulate the production of things for which demand would rise more rapidly, notably meat. This in turn might encourage imports (if the soybean gap is not closed). Under the strain of surpluses, some taboos were more openly questioned than before, notably those about possible controls over production. (The March 1971 action included a general commitment by governments to prevent the expansion of land in agricultural production.) The payments Germany was authorized to make to compensate farmers for the revaluation of the mark moved in the direction advocated by many of supplementing farm incomes without raising prices. These and other possible changes in price and production policies would have a bearing on trade that might be advantageous to outside suppliers. Whether the United States (or any other outsider) can influence the choices the Community will make is another matter, but that possibility has to be borne in mind in shaping American policy.

The Ways of Negotiating

When variable levies were first brought on the scene, trade experts threw up their hands in horror. No possibility seemed to exist of negotiating about the new devices. They could not be reduced or bound like ordinary tariffs without losing their unique character of automatically filling the gap between domestic and foreign prices; *ergo*, there could be no successful negotiation about variable levies. Matters are not that bad. Various ways can be found of limiting the height to which a variable levy may go or otherwise reducing its impact.[12] Of course, such devices would not be acceptable to the

12. For canned poultry, tallow, and variety meats, the Community has agreed that variable levies should not exceed the level of the duties bound in GATT agreements. Other kinds of ceilings can be imagined: a certain percentage of the value of imports, a maximum levy-paid price, or a ceiling linked to some indicator. The Community's variable levy on beef does not come into effect unless the

Community on any large scale precisely because they would hobble the variable levies, and the variable levies are essential to the kind of common agricultural policy the Community has developed. Commitments to outsiders about variable levies and threshold prices would set limits to how the CAP could operate within the Community.

In this aspect, however, variable levies are not radically different from other import barriers geared to domestic farm programs. Often the logic that dictates import limitation to protect domestic price works backwards—if you alter the barriers, you affect the domestic policy. That is why they have been so hard to remove. Consequently, the foreigner anxious to improve his access to the Common Market might do better to ignore the border rules and strike for the jugular—the domestic support price. When that price is high enough, it becomes the begetter of surpluses which lead to the variable levy's shutting off of imports and to subsidized competition in third markets (or even the supplier's own). If the support price is not so high as to stimulate great domestic output, foreign products may come in over the variable levies. A foreign negotiator who obtained a commitment that the support price would not rise above a certain level would be doing far more for his exporters than one who negotiated a commitment limiting the way the variable levy would operate (or, in dealing with other countries, about the level of the tariff). Similar results could be obtained if governments would agree to limit price-supported domestic production to an amount that left room for imports if demand were large enough. Other ways of getting at similar results could be devised. The basic question, prompted not only by the CAP but by the whole history of postwar agriculture, is whether the industrial countries are prepared to negotiate with one another about their domestic farm prices and farm policies as a whole.

The idea sounds unrealistic and politically impossible. Who can contemplate negotiating with other governments about so touchy a subject in domestic politics as food prices? Or production and marketing controls? Will legislatures that hesitate to cut price supports without compensating farmers in some other way dare to do differently because of an understanding with foreigners? Govern-

---

price of imports after the payment of the normal fixed tariff is still below the internal "guide price." An alternative possibility would be to have the levy come into operation only if imports exceeded a certain amount, as is done in the case of tariff quotas. The price rules that buttress the variable levies could also be fixed by international agreement setting ceilings for threshold prices in absolute terms or percentages.

ments have fallen on lesser issues. The difficulties are obvious, but the logic of trying to negotiate about agricultural policy as a whole is compelling—unless nothing is to be done.

The record seems clear that negotiations that aim only at trade liberalization will not produce significant results for major temperate zone farm products so long as national farm policies of the present type are followed. But these policies have not been resoundingly successful. They are costly; they generate surpluses that add to the cost and create international friction as well; the incomes of many farmers in most industrialized countries remain lower than those of other citizens. Consequently, the policies themselves generate pressures on governments to change the policies in more or less important respects. Since there is almost always someone who is also interested in improving his position in foreign trade (at present the United States vis-à-vis the Community), it is not fantastic to think that the two pressures might be combined.

There is more evidence than is sometimes realized that responsible officials in the United States have been acting for some time as if this new kind of negotiation were not politically unthinkable. For example, in the fall of 1962 Secretary of Agriculture Orville Freeman told the Agricultural Committee of the OECD that the United States was willing to discuss international agreements covering "international prices, producer prices, supply management including supply control, import quotas, export shares, stocking, and contributions in the form of food aid to less developed countries."[13] At that point the six countries of the Community were more interested in negotiating with one another than with the United States. Their painful efforts to produce a common agricultural policy delayed agricultural negotiations in the Kennedy Round, interrupted them after they started, and made it impossible to negotiate seriously about lowering either the newly devised trade barriers or the support prices they protected.

Over the course of several years Commission negotiators did, however, put forward several proposals that seemed not too distant from the kind of thing Freeman had suggested. They suggested that the amount each country paid to support agriculture in whatever form—the *montant de soutien*—be ascertained and then bound at a maximum level, product by product. Another proposal was that the height of import levies or export subsidies for products should be limited to the difference between domestic prices and an internationally agreed-on "reference price." In many ways the most interesting proposal of all, advanced first for wheat but potentially

13. *Congressional Record*, January 29, 1963 (Vol. 109, No. 14), pp. 1266-69.

applicable to other products, was that countries should put a ceiling on the degree of self-sufficiency in each product that they were to aim at (which could be over 100 per cent for exporting countries). Output in excess of the agreed level would be kept off the domestic market but might be given away as food aid to poor countries. Thus importing and exporting countries would share the responsibility and costs for contributing to world surpluses, and outsiders would be assured some access to protected markets even when there were domestic surpluses.[14]

In one sense, then, there was in the Kennedy Round, as a key American negotiator said, "full accord" between the United States and the Common Market on the "fundamental objective" that negotiations "should not cover merely the protection at the border but must also deal with the implications of the domestic policies, wherever these have a real effect on international trade."[15] That was almost all the accord there was concerning the products covered by the CAP. Not the principle but the specific features of the Common Market offers made them unacceptable to the United States (or other exporting countries). The Common Market was trying to negotiate from a position it had not yet achieved. The arrangements being proposed amounted to international acceptance of the CAP and its devices; the price levels and self-sufficiency ratios suggested were those the Community hoped to achieve. The results, to American eyes, would not be trade liberalization but increased protectionism; instead of improved access to the European market, outside producers were being asked to acquiesce in arrangements that would almost certainly diminish their share. While some of the Community's initial offers may have been intended as bargaining positions, hard negotiation proved that there was no real chance to get an agreement on lower levels of price support, which was natural enough in view of the struggle the Community had been through

14. My summary of these offers is somewhat simplified. Much of it is drawn from the fuller accounts in Ernest H. Preeg, *Traders and Diplomats: An Analysis of the Kennedy Round of Negotiations under the General Agreement on Tariffs and Trade* (Washington: Brookings Institution, 1970), chaps. 8 and 9; John W. Evans, *The Kennedy Round in American Trade Policy: The Twilight of the GATT?* (Cambridge: Harvard University Press, 1971), chaps. IV, X, and XIII; John A. Schnittker, *A Foreign Economic Policy for the 1970's*, Hearings before the Subcommittee on Foreign Economic Policy of the Joint Economic Committee, 91st Cong., 2d sess., March 16–19, 1970 (Washington: GPO, 1970), pp. 433-44; and, especially, Oscar Zaglits, cited, at pp. 223-29. These participants in the Kennedy Round also elaborate on the points made briefly in my next paragraph.
15. W. M. Blumenthal, "The Kennedy Round," *The Department of State Bulletin*, April 26, 1965, p. 634.

to reach the existing compromises. At the end of the Kennedy Round the position was much the same as in 1964 when Christian Herter, the principal American negotiator, said that the Community's approach "seems to establish as the objective of the negotiations the binding of increased levels of protection rather than reductions in trade barriers and expansion of trade."[16]

The idea of negotiating about farm policy as a whole has survived the impasse in the Kennedy Round. It is endorsed by an increasing number of private individuals, many with enough governmental experience to rebut the charge that their views are "academic" and "idealistic." The U.S. government, too, continues to keep the idea alive. In his farewell report to President Johnson, William M. Roth, Governor Herter's successor, recommended exploring in GATT "the possibility of negotiating adjustments in domestic agricultural policies and related trade barriers in order to further the objectives of fair and equitable farm income and expanding agricultural trade."[17] Nathaniel Samuels, Deputy Under Secretary of State for Economic Affairs in the Nixon Administration, told a farm audience: "Perhaps it is only by a fundamental convergence of internal production and support policies as well as acreage and land use appropriate to each country that we can eliminate the conflicts inherent in different agricultural systems and thereby achieve rational international order. . . . Our thoughts should turn to the harmonization of policies rather than the compromising of conflicts."[18]

Possible Results

If governments proved willing to negotiate about national farm policies as a whole, they might not reach agreement. If they did reach agreement, the results might not be durable or, if durable, beneficial. This section suggests some difficulties and some possibilities with the help of some illustration and some speculation.

The World Grains Arrangement negotiated in the Kennedy Round was not at all a true harmonization of policies but took limited steps in that direction. It soon illustrated the risks of too limited an agreement. Building on the existing (and not very important) in-

16. "The Role of Agriculture in Trade Expansion," *The Department of State Bulletin,* April 27, 1964, p. 673.
17. *Future United States Foreign Trade Policy,* Report to the President submitted by the Special Representative for Trade Negotiations (Washington: GPO, 1969), p. 70.
18. "Agriculture and Foreign Economic Policy," *The Department of State Bulletin,* December 15, 1969, p. 572.

ternational wheat agreement,[19] the new one raised by about 12 per cent the minimum price at which importing nations agreed to buy at least a certain share of their imports from other signatories and the maximum prices at which exporters agreed to guarantee the importing signatories a certain share of their purchases. Unlike the previous agreement, the new one (which in spite of its name also concerned only wheat) applied the minimum prices to transactions with non-members. The main innovation, however, lay in a parallel agreement by which the signatories[20] promised to provide each year, in agreed shares, 4.5 million metric tons of wheat or edible coarse grains or a cash equivalent as aid to poor countries. The United States had pressed hard for this agreement in the Kennedy Round, partly as a way of increasing the European aid contribution while reducing the pressure of supplies, but also because the agreement embodied the principle that, no matter who held surpluses, countries that protected grain-growing had some responsibility for helping to dispose of them.

When the agreement came into effect in July 1968, wheat was much more plentiful than when it had been negotiated. By early 1969 it became apparent that in one way or another a good deal of wheat was finding its way to market at prices below the minimum. Some buyers, like Japan, suspended purchasing until they were offered as favorable terms as other countries. Provisions for consultation when the market was disturbed led not to understandings but to mutual accusations of violating at least the spirit and probably the letter of the agreement. In July 1969, seizing on statements by American and Canadian officials about further price cuts, the Community announced that it would proceed to give even larger export subsidies than before to make possible sales below the agreement's minimum price. Soon little was left of the undertaking, which was later renegotiated on a more limited basis.

If there is a simple lesson in the collapse of the wheat agreement, it is one made familiar by the history of commodity agreements and cartels: International agreements based on price alone are remarkably fragile when surpluses press heavily. The need, it seems clear, is for

19. Which itself was one of the few results of an earlier American interest in commodity agreements for temperate zone farm products. Controversy between the Departments of State and Agriculture about this approach (only partly compromised in the provisions of the ITO Charter) seemed, in the immediate postwar years, highly relevant to the direction of American policy but since then appears to have lost its importance.
20. The United States, the Community, Britain, Canada, Australia, Japan, the Scandinavian countries, Switzerland, and Argentina. It was believed that the Soviet Union, when in an export position, would tacitly conform to the price provisions.

agreements that go further, for example, to limit exports (as is done in the coffee agreement) or total marketing or, most fundamental of all, production. In short, the harmonization of policy must go beyond a certain point if it is to work. The obverse of that clear conclusion is that it will be considerably more difficult to negotiate a complex agreement than a (relatively) simple one.

The great attraction of Mansholt's initial proposal for agreeing to limit the *montant de soutien* was that the governments were asked to agree on a single point on which all else would pivot. Each government would retain a good bit of freedom in working out for itself the combination of price supports, income payments, consumer subsidies, production controls, taxing and credit and surplus disposal arrangements that would meet its domestic situation. But an agreement on a single point would be too simple. How aid is given makes a difference, not least to the level of domestic production. Just as one step has led to another in the construction of trade barriers to protect support prices, so an agreement on price supports raises questions about trade barriers, production controls, export subsidies, and so on. And even if some of these complications can be avoided, what is done about one product spills over into the supply and demand of other products. A simple approach may permit too much freedom of action; the price of a more comprehensive one is to make agreement more difficult because each government has to limit its choices in domestic policy. Even if accepted, such commitments may in the end prove weak spots in an agreement. The results of agricultural policies are rarely just those that were expected, and a government caught between a difficult domestic problem and an international commitment will often strain, or break, the latter, thus starting a process that can well unravel a complicated network of international understandings.

The dilemma of simplicity and freedom of action on the one hand and complexity and the narrowing of national choices in policy on the other cannot be avoided. Governments are likely to emulate Cretan bullfighters and try to balance on the horns; they will devise various kinds of measures, different for different products, that will link trade barriers and domestic policies more closely than before but that will fall short of providing ironclad guarantees against practices that would jeopardize the benefits that others expect to obtain from the agreement. Unsatisfactory as this sounds, such arrangements may have redeeming features; they provide at least temporary help, and one may always hope the worst will not happen. Where alternatives are bad, aims that are too high lead to inaction.

There is, to be sure, no certainty that negotiations about farm policies will always make them more rational. The result may be an

international undertaking that reduces the pressure on national policies, perhaps by some division of the "spoils." For instance, an agreement that keeps up the price of a product in international trade
makes it easier for a country to keep its domestic price supports
higher still, but it gives the foreign supplier a higher return than if
the whole difference were taken up by the importer's tariff. Though
industrial countries have parallel interests in economically more sensible farm policies, their parallel tendencies to pursue less rational
courses are likely to influence international negotiations as well as
independent national action. But there is no reason to think that a
new approach will be any worse than the old one in this respect and
some chance that it will be better.

Without doubt, any attempt to work out international agreements
on national agricultural policies will be messy, annoying, and long.
While the prospects for achieving anything substantial may be ques-
tionable, they would be even poorer if the only forces working in
favor of such agreements were those of reason, the desire for an
orderly world economy, and the interest in lowering trade barriers
(which is strong only in some countries and then usually only for
some products). Even the desire to reduce international political
friction plays only a limited part if its counterpart is rural discontent
at home. But there are other, stronger forces working for change in
agricultural policies, and it is these which make it reasonable to think
that all roads forward may not be closed. These forces stem from the
cost of past policies, their failures, and the conflict between the interests of the majority of the population of an industrial country and
traditional agrarian protectionism, a matter which becomes clearer
the further agricultural policy is pushed while the relative position of
farming in the economy declines. The signs of change in American
agricultural policy that became discernible in the early '60s were
largely responsive to these forces plus a concern for keeping export
markets open.[21] The difficulties of the CAP, about which enough has
been said, move it in the same direction.

In spite of all the differences, it is hard to resist the parallel between the history of American farm policy from the '30s to the '60s
and that of the CAP beginning in the early '60s. For about a generation, the United States went through the process of raising farm

21. John Coppock links the American initiatives for international discussion of
price supports to the story that when President Kennedy reviewed his first budget,
his reaction to the agricultural item was to tell his officials (unavailingly) "that
he did not know how they were going to do what he wanted, but to get that total
down." *Atlantic Agricultural Unity: Is It Possible?* (New York: McGraw-Hill, for
the Council on Foreign Relations, 1966), p. 197.

prices well above the market levels, spending heavily to handle and dispose of the resulting surpluses, and, as a logical consequence, resisting the liberalization of world trade in farm products. Then the tide began to turn. In Europe the turning has not yet come. But— as is not surprising in a world where so much else is accelerated —major strains have shown themselves in less than a decade. It is not inevitable that Europe should change direction; many expedients could delay the time for choice: production control, reforming farm structures, enlarging the Community. But there is also an accumulation of pressure that may encourage more basic changes—though probably not quickly.

This out-of-phase parallel has some bearing on current problems. At the lowest level—leaving aside the avoidance of political friction— there is a common interest of Europe and America in limiting the cost of farm policies. To check competitive subsidies to sell surpluses in third markets may be easier than to take some other steps. It would be a logical starting place. A ceiling on support prices at home is likely to appeal to finance ministers as well as to taxpayers and foreign suppliers. Sometimes a limited balance can be struck between one nation's interest in access to another's market (American soybeans and European cheese). Stability, that appealing but unclear and elusive goal, whether put in terms of prices, supplies, or markets, has not lost all its attractions, and efforts to approach it require some degree of international cooperation. Even within the somewhat arbitrary parameters of national farm policies there are advantages in concentrating resources in their most efficient uses, an aim that usually implies some interest in international trade.

More important in the long run may be certain similarities in the farm problems of industrialized countries that have not been adequately dealt with by past policies. In both Europe and the United States, it has become clear, price-support policies benefit big and rich farmers far more than small and poor ones. There is no escape from this result except through the disappearance of small farmers or a shift to income support geared to need and not output. Modernized farming can yield good incomes to a small number of people even if prices are relatively moderate. To provide the same incomes to all farmers would require even higher prices than those which have produced surpluses and would impose additional costs on taxpayers (and yield even higher profits for relatively efficient farmers). The social aims of farm policy have not been adequately met by price supports. Truly modern farm enterprises, in Europe and in the United States, have resources and competitive strength that permit them to function more or less as businesses do (but sometimes within protected markets only). Though the big farmers remain politically important, governments can treat them differently from peasants. With such a farm sector, the chances increase of directing farm resources into their most economical uses, and there is room for greater reliance on market forces to provide the guidance at which national farm administrators have generally been so inept.

All this is for the future, and a longer future for Europe than the United States. But it is not a dream world, and some parts of it can be fitted into the short run. The Mansholt Plan points clearly to this kind of reform of European agriculture and is essentially intended to hasten a process that is already taking place. In the United States, without benefit of an over-all plan, farming has moved markedly in the same direction.

These similarities point to still another ingredient of the mixture out of which new arrangements for agriculture may come. Without committing themselves internationally, countries might move along parallel or converging lines. A move toward policies that concentrate on supporting farm income while permitting prices to move more freely in relation to demand—an approach that has advocates in every country—would reduce the pressures for trade barriers to shore up domestic policies. A ceiling on some prices in the Community and a change in American practices that eliminated export subsidies on the same products, each a change that could reasonably be made on a calculation of national interest alone, would have the effect of improving international trade in farm products and probably the international allocation of resources as well. Whether governments are more likely to move in these directions when acting alone, each setting its own political pace, or in concert is a matter on which there can be much debate but not, so far as I can see, any firm general conclusion. To appear to do something "for" foreigners can be politically hazardous. To "have" to take certain steps to conform to agreed-on principles and get some advantage from what the others do may be just the extra reason that makes action possible.

Those who have seen many international efforts fail have a right to be skeptical. "There is a long way to go before countries even begin to get together on the underlying problems," says a leading American agricultural economist who advocates coordination of national measures.[22] Another adds, " 'cleaning up' agriculture and its pricing . . .

22. Dale E. Hathaway, "The Search for New International Arrangements to Deal with the Agricultural Problems of the Industrialized Countries," in Ugo Papi and Charles Nunn, *Economic Problems of Agriculture in Industrial Societies* (New York: St. Martin's Press, for the International Economic Association, 1969), pp. 51-69. The comment cited is not a direct quotation but appears in the discussion of the paper, p. 71.

requires a great amount of *national* housecleaning. Not very much can be accomplished by international negotiations so far as agricultural specialization is concerned at this point."[23] But, as he says, it is also true that

> . . . national agricultural problems have been brought under . . . international surveillance because there is no other place for them to be considered, and it is becoming increasingly clear that they must be faced in some arena. Governments find it inexpedient, perhaps even fatal, to do what needs to be done on a national scale to bring their agricultural policies back within the realm of economic reality.

Having presided over efforts at international cooperation, Thorkil Kristensen, then Secretary General of the OECD, observed: "It will be much easier for the individual country to take measures that bring us closer to market equilibrium if other countries do it at the same time." And if production control is involved, "one cannot expect individual countries to take courageous steps . . . unless they have a certain guarantee that others will do the same."[24]

Sometimes separately and sometimes in agreement, moved by domestic considerations and by international pressures—and sometimes, too, by the wish to diminish friction among friends—the governments of the industrialized countries may move in the direction of adapting their farm policies to more economical practices. Their progress is likely to be slow and marked by setbacks as well as gains. No great breakthroughs in trade liberalization are to be expected, much less the radical rationalization of farming in Europe and North America. Much of what is done, if anything is done at all, will be an accommodation of national systems of protection, subsidy and support, not a major extension of competition. The results, at least for some time, are less likely to be liberalization than new forms of international management of agricultural problems. But if there is also an increase in international influence on national policy, some degree of liberalization may follow. At some points, the international pressures will converge with domestic measures to make for a more economic and rational treatment of agriculture than has marked most of the postwar period. To be sure, governments working together can be as restrictionist and irrational as governments working separately. Each will undoubtedly try to get international sanction for

23. Coppock, cited, p. 30; the quotation that follows is from p. 16.
24. OECD *Press Release*, Introductory Statement by the Secretary General at a Meeting at the Ministerial Level of the Committee for Agriculture, November 28, 1968. The first quotation is from p. 6, the second from p. 5.

national restrictions. But there is at least a chance—for all the reasons reviewed in these pages—that new ways could be found of dealing with international agricultural issues. They could hardly be worse than the old ways.

American Policy

Though past farm policies have decreased American competitiveness in world markets for some products, the United States remains a relatively efficient producer of others. To the advantages conferred by nature, man has added those of extraordinary technological progress and investment on a scale that makes much of American farming a capital-intensive activity. The transfer of resources from the rest of the economy to agriculture under past policies has undoubtedly contributed to this development. Though farm exports have done surprisingly well in the face of protectionism abroad, there is little doubt that there is an American interest in measures that open markets further or discourage their closing. If, as is only to be expected, the necessary condition for reducing foreign protectionism is the equivalent reduction of protectionism in the United States, Americans would gain from that step as well, as consumers and in insuring the best use of national resources. This is probably also true even on a traditional, narrow, mercantilist basis since "the output value of farm products which the United States produces at a relatively low cost compared to the rest of the world is several times the value of those farm products which must be protected from international competition if they are to be produced in the United States."[25]

There seems little doubt, then, that the United States has an interest in the general reduction of agrarian protectionism. There is also a good case to be made for the benefits that would accrue to many people in the rest of the world if they were free to buy from the most efficient producers. But the general interest in having the world so organized that nations can live by doing what they do best rarely inspires action. The technique of reciprocal reduction of trade barriers that has worked well in other fields produces few results in agriculture, so if the aim of the United States and others is to give greater scope to the most efficient producers, they will have to move toward negotiation about farm policies.

Unfortunately, the United States is not in a strong position to exercise great leverage on other countries to move in this uncomfortable

25. D. Gale Johnson, "Agricultural Trade and Foreign Economic Policy," in *Foreign Trade and Agricultural Policy*, cited, p. 5.

direction. Europe is an essential partner and will be all the more important (and probably more difficult) as the Common Market is enlarged. There is no symmetry between the United States's interest in exporting farm products to Europe and Europe's interest in selling farm products to the United States. One-fifth of American exports to Europe are agricultural, less than one-tenth of Europe's to the United States (and the figure for the Community alone is still lower). That was why the American strategy at the Kennedy Round was to link agricultural and industrial negotiations, but the technique was not very successful, largely because of the CAP. Those principally concerned with farm exports say the same linkage must be made in the future. But as the European interest in easier access to the American market for manufactured goods is not noticeably greater than the American interest in selling manufactured goods in Europe, there is no great margin for adding farm products to this "package" of tariff concessions. As in the case of nontariff barriers or the industry-by-industry approach to trade negotiations, there is a conflict between the apparent logic of dealing separately with a single subject or a related group of products and the need for a balance of reciprocal advantage before bargains can be struck. Some improvement may be found in broadening negotiations to include other European countries with a stronger import interest than the Common Market and other agricultural exporters, such as Canada, Australia, Argentina, and New Zealand. Still, it will remain true that the lack of a balanced interest in trade-barrier removal will handicap negotiations dealing with agriculture.

If there are no serious negotiations about basic agricultural policies, it is likely that the operation of the CAP will bring out the worst in American policy. By calling forth surpluses and then subsidizing their export, the CAP invites retaliation and emulation. When, in 1967 and 1968, the United States imposed new quotas on dairy products, one of the reasons for the action was the increase in imports of cheese, butter, and butterfat compounds from the Common Market at low, subsidized prices. Measures were taken against Italian tomato paste and Dutch canned hams, again on the grounds of subsidy. After the "chicken war" seemed settled, hostilities reopened when the Community began subsidizing its own exports. Competition was intensified by the fact that Denmark, which like the United States had been seriously hit by CAP levies and price controls, resorted to a two-price policy to keep up exports. By 1967 the American share of Swiss poultry imports was only 3 per cent in contrast to the 67 per cent it had been before 1962. So the United States began subsidizing poultry sales to Switzerland in April 1968. A similar action followed in Greece, and early in 1971 Dutch and Canadian poultry exports were offered at subsidized prices to Hong Kong and Japan. In January 1969 the United States began giving a subsidy of about 25 per cent on exports of lard to Britain where the American share of the market had dropped from 80 per cent to 30 per cent, partly because the Common Market, formerly an importer, was now subsidizing exports.

There is no reason to suppose that this process will stop. On the contrary, the CAP seems custom-made to produce incident after incident, and it is hard to see that any other course is likely to strike an American administration as reasonable but to throw up protective barriers at home and match subsidies abroad. Other countries, whether exporters or importers, will follow suit. Measures to cope with "unfair" competition will shade off into trade barriers and subsidies that have no such justification. The resistance of governments and legislatures to the demands of their farmers will weaken as all troubles and costs are blamed on the foreigner. Disputes can easily go beyond farm policy. If the Common Market moves to increase its protection, the United States's most effective response may be to threaten retaliation in other fields, as the soybean episode shows. A demonstration that CAP was costing the United States x amount of foreign exchange earnings could be transformed by some into an added argument that American troops should be withdrawn from Europe on balance of payments grounds.

In an atmosphere of rivalry and conflicts over farm policy it is tempting to look for measures by which the United States might take the initiative itself to avoid or reduce even temporary loss of a market. Pre-emptive export subsidies suggest themselves, and it requires no great leap of the imagination to think of devices by which export markets might be held by threatening buyers with retaliation if they break old trade links. A quite different line of approach, and perhaps not a very practical one, would be to try to reach agreement with other suppliers to raise the price of commodities shipped to the Common Market. If wheat arrived in European ports with a price tag equal to the threshold price plus the variable levy, the American suppliers would get money that otherwise goes into European treasuries. Less money from the levies means more direct contributions by governments to finance the CAP and its export subsidies, thus adding to the strain. It is, of course, not easy to manipulate prices in this fashion; the simplest expedient, an export tax, is banned in the United States by the Constitution. To play off one supplier against another would be a natural and probably successful response of the Community. Impractical as it probably is, the idea at least has the merit of reminding one that as long as Europe keeps domestic prices well above world levels, the question of who should benefit from the spread and who should bear the cost of the resulting world surpluses is a central one.

Out of conflict can come agreement. Perhaps the best safeguard against agricultural rivalry leading to serious frictions is the visibility of the danger. Moreover, it is hard on even the narrowest nationalistic basis to discern much hope of gain in competitive export subsidies and an endless round of retaliatory trade measures. A truce would appeal to many. The American proposal to drop export subsidies on poultry if others do the same is the kind of approach that should be extended to other products and other activities. Even limited and fragile agreements have the merit of calling attention to the existence of alternatives to simple nationalistic reaction. But the forces working against agreement are strong, and retaliation is a deep-rooted instinct in a world of nations. It is conceivable that as the costs of conflict over farm policy rise, governments will some day reach the point of limiting what they do simply for their own sakes, not that of others. But as Vladimir Nabokov said of another matter in *Ada*, "All this is easier described than imagined."

The foreign agricultural policy of the United States has to be concerned with other matters as well as the friction arising from the CAP. There are, for example, important markets to which access is controlled only by conventional trade barriers. Some of these are in the Common Market, more or less outside the CAP, but the more important ones are in the rest of Europe (at least for the time being), Canada, and Japan, our largest customers. Nontariff barriers flourish in agricultural trade, sometimes as the blunt and overt imposition of a quota and sometimes in the refined forms of safeguards for health, quality standards, and specifications about size and packaging. Having comparable controls itself, the United States is in a position to engage in more or less conventional kinds of trade bargaining, moving toward the reduction or elimination of tariffs, the enlargement or abolition of quotas, and the removal of nontariff barriers or their administration in such ways that the pursuing of the professed public interest does not conceal protection. How much liberalization can be achieved in this way is not easy to say without a careful study of products and markets. The record of the Kennedy Round, in which much better agricultural concessions were obtained from Japan and Canada than from the Common Market, suggests that the conventional approach still has value. It would, however, fly in the face of postwar history to forget that when conventional barriers are used to shield domestic farm policies, they often cannot be worn down or bargained away as effectively as barriers to trade in manufactured goods, which are mostly rooted in simple protectionism. The American record is not good in these matters, and there are limits to what we can expect from others. Of course, an agreement on trade barriers can help to prevent the agricultural policies of foreign countries from becoming more damaging to American exports than they might be, but when the compulsion is strong there are many ways around. Japan, once the world's largest rice importer, has become self-sufficient in that grain and pays a high price for the privilege. While the United States might gain a rice market if the Japanese support price were lower, it is more interested in the shipment of wheat, soybeans, and coarse grains.

More important than anything the United States could achieve by an attack on foreign trade barriers are the things it could do in its own agricultural policies. Here there need be none of the frustration of finding others immovable and none of the cumbersomeness of trying to work out arrangements that combine international commitments and domestic imperatives in a meaningful, workable way. There are fewer risks that the result of international negotiation will be to sanction one damaging restriction as the price of a little progress in loosening another. Looking primarily to its own interests, the United States can remove self-imposed obstacles to the most efficient use of its resources, setting its own pace and choosing its own methods of making adjustments in a politically acceptable fashion.

Unilateral action would not remove other people's trade barriers but might in the long run have an influence on what other industrial countries were willing to do. As John Coppock observes, "a half-submerged position in the gutter is not a good one from which to propose temperance to others, even if they happen to be a little further down."[26] Still, too much should not be expected from the "demonstration effect" of an altered American farm policy, even from people who are, in a sense, repeating a process the United States has already gone through. Reforms in farm policy that strengthen the position of American agriculture might even make others hesitate to open their markets lest the advantage of any reduction in agricultural protectionism accrue to the United States. Nevertheless, it would make sense to move in a direction that improves competitiveness, breaks (or at least reduces) the link between supporting farm welfare and supporting prices, and escapes from the tangles that conceal the real strength and weaknesses of American agriculture behind export subsidies and import restrictions. A more efficient use of American resources and a reduction of the burden of

26. Cited, p. 198.

farm policy on the rest of the economy would increase American competitiveness in more than agriculture. It is on such considerations rather than on possible effects on the rest of the world that the case for reforms in American farm policy rests.

There are no great mysteries about the main elements of desirable reforms. The Wool Act of 1954 was a step in the right direction. Both to make possible a tariff reduction and to avoid putting wool at a disadvantage in competition with other fibers, it seemed unwise to keep the domestic price too far above world levels. Instead American producers were compensated by direct payments equal to the difference between the market prices they actually received and a "support price" set in the law (and kept constant for a decade). Changes in wheat policies in the '60s eliminated surpluses and cut export subsidies in half but left wheat heavily dependent on government support for sales in the world market. The steps taken in cotton have already been described. For other products, too, including soybeans, support prices have been lowered with beneficial results.

In spite of these changes, American agriculture gets a great deal of government help and is far from fitting easily into the international economy. The price which determines a farmer's decision about how much to produce is still often a support price above world levels, even if he receives part of it as a direct payment from the government. Some of the formulas used to allocate payments counteract the guidance that market prices would give. Attempts at production control fail repeatedly as the permitted acreage is farmed more intensively and productively, a process that is greatly helped by the additional capital put into farmers' hands by government payments. Though they had declined by the late '60s, export subsidies remained important for wheat and peanuts, rice, dry milk, and some other products as well. New ones were introduced for tobacco which was long unsubsidized. Import barriers remained important, too, and new ones were imposed on dairy products even though foreigners supply only a small share of the market; in spite of major price increases in the United States, foreign meat producers were held at bay with the threat of tighter controls if their shipments rose too rapidly. The Agricultural Act of 1970 confirmed the trend toward moderate support prices and gave farmers who were paid for taking land out of production more choice about what they grew on the rest of their acres. The history of the gap between expectation and result warns against confident judgments about what changes this step toward a more market-oriented agriculture will bring.

There is a good bit of evidence that a major part of American agriculture could function efficiently and profitably without anything like the amount and kind of government aid it has had.[27] Of course, important adjustments would have to be made, as the least efficient producers in every sector either went out of business or shifted to other products. The output of some products, such as peanuts, would probably be very seriously curtailed. Labor-intensive segments of American agriculture, such as dairy farming and wool raising, would suffer unless great changes were made in production techniques, as has happened in the case of poultry and eggs. Much of the subsidy for some crops has gone to big commercially operated farms; they are among the strong points in American agriculture and contribute much to its export potential but would probably often be capable of functioning profitably without this extra help. Though there are types of agriculture in which a few men and their machines do quite well, lower prices would hit small farmers more than big ones. If for political or social reasons the United States wants to preserve small farms even if they are not competitive, ways can be found of doing so that will minimize the cost of farm policy and not maximize it as is done when prices are put at a level that gives more efficient producers windfall profits at the cost of consumers and taxpayers and leads to surpluses which add to the expense.

For quite a long time an impressive body of economic opinion has supported the view that the best way to subsidize agriculture is through income payments rather than support prices. The resistance to the idea from farmers and others has been equally impressive, though not always clearly explained. Part of the objection seems to be a feeling that a direct "handout" would be more humiliating than the more roundabout subvention to which we have become habituated. Fear that an easily identifiable subsidy that had to be voted by Congress would be vulnerable to attack probably fills out the picture. From the point of view of the public interest, these understandable attitudes should be subordinated to the advantages of the income subsidy. These are, in brief, the ability to match needs and assistance quite precisely; less distortion of production and prices than under the old system; less need for import barriers and export subsidies; better guidance from the market; flexibility and relative precision in the use of public payments to achieve the aims of public policy. As the farming population shrinks, the idea of income support may become

27. Oscar Zaglits estimated in 1967 that if both price supports and export subsidies were eliminated, "the United States would remain a major exporter" of all the important products then being exported under subsidy except for dairy products. "Agricultural Trade and Trade Policy," in *Foreign Trade and Agricultural Policy,* cited, p. 160. D. Gale Johnson's estimate of the balance of effects was quoted on p. 287.

politically more palatable. One of the advantages of income support is its selectivity, a feature that is only clumsily introduced into price supports by such a device as limiting the total payments that can be made to a producer.

There are disadvantages in trying to rationalize farm policy on a national basis. The distortions in trade introduced by the policies of other countries make it difficult to assess the optimum pattern for American agriculture. The case for keeping out subsidized imports remains strong, and that for matching the export subsidies of others in third markets has a certain cogency. Both help to confuse the issue about the long-run interests of the United States in more ways than one. It is harder to be convincing about the wisdom of lowering American support prices if European farmers are guaranteed prices twice as high. "World prices" stop being helpful guides when protection, subsidies, and aid narrow the free market for all but a few products. There is a risk that the country that tries to formulate a farm policy that truly economizes will find itself becoming the residual adjuster to the uneconomic policies of others.

It should not be impossible to overcome these difficulties if a few basic facts are kept in mind. First, the reason for continuing to move American farm policy away from its past method and character is to increase American welfare and strengthen the national economy, not to do a good turn for the rest of the world. Second, the proposal is not to create the kind of *laissez faire* that would throw farmers entirely onto the market to receive what the Physiocrats called their *bon prix*. There are good domestic economic and social reasons for rejecting such a course, and the existing distortion of world agricultural production limits its rationality. The aim is much better put another way: "the overriding requirement is that the economic criterion of efficiency—of proper resource allocation—be restored to its place of primacy in making agricultural policies. . . . public management of agriculture [should] simulate in the results it obtains the kind of resource utilization which would prevail if this were a more competitive world."[28] Third, the rationalization of American agriculture is not equivalent to its elimination; by any reasonable reckoning the United States must be counted as a major agricultural producer for as long ahead as anyone can see. The kinds of changes discussed here will make it a more efficient producer and in many ways increase its potential as an agricultural exporter.

The realization of that potential depends on others as well as itself.

---

28. John Coppock, *North Atlantic Policy: The Agricultural Gap* (New York: Twentieth Century Fund, 1963), p. 189.

The improvement of domestic farm policy should be combined with the active pursuit of three objectives in foreign economic policy. Where possible, negotiations should aim to remove foreign barriers to American farm exports. If that is not possible, at least in the short run, in dealing with CAP Europe, the United States should actively counter any extension of the CAP that would worsen the position of American exports to Europe. The third, and simultaneous, element of American policy would be to work for international understandings on some or many aspects of national farm policies of the sort that would improve the allocation of resources and make it easier to lower trade barriers.

COMMON POLICIES FOR AGRICULTURE IN A WORLD SETTING

There will sometimes be conflicts between the domestic and foreign agricultural policies proposed for the United States and also among the elements of the foreign policy. They involve some nice distinctions. For example, export subsidies to compensate for artificially high domestic prices are to be eschewed, but to hold a market against subsidized competition they might be justified. Some of the conflicts are superficial. There is no real incompatibility between countervailing duties and other import restrictions to keep out foreign surpluses offered at sacrifice prices and the principle of keeping home prices at a level that does not require high protection. The conduct of these policies will be plagued by such questions as whether eventual agreement will be made more likely by intensifying a present dispute or playing it down. The art of this kind of diplomacy will be to find ways of making the domestic and international reinforce one another. For example, a European policy that left opportunities for American feed grain sales to grow might be matched by an American dairy policy that did not restrict imports of European specialty cheeses. Reforms of the CAP might, at least sometimes, be linked with international agreements on price ceilings, income support, and possibly production controls. Political sensitivity will be needed to insure that external pressures are not counterproductive.

Such results cannot be counted on; they will certainly not be achieved smoothly. But the chances for cooperation are helped by a shift in emphasis in the farm policies of the industrialized countries. For quite a long time they were almost all caught up in policies "inspired much more by concern for assuring farmers of markets and of prices that cover their costs than by attention to increasing the productivity of farming, which would have been the right method—though more painful in the short and medium run—of assuring the survival and progress of viable units."[29] Now all are feeling, to some degree, the need to "improve the structures"—i.e., to make more units viable. It will be more natural for governments to try to make these changes by national action than by international agreement, but either way there are some opportunities for linking the two. Whether the opportunities are taken or not, some increase in friction between the United States and Europe is likely. A reasonable economic and political perspective on agriculture will help to keep matters in proportion.

It has been said that the industrial countries are rich enough to afford bad agricultural policies. Past performance certainly bears that out and so does any reasonable look into the future. The 95 per cent of the American people who do not live on farms can afford to support the 5 per cent who do in almost any way they choose. In Europe the proportions are different but the principle is the same. But such a calculation is no criterion of policy. Ragnar Nurkse once said that the world is not rich enough to ignore the advantage of doing something more efficiently. There are gains to be had from rationalizing agriculture, and it is only sensible to try to obtain them. The aim is not to take something away from the agricultural minority and to give to the others but to arrange life in unprecedentedly rich and industrialized countries so that there is more for everybody, including those who perform the essential functions of producing crops and raising livestock. It is not a matter of penalizing farming but of modernizing it.

Such reasoning may be slow to command assent, and it could well be argued that if the industrialized countries insist on having bad farm policies, they should at least not fight about them. As the economies of the industrialized countries become more closely meshed, occasions for disputes increase at the same time that common interests grow. Fights about farm policies that jeopardize the solution of other problems could be costly. An armistice might be in order, especially since the main cost of bad farm policies is paid by the domestic population of each country. But the idea does not seem very realistic. Burdens are shifted, interests are damaged, and national political processes require governments to act; and each action produces its predictable reaction. One can hardly imagine a government in Washington sitting still for the sake of "harmony" while Europe intensified the protectionism of the CAP. Moreover, it may well be

29. Luc Fauvel, "Quarante Ans de Politique des Marchés," *Revue d'Economie Politique*, March-April 1969, p. 463. The phrase in the next sentence comes from p. 464.

that an armistice (which can be made to look like "sweeping the issues under the rug") would accomplish less in the long run than an effort to blunt the sharpness of the clashes by restraint and compromise while at the same time finding new ways to make adjustments that would eventually remove some of the causes of the trouble. The record of past negotiations in agriculture and the difficulties of the new approaches do not justify great optimism.

The farm issue is not just one between the United States and Europe. For Canada, Australia, and New Zealand, agricultural exports are relatively more important than for the United States; if markets for temperate zone farm products are reduced, their problems of adjustment could be serious. Of the three, Canada is best off with increasing exports of manufactured goods, great resources in lumber, minerals, and water power, and special opportunities in the American market. Australia, too, has moved toward diversification, though wheat, meat, and wool exports remain important. New Zealand has the farthest to go in finding alternatives to the export of dairy products, wool, and meat. The export problems of these countries have to be taken into account in the shaping of European and American farm policies, not only because of the common interest in the economic well-being of these advanced, relatively rich countries, but because as efficient producers of a number of agricultural products, they can contribute to the welfare and economic strength of the whole free world—if they are permitted to.

The position of the poor countries is also highly relevant to what the rich do about agriculture. One possibility is that they will offer opportunities to reduce the strains of the competitive disposition of surpluses created by agricultural support policies in Europe and the United States. However, it is no longer as sure as it seemed at one time that the most industrialized countries will for a long time to come have to provide a high proportion of the food of the least industrialized countries. The size of the problem appears to have changed, thanks to a technological revolution in agriculture which greatly improves the chances of some less developed countries becoming self-sufficient in food. For the time being, however, food shipments from Europe and the United States to the poor countries remain important. Some are sold commercially, some provided as aid, and some are sold on terms and at prices that blur the distinction. It is not always easy to determine who benefits and to what degree from these practices. Serious questions arise among the donors or sellers as well as between them and the recipients. The substance of the issues cannot be examined here, but they have a bearing both on the level and pattern of production that is a reasonable target for the rich countries and on the prospects of cooperation or friction between them.

Close to the heart of the issues discussed in this chapter is the question of the rich countries' willingness to import farm products from the poor countries. Plentiful cheap labor and much land (not all of it so good) do not necessarily give the less developed countries advantages over the heavily capitalized, highly skilled farmers of North America and Europe. But there is no doubt that they can produce some things more cheaply and could contribute to their own development by selling them in greater quantities than now to the industrial countries. In addition to purely tropical products, which have problems of their own, there are some that compete directly with the output of farmers in the industrialized countries. Sugar is the most important, but oilseeds, cotton, rice, fruit, tobacco, and, for some countries, meat are also involved. The list could undoubtedly be lengthened if producers in the less developed countries felt sure that they would be allowed to compete in the markets of the rich countries. But agrarian protection in the industrialized countries is a major block. The same barriers that are obstacles to the efficient use of resources in the developed countries stand in the way of the development of the poor countries. How serious the rich countries are about encouraging the development of the poor ones is a matter that will have to be discussed in another context. But if they really want to help, there is no sounder basis than to open their markets to the products the poor countries can produce and sell efficiently.

To do so for agricultural products, the industrialized countries would have to face the kinds of policy questions discussed in this chapter. Two possible conflicts would arise between taking steps favorable to the less developed countries and improving the conditions of farm production and trade in the industrialized countries themselves. One concerns the rather complicated matter of giving preferential treatment to the products of less developed countries, and that is better discussed elsewhere as part of the larger problem of trade policies to aid development. The other is a matter of priorities. That the difficulty of adjustment is likely to set the pace for the reduction of agricultural protection has been a commonplace of this chapter. There is a sense in which a country may feel able to make only a certain amount of adjustment at once. The limit might be thought of as being set by the difficulty of shaping and executing careful policies, or by finances, or, more likely, by how much can be asked of the farmers at any one time. If there is in fact some such political or psychological quantum of possible adjustment, how is it to be divided between measures that will widen the market for the products of poor countries and of rich ones? It is clear, I think, that the priority must be given to measures that would help the poor; they need it more and the gain in total welfare would probably be greater. But the issues will rarely be posed very neatly and the dichotomy may often be false.[30]

Coming on top of the already great difficulties Europe and the United States may have in making adjustments in agriculture and agricultural policy, such questions complicate matters but do not justify inaction. They stress the desirability of dealing with agricultural problems internationally but do not undermine the argument that the United States can make significant progress by reforming its own policies even if others move more slowly. They underline a conclusion implicit in much that has already been said: there are opportunities for progress, but it is unlikely that we are on the eve of a great revolution in farm policy.

New Roads and Old Ruts

This chapter has traced a strange course. It started with a picture of agriculture as a "hopeless case," falling outside the process of cooperation in the liberalization of international economic relations in the postwar period. It concludes with the thought that the way agriculture can be brought into that process is not by a "catching up" but by a leap into a kind of cooperation that has not yet been established in other fields. Past chapters have shown that in their relations concerning such things as trade, nontariff barriers, investment, and the balance of payments adjustment process the industrialized countries will increasingly have to deal internationally with matters that have always been regarded as primarily domestic. This is the result of progress. This chapter suggests that something similar is true of farm policy, but as a result of lack of progress.

Whether anything like a new approach is in fact attempted may well depend on what Europe does next about the combination of new and old factors called the Common Agricultural Policy, and how the United States reacts to the new obstacles that have been put in

30. Need priority for sugar hinder adjustment in wheat if a switch of land-use from one to the other is not involved? Should those who stop competing with the products of poor countries be given added protection against the products of rich ones (or allowed to switch to products already protected)? Are there advantages in moving on a number of fronts at once since each separate slice of adjustment is likely to take some time? If adjustment is made easier by a matching action by another country (so that you gain exports as well as imports), the partner is likely to be another rich country rather than a poor one from which little reciprocity can be expected.

the way of agricultural trade which are so similar in many ways to the obstacles American policy has created in the past. Though it is hard to escape the conclusion that this international clash will be of decisive importance, whether it leads to constructive or destructive action, the chapter suggests that the most cogent arguments for changing farm policies concern not international trade but how each country can best improve the welfare of its own people. For the United States, at least, much can be done by unilateral action alone. No significant broad international action can be taken unless it is supported by national action to clean up the situation in each country.

Oddly, the study of the poor record of agriculture brings into relief a point that is often obscured by the study of the good record of liberalization and cooperation in money, investment, and trade in manufactured goods. Almost always the latter story is told in terms of bargaining, of *do ut des*, and of the balance of reciprocal advantage. Problems are analyzed in terms of each country's concern with what the others are doing. What is lost sight of more often than not is the benefit each country gets from elimination of measures that penalize foreigners. The agricultural story, being one of failure, cannot be told in terms of reciprocal advantage, and so the mind turns to some fundamentals that are not limited to agriculture.

PART III

Choices for the '70s and Beyond

9

Building Blocs or Stumbling Blocs?

The integration of Western Europe, limited though it is, is one of the great facts of the postwar world. Not only part of "the Matter of Europe," as medieval writers would have said, it changes the structure of global relations. In the eyes of many people, it is also an indication of things to come, the first major step toward the spread of regionalism throughout much of the world. About this last idea, one may have some doubts, but Western Europe's regionalism and what may come of it poses central questions about the future organization of the world economy and the relation of the industrialized countries to one another.[1] They fall into three groups.

The first concerns the future of European integration. How broad and deep is it likely to become? What attitude should the United States take toward the new possibilities (or uncertainties)?

1. Regionalism has become a loose term. It should refer to the grouping of nations with some kind of geographical link, as in the European Community, but the idea can be stretched, as in OECD, or strained, as in EFTA; and if the sterling area is a "regional" grouping then the geographical element has become haphazard. Not all less-than-universal groupings are thought of as regional, e.g., GATT or the IMF. For present purposes, a group of countries according one another treatment denied to outsiders and not so numerous that they cover most of the free world will be called regional, when that is convenient, in contrast to GATT, the IMF, etc. The economic regionalism discernible in the less developed parts of the world and among the Communist countries is quite different from that of Western Europe and will be considered in later books.

The second set of questions concerns the outsiders. Who these are depends in part on the answers to the first set of questions. They may be European countries, but if most of Western Europe becomes more or less integrated, the key outsiders will be the United States, Japan, and Canada. In either case, Australia and New Zealand present special problems. Should the outsiders, whether their number is larger or smaller, try to form a grouping of their own, or perhaps more than one? If not, what policies should they follow toward the integrated area?

The third set of questions concerns the industrialized countries as a whole. Should the next step in "regionalism" be to link them in some kind of association? Or is the more promising course to adapt existing organizations, such as GATT, the IMF, and the OECD, to the new shape of the world resulting from Western European integration?

The answers to these questions, as readers will discover, are rather "iffy." Though the issues are architectonic, involving alternative ways of organizing the world economy, the case for choosing one structure rather than another depends on a whole series of pragmatic judgments, some of which will have to be made in circumstances that cannot be predicted.

EUROPE, MORE OR LESS UNITED

The progress of European integration has defied accurate prediction. The French proposal for a coal and steel pool startled the world; its translation into actuality without great dilution was hardly less surprising. When the treaty that would have created a European Defense Community was defeated, in 1954, the tide of integration seemed to be receding but in a surprisingly short time the European Economic Community was established. At the time, the companion treaty that created the European Atomic Energy Community seemed in many ways more important and stronger—but was not. The European Economic Community moved far faster than anyone expected in tearing down barriers to trade among members. Expected to lag, France led in building the Community. By late 1962 England's entry seemed almost certain but was ruled out for the foreseeable future by a few words General de Gaulle spoke at the beginning of 1963. The resulting strains seemed likely to produce, if nothing worse, a standstill in the Community, but in fact big steps toward integration were taken in the Common Agricultural Policy. In the latter '60s, stagnation seemed to give the lie to earlier confident predictions that each step in integration would create new problems that could only be resolved by a further step toward integration.

Of course, each of the unexpected turns had a perfectly rational explanation. There is no need to give up trying to assess future possibilities in a systematic manner, but a glance backward makes one wary and suggests that policy must be ready to cope with unexpected developments. The departure of de Gaulle and the change in France's economic position led to a *relance* of European integration, but its probable pace is hard to judge and even some of the directions in which it will move are uncertain.[2] The entry of Britain into the Community will alter some problems and the balance of forces as well. However clear certain aspects of some key problems appear to be at the beginning of the '70s, there is no way to take full account of the intricate interplay over the years to come among issues and the interests of member governments: agriculture, monetary policy, technology; membership in the Community; national power versus Community power; the possession of nuclear weapons. A major solvent for hard problems is the political will to "make Europe." Who can say with any sense of assurance whether in the mid-'70s that drive will be as strong as it was in the late '50s or as weak as in the late '60s? Judgment about the degree and character of European integration a decade from now, or at any point in between, must be highly qualified. American policy toward European integration must, therefore, be able to cope with a fairly wide range of circumstances.

Matters are somewhat simplified by the fact that one can be quite sure the progress of European integration will not be decided by American policy. The time is long past when American support, and for a time even active leadership, was a crucial factor in bringing the countries of Western Europe closer together. How far and how fast they go, and what form their integration takes, is up to the Europeans, as it has been for some years. American approval and encouragement may help but cannot be decisive on the essentials. On some political and military issues which it is not feasible to explore in this book—for example, a possible understanding between France and Britain on nuclear matters—the American voice would be much more important. With regard to economic policy, American leverage would probably be greater if the United States were trying to hamper European integration than if it were helping. But negative forces unite as well as divide. More than one person has thought it would be easier to unify Europe against the Americans than with their help. The Suez crisis of 1956–57 did much to stimulate the will to integrate—

2. It was not only de Gaulle who stood in the way of the rapid progress of integration. On first meeting his Common Market colleagues after de Gaulle's departure, a French diplomat is reported to have said, "We have lost a general; you have lost an alibi." Quoted by Maurice Faure, *Le Monde*, September 6, 1969.

and not just because Europe learned fear about its oil supply.

But why should the United States disapprove of Western European integration and resist it? Because, some would say, we have had a taste of the way a partially integrated Europe can damage American interests and can expect a stronger, more integrated Europe to be more damaging still. Suppose, for example, a union comprising the whole of Western Europe including Britain were headed by new de Gaulles who commanded as much support in the other countries as the General did in France at the height of his power. Possessing an independent nuclear force, such leaders might believe that the best interests of Europe would be served not only by refusing close strategic ties with the United States but also by resisting the efforts of the superpowers to "run the world" by reaching agreements to restrict the use of arms. Aiming at self-sufficiency in agriculture and energy, resisting the spread of American influence that they thought came with investment and freer trade, anxious to "keep the dollar in its place" and make gold as good as it once was, such a Europe would set its hand against most of the main aims of American economic policy. In relations with the less developed part of the world it would use its wealth and purchasing power to tie certain countries closely to it, thus shutting out American influence in some places and giving no help in dealing with the difficult problems of other great areas. Such a Europe might not only damage American interests by what it did, but also threaten them through the illusions it might develop about its security in the face of Soviet power.

Instead of helping to create such a Golem, would the United States not be better off with a policy that helped perpetuate a weaker, more divided Europe, some of whose countries would inevitably be more dependent on the United States, more in agreement with its views, and more amenable to its pressures? Sensible national policies could make such a Europe stable and prosperous; it could benefit from the same reduction of barriers to trade and payments and multiplication of economic contacts throughout the free world that the United States seeks. As Jacob Viner once said, our view of a divided Europe would be different if instead of Balkanization we spoke of Scandinavianization. And if the policies Europeans followed were not benign, the price would be paid mostly by Europeans; the effects on the United States would be less serious than those of measures taken by an entity that controlled the resources and markets of all Europe.

Most American advocates of European integration have had a third, contrasting vision. They have imagined a united Europe that saw its interests well served by reducing barriers to trade with the rest of the world, lowering farm prices for the sake of efficiency and economy, and cooperating with the United States in the creation of a workable monetary system. Such a Europe might well understand the importance of sharing the burdens of military expenses (and the decisions from which they arise), and would continue to contribute to the development of the poor countries, by aid and trade, on a scale commensurate with its wealth. With internal barriers removed, Europe could allocate its resources more efficiently than when national economic policies clashed. Large European enterprises would grow up that could compete on equal terms with American companies and spread their investments world-wide without fear of the effects of American investment in Europe. No docile partner, such a Europe would have a good influence on American policies, requiring its just *quid pro quo* in bargaining, making cooperation the sensible way of reducing conflicts of interest, creating economic competition, and challenging the United States to emulate its performance.

Americans are not free to choose among these alternatives. The United States is no Pygmalion. It lacks the ability to design the perfect Europe, much less bring it to life. (Even Pygmalion needed supernatural help for that.) Europeans will create Europe, and it will be for a long time a Europe that, in policy and attitudes, will be somewhere between the extreme models sketched above. It may well be much more integrated than now but will not be truly united. National divisions will persist and may make integration a very slow process. There are conflicting forces in Europe and people who have different views of their own and Europe's interest. The willingness to act as Europeans instead of as nationalists fluctuates and is different for different things. The internal pressures for integration are quite real; but the economic advantages it offers can be obtained only by a certain disturbance of the status quo which people are not always willing to accept. Some of the external pressures for integration are weaker than they were in the past; but others are likely to increase, especially if friction with the United States grows. It is not easy to predict, however, whether having a greater voice in the world, more power, and more ability to "stand up to the Americans" will appeal to Europeans more than the prospects of a quiet life. It is possible that the limited integration so far achieved in Western Europe may be partially undone, but it is more likely to be deepened and broadened, perhaps rather sharply. Some of the results may be undesirable in American eyes, and sometimes American interests will be hurt. The United States should resist such developments and try to offset them if it fails. I can find little ground, however, for reversing the judgment of 1947 and afterwards that the United States has more to gain from the advance of European integration than from its interruption or reversal. Among the issues with which this book has been principally concerned can be found a good bit of evidence to support this conclusion, for it is clear that in the management of the world economy of the '70s, a Western Europe approaching economic unity can play a more constructive part than one dominated by divisions.

There are, however, some changes from the late '40s and early '50s in the nature of the American interest in European integration. Then there was great concern about European security, recovery, and the German problem (whether that was conceived as finding a way to live with the division of Germany by fitting the Western part firmly into the free world, or insuring that reunification, if it took place, should not put Germany in a position to dominate Europe). To achieve these aims close economic cooperation among the European countries was regarded as essential and would, it was widely believed, lead to some kind of political unity. Since then, as Harold van B. Cleveland pointed out in 1966, "the ends which European union was to serve according to the classical doctrine have been accomplished by other means, sufficiently so, at any rate, to remove the urgency and dampen the crusading spirit which once characterized the European movement."[3] He was writing primarily about political union and assuming that in economic matters "the Community will go on much as before," but his argument can be extended to economic integration as well. Europe is prosperous; it could probably become more so by further integration, but is it very important to the United States that Europe should move rapidly in that direction? Clearly the urgency of the earlier period is lacking. Even one who believes, as I do, that a Europe more unified than it now is could help make the world economy function better must admit that, while this would be desirable from an American point of view, the objective is not on the same footing as the need for intra-European cooperation in the '40s and '50s.

It is important to be clear that the loss of urgency cannot be turned into an argument against integration or for disintegration. There is a connection between the partial integration Europe has achieved and the solution of its old problems. Not important for military security against external threats, where the key role has been American, integration almost certainly contributed to political stability and the absence of warlike quarrels among Western European countries. It played an important part in economic improvement

3. *The Atlantic Idea and Its European Rivals* (New York: McGraw-Hill, for the Council on Foreign Relations, 1966), p. 132. The quotation in the next sentence comes from p. 130.

and looks as if it had been vital, politically and economically, in making it possible for Western Germany to get along as well as it has without finding any assured solution of the German problem. Some degree of disintegration (for example, in agriculture) may be compatible with keeping all of these gains, but clearly a reversal of the whole process would bring new risks and dangers.

The reduction in the American ability to further European integration and the lessening of the sense of urgency that gave European integration such a high and compelling priority in the postwar years are complementary developments. They mesh well with a third shift, one of emphasis. From the beginning the United States has been concerned with Europe's place in the world economy; that was a key element in the Bretton Woods picture, the British loan, the Marshall Plan, the Kennedy Round and, indeed, the interest in European integration itself. But integration is ambivalent; bringing the participants closer together, it at the same time divides them more sharply from other countries in certain respects. Consequently, an American policy that favors both European integration and the creation of an open, nondiscriminatory world economy has in it conflicting tendencies. Keeping the two tendencies in the right balance is essential to the success of the dual policy and can be very difficult, the more so since the "right" formula is likely to change as time passes. Before the move to integration was well launched, efforts to remove barriers within Europe had a clear priority (reinforced by the circumstances of the dollar shortage). Now, and for some years past, the main emphasis of American policy has properly been on the external aspects of integration—on how Europe fits into the world.

It was never American policy—though some critics have made it sound that way—to favor European integration "at any price." It is true, though, that the United States accepted, even encouraged, measures that were in some respects damaging to its interests (for instance, in trade discrimination and agriculture) in part because they contributed to European integration. There was a case, to be sure, for believing that the short-run economic loss would be more than offset by the long-run gains from European growth and prosperity, both in direct economic relations and in the improved functioning of the world economy. Even if that "compensation" fell short, some or all of the economic loss could be written off against broader political and security gains credited to integration—and, it was generally conceded, the United States could afford it. Equally difficult calculations will have to be made in the future; they are inescapable because of the multiple ends of foreign policy and inherent in a policy that favors lines of action that sometimes conflict. Since, however, major "internal" steps in European integration will rarely be determined by American action, the United States has a greater freedom of action than it once had in putting its primary emphasis on the avoidance of damage to outsiders (the United States and others) even if the result includes some slowing of integration.

It may seem high-sounding to say that the United States should work at making the promise come true that European integration will benefit the international economy, but that course is also a practical and rather mundane one. For one thing, the American ability to influence constructively what Europe does is likely to be greater at the intersection of the internal and external economies —tariffs, farm policy, investment, etc.—than at the core of integration. For another, the United States has good, selfish reasons for pursuing such a course, since it has to be more concerned with exports and the strength of the dollar than it was in the '40s and '50s. In addition, the United States has both a direct and a more general interest in seeing to it that the advantages of European integration are not paid for by non-Europeans. As the compromises necessary for further integration become increasingly intricate, the tendency of the European governments to make bargains that throw the burdens of adjustment on outsiders will not diminish and may well grow. By providing some counterweight, the United States not only protects its interests and those of the others but strengthens the position of the people in Europe who want both integration and a liberal policy toward the rest of the world.

Mention of these "internal allies"—or potential allies—of American policy, the Europeans who are concerned with an open international economy for the industrialized countries, points to still other dimensions of the problem. There is a real European interest in the removal of barriers to trade and payments in other parts of the world; without it the progress made so far would not have been possible. A European contribution to further progress in the same direction can only be expected if the United States continues to pursue policies that offer opportunities and not just objections to what Europe is doing. They must be policies that are more than the pursuit of narrowly conceived American advantages. If issues repeatedly arise as choices between integration and an "outward-looking" policy for the Community, people in Europe who are interested in both objectives will be hard put to find a course of action they can consistently support. They are not likely to find it as easy as Americans to believe that the "external" liberalization is always to be given priority over the removal of obstacles to the creation of a true economic community in Europe. The aim must be to find ways of reconciling the pursuit of both objectives. Sometimes that will mean pressing harder for integration, not moderating it. For instance, a more effectively integrated European Community would probably find it easier to lower farm prices and reduce the level of protection than one in which these things can only be done by the kinds of compromises among national governments that have thus far shaped the Common Agricultural Policy. But to get that degree of integration would require bargains on other matters, some of which would hit outsiders. And so the contradictions continue.

Other outsiders besides the United States are also affected by European integration and often much more severely. Their support and participation in finding satisfactory solutions can only be secured if the American approach to European regionalism is broadly enough conceived to accommodate more than narrow American interests. It may well be to the advantage of the United States to find ways of insuring that the attack on European policies does not become a purely bilateral affair. Combined with what was said in the previous paragraph about the need to enlist European support as well, these considerations suggest that American policy toward European regionalism ought to be thought of at least partly in terms of the shaping of broad agreements about international economic cooperation and, if that proves necessary, the reshaping of international economic organizations. It is, in short, a process of fitting regionalism into a revised Bretton Woods world.

The translation of these broad principles of American policy into concrete terms has to some extent already been made in earlier chapters concerning trade, investment, money, the Common Agricultural Policy, and, in less detail, such matters as energy and technology. Those discussions have also made it clear that this process will not always be easy. Though it is up to the Europeans how far they will carry their integration, one of the main motive forces in a number of cases will be to provide a common front to the United States or to "reduce dependence on the dollar," or whatever. In discussing monetary issues, we saw the opportunities for friction, in agriculture their inevitability. And sometimes, if the Europeans are concentrating on relations with one another, they may all but ignore American interests in what they do. But whichever emphasis is dominant in Europe, accommodations with the United States are possible and it is on these that American policy should focus.

New Members and Others

What has been said about the deepening of European integration applies very largely to its possible broadening as well. The conflicting tendencies in American policy were brought sharply into focus by the possibility of British membership in the Community. That question was long ago thought through by those who shaped and supported the American policy of favoring British membership. The reasoning was essentially the same as that which favored European integration in general in spite of the fact that there would be some disadvantages for American trade, especially in agriculture. If entry into the Community leads to a rise in British growth rates and a durable strengthening of the country's balance of payments, there would be substantial gains for the international economy as a whole. Even if the improvement of the pound's position proves to be a slow process and there are further calls on American help, the United States will gain if the Continental countries' interest in the matter has been sharpened by Britain's having joined them.

It has long been argued that British influence would help make the Community "outward-looking," interested in the benefits of trade liberalization, and so receptive to American initiatives in that direction. Maybe so; certainly the United States should encourage that possibility by what it proposes and the opportunities it offers. But one must be skeptical. The strength of liberalizing forces is not what it once was in Britain. One element in the willingness to go into Europe is a shift in priorities away from other parts of the world. Faced with the problems of adjusting to stronger French and German competition and anxious to exploit their new opportunities, British businessmen will not be eager to tear down the tariff wall they have just scaled. Though British interest in reforming the CAP should be strong, London's influence on that matter may not be great at first. A more reliable line of argument is that the addition of Britain will improve the Community's ability to play a constructive part in managing the world economy. The possibility is clearest in monetary affairs but even there rests on two different assumptions. One is that British membership does not weaken the Community (for example, through difficulty with the pound). The other is that monetary integration is carried far enough to permit the Community to function with a good deal of unanimity. One can, of course, uncork a bad genie as well as a good one. A unified Europe with a strong balance of payments position, the skills of the City of London, and Britain's votes in the International Monetary Fund added to those of the Six (and perhaps more) could be a formidable opponent for the United States in monetary matters. But, like the "bad" Europe that can be imagined without Britain, this is a danger that policy should work against, not an inescapable Moloch.

As this is written, it is uncertain which other countries are likely to follow Britain into the Community, though several have said they would like to do so. None of these is a Britain in economic importance or in the effect its joining would have on the Community's place in the world. But the arguments that made the United States look with favor on British entry can hardly be reversed if the issue is the membership of Ireland, Denmark, Norway, or, indeed, any other European country. For Austria and Finland, the issue of full membership can hardly arise since the U.S.S.R. is in a position to object. Sweden, Switzerland, and Iceland are free agents but may seek an association that falls short of full membership, while Spain, Portugal, and Yugoslavia are also not soon likely to be candidates. If special arrangements are to be worked out, the problems that arise are in the first instance for the Community and the countries concerned, but the United States has an interest. Taken together, the smaller countries of Western Europe have in recent years provided a market for slightly more American exports than Britain and something under half as much as the Common Market. Over one-quarter of American sales to them has been made up of farm products, a number of which would come under the Common Agricultural Policy.

The main concern of the outside countries that are not negotiating for membership is usually trade and sometimes other economic relations with the Community. The Community is the largest market for most of them. Though they do not seem to have done badly, they fear the disadvantages that being outside may bring in the future. Since their own markets are small, they have little to offer the Community. Weak bargaining positions make them vulnerable to pressures to settle for second best. They are often receptive to the idea of special arrangements by which, without meeting quite all of the qualifications of Community membership, they would stop being complete outsiders and gain some privileges by granting some. Within the Community there are always special interests that resist the general freeing of trade with outsiders: the Italians are concerned about Spanish oranges, the French about Norwegian aluminum, the paper industry about Scandinavia in general, and groups of farmers about Danish pigs, poultry, and butter. In addition, there is the more general argument that the distinction between members and nonmembers should not be blurred and that only those who assume the full obligations of joining the Community should have full access to its benefits, including those of trade and agriculture.

In these circumstances, it is possible that the United States will be faced with a Community, including Britain and perhaps some additional members, that is engaged in weaving a network of understandings with other European countries at least on trade, probably on agriculture, and maybe on other matters as well. Predominantly bilateral, with the Community as one party, each of these agreements will be tailored to a special set of circumstances. Privileges will be exchanged which are often not extended to other countries. Some will be valued precisely because of that; some will have been granted only as a price to be paid to get something that was badly wanted— usually freer access to the Common Market. The classical process by which compromises are reached partly at the expense of outsiders will be much in evidence. The results are not likely to conform well to principles of multilateral equal treatment. In terms of the general lines of American trade policy, such a development would be objectionable. Though the amount of trade involved in each case would be small, the cumulative effect on other countries as well as the United States would be of some concern. The damage to the already eroded principle of equal treatment would be appreciable (see chap. 10, pp. 358–64). The choices for the United States might be between going along with a bad arrangement and retaliating against it by means that introduced still more trade barriers and discrimination.

General political arguments about the benefits of European integration that have helped to solve similar problems in the past hardly seem to apply. After all, the reason for most of the special arrangements would be the unwillingness of one or both of the parties to expand the Community. It would seem reasonable for the United States to take the view that a country must either be in or out of the Community and, if out, on an equal basis with others. But what American interest would be served by objecting to an arrangement that helped Austria or Finland (who are not free to become members) and strengthened their links with Western Europe? In other cases as well, would the United States really gain by opposing arrangements that small friendly countries thought essential to their welfare? Moreover, whatever the political leaders of the moment may say about their intentions, the intensification of connections among European countries may prove to be a step toward the kind of strong and more unified European economy the United States would like to see.

It is not surprising that Americans who agree in general on what are the right lines of policy toward Europe should disagree on this issue, and on specific cases. One group says that those who oppose any special arrangements are "too commercial-policy minded" and let their ideology of equal treatment blind them to broader issues and true American interests. The other group accuses its opponents of believing that anything Europeans claim contributes to integration is automatically in the American interest. It is doubtful whether the problem can be solved in general terms; certainly no single formula is likely to prove satisfactory given the differences among cases and the circumstances in which they are likely to arise. At best one might indicate a few aims that ought to guide American policy, without thereby suggesting that they can be made fully effective in all cases or that they may not be overridden by other considerations in some instances.

Except where there are clearly recognizable obstacles, as in the Austrian and Finnish cases, American policy ought to presume that unless countries become members of the Community their relations with it should conform to the rules governing their relations with other countries as well. That would leave open the possibility of their forming with the Community true free trade areas that conformed to GATT rules. Where free trade was unacceptable, nondiscriminatory tariff reductions on the goods of special interest to the smaller countries should be employed. The Community's agreement with Yugoslavia shows that this can be done. To the extent that circumstances seem to justify some discriminatory arrangements, it would be preferable to treat them as exceptions to a rule rather than to act as if the principle itself could be ignored.

The issues of American policy raised by the Community's preferential trading relations with some less developed countries fall outside the bounds set for this book. One should note, however, that they have a bearing on the Community's policy toward poor European states that are not members. The Community's trade treaties with Spain and Yugoslavia and its earlier association agreements with Greece and Turkey[4] have a connection with its agreements with Israel and the Maghreb and the possibilities being explored with other Arab states. Although references increase to the relation between these agreements and the beginnings of a somewhat vague

4. Judged unready for full membership in the Common Market, Greece and Turkey have from an early date been involved in long transitional arrangements during which barriers are slowly being reduced and special problems, such as those in agriculture, worked out. One finds the kinds of exceptions, special arrangements, and safeguards to meet special interests that I have suggested may arise in other cases. It may well be wondered why the two countries were chosen for this special status in the first place. In a dim picture one senses Greek and Turkish fears for their economies if they were put at a disadvantage in Western European markets; Community concern that Britain would add the two countries to its "side" in the economic division of Europe; American expectation that any setback to Greek and Turkish growth would only add to or prolong their need for the support the United States had long been giving to them. Not prominent in Community policy (or American policy toward the Community), the arrangements have a future that is hard to predict but is better considered in the context suggested above than as part of the possible future expansion of the Community.

"Mediterranean policy" on the part of the Community, what has been done so far seems primarily to reflect the feeling of a number of countries, in and out of Europe, that they need to come to terms with the Common Market and get the best access they can to what is at once a promising and a threatening entity.

In contrast to the mixed set of bilateral and discriminatory arrangements suggested earlier, Western Europe may yet move toward creating a free trade area including most countries on the Continent and with the Community (enlarged or not) as one of its members. In one form or another this possibility has been part of the common furniture of European cooperation for decades. Since the failure of the OEEC-sponsored negotiations for a comprehensive free trade area in 1958, the idea has never acquired much momentum, largely because it was seen as an alternative to British membership that was unacceptable to one side at one time and to the other at another time. Perhaps it is not surprising, then, that the idea should have re-emerged as a serious possibility when it appeared that British entry was assured. It was suggested first as a way of helping the EFTA countries that stayed outside the Community and would be hurt if duties were imposed on the entry of their goods into Britain, Denmark, and Norway. Then the thought was put forward that Denmark and Norway might be just as well satisfied to be in such a free trade area as to be in the Community. Although advanced as a way of overcoming some of the political opposition to joining the Community that existed in the two Scandinavian countries, the proposal also responded to the old fear among some champions of integration that the Community would be diluted if so many new countries were added at once.

Whether Denmark and Norway are in or out of the Community, a true industrial free trade area would be greatly preferable, from the point of view of the United States, to a series of special arrangements. The problems of the outsider being at a trade disadvantage and of the enlargement of the area of discrimination against him would still exist. However, the general liberalization required by a free trade area is likely to produce better results than the selective removal of trade barriers resulting from separate negotiations between the Community and individual countries (and avoid further damage to GATT rules as well). To insure this result, the United States and others would have to insist that the Europeans live up to GATT principles and not make so many exceptions that, in the name of creating a free trade area, they produced the same results as if they worked out the kind of special arrangements described above.

From the American point of view there would be a political or psychological gain in the Community's entering a free trade area. That action would weaken the claim that the common external tariff could not be regarded in quite the same way as a national tariff because it was part of the political cement of the Community. To be sure, free trade with relatively small neighbors, much of it following traditional patterns, is not the same thing as free trade with the United States, Japan, and the rest of the world—but it is a big step.

In fact it is a step that the United States should take as a signal that the time has come to think seriously about the elimination of tariffs on trade among the industrialized countries. There are, of course, any number of reasons why Europeans might be less than eager to move quickly in this direction while they are still adjusting to changes in trading relations inside Europe. The United States and Japan have not prepared themselves for such a step. For reasons made plain in chapter 5, further trade liberalization is not likely to be rapid or easy, but a big change in the relation of the Community to the rest of Europe provides an occasion and an impetus. There will, after all, have to be negotiations concerning the effects on American trade of the addition of members to the Community, association arrangements, or a European free trade area.[5] Taken in isolation, some of these might easily become niggling. Approached more broadly, they provide an opportunity to register the ending of a period when the highest achievement of European integration was the creation of a customs union.

American Flexibility

American policy must be able to deal not only with further major steps in European integration but also with a lack of progress in that direction. Even if the post-de Gaulle *relance* proves durable, it will be a long time before Europe has anything like an integrated economy. At best, progress will be irregular and different with respect to different matters. British entry will come in stages; there will be a period of transition before the full meaning of enlargement is apparent in the Community's internal and external relations. No set of clear-cut contingency plans in a policy-maker's file is likely to be adequate for dealing with the combination of slow progress toward integration, setbacks, and an uneven pace of development in different fields. Nevertheless, the United States will have to find ways of pursuing the aims of its foreign economic policy that will be workable whatever the state of European integration.

5. GATT's Contracting Parties would have to pass on whether a free trade area meets the Agreement's standards; discriminatory treatment would require a waiver; British (or other) adoption of the common external tariff would raise questions about the compensation due the United States for any worsening of the terms of entry of its products.

That means being able to deal with an integrated Europe (of whatever number) on some matters and with separate national governments on others, and sometimes with both, for issues do not always rise discretely, neatly divided into those which the Europeans are prepared to deal with together or separately. Very often the issues of foreign economic policy will have to be dealt with in a setting in which political and security issues are also much involved and may dominate the scene. In these matters European integration is even farther in the future. There can be no formula for dealing with such different cases, no calibrated table of values against which the elements of each situation can be measured to discover what is more important and what less. In these respects the future of American policy toward Europe is no different from much of its past or most other international relations.

OTHER GROUPINGS?

As Europe goes its way, what are the other industrialized countries to do, the outsiders? They have a common interest in mitigating the discrimination against themselves that results from European integration, mostly by working to reduce the trade barriers around the Community. But do their common interests go to the point of forming some kind of grouping among themselves?

The United States, Canada, and Japan—to name the key outsiders is to see how unlikely a combination they are for some sort of economic grouping or association, a customs union, or a free trade area.[6] Though they might find some compensation in an intensification of trade with one another on terms that put European competitors at a disadvantage, they could not by such means improve their access to the Common Market. Only negotiation with the Europeans could achieve that. While a certain coordination of bargaining tactics might be useful, working out an extensive agreement for some kind of integration would not only be the long way round to that end but would also involve a degree of travail that might well so preoccupy the three governments as to make effective negotiations with Europe impossible. Though a *club de sans club* has a certain attraction, it does not seem a very promising alternative to a policy of reducing barriers wherever they are found, including Europe.

In monetary affairs things are somewhat different. The Canadian

6. The possibilities and limitations of a tighter American-Canadian link were discussed in chapter 4, pp. 95–100. The relations between Japanese-American ties and the interest of each country in a multilateral world economy was examined in chapter 3, pp. 67–72.

and Japanese economies have been closely linked with the dollar and lacked the possibility Europe had of creating a currency bloc that would in some sense rival the dollar. Things may be different in the future. Monetary blocs need not respect geography; it is imaginable that Japan (though hardly Canada) might be tempted to lean toward a European arrangement quite different from what the United States preferred, though for a number of reasons touched on in preceding chapters this is not too likely. It would, of course, be in the American interest to keep both Japan and Canada in a "dollar area" if the point were reached where that term rather clearly distinguished one group of countries from another. But since a prior objective should be to try to avoid that kind of split, this defensive second-best possibility does not provide a basis for an American policy of bloc-building.

There is another possible grouping Americans have to consider, one embracing the whole Western Hemisphere (or as many countries of it as would be interested). This is an idea with a history behind it; it has appeared at intervals throughout the century and has always been put away again. It emerged strongly when it seemed that the Nazis might conquer all Western Europe. It is heard again now with particular emphasis on the advantage for the Latin American countries of having special access to the United States market to help their development and offset the privileges that African countries have in Europe and some Asian ones in Britain. A proper assessment of the arguments for such an approach, its possibilities and difficulties, belongs in another book that examines the whole range of American relations with the less developed countries. A blunt summary of the conclusions, as I see them now, can be put in a few sentences. The grouping is less natural than it seems and not as acceptable to the Latin Americans as is often thought. To overcome the many objections to moving toward a Western Hemisphere common market, one would have to demonstrate that that course was the least bad of the feasible ways of ordering relations among the rich and poor countries as a whole. The contribution to solving the problems that arise from the fact that the United States is outside an integrating Europe would not be great.

Another idea with a history—and as many shapes as Proteus—no longer needs to be considered in any detail. The idea of a North Atlantic Free Trade Area or Association (NAFTA) has always rested primarily on the wish to provide Britain with an alternative to membership in the European Community. With Britain in the Community, that kind of NAFTA is nonexistent. If, contrary to expectations as these lines are written, Britain should not enter the Community, the old question would re-open. But it would no longer be the same question; there would be a new issue, the character of which would be largely shaped by the reasons Britain did not enter and the reactions, in Britain and abroad, to the failure to do so. To postulate all the hypotheses that would be needed to consider alternative possibilities would go far beyond the limits of this book.

There are, however, two kinds of NAFTA that could be organized with Britain *in* the Community. One underlines the geographical emphasis of the label. There is, according to the proponents of this model, an Atlantic Community, rooted in history and culture and corresponding to fundamental political and economic divisions in the modern world. For their welfare and security, the countries around the Atlantic should cooperate very closely, as in fact they have done in the postwar period. In trade the natural culmination of the liberalization that has already taken place is the creation of a free trade area. By creating one, the countries of North America and Western Europe would not only gain economic advantages but encourage a closer knitting of other ties as well. The argument is commonplace but has the singular feature of seeming to ignore Japan. To a challenge on that point, two answers are possible. One is that, of course, Japan could be included, almost as if its omission were an oversight that could be repaired without throwing out half the argument based on history and culture. This proposal, in which the NA in NAFTA loses its meaning, is the subject of the next section.

The second possible answer to the question about NAFTA and Japan is that the NA is very meaningful indeed and that Japan is left out of the proposal by design. Two kinds of arguments can be used, taken together or separately. One stresses the fact that more than economics is involved and that the affinities of history and culture make the relations between Western Europe and North America unique. The other is more economic and pragmatic, pointing out that although Japan is a modern industrial country, playing a major role in the international economy, it remains significantly different from the other countries in the group. Not only is it more restrictive in trade and investment than they, but the relationship of government and business is such that even if the forms of liberalism are adhered to, its substance will not be there. Consequently, either it will be impossible to create a free trade area which includes Japan, or, if one is formed, it will not work as it is supposed to because of differences between the economic systems of Japan and the others. Closely allied to this argument is the whole set of conditions discussed in chapter 3 that cause the other industrialized countries to treat Japan less than equally.

Though they may sometimes have an anti-Japanese cast, the arguments for having a NAFTA without Japan are not incompatible in principle with the view that one ought to have a liberal policy toward Japan and cultivate its part in international economic cooperation. They also leave open the possibility that some day Japan will be ready for membership in an enlarged NAFTA. Nevertheless, as an objective of American policy the idea of a free trade arrangement that excludes Japan is not acceptable. Though the argument about the difficulty of having free trade with Japan has much validity, there seems little to be gained by building a shrine to the difficulty. The many reasons discussed earlier that make it desirable to try to find a full and equal place for Japan in the industrial world point away from any arrangement which draws a formal distinction between Japan and the others, especially if the result could be interpreted as putting Japan in an inferior position. For broad foreign policy reasons as well as those concerning the shaping of the world economy, the United States should not be a party to arrangements that even nominally discriminate against Japan.

No more, of course, should the United States look with favor on an arrangement under which it would draw more closely together with other countries than with those of Western Europe. One of the key issues in judging the case for the old NAFTA—the one with Britain in and the Community out—was whether it would do more to introduce new divisions in the international world than it would help to overcome the already existing ones. Similar issues in a different form have appeared in a number of places throughout this book, and the pattern of policy conclusions that emerges makes it clear that if the United States pursues the objectives that have seemed most promising to me, it will rarely be engaged in bloc-building. Would things be different if a bloc were proposed that would include all the countries of the industrial world?

A Bloc for the Rich?

A NAFTA that included Japan has been called by some of its advocates MFTA or WFTA or IFTA (for Multilateral or World or International Free Trade Association). Like most designs for major changes in the world order, this one can take a number of different forms and accommodate a wide variety of differences in detail. For present purposes it is enough to think of it first as simply a free trade arrangement and later as a possible vehicle for a wider range of economic cooperation. Clearly it fits well, at least at first glance, with some of the major arguments of this book such as that elimination of the remaining tariffs on manufactured goods and industrial raw materials is a realistic goal. Even more to the point, it appears as one way of embodying the theme that economic relations among Western Europe, Canada, Japan, and the United States are in major respects quite distinct from their relations with the poor countries or those of the Communist world.

The strongest argument in favor of MFTA is that if governments will commit themselves to move to free trade on some sort of schedule, they will have created a very different situation from that surrounding tariff bargaining in GATT. The formal commitment would itself become part of the dynamics of trade barrier reduction. Business would be given an assurance about the future that it can never have as long as the bargaining process is not linked to a specific objective. Like European businessmen when the Common Market was started, world traders might begin to anticipate the future by behaving almost as if trade were already free. Investment, production, and marketing plans would be made with an eye to a known future. With a known time limit, the pressures for adjustment would grow. The commitment would stiffen the spines of governments in resisting domestic pressures to hold back and in taking steps necessary to bring about a transition to a new situation.

The point is a strong one and might, when the time was ripe, be the decisive factor in making the MFTA approach preferable to carrying on in a more traditional way. But there is, of course, another side to the coin. May not the commitment to free trade itself prove to be an obstacle that will make governments unwilling to act? Much of the postwar progress in liberalization has been made by governments not committed to a specific goal. Few, if any of them, would have committed themselves in 1945 or 1950 or even 1960 to move even to where they are in 1970, much less to free trade. When there were more limited commitments to free trade (the Common Market, EFTA, and the Trade Expansion Act of 1962), there was always an extra impetus of a broadly political character that was crucial to making the free trade commitment acceptable. It is possible, of course, that the idea of MFTA may some day take on such a dimension, perhaps simply because the feeling of solidarity among the industrialized countries of the free world grows greater than it has been in recent years. It is clear enough that the idea of free trade has not yet acquired that kind of charisma.

If, at some future time, most but not all of the industrial nations overcame their present inhibitions about free trade, they could launch MFTA, planning from the first that it would include the others as soon as they were ready. At least, this is the claim made by some MFTA advocates who see it as a way of escaping the "convoy effect" of multilateral trade negotiations in which the pace of the slowest limits what the rest can do unless they are willing, under the most-favored-nation clause, to give it the benefit of reductions they make in their own tariffs that are not matched by what it does. MFTA, according to this view, provides a way of sprinting ahead, as Sperry Lea has put it,[7] so that the pace is set by the fastest and the laggard is given an incentive to catch up. The idea is attractive, but it may also be dangerous. Everything depends on who is left out and how he reacts. It is conceivable that the country that is omitted will work harder to move to free trade and join the others. But it is also possible that it will react sharply, withdraw benefits already given, seek compensation in other quarters, and, if it is strong enough, start a process that may become economic warfare and will certainly represent a lowering of the level of economic cooperation already achieved. One would certainly have to move carefully if the recalcitrant were Japan, the European Community, or the United States. This is not the kind of issue about which one can make good judgments in advance, but it opens the possibility that MFTA, too, is caught in a convoy effect.[8]

There could be long discussions about whether one or another country should be in or out of MFTA (Australia, New Zealand, South Africa) or whether some would need special arrangements (Portugal, Greece, Turkey), but it is hard to believe that any of these issues would be crucial to the decision if the major trading countries were ready to move to free trade. A decisive issue could, however, arise about the relation of MFTA to the less developed countries.

In 1962 President Kennedy said that although the Trade Expansion Act concentrated on the trade of Europe and the United States, it was not intended to lead to the formation of a rich man's club. Writing shortly afterwards, Randall Hinshaw stated more precisely a widely held view: "The United States should never become a member of an exclusive Atlantic free-trade zone . . . it surely would not be wise or right . . . to move toward free trade with the richer countries while retaining protection against the poorer countries."[9] Most advocates of MFTA agree wholeheartedly. They are quite willing to contemplate arrangements that would keep MFTA from increasing

7. "The Future Shape of U.S. Trade Policy: Multilateral or Free Trade Approaches?" Kiyoshi Kojima, ed., *Pacific Trade and Development,* II (Tokyo: Japan Economic Research Center, 1969), p. 29.

8. It would, of course, be possible to have members who eliminated tariffs more slowly than the rest, but this device would still require them to make the commitment to free trade and so is a different matter.

9. *The European Community and American Trade* (New York: Praeger, for the Council on Foreign Relations, 1964), p. 140.

discrimination against less developed countries. Prescriptions vary, but one way or another they insure that products from less developed countries enter the markets of the rich countries on the same basis as those of MFTA countries.

For the developed countries to accept that view would be quite a change from their past practices—perhaps greater than that of adopting MFTA. The progress that has been made in liberalizing trade among themselves is in considerable contrast to the extensive restrictions that still exist on imports from the poorer countries. Perhaps by the time they are ready for MFTA, the rich countries will have changed all this. Progress in that direction is suggested by the agreement to give tariff preferences to many products from less developed countries; doubt is spread by the kind of action taken. A willingness to import fairly freely from the less developed countries might be a stimulus to MFTA, for why then cling to relatively minor restraints on imports from other industrialized countries (except, indeed, to give the poor countries the benefits of preferences)? But if the improved treatment of imports from the LDCs is limited to certain products and hedged round with safeguards and limitations, then the question would still arise: Would MFTA amount to discrimination against the poor countries?

For some people that possibility may be an attraction. As a free trade area conforming to GATT rules, MFTA would legitimize discrimination against a form of competition they particularly fear. If that view is rejected and the aim is to keep discrimination to a minimum, some complicated questions arise. Should unwillingness to expose a domestic industry to the competition of low-cost production from a poor country—the seriousness of which may well be exaggerated—be allowed to stand in the way of an important step toward liberalization of a much larger volume of trade among developed countries? If the answer is "yes," MFTA provides no escape from the convoy effect. If it is "no," the case for MFTA must balance progress in the relations among rich countries against the creation of a new division between rich and poor.

The question is simply a new version of the old basic one about regionalism: Is the gain from greater liberalization within a small group larger than the loss from the introduction of new discriminations into international trade as a whole? We have seen that there is no simple answer to this question when it applies to arrangements among some of the industrialized countries. Whether one's judgment would be different when the discrimination is between two worlds depends on an estimate of the importance of future relations between the rich and poor. It is true that the problem already exists; negotiating under most-favored-nation arrangements, the industrialized countries will not go as far in freeing trade as they would if they did not have to reduce barriers to imports from LDCs as well as among themselves. There is a difference, though, between slowing down the process of liberalization and introducing new and formal discrimination against poor countries.

The difference may be of special importance for the future. The less developed countries vary greatly in what they produce or could soon produce if they had the markets, in what they can sell in competition with producers in developed countries, in their ability to get and use capital, and in the kinds of policies their governments can carry out effectively. The more advanced of the less developed countries already have more in common with the least developed of the more advanced countries than they do with the most backward countries in the world. In a decade there will be countries in Latin America and Asia as developed as some European countries that now participate in the cooperative arrangements of the industrialized world, albeit sometimes with special provisions. Not only will such countries be better able than the least developed to take advantage of relatively free access to the markets of more fully industrialized countries (and would therefore be more heavily penalized if they were discriminated against), but there will be less justification—in their own interest—in exempting them from the obligations to reciprocate in the removal of trade barriers. But they are not likely to be ready to open their economies as widely as the rich countries already do. We may never see another Japan, but the path that country has traced in a generation or so goes in the same direction as those which others are climbing. The place of these countries in the world should change as their economies develop. For some period they will live in an intermediate status. Can it be more easily accommodated in relation to a formal grouping with rules about free trade and attendant matters or under looser systems like those of GATT and the IMF, which have provisos to take care of circumstances and procedures for determining which countries are eligible to take advantage of them? Is there any reason MFTA and the broader organizations could not co-exist? The answers are not obvious and the bounds set to this book prevent a full exploration of the issues. But the questions themselves indicate a major set of complications that would be encountered if the industrialized countries were seriously to contemplate forming something like MFTA.[10]

10. Also omitted are: the possibility of alleviating the problems for LDCS by special treatment of products of particular interest to them; the implications of the fact that a free trade area does not require that members all treat outsiders the same way; and the claim that MFTA would make it easier for the rich countries to cooperate in their treatment of LDCs.

Advocates of free trade areas usually claim as an advantage of their proposals that they are simpler than customs unions, which require a common tariff against outside products, and economic unions such as the European Community, which call for common policies in a number of fields. Sometimes this claim is based on the view that relatively little coordination of policy is necessary to make free trade work effectively. It is hard to believe, though, that MFTA would ever be acceptable in so simple a form. The great concern with all kinds of trade barriers and distortions, the strong tendency to link tariff and nontariff negotiations, and to take into account investment and other aspects of economic policy as well, all make this unlikely. Indeed, it is easier to reverse the argument, as some of its advocates have done,[11] and say that one of the advantages of MFTA is that it would permit the countries to work on the difficult problems of the "conditions of competition" more effectively than they can in larger organizations. Put that way, the argument provides one more reason for believing that MFTA can only become a serious possibility at some indeterminate time in the future. For we have seen that, on the one hand, the industrialized countries are already heavily engaged in the process of negotiating about more than trade matters while, on the other, they are far from developing enough of an area of agreement about even the objectives they are seeking to be willing to take on broad commitments to deal with such matters in a comprehensive way and in a new and untried framework.

Much of the difficulty that many people have in believing that MFTA will soon become a serious subject of discussion is summed up in two reactions. Told that its single most obvious benefit, free trade in a number of products, would quickly have to be extended to the LDCs, many people say, "In that case why bother with the difficult task of negotiating MFTA in the first place? The same thing can be done under GATT." When the added point is made that MFTA would also deal with a wide range of other forms of economic cooperation among its members, the same, or other, people say, "But we are already engaged on that process bilaterally and in a number of international organizations; progress is slow and we cannot be sure where we are going; MFTA would only complicate matters and seems the long way round to a goal that we are in any case already working toward." Coming as they do from practical people, these reactions

11. Theodore Geiger and Sperry Lea, "The Free Trade Area Concept as Applied to the United States," in *Issues and Objectives of U.S. Foreign Trade Policy*, compendium of statements submitted to the Subcommittee on Foreign Economic Policy of the Joint Economic Committee, 90th Cong., 1st sess. (Washington: GPO, 1967), pp. 43-64.

represent a realistic assessment of the present. As to the future, when present processes of negotiation about trade and other matters have advanced further and succeeded or failed in varying degrees, one cannot be so sure. That MFTA is not on the current agenda of the free world is clear, but it may have some future life. Paradoxically, the date at which MFTA might become a more lively issue could be brought closer by either the success of other measures of cooperation (widening the area of agreement) or their failure (suggesting that a more radical commitment was needed).

BLOCS AND NATIONS

There are those whose sense of the future tells them that the world will some day be made up of blocs of countries instead of the individual nations we have known in the past. They may be right, but up to the present the evidence is far from conclusive. At least that is so with regard to deliberately formed groupings of nations seeking to do together what they are no longer big enough to do separately. If, however, a bloc is thought of as less a consciously created entity and more a drawing together of a certain group of countries in response to political, economic, and cultural forces, the evidence is stronger. Then two kinds of questions arise: Will the magnetic forces come to operate over an ever-widening area? Will different kinds of forces pull the same country in different directions so that what seems a "natural" grouping from one point of view cuts across strong affinities of another sort? In either case there may be a conflict between the forces that tend to absorb a country in a larger unit and the will to remain separate or "independent."

Quite a few of the issues about the future of the industrial world that have been discussed in this book could be translated into these terms. The exercise would, however, leave us unable to come to firm conclusions on what the growing interpenetration of the economies of Western Europe, Japan, Canada, and the United States portends, at least until we have given comparable attention to their relations with the rest of the world, and especially the majority of humanity that lives in the poor countries.

When we deal with blocs in the more usual sense, we are really talking only of Western Europe and especially of the European Community (for the history, and probably the future, of EFTA must be seen as ancillary to it). The case for calling it a building block rests in part on things already achieved and even more on its potential role in the world economy if it is broadened and deepened. The senses in which it is and will continue to be a stumbling block have already occupied a good bit of our attention. One of the central issues of future relations within the industrial world is how to strengthen the former aspect and minimize or offset the latter, something that does not depend on Europe alone. When we talk of other possible blocs within the industrial world, it is easier to see the difficulties they would create than the contribution they would make. This may, of course, be due to shortsightedness just as my emphasis on the difficulty of creating them—a different kind of argument but a highly relevant one—may be due to a lack of imagination or the sense of need that enabled Europeans to overcome difficulties of a high order. If, however, the conclusion that the future of the industrial world does not lie in further bloc-building is correct, it combines with other considerations to support four points emerging from this chapter that point to the continuing importance of the kind of multilateralism that was a key feature of the Bretton Woods approach.

First, if there are to be no new blocs, the relations of the other countries of the industrial world with the European Community will involve the same kinds of problems that the Bretton Woods approach tried to deal with, so that its principles, rules, procedures, and organization (or some modification of them) continue to be necessary. This view is not just an American idiosyncrasy. Indeed, as the Community is enlarged, it is the Japanese above all who would have cause to worry if it seemed that the future of the industrial world was being shaped by negotiations between the representatives of two massive economies instead of by broader multilateral processes.

Second, though the Community is in some respects a bloc, in others it is not a bloc at all and in still others it is at some sort of halfway house. Thus to deal even with Europe, an essentially multilateral framework is required and especially in that great range of major issues which promise to be the most important items on the agenda of the industrial world in the years to come as trade negotiations in the old-fashioned sense fall more and more into the background.

Third, the relations of the industrialized countries with the rest of the world cannot be wholly separated from their relations among themselves; and since the rest of the world is made up of a large number of countries, each of which wishes to make its decisions about how to pursue its own interests, it is hard to imagine any but a multilateral framework.

Fourth, in all three of these sets of relations, the sense in which a bloc can be a stumbling block is often closely linked with the developments that might in one way or another either threaten a degree of cooperation already achieved over a wider range or deny an outsider benefits to which he thought he was entitled. Since the past pattern of cooperation has been to a high degree multilateral, it cannot easily be shifted to some new framework without serious risk of undoing or at least throwing into doubt past accomplishments.

Four sets of relations, then, make multilateral elements of the sort embodied in the Bretton Woods approach still relevant for the future. But whether the need can be translated into some policy depends to an important degree on how the Bretton Woods machinery still functions, how it may have to be altered to work better, and above all on whether its fundamental principles are well adapted for a world that is in many ways different from the one to which they were first applied. To consider these possibilities is the main task of the next chapter.

10

On the Restoration of Old Pictures

At the beginning of the postwar period the United States, facing a
world full of destruction and disorganization, had rather clear ideas
about what could be made of that world and how to set about the
task. At the beginning of the '70s, the United States, facing a world
in which there is more prosperity than has ever been known and a
high degree of international cooperation, does not feel sure of how
the problems of that world ought to be approached. There are many
reasons for this. One—or is it symptom rather than cause?—is the
lack of a clear idea of what kind of future international economy
would be desirable, such as was provided by the Bretton Woods
world picture. Is the difficulty one of looking forward or of learning
from the recent past?

BRETTON WOODS REFOCUSED

The Bretton Woods approach was forward-looking but to an important degree reflected the past. It aimed not simply at restoring what
the war had destroyed or disorganized but at creating a new world
economy without the faults that had caused so much trouble between
the wars. The methods to be used were sometimes modernized ver-
sions of familiar techniques too little used in the past, such as the
reduction of trade barriers, and sometimes inventions to replace and
improve on functions once carried out in more automatic, or at least

less deliberate, ways, like the International Monetary Fund. New problems were recognized, notably those arising from general acceptance of governmental responsibility for full employment; but naturally enough it was hard to know how to deal with these, so arrangements were less explicit and, in some cases, never properly put into effect. Some of the objectives, it was thought, could be attained in a fairly short time; others were known to lie much further in the future. Indeed, it is misleading to speak of the objectives in terms of the ultimate creation of a specific condition, such as free trade. More often the aim was to set the world moving in a certain direction and to establish a process of international cooperation with rules, organizations, and means of settling disputes and reconciling conflicts of interest. By these means governments were to move in the direction of freeing international economic life from unnecessary trammels without committing themselves to some well-defined state of affairs as the eventual ideal.

Some of the processes set in motion in the '40s are still working well and are almost taken for granted; others work only with difficulty or not at all. Some of the problems the world faces in the '70s are, to an important degree, the results of progress that has been made in giving reality to the earlier vision. Some stem from the failures, while some are simply new or at least were unthought of or seemed unimportant before.

In these circumstances, has the Bretton Woods picture any relevance to the relations of the industrialized countries in the '70s? Can the new problems be dealt with in the existing framework? Is that framework useful even for the old problems it was intended to deal with? Is the issue one of finding a wholly new approach?

These questions are not asked to elicit historical answers—how we got here or whether one American policy succeeded while another failed. Nor is the aim to judge whether the Bretton Woods approach rested on an accurate or adequate understanding of the problems of the world economy in its time. Since the Bretton Woods approach was comprehensive and well articulated, its picture of the world economy provides a convenient way of ordering a mass of material. But if that were all, the framework could soon be discarded as a scaffolding is dismantled when the building is up or the mold cracked when the sculpture is cast. Such analogies are false; in whatever distorted or incomplete form it has come through, the Bretton Woods approach has left not an external framework but a number of elements that are central to the world economy at the beginning of the '70s: organizations, rules, principles, concrete commitments, national policies, and, not least, a continuing influence on the thinking and attitudes of the people who concern themselves with these matters. Any picture one could draw of a world economy for the '70s or '80s toward which American policy should be directed is bound to have some meaningful relation to the Bretton Woods picture. But it will not be the same picture, and the vital question is: What is to be changed and what is to be kept?

No simple answer can be given by subtracting from the original Bretton Woods list those problems which have been "solved," keeping those that remain and adding the new ones, not known or thought of twenty-five years ago. Much space has been given in preceding chapters to showing how some old problems have transformed themselves into quite new ones. Moreover, the old, the new, and the transformed converge to a much greater degree than they seemed to in the past. For example, the removal of tariffs and quotas makes businessmen more sensitive than before to other factors that affect the terms on which they must compete with foreigners. The fluidity of capital and the mobility of industry combine to expand international production, which links trade policy with investment policy in complicated ways. The increased links of trade, investment, and money make economies more sensitive to one another so that each government develops a great interest in what the others do about a wide range of matters. The operation of the international monetary system entails a combination of collective action and national measures of adjustment that depend heavily on one another for their success. As a result of this drawing together, the line between what is domestic and what is foreign has become blurred. Actions traditionally the sole responsibility of each country are increasingly matters of international concern and, frequently, of negotiation. The need for —if not always the supply of—common or coordinated policies grows.

Much of this closeness and openness is the result of the reasonably consistent pursuit for a quarter of a century of the ideas and methods of the Bretton Woods approach. Much of it is the result of other things: technology, communications, economic growth, general political stability, a drawing together for security, the absence of a depression. These multiple causes have endowed the problems that will arise among the industrialized countries in the '70s with two characteristics that are highly relevant to the shaping of national policies. On the one hand, there is much that is new; with novelty comes uncertainty; questions can be foreseen more easily than answers. On the other hand, we can see that even to deal adequately with new issues it is essential for governments to retain some features of the Bretton Woods approach. How this duality affects policy on a number of issues has been examined in earlier chapters. This one is an effort to draw together the implications of duality, first for the character of foreign economic policy as a whole in the '70s and then for some of the fundamental principles of the Bretton Woods approach which have not been separately discussed earlier but have to be kept, dropped, or adapted.

A FUTURE DIFFERENT FROM THE PAST

Much of the aim of the Bretton Woods approach could be summed up as the removal of barriers to the movement of goods and funds across national boundaries. Since it was obvious that barriers would not be completely eliminated, a good deal of the effort was put into devising ways to regulate their use, usually by a combination of rules concerning national behavior and procedures insuring some degree of international surveillance. Is the same emphasis right for the '70s?

There is hardly need to explore the antithesis: the restoration of barriers. The occasional appearance of theoretical justifications of protectionism as a general policy seems to have little to do with the modern life of great industrial nations. (Matters are somewhat different in the less developed world.) Given the degree of interpenetration and openness that exists among these countries, it is difficult to imagine one of them adopting as a general policy the re-erection of barriers and the cutting of international ties. Such a policy would have to be based on the wish for some kind of autarky, an impractical aim that is not compatible with the other things the people of industrial societies have shown they want.

The protection of certain industries, the resistance to certain kinds of foreign penetration, the need for restrictions and controls in certain circumstances, the reluctance to remove some barriers or to accept the adjustment required by further openness and interpenetration, nationalistic responses to new problems, and the renewal of challenges—all these will probably be as characteristic of national policies in the future as in the past. Allowed free play, they could undo much of the work of a generation. They feed on one another and stimulate retaliation. No one can be certain that in the '70s governments will restrain these impulses as well as they did in the past two decades.

If they do not, the removal of barriers may once again become the first order of business in international economic cooperation. But if there is no reversal of direction, the removal of barriers may not be regarded as so central and urgent a task in the '70s as it has been. The authors of Bretton Woods had vivid memories of the heights to which barriers had been raised in the '30s and knew that in a disrupted postwar world it would take an extraordinary effort to separate the controllers from their controls. Today, with industrial tariffs at 10 per cent, it is much harder to get excited about their cost to prosperous nations. Even obviously burdensome agricultural policies have not prevented impressive growth. Large corporations can organize their activities so as to minimize the impact of national trade measures that would be more damaging to an atomistic structure of production and trade. In other words, twenty-five years of trade barrier reduction has, naturally enough, made trade barrier reduction seem less vital in the '70s.

This drop in the sense of urgency should not be translated into a judgment that further liberalization of trade and payments is unimportant. The remaining tariffs are far from negligible. There are still some quotas. Other nontariff barriers and trade-distorting practices now seem more important than they did in the past. No major effort to deal with international economic issues in the '70s could neglect them. They lie along the route between the more familiar trade barrier reduction of the past and the continuing work on conditions of competition and coordination of national economic policies that will clearly be important tasks in the '70s. The more open economies become to one another, the more sensitive they seem to be to hindrances to the free movement of goods and funds that seemed minor when compared with the tariffs, quotas, and exchange controls of the mid-'40s.

A final compelling reason for not putting further liberalization of trade and payments in the category of unimportant issues for the '70s is that to do so might well result in an increase in barriers and the undoing of much of what has been accomplished in the past. In all countries there is a constant stream of demands for the imposition of one or another kind of trade barrier. Sometimes interested parties are simply trying once more to get what was denied them in the past; sometimes they claim injury or otherwise raise questions about the wisdom or justice of past decisions. They may want major legislative action or they may settle for less overt forms of help. There are any number of governmental decisions that could be influenced by the fact that local interests feel strongly about foreign competition —almost always thought of as in some sense "unfair." The ability of a government to resist these pressures is weak if trade liberalization does not rank high as an objective of policy. When one government imposes a new control or tightens an old one, others will retaliate— and more quickly if there is no strong feeling that trade barriers are dangerous and undesirable. Even if a backward-moving process of blow and counter blow does not set in, what is permissible for one must be permissible for others; so when one government succumbs, the next pressure for protection somewhere else will be harder to resist.

For all these reasons, the removal of barriers to trade and payments remains high on the list of objectives for the '70s. There are, however, some important differences in how governments will have to go about the matter and also in how they will define what they mean by further liberalization.

The aim set in the trade negotiations of the late '40s was to eliminate quotas (except when they were used in agreed-on circumstances) but only to reduce tariffs. The distinction was made partly because it seemed unrealistic to expect governments to commit themselves to the complete abolition of tariffs, even as a distant objective, while quotas, which were considered more vicious, were also usually alleged to be temporary or emergency measures. In the '70s it is quite reasonable to make the complete removal of tariffs on most of the trade among industrial countries a goal for the next decade or so. But nontariff barriers cannot be so sweepingly dealt with. They will have to be treated somewhat as tariffs were before; governments can agree to work for their reduction or removal but with the emphasis on the process rather than the ultimate condition to be achieved. Some, no doubt, may eventually be altogether eliminated, but in other cases the only reasonable objective will be regulation of their use, since trade-impeding effects may result from the pursuit of governmental policies of greater priority than trade liberalization.

The authors of Bretton Woods knew that the removal of barriers would not solve all problems, even if the Fund Agreement sufficed to make the international monetary system work well. They were aware of the problems of reconciling domestic economic policies with international commitments and of the possible conflicts between economic planning and the removal of controls or between the maintenance of full employment and trade liberalization. The issues for which "the international adjustment problem" is shorthand were familiar to them. They were aware of the fact that trade in raw materials and agricultural products had special characteristics, that restrictive practices by private business could frustrate official liberalization, and that it would be desirable to get international agreement on conditions of investment. The awareness of all these things was only to a limited extent translated into provisions of various international agreements, sometimes in a rudimentary fashion and with results that were less clear and firm than the arrangements for the removal of tariffs and quotas. In part this was the result of not knowing quite how to cope with some of the problems; in part it was a failure to get substantial international agreement on detailed proposals; in part the result came from the abandonment of the International Trade Organization (ITO), the most compendious of the proposed agreements. There was, too, a sensible belief that not everything could be done at once and that if some of the imaginable but not sharply defined problems either interfered with the removal of barriers or otherwise became more prominent in the future, then the future would have to find its way of dealing with them.

That time has come, at least for a number of the issues that were, for one reason or another, not fully dealt with under the Bretton Woods approach. The range of tasks has been surveyed already. No simple label applies to them, but they certainly go beyond anything for which "the removal of barriers" would be regarded as an adequate expression. What these tasks have in common is that, although some of them result from past measures of liberalization, they are more nearly the tasks of managing the international economy than of simply eliminating governmental interference with the flow of private activity.

Some elements of this kind have long been a part of foreign economic policy: for example, the management of the international monetary system; collective action to help a country in balance of payments difficulties, provided it conformed to standards set by the countries giving aid; the application of domestic law to American-owned firms abroad; the negotiation of international treaties about taxation; and some governmental measures bearing on foreign investment. In the future, however, the relative weight of what might be called "positive" governmental actions, as contrasted with the "negative" ones of removing impediments, seems sure to grow. We have already seen how this process works in the matter of nontariff barriers. At first the objective appears to be just a new kind of trade barrier reduction—a "negative" measure. So it is in some cases, but the further the process is pushed, the more complicated the issues will become because so many nontariff barriers are closely linked with governmental policies that are not going to be given up simply in order to liberalize trade. Governments will increasingly be called on to modify measures they are taking for the management of their own economies (or the pursuit of particular national aims, some of them quite specific) because of their impact on the trade of others. In effect, even if not explicitly, the industrial countries will be trying to achieve an unprecedented harmonization of at least some parts of their national policies.

Because their economies are so open to one another, the governments of the industrialized countries will find that in dealing domestically with inflation, deflation, growth, and stability they sometimes have to choose between retaining some degree of international co-operation and taking purely national measures which deprive them of some of the benefits of openness. In some other matters, international cooperation will be increasingly necessary to make national policies effective; for example, in coping with massive flows of short-term capital. It is, incidentally, mildly ironic that this need arises precisely in a sector which the Bretton Woods arrangements did not try to liberalize for fear of unsettling consequences. A widening area of agreement on standards governing national adjustment to balance of payments changes seems needed. The more governments are concerned not only with the general condition of their economies but, rather specifically, with their structure, the more they will be drawn toward a variety of measures that affect the interests of other countries in ways that cannot be dealt with adequately by negotiations confined to trade barriers. Agriculture provides an old example; but for the future the mixed category of activities that can be labeled "industrial policy" is likely to be far more important. Finally, governments face problems arising from the fact that a largely private international economy has developed that in many ways escapes the effective supervision of national governments or can be dealt with by them only in ways that impose undesirable economic costs. To assure the dominance of public interest over private interests and at the same time reap the benefits of business dynamism and the ability of entrepreneurs to produce and distribute efficiently in the contemporary, interpenetrated world, governments will have to find new ways of working together.

The shift in emphasis toward the need for more "positive" measures in international economic cooperation will make the carrying out of foreign economic policy more complex and therefore more difficult than it has been in the past. It has not been easy to reduce tariffs and other trade barriers to their present low levels. And yet that has been, in at least some respects, a relatively simple task. The objective could be clearly stated; the methods, though tedious and in their detail complex, were basically quite obvious; there was a hundred years of economic theory to provide the rationale for what was being done. Now new problems have to be faced which are often not fully understood. There is frequently little agreement as to what should be done about them even if governments were ready to act and wholly free to do so. The methods of dealing with many of the issues are still in the realm of suggestion, not experience.

Even when the intellectual problems are not so difficult, there is the obstacle that it is probably always easier to take "negative" action than to get the agreement of several governments on "positive" measures. Problems that are difficult and touchy enough on a national basis become more troublesome to deal with if foreign interests must constantly be taken into account. In reaching a compromise among conflicting domestic interests, different countries may arrive at quite incompatible policies. In each country, the constituency concerned with foreign economic policy is enlarged, and new resistances may develop.

To argue that a wide range of subjects will be drawn into international negotiation is not to imply that agreement will be reached about them. To point out that in many instances purely national regulation deprives the people of the regulating nation of some of the advantages of international specialization and openness is not to say that governments will always opt for the economically "rational" decision. They may act to preserve the position of a domestic group or they may set "political" values higher than "economic." To preserve national control of an industry may well seem more desirable, if more costly, than to let in a more efficient foreign investor. Sometimes the sense of urgency about a problem calls for action long before a more satisfactory method of dealing with it by international agreement can be devised. Governments will try to shield themselves from the impact of short-term capital movements before effective international supervision of the Eurodollar market can be created. To revive depressed areas, they will make decisions expanding industrial output of certain products long before they and other governments are ready to compare notes about the international implications of what each is doing. Sometimes, as we have seen, the clash of national policies is the spur to ultimate agreement. But there is no inevitability in this process and the open, interpenetrated economy the industrial countries built by twenty-five years of successful international agreement on "negative" actions could be destroyed by a long enough period of predominantly national action of a "positive" sort.

Even in the familiar "negative" sector, the future may hold more difficulties than the past. Though trade barriers are by historic standards low, governments have been unwilling to remove some of those that remain for fear of the supposed consequences for domestic producers. In some cases the fears are undoubtedly exaggerated, and the reduction of these barriers would be little more disturbing than what has already been done. But it is also quite possible that further trade barrier reduction will entail a greater degree of adjustment in domestic economies, for which governments will have to assume responsibility. Even if there were no further trade liberalization, the adjustment problem will almost certainly become more serious in the

future than in the past. The reasons are familiar. Accelerated technological change, the international mobility of capital and management, general expansion accompanied by increases in the optimum
size of new productive units, and the amounts of capital required
combine to speed up the rate of change and to increase its impact on
whatever enterprise, area, or process is being superseded.

The consequences for policy are marked. To make the changes
called for is more difficult than before, with or without government
help. Dislocations follow one another with considerable frequency.
A good accommodation in one case is upset by the onset of a new
problem. Planning is made more difficult, and even the direction in
which adjustment should move may become uncertain. The pressure
increases to restore old trade barriers or to impose new kinds of
restrictions. Sensitivity rises to foreign prices, taxes, dumping, and
other elements of "fair competition." The point is soon reached
where the "negative" task of barrier removal merges with the "positive" one of coordinating national policies, one of the most difficult
parts of the terrain of the future.

More is involved in adjustment than changing the structure of
production in response to new trade flows. The industrialized countries are always adjusting to one another in a variety of ways. Their
openness makes the inflation, deflation, interest rate changes, and
other fluctuations of one a force to which others must adapt. All this
takes place on top of a continuing major adjustment in the industrial
world, something that might almost be called a continental drift.
One phase of it has been the recovery of Western Europe from its
postwar low and its expansion to a point of substantial economic
strength relative to the United States, in financial as well as physical
terms. The other major phase has been marked by the unprecedented
growth rates that have brought Japan to near the top of the list of
industrialized nations from a position at the end of the war which
was certainly weak and which seemed to many to be closer to the
less developed countries than to the rich nations. These great movements are, plainly enough, not finished; both the progress they make
and the factors that hamper their progress, notably those in Japan
and between Japan and the rest of the world, pose new problems and
have an influence on the way other problems present themselves.
These very large movements, though they may be described in
economic terms, inevitably have at least political overtones and sometimes sharply political leading edges.

When large adjustments are in question, a quite proper concern
for social values and for not burdening the weak easily slides over

into a defense of the status quo and an implicit acceptance of the idea that people have a right to go on doing what they have always done. Affluence may strengthen this conservative bias because it makes it easier for a country to accept the cost of a less efficient use of its resources than could be obtained. Affluence plays its part, too, in creating an atmosphere of changing values that still further complicates the tasks of the industrial countries as they try to cope with their lengthy agenda of international economic problems. With record industrial output and new high levels of consumption has come intensified concern for pollution, congestion, conservation, and forms of welfare not attainable through material progress alone. It is not true that the quality of life and the quantity of goods produced are always in conflict, but sometimes they are. In all the industrial countries the opinion is growing—or at least finding more frequent expression—that a calculus that always gives first place to output and efficiency is not acceptable. Very complex questions arise for national economies. Some of their international impact takes very specific forms, such as the spawning of nontariff barriers by the introduction of standards in one country that are not adopted in others. But the more fundamental impact, with effects not easy to predict, comes from introducing still one more set of variables into a system that is already most difficult to operate because it consists of a group of policy-making units that are largely national but have to deal simultaneously with a series of problems that lie along a continuum from the purely internal to the global and mostly combine domestic and international elements.

The co-existence of old and new problems in international economic relations makes it look as if the conduct of foreign economic policy would be more difficult in the future than in the past. Not only are there new complexities but the number of tasks grows. Governments will have to find ways to negotiate almost simultaneously about a large number of issues that differ greatly in character. To translate new ideas and approaches into action is always difficult. It is made harder in this case not through the widening of the range of issues relevant to foreign economic policy—they were always relevant —but through the widening perception of what is relevant and a sharpening sense of the importance of taking into account issues once left aside. The question naturally arises whether some of the fundamental elements of the Bretton Woods approach are still usable in this considerably changed world. Does it still make sense to emphasize international organizations, aspire to the equal treatment of nations, rely on reciprocal bargaining among governments as the mechanism of reaching agreement, and speak as if "national interest" were a meaningful concept?

ORGANIZATIONS SURROUNDED BY RULES

We have grown very used to the idea that much economic cooperation takes place through international organizations with prescribed purposes, rules for pursuing them, membership of a sort that promises reasonable performance, and a suitable secretariat. It is worth recalling that this idea is a direct contribution of the Bretton Woods approach and one that marks an important difference between the postwar world economy and the past—not only the interwar period but the century before World War I as well.

When Britain tried to get other countries to adopt free trade during a certain period in the nineteenth century, its vehicle was national treaties, not an international organization or a multilateral convention. When the United States tried to turn the tide of protectionism in the '30s, it too used bilateral agreements. The idea of establishing GATT lay in the future. The gold standard of the nineteenth century operated through national responses to events, not international negotiation; such management as there was, was largely in the hands of men in London, not officials of an international body. Between the wars, international efforts to cope with monetary problems called forth conferences and committees and involved a high degree of collaboration among central banks but no continuing organizations except for the Bank for International Settlements, created originally for rather limited purposes but in a way something of a harbinger of things to come in spite of its difficulties in the years of fascism and war.

When the authors of Bretton Woods set about changing things, they thought partly in terms of international organizations to match problems and partly in terms of international agreements, of which the organizations were a part. Obvious enough, the distinction has sometimes escaped people who have tried to describe the postwar structure of international economic cooperation in terms of organizations alone. It is hardly surprising, though, that organizations like GATT and the IMF, which are embedded in agreements imposing obligations (and conferring privileges) on members, have had a far greater impact on national policies than bodies like FAO and ECOSOC. This simple distinction does not, however, exhaust the subject, since one also has to take into account the real influence on national policies of OECD and UNCTAD, which does not stem from obligations laid down in written agreements.[1]

Sometimes emphasis on international organizations encourages the illusion that the creation of a properly constituted body is tantamount to the solution of a problem. Habits of speech encourage further illusions. "Why doesn't the U.N. do something about it?" is a frequent plaint. That it is not "the U.N." but its member nations that have to "do something" should be clear enough. Much the same is true of international economic organizations, at least most of the time. Still, the common formulation is not quite as obtuse as it sounds when referring to bodies like the IMF and GATT. Their secretariats have certain powers and responsibilities; other organs can be brought into action by a single country's complaint or petition and have a responsibility for policing the behavior of members who slight their obligations; countries can be bound by decisions on which they were outvoted. The other oversimplifications, too, contain kernels of truth. While the creation of an organization does not solve many problems, the existence of the organization may insure more continuing, organized attention to a problem than would otherwise be given. And the absence of an organization may contribute to the neglect of an issue.

Sometimes the most important result of establishing an organization is to institutionalize the degree of cooperation that governments have achieved in their best moments. In such cases the organization provides a degree of continuity and consistency in the definition of objectives that individual governments find difficult to sustain. A government's past agreement to a principle becomes a present force affecting its behavior; the application of rules to cases can be more consistent and more objective in the framework of an international organization than it can if the only guides are day-to-day diplomacy and *ad hoc* arrangements. Past achievements may, of course, become outmoded or disregarded; but even then, if someone complains, the need to consult about the interpretation of rules and principles can contribute to the evolution of policy. No organization can prevail against general neglect or the refusal of many of its major members to abide by their obligations, but it is usually to someone's interest

1. The organs established under regional agreements like the Treaty of Rome present still a different case, as do bodies created primarily for special and probably temporary purposes, some of them quite technical but others as broad as those of the OEEC when its main task was advancing European recovery and arranging for the cooperation necessary to make effective use of Marshall Plan aid. Still different characteristics distinguish the International Labor Organization, one of the oldest of the international economic institutions.

to complain and call others to account, so life may be breathed into the organization and the agreement on which it is founded.

Membership has had an important bearing on how international economic organizations have worked. The Bretton Woods approach aspired to universality but largely escaped damage from the fractures brought on by the cold war that reduced the effectiveness of such bodies as ECOSOC and the ECE. UNCTAD exists because the less developed countries felt the need for an organization that focused on their needs and wishes. That emphasis has helped make the OECD a place where the industrial countries can discuss policy toward the LDCs as well as the special problems of relations among themselves. The size of the memberships of GATT and the IMF is a matter of considerable importance in determining how they can be used. They have the advantage of including most countries and the disadvantage of not lending themselves to the kind of work that can be done in a small body like the Group of Ten or the OECD. Sometimes this last difficulty can be partly overcome by the use of small committees or restricted groups within the larger framework.

From the analysis of past chapters, three questions stand out about the use of international economic organizations in the '70s. Where are the new kinds of problems to be dealt with? What revision ought to be made in GATT and the IMF to adapt them to the changing world while helping them to continue performing their established functions? Should the industrialized countries make the OECD a stronger body than it has been?

New Problems

New problems could be lodged in new organizations, existing ones, or, for the time being, nowhere, to avoid freezing patterns prematurely. The merits and defects of the three possibilities or combinations of them will differ according to the problem, and it would be tedious to ring all the changes on the arguments. A brief consideration of how nontariff barriers might be handled will suggest some of the issues that need to be thought about.

GATT seems a natural place to start. Nontariff barriers are closely related to the general run of GATT business; some are already dealt with there; there is an inescapable link between the removal of nontariff barriers and the further reduction of tariffs. Though GATT lives by rules, the inability to get general agreement on precise codes for some nontariff barriers is no reason to leave them outside of GATT's scope since that organization can have an "open table" or complaints procedure just as well as anyone else and has the advantage of being a great repository of fact, analysis, and, in a sense, habit concerning the treatment of trade barriers. Moreover, its staff is used to playing the part of intermediary and proposer of solutions and compromises.

The case is strong, but there are some difficulties with it. The membership of GATT is now very broad, but the concern with some nontariff barriers is heavily concentrated in the industrialized countries, where conventional trade barriers are lowest. It is their pressure on one another that gives the best chance of limiting the use of nontariff barriers.[2] Can they negotiate successfully with one another "in GATT" without having their work impaired by the size of the membership? If they agree to get rid of some nontariff barriers and regulate the use of others, will they be allowed to withhold some of these benefits from GATT members that do not undertake comparable obligations? If not, will they hesitate to tie their hands? It is not easy to answer these questions. They involve matters of principle, such as equal treatment, and very practical questions about how to exert enough pressure on countries to get them to change their ways. Because nontariff barriers are such a mixed lot, the answers may not be uniform in all cases. Work on some matters might take place in GATT, on others in the OECD; agreements reached in the latter forum might at some point be formalized in GATT.

The idea of creating a new agency to deal with nontariff barriers is not likely to be very appealing because of their variety and their links with other trade barriers and domestic policies. The third course, dealing with nontariff barriers outside of organizations, is fairly likely to be followed in some cases (though it might be arrived at without any conscious choice). Informal but continuing methods of dealing with certain practices could quite easily take shape as a few countries tried to work on problems of special concern to them. Some of the issues are sure to arise in formally constituted but not highly organized bodies, such as the cabinet sessions (with supporting committees) between the United States and Canada and the United States and Japan or in the commissions occasionally provided for in treaties. Bilateral negotiations are rarely likely to be adequate to handle major problems in international trade distortion, but may be crucial to any agreement on how national behavior is to be altered, whether a formal understanding is reached or not.

Similar reasoning about other new problems might lead to quite

---

2. Some of the more esoteric barriers probably do not exist at all in less developed countries, but others, like government purchasing arrangements, are sometimes mainstays of trade and development policies. If the LDCs are not expected to remove conventional barriers as freely as the industrialized countries do, is it reasonable to expect them to treat nontariff barriers differently?

different results but always there would be uncertainties. It may seem obvious, for example, that agreements about agricultural trade belong in GATT; but if the process of reaching them is going to involve wholly new kinds of negotiation about some national farm policies, the serious spadework may well have to be done elsewhere. Perhaps *ad hoc* sessions between the United States and the European Community would be best. But should it not be possible for the OECD's agricultural committee to reach a point one day at which countries criticize one another's farm policies—and perhaps influence performance—just as they do monetary and fiscal policies in Working Party No. 3? Investment problems, too, are likely to arise initially between two countries, but sometimes involve more; rapid progress is not likely to follow if the difficult questions about international production are thrown too early into a general forum. If any significant degree of agreement is reached to cooperate in regulating the Eurodollar market, or otherwise dealing with short-term capital movements, it will surely be as the result of negotiations among the central banks and treasuries of the Group of Ten.

As people become more aware of the wide range of interconnected issues about which the industrial countries have to negotiate, the proposal will be made that sooner or later a comprehensive understanding should be drawn up embodying as much agreement as can be reached on a wide range of topics along with provision for negotiation and exploration of others. The idea is a poor one. The lesson of the ITO is that the apparently logical effort to take account of interrelations, and to provide assurance that concern with one problem (for example, trade liberalization) will not be permitted to interfere with the effective pursuit of another aim (for example, full employment), can quickly lead to failure. There were a number of reasons for the ITO's failure, but not least was the overloading of the agreement and the concomitant watering-down of provisions to secure general acceptance. It seems only too likely that another effort to be comprehensive would lead to the same results.

It is true that the effort to deal separately with a number of issues will lead to overlap and at the same time leave gaps. It would be desirable to avoid the worst of these defects, but neatness is not the ultimate virtue in this matter and may be the will-o'-the-wisp that leads into the swamp. There is no insurmountable reason why the same governments cannot meet one another in different places to deal with different problems or establish whatever links among the issues seem to them appropriate. For many matters, especially new ones, it may be the best approach to negotiate in different places, testing the many-sidedness of questions to see with what others they can most profitably be linked, or to find what group of governments, inspired by what *genius loci*, can make the most progress on a certain matter. For a single government, anxious to bring certain issues into international negotiation, this multiple approach may be almost mandatory. As one of the closest students of the OECD said: "A variety of instrumentalities, used pragmatically and flexibly, provides a range of options; moreover, several can be used, simultaneously or alternatively, as the situation demands. And always, there are the conventional and enduring methods of bilateral talks and negotiations."[3]

There are, of course, some qualifications to such a free-handed prescription. There needs to be more coordination in the handling of related issues than in the past; that is a matter partly of the organization of national governments for the conduct of foreign economic policy and partly of better cooperation among such organizations as GATT, the IMF, and the OECD when they deal with interrelated or even overlapping problems. The multiplication of channels must not become a substitute for effective concentration on problems but a means of finding the most effective way of concentrating (while at the same time taking account of the links between each new issue and several old ones). It is an approach better suited to the problems that do not (or not yet) lend themselves to elaborate written agreement and procedures. When the latter stage is reached, the case is often strong for attaching such arrangements, subject to some of the conditions discussed above, to existing agencies, notably GATT and the IMF.

Adapting GATT and the IMF

For many people, "Bretton Woods" means the IMF, one of its original cornerstones. In the broader sense used in this book, the Bretton Woods approach gives equal pride of place to GATT, originally intended to be a temporary arrangement. The key roles these two organizations have played in postwar economic cooperation is evident. It is equally evident that if the agreements were to be newly drawn, draftsmen with a sense of the '70s would make significant changes in some of the rules and, perhaps especially, in the scope of the agencies' responsibilities. What is not obvious is whether the kind of agreements that could be negotiated today would be at all as liberal as those on which the Fund and GATT rest. Many experienced people believe they would not. That conclusion—or even just the suspicion that it may be correct—has an important bearing on

3. Henry G. Aubrey, *Atlantic Economic Cooperation: The Case of the* OECD (New York: Praeger, for the Council on Foreign Relations, 1967), p. 84.

how these valuable parts of the Bretton Woods heritage can best be adapted to the needs of the future.

The case of the Fund is in many respects the easier. The practice of working out major monetary reforms among key countries, notably the Group of Ten, and then lodging them in the Fund structure works quite well. The review required every five years of national quotas (not import restrictions but shares in the Fund which also determine votes) has made it possible to take some account of the shifting economic importance of countries. No regional monetary arrangements have taken a form that challenges the Fund's pre-eminence or even strains its rules. Adaptations to other changes, such as the provision of additional facilities for less developed countries in certain circumstances, have been made either by amendment or the adoption of new procedures.

Few people question the value of the Fund, but GATT has come under increasing attack in recent years. Many of the complaints arise from the erosion of the principle of equal treatment, of which more will be said later. Closely connected, however, are objections about the number of exceptions made to rules, slowness or lack of enforcement, and, in general, a sense of flaccidity. A specifically American version of these complaints is that the United States does not get as good treatment as it gives because others are not made to live up to their obligations; i.e., a lack of reciprocity is charged, always a serious failing in American eyes. To complain about GATT is, of course, to complain about its member countries and how they act in GATT. Some people attribute much of the trouble to the large increase in membership. Others trace the main difficulties to the European Community's departures from GATT principles and the unwillingness of others, including Britain, to challenge the Community because they are concentrating on working out their own relations to it. Still other people see the main source of trouble in the lack of American initiative (in the period since the Kennedy Round) and the failure of the United States to devote to GATT the energy necessary to get the most out of the organization in, admittedly, difficult circumstances. To some Americans GATT is not satisfactory because "the United States can always be outvoted"—a strange objection from those who stress the importance of international cooperation, but a long-standing prejudice of congressional committees.

It is easy to draw up lists of ways in which GATT might be strengthened. Some would amount to improving or elaborating the rules on such matters as customs unions and free trade areas, subsidies, the use of trade barriers in balance of payments adjustments, state trading (related to government procurement), and international supervision of the use of escape clauses. Another list would concern the extension of GATT's rules to cover additional problems, some old and some new, connected with trade, such as "voluntary" export quotas, private business practices, pricing, various kinds of industrial policies, other nontariff barriers, and, in general, those things that could be considered to fall under the heading of the rules of fair competition. The list quickly becomes formidable, and the obstacles to acting on it stand out: the risk that the results would be to weaken the rules instead of strengthening them; the danger of destroying the organization by overloading it; the large number of countries involved; the fact that not all the problems are ripe for solution by rules. Whether it would be wise to try to amend GATT in one respect or another is a question on which only the most pragmatic judgments can be respected.[4] A general revision runs afoul of the suspicion mentioned earlier, that nothing as liberal as GATT could be negotiated today. Lack of agreement on how a wide range of new problems should be handled makes the idea of a general revision seem premature. The main virtue of such a proposal would be to call attention to the importance of trade issues and of GATT's potential.

There is a risk that "the falling tide of expectations," as John Evans has called it,[5] will cause people to underestimate the potential of GATT and so contribute to the deterioration that creates the discontent in the first place. Perhaps too much is taken for granted. In spite of the waivers and violations, there are GATT rules and decisions that are adhered to. How many new restrictions might be imposed if GATT did not forbid them? Even the need to consult about the application of principles to cases and to explain why one has done something plays its part in shaping national action. At the same time that GATT is so frequently criticized, one repeatedly encounters the thought that we need "a GATT" for investment, adjustment, capital movements, or the multinational corporation. These ideas, some of them referred to in earlier pages, come from serious-minded men. The striking frequency with which they use the GATT analogy suggests that in international economic relations there is a growing, not declining, need for acceptance by governments of a combination of principles, rules, procedures and a place to negotiate about them. This is what GATT has provided for international trade

4. Some GATT amendments require unanimity, others a two-thirds vote. The latter become binding only on those countries which accept them. A country may not be willing to accept new obligations unless certain others do so as well.
5. *The Kennedy Round in American Trade Policy: The Twilight of the GATT?* (Cambridge: Harvard University Press, 1971), p. 325.

since 1947, and before dissatisfaction turns to deprecation one should try to imagine what the period would have been like without GATT.

Whether GATT can be made to work better depends on how much agreement there is among the leading countries about the kinds of rules that should govern international trade. That agreement depends to an important extent on a judgment about how costly or dangerous it might be not to agree. The sense that arose in the '60s that it was vital to the coherence of the international economic system that the principal nations agree on monetary reform has not existed in relation to trade. While it is true that many of the issues that cause the most dissatisfaction with GATT are neither dramatic enough nor materially significant enough, when taken one by one, to threaten the survival of the international economy, they are of great importance when taken cumulatively and with a feeling for the ultimate results of a chain reaction of retaliation. If a sense of danger grows, the decline of GATT could be reversed. While some amendments may be useful, the principal road to improvement would lie in how governments use GATT. If they took it more seriously, both in conforming to its rules and in using its procedures as much as possible, they would not only overcome some of the deficiencies that led to dissatisfaction with GATT but would open up its potentialities, which have in many respects been ignored in the years since the Kennedy Round. One government alone cannot bring about this transformation, but a serious effort by any one of the major trading nations would get some response, and a combined effort by a few would force the rest to pay attention.

Even in the absence of agreement on how GATT should be changed, there may be ways to make it more useful. One would have thought that the thousands of man-hours spent every year in bilateral and multilateral discussions would provide more than enough talk about trade matters. Oddly enough, though, thoughtful practitioners of commercial diplomacy feel the need for still more extensive consultation. An experienced Dutch diplomat, who represented his government at GATT, has said: "The present G.A.T.T. Council is, apart from its routine business, usually convened only *after* some disputed measure has been taken. . . . A periodic meeting, perhaps once or twice a month, would have the advantage of giving governments contemplating specific measures a chance to explain them."[6] One

6. Johan Kaufmann, "International Trade Policy at the Crossroads," *Progress, the Unilever Quarterly*, No. 4–1968/69, p. 48. He would not confine membership to countries in GATT and thinks of the Council as functioning sometimes as a GATT organ and sometimes as a joint GATT–UNCTAD body, but these points raise questions which it is not necessary to go into here.

may have doubts whether a forum of the size proposed would really provide adequate close consultation. What is wanted is something different from the annual meeting of the Fund and Bank or the debate in the U.N. General Assembly's Second Committee. Perhaps the problem could be resolved by committees and restricted groups operating within a larger framework. In the summer of 1970 high officials of the United States, Britain, Japan, and the Community met at (though technically not in) GATT to talk about textiles and related matters. Whatever the right formula (and there may not be a single one), other practitioners share Kaufmann's view of the need for more consultation than before. The conclusion fits well with points made a number of times in this book about the need for extensive negotiation for a number of purposes: to prevent problems from arising, to settle them when they do, to provide ways of handling similar issues in the future, and above all to explore the ways of dealing with a growing list of unfamiliar and complex problems.

More active use of GATT might well include an effort to deal informally with some issues, perhaps in a way that might eventually produce an agreement that would be formalized. There might well be ways of bringing both GATT and the Fund more fully into the adjustment process. Other issues may be best attacked by negotiations outside GATT, perhaps in the OECD, with the possibility that the results will ultimately be embodied in GATT. The idea of copying the technique used in monetary matters is attractive, but the analogy is not complete. No small set of countries has the almost unchallenged authority of the Group of Ten. Nevertheless, unless GATT manages to retain its old ability to combine negotiation among a few countries with the devising of arrangements acceptable to the membership as a whole, it will not be able to cope with evolving issues, at least when they are of primary importance to a few countries and only secondary significance to the rest.

To adapt GATT and the IMF to the changing world of the '70s may not prove easy. While the case for doing some things outside the GATT–IMF framework is strong, major efforts should be made to do this in ways that do not weaken the basic structure and principles of the two Bretton Woods pillars. In addition to what they do to enhance cooperation among the industrialized countries, both GATT and IMF are important because they are global (or nearly so) and concern the relations of all member countries. Even though less developed countries may for a long time be excused from many obligations, the existence of the agreements provides a setting into which countries can enter more fully as time passes. The value of the Fund and GATT in these respects is clear. On the other side of this coin, however, are the disadvantages of organizations with many members and the discrepancy between the level of cooperation achieved among the industrialized countries and between them and the rest of the world. There is no escaping the thought that the industrialized countries might achieve most by concentrating on cooperation among themselves, perhaps inside an organization of their own.

The OECD

They have such an organization, the OECD. It stands in contrast to GATT and the IMF not only in membership but in the limited number of obligations it puts on governments. No great body of rules says what may or may not be done, provides means of acting against a country that violates them, or assures the help of others when a country is in difficulty. For the most part the obligations are to consult or notify, and, if some action is agreed on, it usually binds only those countries that consent to it. Consequently, it has been easy for critics to deride the OECD as a talking shop. But we have seen that consulting is one of the major activities in which the industrialized nations have to engage if they are to find ways of dealing with a growing list of questions, especially those for which there is no agreed body of rules. Moreover, a major characteristic of many of these problems is that they do not fall neatly into traditional categories but involve matters that are both domestic and international in their effects and that concern several different kinds of international economic relations. The OECD's mandate is broad and loose enough to make it the one place where the secretariat and the staffs of national delegations can consider a whole range of subjects and their interconnections without running afoul of jurisdictional problems.

Interestingly enough, OECD's principal achievement in the '60s was of just this character. Several times a year, leading economic officials from the member countries meet in Paris at the OECD's Economic Policy Committee or in the guise of its more restricted Working Party No. 3. In these sessions national economic policies are discussed, explained, and criticized. National experts' assessments of the state of their own economies are accepted or questioned by their foreign peers. Policies being followed or contemplated are attacked and defended. What, precisely, the consequences have been in terms of changes in what governments have done are matters about which the public record is naturally not clear. There can be little doubt, though, that knowing that others question one's judgment or that to persist in a certain course will stimulate a bad reaction abroad has an influence. On most issues, differences exist within each government, and foreign reactions may play their part in shifting a balance. And in the shaping of future policy, decisions must surely be influenced by knowing what others intend to do, or at least how they see certain problems and what they expect to happen.

Some of the same elements are found in the work of OECD's Development Assistance Committee (DAC) where countries discuss their aid policies. In other fields, too, a certain degree of confrontation, explanation, and mutual criticism takes place but not as consistently as in Working Party No. 3 and often not at as high a level. No doubt there are historical, perhaps even accidental, reasons that explain why governments seem to take much of the other work of the OECD less seriously than that in Working Party No. 3. But there is no reason why this must always be so. Discussions in chapters 5 and 8 have suggested that agriculture and the whole cluster of issues comprised in the idea of the conditions of fair competition might well be dealt with more seriously in the OECD in the future than in the past. A somewhat different route to potentially useful competition was set out in a "Procedure for Notification and Consultation on Measures for Control of Substances Affecting Man or His Environment," established in May 1971. With the secretariat acting as a kind of message center, governments are to report measures "likely to affect adversely and to a substantial extent the economic interests of other Member countries or international trade."[7] The others will express their reactions and may ask for consultation. If used more actively than some other complaints procedures, this one could in time provide the rudiments of a code of behavior (if not precise rules) that was accepted in practice (if not in law) and that began to establish common standards (at least among member countries). Like so many of the early steps in environmental matters, this one poses the question: Why here? Why OECD and not GATT or, indeed, the U.N.'s Economic Commission for Europe, since the concern for pollution is well known to be one of the shared values of Marxists and non-Marxists alike? The only answer one can give at the outset is "better here than nowhere." Plainly, when agreement can be found, it should be acted on, but what is done in one organization should not become a barrier to taking complementary action elsewhere. In the long run, questions will arise about how the extensiveness of coverage of one arrangement is to be compared with the effectiveness of action under another and the costs of duplication versus its possible advantages. But these are questions for the future.

In a second line of activity, the OECD record is weaker (that is to

7. *OECD Notification Procedure for Environmental Control Measures*, from OECD Press Release/A(71)10, Annex, Paris, May 26, 1971.

say, the governments have not been willing to go very far). A limited arrangement has been made for consultation about national policies toward private business practices. Some progress was made in drafting a code on government purchasing, but it was never acted on. For years the OECD has had codes of liberalization concerning current invisibles and capital movements. While the rules they lay down probably determine what happens in some cases, the codes have no teeth to speak of and quite often seem to be forgotten. A strong case can be made for taking a hard look at the codes to see whether they provide a basis on which cooperation about investment policies and capital movements might be built. The more the OECD's work in these and related matters expands, the more problems arise about how the arrangements worked out in OECD and possibly applying only to the advanced countries are to be related to GATT and the IMF. There are also issues affecting both these organizations (and sometimes others) that can usefully be discussed in the OECD even if no formal agreements are reached. An example is the adjustment process which was the subject of an extensive exchange of views in Working Party No. 3 in the mid-'60s, resulting in a sound report and perhaps some influence on national policies.

A third way that the OECD can be used is to try to work out understandings about how member countries will conduct themselves in other international organizations. There is an element of this in DAC's work, but the most notable case is the agreement on a preferential tariff system for LDCs that was then offered to them in UNCTAD and would eventually involve changes in GATT. Comparable approaches to economic relations with the Communist countries have been suggested from time to time but without much success. There need not always be some outside group toward whom the OECD members are coordinating their behavior. A potentially major step toward dealing with trade matters came when the OECD agreed to set up "a small high-level group" to help explore "broader opportunities for progress" toward trade liberalization.[8] The need for

8. *Communiqué* of the Council of the OECD at Ministerial Level, from OECD Press Release/A(71)18, Paris, June 8, 1971, p. 3. The group's mandate stresses trade problems and not their relation to other matters such as investment, capital movements, the adjustment process, and monetary affairs. Not only out of tune with the intellectual currents of the time, this maneuver is especially ironic in an organization with the special advantage of being able to draw different kinds of things together. The explanation seems to lie in the belief of at least some monetary authorities that existing arrangements for exploring their field of policy are quite satisfactory.

the action arose from "the changing nature of trade and related problems"; and the results, if they are concrete at all, could hardly fail to point to action that member governments ought to take, separately and together, in relations with others as well as among themselves, in GATT as well as in the OECD.

A fourth possible line of development sometimes envisioned for the OECD is not very promising, at least for the foreseeable future. This is the thought that, because the industrialized countries have a better chance of pressing ahead with closer economic cooperation when they concentrate on relations with one another, they should aim to give the OECD more authority, put obligations on members, and generally make it the central economic organization of the industrial world in the sense that GATT and the IMF are the centers of their "worlds." One form of this suggestion is that a set of rules about trade paralleling that of GATT should be built up in the OECD; indeed, the GATT rules might be transferred to OECD, leaving GATT (if it remained anything at all) the place where only global trade matters were dealt with. The case against this approach has already been made in discussing other questions. The risk would be high that, in being transferred, the GATT rules would be weakened even as they applied to the industrial countries. To weaken the effort to deal with trade problems on a global basis is in many respects undesirable. A formalized rich man's club might well result in discrimination in some form against the poor countries and damage to their interests. Given the limited load that the governments can carry at any given time in negotiating about international economic relations, it seems highly doubtful that this kind of reordering of the organization framework—which would undoubtedly be tedious and difficult, opening up new issues as it proceeded—would be the best use of their efforts. Much of what has been said about the difficulties of MFTA applies here as well.

Perhaps some day a radical reformation of the OECD will seem desirable. For the foreseeable future the emphasis should be on making more effective use of the OECD to deal with the intricate problems the industrial countries face. For the most part, the OECD should probably be thought of as an organization where consultation and negotiations take place. Sometimes agreements may be reached and sometimes the application and enforcement of the agreements may be lodged in the OECD. No doubt the strengthening of OECD will require some changes in staffing and organization, but these should not prove too difficult to work out if governments show they are willing to make fuller use of the possibilities they have created for themselves.[9] That they should try to do so is clear enough. If the main lines of analysis worked out in this book have validity, and if the industrial countries do not choose to ignore the advantages of openness and cooperation, then it would be logical to suppose that the OECD would have a future far greater than its past. That possibility, and the organization's ability to live up to it, depends on the governments of the member countries—or at least a few of them.

Choices

It is not very fruitful to pursue questions of the proper allocation of functions among organizations in any detail or to fashion hypothetical new organizations to take care of future problems. Neither elegant pigeonholing nor ideal designing will advance thought or policy very much. A few conclusions stand out from this review of problems and possibilities. If changing problems are to be dealt with effectively, there will have to be some changes in existing organizations, the development of new functions, and possibly the creation of new organizations. From time to time, progress may be made in large jumps, when whole new areas of policy or practice are subjected to this kind of international legislation and even constitution-making. More often progress will be piecemeal, made by adding provisions to existing agreements or developing new patterns of behavior within existing organizations.

The choice of what to do was in one sense easier when the Bretton Woods picture was drawn than it is now. Then there were no international economic organizations that could serve the purposes intended, and it was not hard to see which were essential. Today's need is to proceed organically, building on existing bodies which are firmly embedded in international economic life, and the difficulty, as in all organic matters, is how to encourage growth in the right direction without bringing on debilitation, deformity, or death. The problem is further complicated by the divisions in the world, between rich and poor and between the socialist economies and the market-oriented ones. These divisions call into question the univer-

9. One rather drastic change that would be compatible with the emphasis on consultation and negotiation would be the creation of some kind of parliamentary organ in OECD. The objective would not be international legislation or control over the secretariat but the regular exposure of national law-makers to the views of those in other countries about some of the issues being discussed in OECD. A number of objections have made this idea a non-starter in the past, but it seems worth reconsidering from time to time for some of the reasons singled out in Henry Aubrey, cited, pp. 133-36. One possibility that I have not seen explored is to organize something less sweeping than a general parliamentary assembly and more like a set of committees on certain problems.

salism of the Bretton Woods approach, not for reasons of justice or selfishness or because the industrial countries do not need to take account of the global impact of what they do, but on highly practical grounds of relevance and pragmatism. Relevance becomes a question because the Bretton Woods approach lacked means of coping with the problems of international economic management faced by the industrial countries. Pragmatism enters because to make progress it may be necessary to push ahead where opportunity offers and not let doors be closed because not everyone is ready to go through them.

Relevance and pragmatism do not, however, always point to exclusion and the virtues of the small group. There are significant issues in international economics that primarily affect the relations of the rich market-oriented countries with one or both of the other two parts of the world. Sometimes those relations are so importantly affected by what the industrialized countries do among themselves that the smaller group cannot wisely or decently refrain from drawing the others into the final settlement. And there are some issues, from the environment through communications to transportation, that simply have to be handled either globally or at least in groupings that cut across the divisions of rich or poor, Communist or capitalist. So a dualism remains. There is need for both limited and larger groups. There is still another kind of dualism involved, concerning not who is in which arrangement but what is done there. Sometimes results can be achieved only if governments are willing to lay down and accept internationally binding rules and to abide by established procedures for settling disputes about those rules. In other cases, an intensification, sophistication, and better ordering of processes of consultation and negotiation are the most that should be attempted.

In these circumstances it is hard to escape the conclusion that the industrial countries have to follow multiple ends in the organization of the world economy. The "global" organizations inherited from Bretton Woods ought to remain the centerpieces of much international economic cooperation, but they have to be supplemented by a considerable strengthening of the OECD and probably the design of other means of closer cooperation among the industrialized countries as well. Not all cooperation requires formal or even lasting arrangements. Multilateralism, whether global or within the industrial group, does not eliminate the need for a good bit of bilateral (or trilateral or *n*-lateral) cooperation as well, but it makes unacceptable certain kinds of results from such activities. Among multiple ends and a variety of means, there will sometimes be conflict, often tension, and always an element of uncertainty about the best way to proceed. But in these respects the problems of organization are not different from the rest of international economic relations. The option that must be excluded from a list of intelligent alternatives is to go back to the pre–Bretton Woods pattern of trying to conduct international economic relations with only the barest minimum of international organizations and agreements.

EQUALITY FOREVER?

Close to the heart of the Bretton Woods ideal was the concept of equal treatment of all countries in international economic relations.[10] Its most familiar form, most-favored-nation treatment in international trade, was enshrined in the opening article of GATT. The Fund Agreement's rules about exchange rates and the eventual ending of controls on current transactions were expected to do away with some of the instruments by which discrimination was practiced. In the minds of the authors, and especially the American authors, these steps embodied some of the greatest lessons learned from the bad interwar experience and provided vitally needed insurance against the discriminatory practices which had so distorted world trade and payments in the '30s. In addition, they were seen as a major defense, on the one hand, against the political friction generated by measures that treated one country better (or worse) than another and, on the other hand, against allowing political considerations (whether intended to favor or hurt) to interfere with the sound long-run development of the world economy.

The non-American authors were less sure. Even if they accepted the ideas as sound for the long-run organization of the world economy (and not all did), many had qualms about the immediate future. A commitment not to discriminate might prove to be a costly restriction on their freedom of action to make the most of their limited resources during recovery. A compromise was reached in the "fine print" in GATT and the Fund Articles that permitted discrimination (and other generally forbidden practices) when countries were in balance of payments difficulties. For more than a decade, in-

10. Some people prefer the term "nondiscrimination," arguing that this emphasizes policies that apply uniformly to all regardless of whether all can benefit equally from such treatment. They would reserve "equal treatment" for measures that apply uniformly to countries in comparable positions, so that it could be assumed that the result would be more or less equal. There is something to this point, but I find it more convenient to use the terms interchangeably. I shall also ignore, for the general part of this discussion, the limits on equal treatment that arise from having the commitment to provide it confined to relations with others who make the same commitment (which is the form the "universal" principle takes in GATT and the IMF, for example).

terpretation of these elaborate provisions along with decisions as to when they were and were not applicable did much to shape the international transactions of the developed countries. As the dollar shortage ended and more currencies became convertible, the exceptions became less important (though some hung on), and the rules of equal treatment were more generally applied. The original compromise paid off magnificently. Countries were allowed to discriminate rather fruitfully when they needed to; when the need was over, equal treatment was more or less automatically introduced. Had the principle not been established at the outset and incorporated in concrete rules, it is hard to believe that there would not be much more discrimination than now exists in world trade.

In spite of this achievement, the status of the principle of equal treatment was far from secure as the world entered the '70s. This was less the result of a direct challenge or careful calculation of alternatives than of a kind of erosion combined with efforts to deal with specific problems without much regard for general principles. The erosion stems partly from the importance in world trade of two groups of countries that trade freely with one another but levy tariffs on imports from outsiders: the Common Market and EFTA. The expected enlargement of the Community and the association of some nonmembers with it will increase the area of preferential trading. Though the automotive agreement between the United States and Canada has a number of peculiar features, the great growth of trade under it is regarded by most people as another big departure from equal treatment. A number of less developed countries receive preferential tariff treatment from the European Community (and accord some preferences in return). A fairly extensive preferential system remains within the British Commonwealth. The idea has been accepted that some exports from almost all less developed countries should be given preferential tariff treatment in the markets of all the industrialized countries. Thus the volume of trade conducted under exceptions to most-favored-nation treatment looms very large and may well grow.

A number of less developed countries practice discrimination in their exchange rates. Trade with the Communist countries is shot through with discriminatory arrangements. Discrimination against many Japanese goods persists in one form or another even when rules are not violated. For a number of reasons, some more and some less meritorious, countries frequently seek GATT sanction for discriminatory trade practices. Sometimes the practices go on without approval and may even survive challenges. The willingness of a government to accept another's departures from the rules is enhanced by the thought that it may wish a similar indulgence on another occasion. The very process of protecting the principle may lead in hard cases to acquiescence in arrangements by which the rules are bent in order to avoid strains that might overtly break them and so lead to the dilemma of retaliation or apparent acceptance of further disrespect for the rule.

Such erosion is dangerous for the future of the principle of equal treatment. There is, however, another side to the story. For one thing, distinctions need to be made between different kinds of departures from equal treatment. Those that are covered by an agreed-on general principle—the formation of customs unions or free trade areas or the formally accepted granting of preferences for exports of less developed countries—must be distinguished from those in which countries violate the rules or circumvent them. In the former case, whether the exception was wise or not, it was at least made in a conscious effort to modify the principle of equal treatment for the common good. In the latter case, countries are abusing international agreements in what they conceive to be their own interests. The third category of departures from equal treatment—agreed-on waivers in specific circumstances—falls beween the first two. It is the vehicle of flexibility and flexibility is a virtue, as the experience of the period of the dollar shortage shows. But flexibility can also be abused until the values of the rules are lost in a sea of exceptions. The danger is that the growth in importance of the first category and a failure to make progress in eliminating the second will lead to the third category's becoming not a useful way of adapting principles to circumstances but a demonstration of the often-heard cynical remark that "anything is 'Gattable'" if the interested parties are strong enough and firm enough in their stands. The reasoning would be somewhat like that of Seithenyn in Peacock's *The Misfortunes of Elphin.* Accused of letting the embankment entrusted to his care decay, he said, "Decay is one thing, and danger is another. . . . I say, the parts that are rotten give elasticity to those that are sound."

Not all the pressure is in one direction. Governments continue to be very much concerned about discrimination when it hurts them. The countries in EFTA and the Community object to discriminatory rules within the group; equality in the broader sense of a balance of advantage among the members is crucial to their cohesion. British entry into the Community and whatever arrangements follow with regard to the rest of EFTA result in part from the wish to get on an equal footing with competitors. A key element in the debate about existing or proposed preferences for the exports of the less developed countries concerns discrimination among them by the developed countries or some of them. Many Americans argue that, because Europe discriminates against Japan more than the United States does, the pressure of Japanese goods on the American market is increasing. Countries cannot be too complacent about the persistence of discrimination (or too easy-going in their support of others' requests for waivers of GATT rules) lest they find themselves in the future at the losing end of a comparable arrangement. For small countries, or those in a weak bargaining position, the most-favored-nation clause is one of the best protections ever invented.

In addition to pressures for equal treatment motivated by a concern for exports, there are others, usually much weaker, based on the cost that discrimination puts on economies through imports. To deny oneself the freedom to import from the cheapest sources in the world is to impose a burden not only on consumers but also on producers if the result is to make their materials and equipment more expensive than they need be. A trade grouping valued for the export opportunities it opens may entail costs if it encourages the growth (or continuation) of relatively high-cost production in other countries within the group. Inflation is fed by any measure that restricts imports or raises their price. In the end, the concern with imports may become a concern with exports if producers find themselves less competitive in world markets than those in countries that import more freely. Reaction to such considerations is apt to be slow since congenital export-mindedness will focus first on the advantages of a privileged position in someone else's market. Nevertheless, in the best study of postwar trade discrimination that we have, Gardner Patterson has found that in the '50s concern about the costs of postwar trade discrimination played a significant part in renewing interest in equal treatment.[11] But the onset of trade regionalism and the attractions it offered many countries seemed, when he was writing in the mid-'60s, to have overwhelmed this concern. It may well show itself again (for example, through the European Community's Common Agricultural Policy), but its potential force is hard to judge and at best a long-run matter.

The challenge to equal treatment does not come from support for some contradictory principle. It would, indeed, be hard to imagine how a principle of unequal treatment could be worked out as a general guide to policy. Regionalism is spoken of by some as an alternative principle to equal treatment. But unless it is seen as an agreed-on departure from equal treatment (as in the creation of a customs union), it lacks any principle for relations between regions. Dis-

11. *Discrimination in International Trade: The Policy Issues, 1945–1965* (Princeton University Press, 1966), pp. 39-43.

crimination in favor of the poor is conceivable as a general principle, but it is hard to imagine a world in which the main threat to equal treatment comes from the insistence that tariffs be higher in trade among the rich countries than on their imports from the poor. Beyond that, the principle gives no guidance about relations among the non-poor (or even among the poor alone). Discrimination is almost certainly less important than improved access to rich markets as a means of helping the poor. Economic theory lends support to the view that nondiscrimination maximizes general welfare only under conditions which rarely, if ever, prevail in the real world. A certain amount of discrimination of just the right kind would increase world welfare more than completely nondiscriminatory treatment.[12] It is, however, difficult to translate this proposition into policy in any very convincing fashion. If there were no international agreement on a formula (which might require frequent changes in the pattern of discrimination), efforts by individual countries to follow their own calculations could be upset by the decision of other countries to respond in kind. The strong may make out well at this game, but that is another matter.

The real alternative to equal treatment is not the substitution of a different general principle but acceptance of the idea that each country should be free to calculate its own interests as well as it can and discriminate as it deems best. The likely result will be counterdiscrimination. As each country seeks to offset the behavior of others or get compensation by seeking privileges of their own, international friction will result, with two possible outcomes. By compromising conflicts and exchanging privileges, two countries, or groups of countries, may remove the friction and come to acceptable arrangements. Some of these will be damaging to outsiders; but even if there were a global compromise, there is no reason to suppose it would be better for all (or even for the countries involved if it were not global) than adherence to the principle of equal treatment. The second outcome, which could be concomitant or alternative, would be a hodge-podge of discriminatory practices, which only by the remotest coincidence would be likely to serve the general interest or even many national

---

12. One of the winners of the first Nobel Prize for economics gained part of his fame by an essay on how, in some circumstances, trade could be maximized by discrimination. Ragnar Frisch, "On the Need for Forecasting a Multilateral Balance of Payments," *The American Economic Review*, September 1947, pp. 535-51. Of course, trade is only a rough measure of welfare, but the real trouble with the approach is that the models showing what pattern and degree of discrimination would maximize trade must depend on assumptions that may or may not correspond to real conditions just as the theory of nondiscrimination does. Moreover, these conditions change, whereas sensitive, quick changes in policy are rare.

interests better than a system based on equal treatment. The hodge-podge would be dynamic; retaliation, imitation, and the hope of gaining political or economic advantage plus the need to respond to domestic pressures, with no support for resistance from international obligations, would almost surely lead to more restriction and distortion of international trade rather than a rectification of the deficiencies flowing from a rigorous application of most-favored-nation treatment. Nor is it likely that discrimination will stop at trade measures. The competitive economic nationalism of the '30s from which the authors of Bretton Woods drew back in revulsion and tried to protect the postwar world is the authentic picture of the conditions to which this course leads.

It is too much to say that the industrialized countries have started down that road at the beginning of the '70s. Nevertheless, the erosion of the idea of equal treatment removes some of the roadblocks. The justification that a given expedient yields immediate gains gets around some others. A failure to reassert the principle of equal treatment will result in further deterioration. Rumination on alternatives supports no conclusion other than that reached by Gardner Patterson:

> The world will be well served by holding to the general policy of non-discrimination, requiring that departures from it be justified in each case. It will also be well served by continuing to demand that any such departures be subject to international approval and supervision. Despite all the outright violations of the IMF and GATT nondiscrimination rules, and the even more frequent bending of them, the two decades since the end of World War II have demonstrated that such rules and such institutions not only mean that retaliation is less likely, but also that if a nation or a group of nations wants to discriminate they have to give more attention than they probably otherwise would to long-run as well as short-run consequences, to the impact on others as well as on themselves, and to secondary as well as primary effects. This surely is in the interests of the world's welfare.[13]

This moderate and carefully phrased conclusion does not answer all possible questions about equal treatment. It leaves open the matter of what exceptions ought to be approved. Enough has been said throughout this book about blocs, national adjustment to balance of payments changes, and the difficulties of adapting domestic industrial and agricultural production to changes in world trade to show some of the difficulties. A study of relations between rich and poor countries would reveal others. As always in considering economic policy, one must bear in mind that cases will arise in which governments will want to discriminate in favor of a certain country to symbolize po-

13. Cited, pp. 395-96.

litical good will. Such practices contribute to the erosion of equal treatment even if their economic importance is minor, as it often is. If major, the results are likely to be retaliation and the kind of friction the emphasis on equal treatment was intended to avoid in the first place.

A different set of problems concerning equal treatment arises from the relative decline in importance of tariff barriers and the increase of other kinds of problems among the industrialized countries. The most-favored-nation principle is the invention of a world in which tariffs were the great issue. Its application to quotas and exchange controls was never entirely satisfactory (but was better than a failure to try to apply it). In investment, equal treatment among foreigners is rarely regarded as an adequate substitute for equal treatment of foreigners and nationals. A serious attack on nontariff barriers will raise new questions touching both issues, national treatment and the attempt to find satisfactory, relatively simple ways of defining equal treatment and detecting departures from it. The answers are not simple, but the process of finding them may give new support to the principle of equal treatment, since countries in a reasonably strong position to bargain are not likely to settle for less. In that case, the erosion of regard for equal tariff treatment may be checked since it will be hard to see why logic should run in different directions according to the type of trade barrier. But the difficulty of establishing general criteria for equal treatment in matters more complex than tariffs and quotas may obscure the point.

If the industrial countries want to keep to the principle of non-discrimination, they will have to do something about it. The drift of affairs at the beginning of the '70s is not conserving the principle but undermining it. Only an increase in attention to how the principle is applied, a reassertion of its importance in its familiar forms, and a continuing effort to work out its implications for the growing complications of international economic life will preserve it as a central feature of the world of the future. If there is no such revival, the way will be opened for further economic distortion and destructive economic nationalism.

RECIPROCITY

In American policy, the path to Bretton Woods starts with the Hull trade agreements program in 1934. Much was made, at that time, of reciprocity; the United States would reduce tariffs only in exchange for equivalent trade barrier reductions by others. By the time the Bretton Woods institutions were being built, much less was said about reciprocity because, I believe, it was taken for granted. How else but through bargaining between independent governments, each of which would have to be satisfied with the results, could new agreements be arrived at? Less an objective of the Bretton Woods approach than a part of its mechanism, reciprocal bargaining plainly remains a fact of international life in the '70s. And yet, since so much else has changed, in form if not in essence, it is worth considering whether in the future "reciprocity" should play the same part in the process of economic cooperation as it has in the past.

"Cooperation" is the bland, *good* word for the result, sometimes slightly smoothed over, of bargaining; it is a word of aftermath, of the process viewed in tranquillity. Close to, the process is one of sharp encounters, toughness about alternatives, insistence that one thing is essential and another completely unacceptable, and a firmer tone of voice about the true national interest than the intellect allows. The Kennedy Round became a milestone in cooperation only after years of exhausting and frustrating battles full of threats and near breakdowns. The cooperation that produced the Special Drawing Rights and other major reforms in the international monetary system included muscle-flexing, accusations that economic realism was being sacrificed to political ambition, and essays in brinkmanship of a sort usually associated with other aspects of international life. All this is well recognized and can be looked at with some equanimity, especially in retrospect and when one considers how much good this rather rugged procedure has accomplished during the postwar period. But the method has its price, and not only in the human terms of the heart attacks that have marked some of the marathon negotiating sessions that led to the peaks of cooperation among the Common Market countries. The price of the bargaining approach is some slowing-up of progress in removing barriers if one country will not do as much as others think it should, some refusal to take perfectly feasible and desirable steps in the hope of being "paid" to take them later, and a good bit of confusion about real interests. The facts about who gains and who loses from what has been done are sometimes concealed by beliefs about who won in the maneuvering (or more likely the wish to demonstrate that everybody won). Quite naturally the feeling has arisen that it would be desirable to moderate this process of nationalistic bargaining in a world of increasing interdependence and to put cooperation on a somewhat more sophisticated (some might say "higher") plane.

Much of the criticism has centered on trade bargaining. One line of attack is that the whole depiction of tariff bargaining as a form of combat is a caricature: the "concession" a country makes to another by reducing its tariffs is in fact a favor to itself. Another set of criticisms (which can be complementary or independent) is directed against the idea that each bargain should result in a close balance of calculable advantages for each country. The results of that practice, it is said, are misdirection of effort, a degree of dishonesty, and a narrow view of what trade barrier reduction really means. Both cases have much merit.

The first line of argument is essentially that of the free trader who says that a country reduces its own welfare (or otherwise damages its economy) by restricting imports and should rid itself of the burden as expeditiously as possible, whether others do so or not. The advice is often good but not the chances of its being taken. The repeal of the Corn Laws, the short-lived episodes of unilateral American tariff reduction, the cutting of duties as an anti-inflationary device in Erhard's Germany, and a few other cases look like exceptions to a strong bias of industrial nations. Moreover, it is hard to gainsay the argument that if a willingness to do away with protection can be used to induce others to do likewise, the results would be better than those of unilateral reductions. Balance of payments considerations are apt to point to the same conclusions. The success of the bargaining approach during the postwar period stems partly from the fact that external pressure and the offer of specific advantages can be more persuasive than counsels of unilateral action. It is hard to believe that the situation will change radically in the future.

There may, however, be some shift in the possibilities. For those tariffs which are very low, perhaps little more than nuisances, unilateral action may be a good bit cheaper and quicker than multilateral negotiation. The discovery that the removal of tariffs is not as traumatic an experience as was once believed and the realization that leaving some tariffs untouched while others are reduced may damage an industry's competitive position (if, for example, duties have to be paid on components used in the production of duty-free items) may increase the number of cases in which the United States or other countries would simply be willing to act without waiting for another round of international tariff bargaining. In agriculture, as we have seen in chapter 8, the case for reducing restrictions rests much more heavily on domestic advantage than on any gain a foreigner can be expected to pay for by a matching concession. If a country were party to an agreement to eliminate tariffs (or other barriers) by stages, it might find it advantageous to move more quickly than its obligations required even if others did not do so.

It seems unlikely, though, that the resulting changes will be more than marginal. Even if one expects to gain from removing a barrier, it is tempting (and often reasonable) to see whether someone else will not sweeten the process by trading even a small "concession" for it. An experienced negotiator observed:

> In the few postwar instances in which governments have reduced tariff rates without compensation, they have usually sought to keep as much as possible of the bargaining power associated with previous, higher rates. In some cases, the reductions have been characterized as "temporary," and the previous rates carefully preserved in a showcase labeled "statutory tariff." Rarely, if ever, has the reduced rate been consolidated in the country's GATT schedule until the maximum compensation could be extracted in a subsequent negotiation.[14]

The linking of tariff reductions with the removal of nontariff barriers, which seems inevitable (see chap. 5, pp. 122–23), will provide another reason to avoid unilateralism.

The second line of criticism mentioned above concentrates on the fatuity with which the honest idea of reciprocity has come to be interpreted. Not only must every *quid* have its *quo*, but each must be assigned the same money value by processes which will not always bear close scrutiny, much less reflect the real effects of the bargaining on trade or welfare. The make-believe, long familiar to those who have paid attention to international trade negotiations, is rather disreputable but still seems a secondary deficiency, the kind of clumsiness we accept as one of the occasional necessities of our complicated ways of governing ourselves. There is, however, a more serious side; "the drive of each participant to obtain reciprocity in its bargain with the others" was the reason the industrialized countries could not "achieve the full benefits of linear reductions" in the Kennedy Round.[15] "Concessions" that a country was perfectly prepared to make were withheld because other countries would not come up with matching concessions. Bargaining positions had to be preserved for "next time." This was not the first time the progress of trade liberalization was held to the pace of the slowest major contributor.

Improvement looks easy. One step would be for governments to stop acting as if balancing assorted numbers proved equal advantage. Or at least the numbers could be estimates of future trade instead of records of the past; then the false impression of precision would be reduced and attention would be focused where it belongs, on the future. The need to take increasing account of nontariff barriers in

14. Evans, cited, p. 31. Evans's whole chapter is a very interesting discussion of the idea of reciprocity and its persistence.
15. John W. Evans, *U.S. Trade Policy: New Legislation for the Next Round* (New York: Harper & Row, for the Council on Foreign Relations, 1967), p. 29.

tariff negotiations should help in this process as the effects of such barriers are so difficult to measure that explanations of why they were removed are almost bound to emphasize future advantage rather than the "sacrifice" of past practices. If governments agree on a process for moving to free trade or on one of the formulas for reducing tariffs, then close calculation of what is given and received becomes irrelevant. If one set of trade negotiations is conducted more or less in isolation from others, the pressure to show that the resulting bargain is balanced will continue to be strong. In general, though, the widening scope of international trade negotiations and the need to see them in relation to international economic relations as a whole will militate against narrow ideas of reciprocity.

More is involved than achieving a higher standard of honesty in presenting the results of negotiations to Congress and the public. The negotiating dilemma of making the maximum possible progress without unnecessarily giving away bargaining power that will be valuable in the future can only be resolved, as Evans points out, by interpreting reciprocity more broadly than in the past. Such a step contributes to the whole process.

It is not hopelessly idealistic to think in these terms. The United States, while insisting on the hallmark of reciprocity, accepted as equal bargains arrangements that were in fact one-way concessions for as long as other countries were short of dollars (but still went through the process of totting up the past trade affected by each duty rate that was cut). Since it abandoned conditional most-favored-nation treatment in the '20s, the United States has given most countries the benefit of concessions it made to others without asking for strict reciprocity (though it limited what it would "give away" in this fashion by refusing to cut duties on products unless their principal supplier was a party to the bargain). The rich countries as a whole have agreed that they will not ask poor countries to reciprocate in the usual way for reductions in barriers to their exports (which is not quite the same as saying they will ask nothing of them). In negotiations about investment matters, formal reciprocity often has little meaning if the flow is expected to be mainly one way. In negotiations about monetary matters, everyone must believe he gets a fair benefit, but no one pretends that a strictly balanced reciprocity is achievable and the improved operation of the monetary system as a whole is regarded as an important objective. Countries in balance of payments difficulties are helped for the common good and not just because of what they promise to do in return.

A broader conception of the benefits to be derived will not alter the basic mechanism of cooperation. Reciprocity and bargaining come naturally to governments. We shall not get away from them. Nor is that a matter for great grief so long as a fascination with the narrow process does not blind the parties to their true interests, which are broad. Without the demand for reciprocity there would have been far less reduction of trade barriers in the postwar world, and probably less cooperation in other matters as well. It is not merely that the United States insisted that other countries get rid of quotas and lower tariffs if they wanted better access to its rich market. Without reciprocity the United States could not have been brought to change its position in the world from that of an exceptionally high-tariff country to one with near-average tariffs.

The other side of reciprocity is retaliation. Fear of it can play a great part in keeping countries from letting domestic pressures or temporary international difficulties push them to restore trade restrictions. In domestic debate, the risk of retaliation provides some common ground between those who are moved by a general wish to see trade barriers reduced and those who consider themselves strictly pragmatic and stick to a narrow idea of reciprocity. The specter of what other countries would do to American exports was one of the strongest weapons of both the Johnson and Nixon Administrations in resisting the protectionist surge in the United States after the Kennedy Round. It is also important to know when other countries will refrain from retaliation. The adjustment process for countries in balance of payments difficulties is kept from becoming a downward spiral partly by the debtor's willingness to listen to the advice of others for fear that they will retaliate against his import restrictions, while the others refrain from retaliating because they accept his need to take restrictive measures as long as they are temporary. GATT tries to fence retaliation round by applying to it standards of reciprocity; if a country raises a tariff it has lowered or bound, it is given a chance to buy off the retaliation of others by "equivalent" concessions on other items; if it fails to produce good enough offers, the others' legal retaliation is confined to imposing new barriers (or restoring old ones) on amounts of goods estimated to be of similar value. The somewhat dubious calculations may be no better than those used to justify bargains in the first place, but they serve a good cause.

The use of reciprocity for broad and narrow purposes is not yet at an end. Neither of what Evans calls "the two faces of reciprocity" will completely disappear in the '70s. It will continue to be a force for international cooperation and a basis for national insistence on not giving more than you get. The fear of retaliation will continue to be a major disciplinary force in a world where countries sometimes need external discipline to act in their own best interests. One of the greatest arts in economic diplomacy is to play on the division of interests within a foreign country to create a disposition to agree to something you want or at least to avoid a damaging step for which there is strong domestic support. It is the Janus of retaliation-reciprocity that keeps this door open.

The iconoclasts are right that reciprocity should not be an idol. The character of economic relations among the industrialized countries makes it important to see reciprocity broadly, not narrowly—and to a degree helps the process along. Dangers remain. The days of a one-sided policy of giving without appearing to get are probably over in the United States. Others will have to show the kind of concern for the international economy as a whole that the United States did in the best days of its postwar policy. But so will the United States. The question is one of seeing one's interests broadly enough. The mainspring of cooperation continues to be mutual advantage. Therefore, some sense of balanced gain (i.e., reciprocity) is inherent and necessary. In these respects the world of the '70s will not be very different from that of Bretton Woods.

NATIONAL INTEREST

Behind what has just been said about reciprocity and equality and, indeed, behind all the conclusions about foreign economic policy set forth in this book lie judgments about the national interest of the United States and of other countries. Not everyone will share these judgments or agree with the conclusions drawn from them, as is natural in any discussion of policy. Often, the reasoning on which my judgments about national interest are based has been made quite explicit, though sometimes in rather general terms. Because this is a book about foreign economic policy, the rationale for most recommendations has been cast in terms of steps that would help to bring about the kind of world economy that would be beneficial to the United States and the other industrialized countries of the world. At the same time the book has always recognized that other kinds of considerations might alter these conclusions or make them unacceptable. Some of these considerations concern national power or independence; they may have military dimensions or bear on cultural autonomy. Some are as much concerned with maximizing the welfare of society as any economic argument, but they put less stress on increasing efficiency, productivity, and production and more on the equitable distribution of benefits, social justice, the protection of the weak, the sacrifice of growth for the sake of being able to control some of the results of growth (as in environmental pollution), and generally on insuring that other values are not ignored for the sake of buying cheap and selling dear in the largest possible volume.

To weigh all of these factors in connection with every policy suggested in this book would have been impossible. The multiple ends that governments pursue are sometimes in conflict with one another, but not always. Economic policy may help the pursuit of other ends by increasing the resources available for them or assuring the more efficient use of what is available. An emphasis on national measures may be illusory if an objective can be attained only by cooperation with others or by accepting an increased degree of interdependence. As time passes and circumstances change, governments may, and sometimes must, shift the relative importance they attach to aims that conflict with others.

Desirable as it would be to have a consistent way of interpreting "national interest," there seems to be no intellectually satisfactory way of doing so except at a very rudimentary level. "Security" is a favorite word of those trying to define fundamental national interests. No one would question that to provide it is one of the purposes of governments, but their ability to do so is limited. Except in obvious cases, the key question is likely to be whether or not a certain course of action in fact promotes security—or even increases national power. Other political values are likely to seem relevant to the national interest: independence, internal stability, individual liberty and, for some people, democracy, for example. To them must be added some economic objectives and whatever combination of other factors a society designates as "welfare." Each term must be interpreted and some way found of resolving conflicts in the pursuit of each end. Only then can the next step be taken and "national interest" translated into foreign policy terms.

One can sympathize with those who have taken refuge in the view that the only usable idea of national interest is that it is what a government says it is at any given time. This operational definition helps when the frame of reference is limited—for example, in the analysis of bargaining about a particular problem. It is, however, of no use at all for broader analysis or the discussion of what policy should be.

Quite a lot can be done by leaving concepts of national interest aside and concentrating on the analysis of issues and the effort to assess the probable results of alternative courses of action. Economics has made progress as a tool of understanding by giving some of its findings in terms of an unfocused "general interest" (e.g., maximization of product or efficiency, leaving aside questions of distribution) or in showing how the gains and losses of each party to a transaction can be maximized (in purely quantitative terms), but providing little or no basis for choosing between conflicting possibilities. Such analysis helps, but judgment about "national interest" must include choices and take account of nonquantifiable factors. Moreover, a reasonably long time perspective is essential to sound policy judgments. It is always difficult for governments to take the long view, and one of the shortcomings of much economic analysis is that it deals less well with dynamic factors than with static ones.

In matters of foreign economic policy, the determination of national interest has a number of special characteristics. Unlike the situation in power politics when one country's gain is usually seen as another's loss, economic policies can often be arranged so that both (or all) countries gain. An increase in another country's economic strength may contribute to one's own strength, while a decline in the welfare of one country may damage the welfare of another. It is not always easy to determine whether a proposed course of action will in fact result in mutual gain. Much may depend on balancing an easily perceived and fairly certain short-run disadvantage against a presumed but naturally not guaranteed course of development over a longer period. And, of course, even a clear demonstration of balanced economic advantage may not be persuasive if undesirable noneconomic consequences are feared by one or another government.

In matters of economic policy, a high proportion of the conflicts of interest are not international but internal. It is the consumer who is asked to pay to protect the manufacturer, the worker whose real income is reduced for the benefit of the farmer, the farmer who must quit the land so that the housewife may buy cheaper food from abroad. Labor may make common cause with employers about imports and exports but disagree about investment abroad. The workers in an expanding industry may sympathize with those in a contracting one but have some hard choices to make if import restrictions that protect the jobs of others lead to foreign retaliation that jeopardizes their own jobs. And so on.

As if matters were not complicated enough, the developments of the postwar period have raised doubts about the traditional concept of a national economy, the "interest" of which a government is supposed to represent. The growth of foreign investment, as we have seen, has greatly increased the part of the world economy that is in some sense American and in some sense foreign. American-owned plants in Europe are outside the American economy in the usual sense of the term. Much of their effect on it can still be thought of in conventional terms, by what they do in creating markets for exports (or displacing them), in their effect on the balance of payments with the inflow of profits and other payments being compared with the outflow of funds for investment. But we have also seen that conventional balance of payments accounting no longer provides an accurate picture of America's place in the world. The same plants are in some sense part of the European economy. Their workers, the goods they use, their markets, even their capital may be entirely European; the corporations are European legal persons; the human persons who run them may be Europeans who may conceivably act just as they would if their owners were rentiers in Rwanda—but probably do not.

The situation is not entirely new. Flemings wove wool in England in the fifteenth century; Englishmen raised cattle in Texas in the nineteenth; and Texans drilled for oil in Latin America before the war. Whether production overseas is more important in relation to domestic production in the industrial countries now than British foreign investment was at its height in the nineteenth century is not altogether clear. Perhaps the change is primarily one of perception, but it seems clear that there has developed an international economy (largely but not entirely private) that does not fit the conventional boundaries of what is national or international, or at least not always. Matters cannot be put right simply by deciding which government's laws should apply or how statistics should be kept. It is not enough to substitute "control" for "ownership," to ask who gives the manager orders, or to trace in a sophisticated fashion the true beneficiaries of the usufruct. Not only foreign direct investment is involved but the existence of pools of capital whose legal nationality is only of nominal importance compared to the way they flow across borders. One is left puzzled to find a suitable image for contemporary national economies—interlocking pieces; gas chambers with filters; ganglia connected to other parts that are sometimes dominated by another center. But the old tacit assumption of sovereign boxes stacked with flat sides against one another and sliding panels that control access from one to another, though it is valid for much of international economic relations, is clearly inadequate. Consequently, the already perplexing subject of defining national interest takes on still greater complexity. That is true whether national interest is conceived broadly or narrowly, in liberal or mercantilist terms, with emphasis on production or consumption. The possibilities of conflicts of interest among private groups of the same nationality are increased. Even so unexceptionable an ideal as "international cooperation" takes on a subtly different meaning from that which it used to have.

A NEW PICTURE?

If this book had examined the relations of market-oriented industrialized economies with the Communist countries or the less developed world, it would have found additional, but quite different, departures from the Bretton Woods world picture. But those already traced in relations among the industrialized countries are enough to show how different the problems of the '70s are from those of the '40s and '50s.

Bretton Woods was a beginning. Though its prescriptions for the future rested heavily on an analysis of the past, they were put forward at a time when no one could deny the need for new building. There is no such clear starting point as the end of the war for the building that is needed for the '70s and beyond. That lack complicates the process of persuading governments of the need to take major new steps and adds to the uncertainty that the process of economic co-operation among the industrialized countries—so marked and important a feature of the postwar landscape—will keep pace with the changes resulting from the dynamic interplay of economies increasingly open to one another. Openness and interpenetration, partly the fruits of the Bretton Woods approach, have themselves become agents for introducing greater complexity into the relations among the industrialized countries and making the tasks of the future different from and in many ways more difficult than those of the past.

No effort has been made in these pages to draw for the '70s a picture corresponding to the Bretton Woods picture. My emphasis has been more on a process than a set of objectives. At least some of the features of that process emerge quite clearly, mostly because the problems to be dealt with are obvious: for example, the need to deal with nontariff barriers, to improve arrangements for international adjustment, to control capital flight, to cooperate more closely in the management of the international monetary system. Less obvious, but discernible in what has already been said, is the predictable need for a widening of the range of international cooperation to bring about greater harmonization of domestic economic policies and the better management through international action of an international economy that cannot be satisfactorily managed by national action alone.

While the changes in the world lead naturally to an emphasis on what is new and different, it is vitally important to understand that any new picture must incorporate much of the old one. There is little of the Bretton Woods picture that should be discarded; indeed, some of what was left aside, for instance, when the ITO was abandoned, may need to be restored in a modernized and revised version. A certain continuity is guaranteed by the extent to which national interests, policies, and practices are embedded in the old matrix. What has been done needs to be supplemented, enhanced, and sometimes redirected, but not ignored. Whether we emphasize the old picture or a new one, the basic need is a three-part one, for preservation, adaptation, and innovation.

11

American Action

Though the forces that are opening the economies of the industrial countries to one another are strong and to a degree autonomous, they are not irresistible. National measures can block or hamper the process, intentionally or otherwise. They can also hasten it; barriers do not fall, they are removed. To garner the greatest benefits of openness, governments must foster it; to insure the reasonable management of the international economy requires deliberate, well thought-out and sustained efforts; both activities need a high degree of cooperation among a strong majority of the main industrial powers. Successful cooperation requires American participation and perhaps leadership. What the United States will do in the '70s depends on the outcome of a far more complicated play of forces than shaped American policy in the years when it first set the process of cooperation in motion and then sustained it through some bad periods.

It would be hard to find anyone seriously arguing that the United States should refuse cooperation or try to cut itself off from the rest of the world economy. But some of the policies and courses urged on Washington move in that direction. And even when there is full agreement on adhering to the principles and aims of past policy, quite different results may be obtained from choosing one specific objective rather than another and from differences in judgment about methods, timing, and tactics. A government's policy is what it does as well as what it says, even if it speaks with complete candor. When there is a sustained discrepancy between pronouncement and behavior, the latter must be considered the real policy while the former is written off as hypocrisy, illusion, or failure.

No country is ever wholly free from such discrepancies. None is completely consistent in what it does. Every government makes compromises in which the interests of domestic groups, the exigencies of hard cases, or a narrowly conceived national advantage is allowed to dominate over adherence to policies and principles that are acknowledged to embody the true, broadly conceived interest of the whole nation. The short run is constantly at war with the long run, and governments respond more to the first than the second. In spite of these facts of life, it is possible, as the history of the postwar period has shown, for the governments of the industrialized countries of the free world to make enormous progress in working together to their mutual advantage. The United States initiated this process and was its acknowledged leader for years. It need not—probably cannot—lead in the same way in the '70s. But, unless it can overcome the difficulties of providing a new kind of leadership, the process of cooperation that has been so fruitful in the past will be seriously threatened.

This final chapter is concerned with some of the difficulties the United States faces, the possibilities of overcoming them, and the kinds of policies that will both take advantage of those possibilities and give reasonable promise of good results. Since the bulk of the book has dealt with this last point, a rough summary of what has already been said about aims and objectives seems the natural starting place and occupies the next few pages.

The Elements of Policy

As exporters, consumers, and producers, Americans must be concerned about economy and efficiency and, therefore, have an interest in the better allocation of world resources and a wide play of competitive forces. This is the main *economic* objective of foreign economic policy. To pursue it requires attention not only to the international effects of policy measures but to their impact on the American economy. The strength of the economy, judged in large part by its ability to function well in changing circumstances, is a prime requisite for the pursuit of a successful foreign economic policy. A second requisite is that American policy must be broadly enough conceived to be concerned with the operation of the international economic system as a whole and not just the pursuit of "national interests" as conventionally conceived. The ability of the United States to meet both requisites in the '70s is in question.

Further reduction and, indeed, eventual elimination of the tariffs that remain on manufactured goods seem natural objectives in the light of what has been accomplished over the last twenty-five years. Many tariffs can probably best be dealt with by a commitment to reduce them steadily over a period of time, preferably to zero. An extension and expansion of the kind of legislation that has been the basis for American trade bargaining in the past would suffice to meet this purpose. Since it is unlikely that all the key countries will agree to the reduction of all tariffs by some kind of formula, other ways will have to be sought to deal with the hard cases. Negotiations will have to include other barriers than tariffs, provide time and means of adaptation in certain industries, and take account of more objectives than just the liberalization of trade. American participation in activities of this sort may well call for measures going beyond the familiar patterns of tariff bargaining with powers delegated to the President.

Efforts to deal with nontariff barriers and trade-distorting practices should be a major element in American policy in the '70s. No single negotiating technique and no common formula for dealing with these activities will suffice. Even where relatively simple kinds of agreements may be called for, the process of arriving at them is likely to become entwined with other matters. A successful attack on some of the most obvious barriers will reveal new and more complicated problems as more and more domestic actions are seen to have a bearing on foreign trade and payments even though their primary purpose is quite different. Indeed, there is no ultimate objective to this process, not even a utopian one such as "free trade" seemed to be when that term meant the complete elimination of tariffs and quotas. The conduct of national affairs, whether in managing credit, regulating pollution, checking inflation, raising revenues, or doing almost anything else, is always liable to take a turn that appears, to someone at home or abroad, to alter the conditions of competition in international trade and hence to call for correction by national or international action. Many rules may eventually be agreed on, but they will never suffice to dispose of all the cases that will arise.

In agriculture, too, the future is likely to be more complicated than the past. The most serious barriers to American farm exports, notably those of the European Community, and the main American barriers to farm imports as well, are rooted in domestic policies and will be impervious to simple reciprocal bargaining. The only promising course, and a difficult one, is to try to reach international understandings about the objectives and methods of domestic agricultural policies, such as support prices, production control, and export subsidies. Quick results are not to be expected, but the wish of Europeans to make changes in the Common Agricultural Policy to reduce costs and surpluses may help the process. The American bargaining position is not strong. A series of hard decisions will have to be made about such matters as competitive export subsidies, retaliation against European exports of nonagricultural products, and the weight to be given short- and long-run considerations.

In its own interest, the United States ought to avoid the kinds of farm policies that in the past have produced high prices, high costs, and surpluses, aiming instead at policies that encourage the most efficient parts of American agriculture, avoid supporting prices that make exports impossible unless they are subsidized, reduce barriers to imports (except when foreign products are being dumped or subsidized), and provide whatever support is given to farmers through direct subsidies or income payments. Such a course will not open foreign markets to American exports but will put the United States in a sounder position than a more protectionist policy while leaving open the possibility of expanding production if others subsequently reduce their protection (as they may, in time, in their own interest).

The close tie between much overseas investment and the flow of international trade is now generally acknowledged, but there are important differences in judgments about how the two processes affect one another and how best to pursue American interests. In future negotiations the United States will undoubtedly want to link the two subjects more closely than in the past, but just how it is not easy to say. The removal of foreign barriers to American investment remains an important objective, but it cannot realistically be pursued without a sensitive understanding of the reasons for foreign resistance to American domination of some economic activities. Such resistance may well grow in the '70s, forcing the United States to work out a fuller and more precise set of investment policies than was needed in the '60s. One key question will be how much the fostering of private investment abroad need be seen as a matter of public interest to the United States. Another is how much control the United States feels it necessary to exercise over American firms abroad, an activity that makes it harder to persuade other governments to treat American companies without discrimination and to widen the area of business freedom. An increase in foreign investment in the United States, to be welcomed on many counts, may, if it becomes large enough, begin to generate domestic reactions that will have some bearing on how other countries treat American investment.

Increasingly in the '70s, issues once thought of as concerning "foreign investment" (largely American) should be seen as part of the problems surrounding "international production" and the "multi-national enterprise" (still largely American but with the foreign share likely to grow). A primary aim of American policy should be to permit businessmen a wide freedom of choice in locating, financing, and conducting their enterprises. However, a policy that is concerned only with the removal of obstacles is unrealistic and inadequate. In a modern economy, business must be regulated in important respects, and matters cannot be different internationally. The rise in importance of international production and the multinational corporation poses two related sets of problems: those of minimizing the clash between national policies and the economic advantages of carrying out business internationally, and those concerning the possibility of developing international techniques for the supervision of business. Because of the predominance of American interests in international production, the United States cannot escape these complex problems and should, therefore, take the lead in devising sensible approaches to them. Even if it does so, the long, difficult process will be marked by clashes between the United States and other governments, foreign governments and American business, and the United States government and American businessmen.

Many strands of international economic relations come together when countries adjust to changes in their balances of payments. The international monetary reforms of the '60s have improved the setting of this process but there is no doubt that a central issue of American policy in the '70s will be to find ways of making adjustment less disruptive to the international economy than it has often been in the past. Recognizing that some governmental interference with the flow of goods and payments is often unavoidable in the adjustment process, the United States ought to favor arrangements in which as much as possible of the weight of adjustment rests on sound management of national economies supplemented by adequate international liquidity (including credit for adjustment purposes on suitable conditions). The entire adjustment process should be recognized as a matter of international concern calling for cooperation, international surveillance, and perhaps the development of more or less common standards of behavior. More will have to be done to control or offset short-term capital movements and to find ways to curb the excesses of the Eurodollar market without losing the benefits of its versatility. An important objective (and one difficult to achieve) will be better cooperation in the prevention of crises, a process in which some greater ease in changing exchange rates would prove useful.

While there is little basis for drawing up a detailed program for further monetary reform, much less a timetable, the fundamentals of what American policy should be are clear. The gains already made by the reforms of the '60s should be strictly safeguarded, and further reform (if there is to be any) should move in the same direction. Gold should not be allowed to become any more important in the monetary system than it is under the two-market system and might well be altogether demonetized when that can be done without causing very much disturbance. The management (and creation) of money should be accepted as a normal international function just as it is nationally. For the United States there are some difficulties in this position. It will remain the major monetary power in the world, but the voice of other countries in money management will, and should, grow stronger. If there were serious disagreements, especially between the United States and several countries in strong monetary positions, an American effort to prevent retrogression might risk fracturing the system. An aim of monetary diplomacy should be to avoid having such a choice forced on the United States and other countries; but at the same time the possibility should be kept open of creating, if necessary, a kind of dollar area, a poor alternative but one preferable to moving backwards (for instance, toward a gold-centered system). The United States should, in any event, stand ready to cooperate in serious efforts to create a monetary system in which there are alternatives to the dollar as a reserve currency.

Whether the prospects for pursuing these kinds of reforms have been enhanced or reduced by the exchange rate alterations and monetary uncertainties of August to December 1971 is discussed in the epilogue. There, too, is an examination of the extent to which the arguments set out in chapter 7 about the management of the American balance of payments apply at a time when the dollar's place in the world economy may be on the verge of changing.

Trade, investment, agriculture, and money do not make up the whole of foreign economic policy, but they account for enough so that what is done about them will decide the character of American relations with the developed countries of the free world. There is enough homogeneity in this set of relations to make it important that policies be coherent, consistent, and therefore, in a sense, general. There are also enough peculiarities in each set of American relations with Western Europe, Japan, and Canada to call for differences in policies and priorities.

Western Europe, if it is taken as a whole, is the largest of the segments of the industrial free world outside the United States. Just because it cannot be taken as a whole for most purposes and yet may have to be in other respects in the course of the '70s, Europe presents particularly complex issues for American policy. How fast, how far, and how deep the process of European integration will go is not a matter that can be safely predicted and not something the United States can settle. Consequently, American policy must be capable of dealing with "Europe," with the separate nations of Europe, and with a Europe in which certain groups of nations are more or less unified. The need will change over time and at any given time be different for different purposes. For reasons that are not confined to foreign economic policy, the United States ought to look favorably on further integration in Europe (of both the widening and the deepening kind). Without putting obstacles in the way of a process that is bound to be difficult and fairly slow, it should also be diligent and active in trying to find ways that minimize the damage to American interests resulting from integration. This means, for example, working to lower barriers to trade between Europe and the rest of the world and resisting arrangements within Europe that provide more trade discrimination than true integration. Some aspects of integration may encourage discrimination against American firms and add to the resistance to American direct investment that is likely to grow in Europe in the '70s. If the time comes when all or most of Western Europe is able to speak with one voice in international monetary affairs it will become a formidable force, comparable in strength with the United States, making the potential danger of a conflict of interests, or views, greater than in the past but also improving the capabilities of the world for managing the international monetary system properly.

A failure of European countries to draw closer together in an integrated economy, or any last-minute failure of Britain to join the Community, would have three major implications for American policy. There would be little chance of Western Europe speaking with one voice in international affairs. The risk would increase that discriminatory arrangements within Europe would become more complex and troublesome. American policies emphasizing multilateralism and equal treatment—with nations rather than blocs as the main participants—would become more important than ever (and more attractive to some Europeans, including some inside the Community).

Japan presents different problems. The process is not yet completed of bringing that rapidly growing and changing country into the economic counsels of the free world on a basis of equality with other industrialized countries. There is less need than in the past for the United States to act as a sort of sponsor for Japan, but it has a key part to play in ending the remaining discrimination against Japanese trade (including export limitation forced on Japan as on no other country). The counterpart of this process—and the two will inevitably be linked—is that of bringing Japan to reduce its barriers to imports and restraints on investment in the same degree as other industrialized countries have done. Even if this is done, the relation of government and business in Japan will give rise to a continuing series of questions about the kind of accommodation that can be found between Japan's patterns of behavior and those familiar in the West. If Japan's strong balance of payments proves durable, Washington should press Tokyo to take on greater responsibility in international monetary affairs and in the improvement of international adjustment processes. There are ample stimuli for disputes and opportunities for serious friction. The accommodation of Japan in the open economic system of the industrial countries will, by any standard, be a troublesome process for some years to come. However, the postwar record is encouraging in spite of frequent friction and occasional crisis. What has been achieved plus the fact that the two countries share a significant range of common interests encourage persistence in working at their continuing problems.

Canada's dependence on the American economy is greater than that of Japan, which is greater than Europe's. From that dependence arise the main problems in the two countries' economic relations. The American economic stake in Canada—conceived in conventional, narrow terms—is far greater than the discrepancy in size of the two economies suggests. In its policies toward Canada, the United States needs to be sensitive and forbearing. Since most American economic policy affects Canada, more than just foreign economic policy is involved. In the narrower field as well, relations are of a somewhat different order from those of either country with the rest of the world. This is particularly true in investment, finance, and money, where new patterns are evolving which to a significant degree bring Canada within what could be called the American balance of payments perimeter. Because the scale of adjustment to the freeing of trade between the two countries is so much greater for Canada, the United States should leave to Canada any major initiatives in this matter. In the future, as in the past, relations between the two countries will be shaped to a significant degree by the course of the inescapable and unending conflict between feelings of nationalism and judgments about economic interest in Canada.

Though much foreign economic policy can be successfully carried out through bilateral negotiations or *ad hoc* consultation and agreement among groups of countries, effective international organizations are of great value to the kinds of policies the United States should pursue (and has been pursuing). They and the agreements about principles and rules on which they rest do much to capture and make lasting the benefits of those periods when the willingness to cooperate is high, and preserve them during times when the will to move forward is weak. IMF and GATT need some refurbishing to deal adequately with the problems of the '70s, but the United States should work to keep these organizations in good running order and not let them be weakened. That means not only defending their rules and principles but applying them to the behavior of the United States as well as to other countries. The OECD seems especially well suited to play an important part in the shaping of future cooperation among the industrial countries. Three of its salient characteristics are especially apposite to the needs of the '70s: an emphasis on consultation, an ability to link discussions of several different subjects, and a membership that comprises the main industrial nations and a few others. These advantages confer no monopoly. While strengthening OECD, the United States should continue to pursue a multi-channeled economic diplomacy.

While much of the emphasis of American policy in the '70s will have to be on finding new ways of dealing with problems that are either new or more important than they used to be, not all old principles embodied in old agreements should be allowed to decay. One of the most important is the principle of equal treatment, as applied both to trade and, in less explicit forms, to other aspects of economic relations as well. The principle of equality is essential to a world economy that aims at international specialization, open frontiers, and a fair sharing of benefits, and that operates through cooperation among national governments, each of which must justify its policies by the benefits they bring to its people. Even when discrimination is inevitable or desirable to achieve these purposes, it should be conceived as a reasoned and, if possible, regulated departure from the norms of equality.

The United States has a special interest in checking the decline into which the idea of equal treatment has fallen. Unlikely to become a member of a bloc, the United States has an interest in seeing to it that the discrimination between members and nonmembers of blocs is kept to the unavoidable minimum and that blocs do not use their power to make discriminatory arrangements with favored outsiders. Equal treatment is a key element in pursuing the dual policy of fitting Japan more fully into the world economy and persuading Japan to reduce restrictions at home. Although the United States is a very strong nation, its bargaining position in a number of situations is not so strong (or can be used only at an undesirable cost), and adherence to the principle of equality is a major defense of its interests as well as those of weaker countries. Finally, although equal treatment will for a long time mean something different in relations among the industrialized countries than in their relations with others, maintenance of the principle and its application as far as possible can be a major step in helping to reduce the differences over time.

THE CHARACTER OF POLICY

Condensation loses nuances, flattens emphasis, and produces occasional ambiguities, but readers will recognize in the last few pages a rough summary of the main findings of earlier chapters as they bear on American policy. As chapter 10 made clear, what is being proposed here is not just "more of the same"—a continuation of the policies the United States has followed more or less consistently since the end of the war, a filling out of the Bretton Woods picture, an extension of old approaches into the '70s. There are elements of that sort, but they are overshadowed by new approaches to old problems, new emphasis on issues that were formerly secondary, and the need to deal with completely new problems. Nevertheless, the elements of continuity are very important. They include, for instance, a stress on multilateralism. Therefore, even if Europe forms a bloc roughly equivalent to the United States in economic weight, the affairs of the world should be conducted in ways that take full account of the interests of other countries as well. It means, too, that the intensified cooperation of which the industrial countries have proved themselves capable will be directed so as to avoid sharpening the differences between them and the rest of the world (unless the price would be a great sacrifice in what could be achieved by cooperation in the smaller group). Another element of "continuity" is the recognition that there is still room for progress in the kind of liberalization of trade and payments that was the hallmark of the Bretton Woods approach. Even to preserve the benefits already achieved, the pursuit of liberalization and the strength of the organizations that reinforced it, notably GATT and the Fund, must be high on the list of policy objectives.

That list is longer than it used to be. Not only has the scope of international economic affairs been greatly enlarged, but the objectives have become more complex. It is more difficult than it once was to summarize American aims and the policies for pursuing them. "The removal of obstacles to trade and payments" and "the creation of international organizations that will foster cooperation," though they remain important objectives, no longer come as near to exhausting the subject as they once did. To describe what has been added is not so simple. The task of analysis should be to stress complexity rather than to encourage oversimplification by the use of terms that easily become slogans. But if some kind of shorthand is wanted, it might be said that the objectives of American foreign economic policy vis-à-vis the developed countries should be to continue the process of opening their economies to one another while at the same time providing means of exercising internationally the degree of supervision or management of economic affairs that is normally exercised domestically by national governments, whether for political, social, and welfare objectives, or simply for the better functioning of the economy, both national and international.

This is a difficult assignment. It was not easy to devise and carry out the Bretton Woods approach, adapting it all the while to changing circumstances and political possibilities. The next stage will be harder. Some of the difficulties are rooted in the novelty and complexity of the new kinds of issues that have to be dealt with in foreign economic policy. But in addition, as the last chapter explained, some of the greatest difficulties arise in the most familiar of fields, the reduction of trade barriers. The question is not simply whether the barriers that remain are in some sense more deep-rooted than those that have been removed. The most sensitive part of the whole issue is that the pressure for industrial change is probably going to be greater than ever before and the need for adjustment accelerated (even without further reduction of trade barriers). A general problem for the industrial countries, this one may have a particular impact on the United States.

The achievements of the last twenty-five years in lowering trade barriers that have endured for a century, as well as those spawned by the Great Depression, encourage the belief that modern, competitive industrial states can continue the process. In the United States, there has been a good bit of change in attitudes. As John Evans has pointed out, even lobbyists are now likely to say, "I am no protectionist but . . ."; while at the time of the Hawley-Smoot debate the objection to raising rates often began, "Of course I favor protectionism, but . . ."[1] Nevertheless, no one is entitled to be certain that American commitment to reducing trade barriers will endure into its fifth decade. The initial decision was taken under the impact of the depression and with exports more in mind than imports.

1. *The Kennedy Round in American Trade Policy: The Twilight of the GATT?* (Cambridge: Harvard University Press, 1971), p. 29. I have paraphrased the passage except for the second quotation, which comes from Raymond A. Bauer, Ithiel de Sola Pool, and Lewis A. Dexter, *American Business and Public Policy: The Politics of Foreign Trade* (New York: Atherton Press, 1963), p. 147.

From, say, 1940 to some time in the '50s, trade barrier reduction did not put many American industries under pressure. As imports of manufactured goods rose, trade policy became more timid until 1962, when the passage of the Trade Expansion Act looked as if it might have been a watershed. After the Kennedy Round, protectionist pressures rose markedly and remained strong into the early '70s. That was not particularly surprising, for a number of reasons touched on earlier. It is not unusual for the United States to go through periods of strong protectionist pressure and even some raising of import barriers; a main requirement of far-seeing policy in these circumstances is to contain the pressures as well as possible while laying the groundwork for new steps forward. The Nixon Administration, like the Johnson Administration before it, worked hard to keep the protectionists at bay, but there was no indication by the beginning of 1972 of when—or whether—the tide might turn.

Even if the old pattern reappears and the President not only holds back protectionist pressures but moves toward further liberalization, the record of the Kennedy, Johnson, and Nixon Administrations in textiles shows how unlikely it is that some of the most obdurate barriers will be removed by traditional trade policy approaches alone. Exhortation will fall on deaf ears; the political strength of protected groups, always more focused than contrary interests, will persuade Presidents that freer trade is not worth fighting for. What is done for one is hard to deny to another. What is missing in the American approach to trade policy is the idea that if an industry continues to need protection, year in and year out, there is almost certainly something wrong with that industry and the deployment of American resources in it. The question to be asked is not whether to continue or remove protection, but how to make that industry competitive if that is possible. The aim is not to be nice to foreigners, but to make the best use of American resources—capital, labor, management, and materials.

Both as producers and consumers, Americans have a very real interest in having American industry work at what it does best and in buying from other countries the things that are best produced there. Whether this means that any particular American industry would produce as much as before (only more efficiently) or that it would produce less, the deficiency being made up by imports and resources shifted to the production of other things, is a matter that will differ from industry to industry. In terms of the economy as a whole, the best use of resources might be achieved either way. The strength of the economy would be judged not by which answer is given but by the ability to adjust to either condition.

The American economy is no stranger to adaptation and adjustment. The rise and fall of firms, industries, and segments of industries, the shift in production from one part of the country to another, the displacement of old products by new, take place all the time on a scale far larger than anything likely to result from the removal of most remaining barriers to imports in an orderly way. Domestically, it is called progress and looked on as the natural and desirable result of competition, enterprise, and innovation. But when the competition is foreign, it is regarded in many industries as something quite different: not a pressure to which one should have to respond but one to be resisted, in the first place by discriminatory taxation in the form of tariffs and, if these fail, by limiting the quantities that can be imported or otherwise putting foreign suppliers at a disadvantage. Public power is invoked for what looks, in most cases, like private purposes; a cost is borne by the economy as a whole for the benefit of one part of it.

The argument need not be elaborated. It is the familiar one for free trade and, therefore, subject to all the qualifications and limitations of that argument. Of course, foreign trade is different from domestic trade. It involves the relation of the national economy to the world economy and raises questions about the balance of payments, exchange rates, and other matters. Of course, some foreign producers have advantages that no domestic producer can have (just as American producers have advantages over foreigners in some things). Of course, some foreign competition is "unfair"—trade policy has to include measures to combat subsidies or dumping or other trade-distorting practices. Working toward new concepts of fair competition in international trade will be a major task of future policy. Sometimes the volume or price of imports reflects foreign conditions that are temporary or that for some other reasons should not be "adapted to" in the general sense of the argument. And, of course, there is more involved in national policy, even national economic policy, than buying cheaply. There are times when maintaining the full use of resources or combating unemployment, whether general or in pockets, would make trade restrictions less costly than free trade; but as a rule those matters are better dealt with by other kinds of policies. There are, too, times when national security warrants the maintenance of a domestic productive capacity even if it cannot match foreign costs; but these cases are few, and there are usually other ways of securing the same result than by tariffs or quotas.

In the past, time and occasional emergency measures have provided all that was necessary for adjustment to the removal of trade barriers. Perhaps that is all that will be required in the future—and the world can well afford a slow process so long as it moves in the right direction. But the need for adjustment is likely to be greater in the future than in the past and to arise more frequently. This would be true even without further trade barrier reduction. Technological change, the expansion of production abroad and increased efforts to sell to the United States, or a number of other factors can add to the pressure of import competition. Without doubt, the United States needs more effective programs of adjustment assistance than it has had in the past. But it needs more than that. For reasons made plain in a discourse in chapter 5, adjustment must be seen in a broader perspective than before. Not just imports are involved but multiple sources of change; not just aid of many sorts but a view of the future needs of the economy; not just governmental measures but the conditions in which the economy functions are the ingredients of sound adjustment.

Not much has been done as yet to persuade the public or Congress that the argument of these pages is correct or that the difficult task it implies is really necessary. A President who undertakes a policy of inducing adjustment will face not only a task of education and leadership but a continuing series of problems in resolving conflicts of interest of the sort that inevitably arise from change. There are limits to how much can be done by government aid to make domestic adjustment palatable to all who are affected by it. An inescapable question would be whether the foreign competition to which domestic producers are asked to adapt themselves is "fair." There is, in short, a link between the hard domestic problem of adjustment and the hard international problem of doing something about nontariff barriers and trade-distorting practices.[2]

2. The link should not be understood to mean that until "conditions of competition" are harmonized, other barriers should not be removed. Some Europeans use that argument when justifying retention of the common external tariff. But they wisely did not let that view prevail when they set up the Community, since it can easily become a barrier to taking any action at all. A more constructive approach is to remove the obstacles to trade with the expectation that this will lead to the need to deal with conditions of competition. Nevertheless, some of the more glaring discrepancies that favor one group over another will probably have to be eliminated before others will agree to forgo the protection they are used to.

A sense that the United States has been unfairly treated in some important respects showed itself strongly in President Nixon's speech of August 15, 1971. The epilogue to this book says something about this, and rather more about the effort the United States subsequently made to initiate major trade negotiations on a wide front. To forecast how these may proceed is not the task of this book. However, some of the problems that will be encountered and some approaches that might be tried are described in the next few pages (which I have left as they went to the printer before the new initiative).

For reasons made clear in earlier chapters, it is unlikely that rapid progress will be made in the removal of nontariff barriers and the elimination of other trade-distorting practices. Not only will they continue to impede trade, but they will be seen to do so more clearly than ever before because negotiation will have focused attention on them. Frustration will grow. Perhaps that will itself force governments to act more energetically, but an unequal distribution of frustrations among countries may, like different rates of inflation, also encourage some to hold back. The consequence could be particularly bad in the United States. Too much delay, too few results might well deprive a liberal American trade policy of one of its few dynamic supports.

Rightly or wrongly, American businessmen believe at the beginning of the '70s that they suffer more from the nontariff barriers and trade-distorting practices of foreign countries than foreigners do from American practices. That belief is an important asset for an American government that wishes to carry on an active trade policy. To use the asset requires energy, ingenuity, and caution. The technique is to supplement the essential and more or less continuous process of international study and slow negotiation with frequent and calculated challenges of foreign practices of particular concern to Americans. For the approach to promise any success, three conditions are essential. First, the targets must be well chosen: they must be important enough to warrant making a serious effort to deal with them and reasonably susceptible to change without asking too much of a foreign country. Second, the United States must have bargaining power either in the same segment of trade or some other of interest to the other country or countries.[3] Third, it must be expected, indeed intended, that whatever is done about the immediate issue at hand, the purpose of bringing on negotiations about specific matters should be to reach agreement about broader issues. Countervailing duties should be used not just to stop a particular importation, but to open the way to agreement on the kinds of subsidies that are acceptable in trade among the industrialized countries and those that are unacceptable. A claim that a country discriminates in the application of sanitary rules should be accompanied by proposals for agreeing on standards or otherwise avoiding recurrence of the same problem in the future.

3. Whatever substance there is to the belief of American businessmen that they are worse off than others, there is no serious possibility of persuading other governments to make one-sided concessions. The only hope is that a broad enough attack on nontariff barriers will be seen to have sufficient mutual advantage to permit governments to accept agreements without too narrow a focus on the supposedly precise exchange of *quids* for *quos* in each one.

There is little point in asking that American firms be allowed to bid on certain kinds of foreign business if we are not prepared to give foreigners equal privileges in the United States. A major handicap for this kind of policy is that, years after the Kennedy Round, American Selling Price, an archetype of nontariff barrier, remains unchanged in American law.

Foreign walls will not fall when the American trumpet sounds a sufficient number of times and the proper shouts have been raised. There is no certainty that a series of complaints will produce better results than an international study aimed at the drafting of codes and rules. In the long run those efforts are quite essential to a constructive solution. The activist line is not just window-dressing, however, or a gesture for domestic consumption. One of its purposes is to bring about a more rapid engagement over serious issues than might otherwise take place. If the United States imposes countervailing duties, for example, it puts a different kind of pressure on foreign governments than if it simply proposes a discussion of subsidies. Properly handled, such a policy can play an important part in the educational process which, it was argued in chapter 5, is an essential element in discovering what practices are most serious in blocking or distorting trade and how good the chances are of eliciting effective action from governments to deal with them. Like most educational techniques, this one could also produce bad results.

There are several risks in this kind of policy. Issues may be partly dealt with bilaterally that would be better handled, even if more slowly, on a multilateral basis. Accommodations to get rid of specific irritants may displace larger understandings as the goals for which governments are willing to work hardest. Quick compromises may reduce the pressure for more basic change. The greatest risk, however, is the danger that enlightened activism will degenerate into economic warfare. When complaints meet nothing but countercomplaints or dilatory tactics, governments will be moved to threaten and then to back up threats by action. Each step will stimulate retaliation. To equalize pressure, counterblows will be taken in a different field from that of the original controversy. Action will spread to additional products, thereby bringing in more offended parties on both sides. The criterion for choosing cases that can be settled constructively will go by the board. The demands of each domestic interest that the government take up its case will rise and the arguments for not doing so will decline. Existing negotiations and the prospects of broader agreement will be jeopardized. The risk is real; how well it can be controlled is hard to judge. The conclusion to be drawn, I believe, is not that one should abandon the idea of an "activist" approach to nontariff barriers, but rather that the risk should be recognized and then minimized both by the way issues are raised and proposals made for dealing with them and by forbearance in conduct and realism in expectations.

There is a comparable, and probably greater, risk in agriculture. Europe's Common Agricultural Policy is double-barreled. It frustrates Americans by narrowing their important European market and then confronts them with the sale of subsidized surpluses in the United States and in third countries. The United States complains about what the Community does, imposes countervailing duties or other barriers to subsidized imports, and subsidizes its own exports to third markets. One step begets another, friction increases, and each party feels the pressure of its own surpluses. Within Europe, bargaining about CAP leads to its extension to additional products. Third countries seek preferential arrangements with the Common Market that add to the discrimination against the United States. President Nixon asks for authority to penalize imports from countries that subsidize competitive exports to third markets.

Sometimes threats work, as in the soybean case, but the potential gains from a process of threats and counterblows are not large. Without changes in agricultural policies on both sides, the pressures for new restrictions, more subsidies, and growing economic warfare can hardly be avoided. Though the new kinds of negotiations outlined in chapter 8 are not likely to produce quick results, their existence may provide a basis for a truce that would mitigate clashes in the short run. The poor prospects in agriculture reduce the chances that a liberal American trade policy will receive strong support from farm groups. It is important, therefore, to keep the agricultural issue alive in international negotiations and push for such openings as may be found, including those outside Europe. It will require considerable delicacy to make the most of the limited American bargaining power while at the same time keeping the chronic struggles in agriculture from spilling over to damage other parts of trade relations.

As often before in this book, issues of trade policy have been given pride of place, this time because of the considerable risks of increased international friction and the sizable effort required at home both to check protectionist pressures and to develop the kinds of policies and attitudes toward adjustment that seem necessary. But monetary problems have given rise to more dramatic crises, full of passion and psychological strain. The risks and dangers are so clear that fear has played an important part in limiting and then ending the crises. While each episode did something to make changes in the system (such as those agreed on in December 1971), slow and steady discussion is also essential in paving the way for reform. Conflicts of interest are equally real in trade policy, but the domestic public concerned with monetary diplomacy is apt to be smaller, except in times of crisis.

In investment policy, a changing, sometimes subtle mixture of issues promises difficulties ahead though the major stresses and strains may be farther off than in trade. Past policy had three main parts: government encouragement to foreign investment; negotiation of fair conditions, preferably national treatment; and support for business in defense of its rights. Not only is this too narrow a policy for the future, but some of its premises are being challenged at home and abroad. There seems little doubt that in the '70s many foreign governments will in one way or another lay down an increasing number of conditions determining how American companies can operate abroad. When the U.S. government should intervene in these matters, how, and with what end in view appear as considerably more difficult questions than they once did even in the minds of many businessmen. Conflicts of national jurisdictions and the sense that a common public interest requires cooperation to regulate internationally those aspects of business that cannot be satisfactorily regulated nationally combine to produce situations in which the U.S. government, alone or in combination with others, will be acting in ways that sometimes garner support from American business and sometimes generate opposition.

Domestically, there is friction between government and business about the controls over investment and lending established for balance of payments purposes. Irksome rather than serious, this dispute may be overshadowed in the future by labor opposition to any investment that it considers to have the effect of "exporting jobs." This issue is complex as a matter of analysis and hard to handle in policy prescription. No formulas for control that come close to providing what labor wants seem at all satisfactory. The discussion in chapter 6 suggested a combination of approaches, including clarification of the issues; understanding of the fact that the labor interest is different from that of business and that some groups of workers could be hurt; some sharing of burdens, when there are any, by the businesses involved; and a broadening of the concept of adjustment to which government policy will address itself. Whether these lines of approach will be acceptable or, if accepted, would prove workable is hard to say. Growth and full employment will be major determinants.

As these sketches indicate, the range of issues on which the U.S. government will have to act to conduct foreign economic policy will be wider in the future than in the past. Inevitably, questions arise about the need for legislation and relations between the President and Congress. In trade policy, we have grown so used to a system in which the President has power to negotiate within bounds set by a periodically reviewed congressional delegation of authority that we forget how much more difficult his position would be if he had to submit most of what he did for congressional approval before it was put into effect. While it may prove possible to avoid the extremes of pre-1934 tariff-making, when Congress undertook to work out the details itself, it is quite possible that Congress will keep the President on a shorter tether in the future. In dealing with nontariff barriers, legislation is sure to be required more often than in tariff matters. While monetary diplomacy may raise no more questions of legislation in the future than in the past, Congress will certainly be involved in many aspects of investment policy, agriculture, and the broad steps to which a recognition of the need to keep the economy flexible might lead. The interplay between Congress and the President, which constitutes the normal way of doing business in American politics, presents singular difficulties when a third party is involved. The choice is not a very happy one between offering the rest of the world prearranged compromises between the two parts of the American government or subjecting an internationally agreed compromise to rearrangement as the result of the play of internal American politics.

The President's ability to persuade Congress to accept internationally negotiated agreements has usually depended heavily on showing that what the United States "gives up" is at least matched by what it gets. Only in that way can it be demonstrated that American officials have not been outdone by foreign negotiators and, more importantly, that the objections of some domestic interest groups have to be overridden for the sake of promised benefits to the country as a whole. But in the future, as we have seen, it will often be more difficult than in the past to show that each specific arrangement contains a neat balance of advantages. The linking of otherwise not very closely related matters to demonstrate such a balance will sometimes be feasible, but the effort may also slow progress. To cultivate a broad conception of reciprocity is highly desirable but will take time, and, meanwhile, the process of getting agreement between the executive and the legislature about what is in the interest of the United States—never an easy task—may well become a greater stumbling block to American foreign economic policy than before.

The presidential task of finding politically tenable balances among conflicting partial interests while at the same time advancing the national interest will be still further complicated by yet another of the new elements in foreign economic policy discussed in preceding chapters. It is a great help in arousing support for policy to have a clear-cut objective or, at least, to be able to call for a specific action, such as approving a treaty or appropriating a certain sum, which can be presented as having decisive importance. No doubt it will be possible in the future, as in the past, to find certain finite goals of policy and propose concrete actions that will bring about easily described changes in international practices and institutions. But much of what has to be done in the '70s requires continuing work to handle ever-changing problems arising from the interpenetration of national economies. Even when discrete steps can be clearly understood, the larger goals to which they may lead will not be easy to describe with great precision, for, as the Director for Industry and Energy of the OECD has said,

> . . . the complex world of industry and energy can be fully understood only as a constant endeavor to achieve or to maintain a state of equilibrium between different forces, constantly subject to change, and between conflicting interests and opposing trends. . . .
>
> The life of modern industrial societies may, indeed, be regarded as a continual struggle towards a balance that can be achieved for a fleeting moment, but never definitively.[4]

It is easier for Fausts than for Presidents to explain why their aim should be to catch the fleeting moment.

Is the Road Blocked?

One of the commonplaces of the early '70s is that Americans are increasingly preoccupied with domestic problems. Foreign affairs are noticed mostly when they intrude dangerously, as in Vietnam and the Middle East, or unpleasantly, when defense spending and foreign aid consume funds that some people would rather devote to domestic objectives and others would like to return to their own pockets by lowering taxes. The atmosphere is not one in which much public enthusiasm is likely to be generated about nontariff barriers, foreign restriction on investment, or the idea of discussing American farm policy with foreigners. Political leaders find other subjects more promising for attracting attention, building reputations, and increasing their influence and following.

These are real disadvantages, but one should think twice about how much weight to attach to them in the long run. What is easily labeled neo-isolationism may come to look somewhat different as

4. Karl Schmidt-Lüders, "On Industrial Policy," *The OECD Observer*, December 1969, p. 14.

time passes. Revulsion from foreign affairs will diminish if Americans are not being killed in distant places. New vitality in the attack on such problems as urbanism, race relations, and poverty may sharpen awareness that these and other ills that man is heir to are not confined by national boundaries. Some attractive goals, like the improvement of the environment, cannot be adequately pursued except by international action. An American administration that was using every international forum to make practical and imaginative proposals to reduce pollution and also forging ahead at home might well give "foreign policy" a new face. Though much of the discontent with society and the dissent from past policy is self-centered and reflects a wish to withdraw from complications of a world beyond one's control, these reactions also have strands of universalism and globalism that may in the end prove stronger. Compelling as a public mood is in the shaping of practical possibilities at any given moment, it cannot be projected far ahead. Too much depends on unpredictable facts and unknown reactions to them, as well as on unpredictable reactions to predictable facts. At most what one can say is that for some time to come there will be uncertainty about what priority the American public and its leaders will accord to foreign economic policy, what objectives they will want to achieve by that policy, and how much success a determined President might have in rallying congressional, business, and public support for an active policy of the sort outlined in this book.

To forecast uncertainty is easy and not very helpful. One can do a little better by asking some questions. Is active popular interest necessary to make progress in foreign economic policy? If a low priority discourages dramatic moves and comprehensive new initiatives, is the result likely to be fatal to sound foreign economic policies? Since, in a pluralistic society, a government must have multiple aims, may it not be able to pursue a successful foreign economic policy even if it is preoccupied with other matters? It seems unlikely that these questions have flat answers, valid for all circumstances. Some comparisons of the present with earlier periods of postwar history, while not encouraging great optimism, help clarify the issues.

With the possible exception of the Marshall Plan, postwar foreign economic policy can hardly be said to have had wide and active support in the public at large. No doubt massive public opposition would have made it impossible to adopt the Bretton Woods approach, aid to Europe, the Trade Expansion Act, and other major features of policy. What made them possible—and perhaps prevented general opposition from developing—was a combination of several factors: strong leadership in the executive branch based on the conviction that the measures were in the long-run national interest, coupled with an explanation of that conviction; sufficient support in Congress, which in the long run (and often in the short run) had to be bipartisan support even though party regularity and cohesion were often crucial;[5] enough support from the groups actively interested in foreign economic policy, especially those with a direct economic stake but including others as well, to outweigh the opposition of those who believed their interests would be damaged. The weakness of one of these factors can be overcome by greater strength in others. Support often has to be bought at the price of compromise. The ability of a President to put together the right combination of factors depends to an important degree on the expected or actual response of other countries. At the beginning of the '70s, conditions at home or abroad are unfavorable for applying formulas that worked well in the past.

When the Bretton Woods approach was new, Washington was the only possible source of a major international economic initiative. The preponderant position of the United States made it likely that agreements would conform, in the main, to American conceptions of what was desirable. The need to provide some kind of framework for world economic reconstruction was clear and urgent. Now, although one may believe that the need for new measures in the '70s is demonstrable, the existence of a working system capable of dealing more or less adequately with a large range of problems dulls the sense of the imperative need to do something. The end of the war provided a natural starting place for action along lines that for the most part had been quite thoroughly discussed for a number of years. Now we are uncertain about the direction in which to move.

It would be hyperbole to speak of the Bretton Woods picture as a vision that guided American policy in the years immediately after the war. And yet there are elements of truth in the idea: there was a grand design, even if the passion to carry it into effect was felt by a relatively small number of people; it was a design that was intended to give shape to a world that would be in many ways new and that would avoid major defects of the prewar world. The result, it was firmly believed, would serve a common interest, not just an American

---

5. Whether congressional support is garnered by persuasion about where the national interest lies or through the deployment of the executive's many means of influencing congressional votes may be immaterial in any given case, but over a period the assurance of bipartisan support is likely to depend on a degree of conviction by a fair number of legislators, plus arguments about the advantages of continuity and the need to meet American commitments. Even when legislation or appropriations are not needed for the President to act—as in much monetary policy or the use of trade-bargaining power already granted—a certain level of congressional support, or at least tolerance, is a necessary safeguard for the future.

one. The main architects understood the importance of devising arrangements that took account of the special interests and concerns of other countries and of getting true consent to what was being done; persuasion, not imposition, was the method. At the same time, it was also believed (as was necessary to the acceptance of the idea) that what was being built was in the long-run interests of the United States. On the definition of those interests there was not always agreement, any more than there was always wholehearted agreement among governments about how the common international interest could be served. Perhaps others had to accommodate themselves to American views more often than Americans to theirs. There was, however, an inner logic in this approach that was, in a sense, self-sustaining. The idea that it was important to build a new international economic order and that this could only serve the American interest in the long run if it served the common interests of "like-minded" countries provided a built-in rationale for not pressing short-run American interests in ways that would damage the larger structure.

Matters are very different in the early '70s. It is too much to say that there is a general rejection of the foreign economic policy followed by the United States since the end of the war; but there is some disillusionment, some disappointment, and enough change in the atmosphere to make the mustering of support for another round of efforts look like uphill work—and some would say an impossible task. Revisionist history and a new popularity of old-fashioned ideas about how capitalism works have taken some toll, but more important, in my opinion, is an accumulation of other factors. What were once novel, venturesome, and promising policies are now largely taken for granted. Four years of hard and sometimes frustrating negotiation dulled people's appreciation of the Kennedy Round as the culmination of a generation's reduction of trade barriers. The immediate aftermath of that great step in liberalization was less a sense that trade was freer than a new awareness of border taxes and nontariff barriers. The European Community is seen as pursuing a selfish course, not the long-promised "outward-looking" one. It is irksome to find Japan controlling trade and investment more tightly than other industrialized countries (and all the while growing faster than the rest and producing large export surpluses). Faint progress in agriculture has turned into a setback that threatens to become worse. The feeling is abroad that the American economy is far more open than those of Europe and Japan and in consequence bears the brunt of stiff competition and the forces of change. Moreover, the United States economy carries a burden of military spending larger

than that of its allies, and Americans are quick to see in that difference one of the roots of the competitive advantages of others, especially the Germans and Japanese. Long years of "reciprocity" seem
in the end to have produced one-sided results.

Along with annoyance has gone anxiety. A decade of trouble with
the balance of payments, though it could well be interpreted to mean
that the problem was not as bad as it first seemed, makes people
cautious, even fearful. The deterioration of the traditional export
surplus of the United States has a similar effect. Both developments
are frequently translated into statements about the decline in American competitiveness, which in turn weakens the will to liberalize. Adjustment problems in steel, shoes, textiles, and clothing hardly warrant
the conclusion that it would be dangerous to lower barriers to imports
of other products, but they are taken by some as warning signs. Protection accorded to one provides others with a claim to similar treatment. Instead of sharpening their competitive edges, industries that
complain of foreign competition raise wages and prices, and the sense
spreads that American costs are out of control.

These unfavorable economic and psychological circumstances create difficulties for a President who wants to pursue an active and
progressive foreign economic policy. In exceptional circumstances it
may be possible to take strong action that generates positive response
in part because it appeals to some of the elements of American dissatisfaction, as President Nixon showed in August 1971. It is far from
clear, however, that the initial impetus can be transformed into the
dependable support needed during long negotiations and the hard
work that only slowly produce results which then take the form of
balanced bargains, not clear-cut American "victories." Perhaps there
is never a good time to embark on a difficult policy. Matters are further
complicated by a shift in the combination of political forces which
have fairly consistently supported such a policy since the '30s. The
most important part of this shift has been organized labor's adoption
of a sharply protectionist position. An ominous development, it is to a
degree a reversion more than the "historical reversal" many people
have dubbed it. Organized labor was protectionist when the country
was protectionist. The shift to support for liberal trade policies
was at least as much a product of the alliance with the Democratic
party that developed in New Deal days as of any close reading of labor's
real interests in freeing trade. In spite of the position of the national
leadership, there were always some unions and groups of workers that
opposed tariff reduction. Perhaps a few unions will continue to support liberal trade policies even if the AFL-CIO continues to call for
restrictions on imports. But in the new phase of the '70s, the situation

is more complicated than ever before because labor has also mounted an attack on American investment abroad as an "export of jobs."[6] Though the two issues are different, they overlap at a few points and blend to add to the intensity of labor feeling.

The substance of these complaints has been examined at some length in foregoing chapters. The long-run national interest, it is clear, requires more flexibility in the economy, and more adaptability of its parts, than is compatible with the view (implied in the labor attitude) that people have a right to continue in the same kind of work at the same places even when that activity is no longer justified by the economic contribution it makes, thanks to the shifting patterns of supply, demand, and technology that mark the world economy (and especially the economies of the industrial countries). There can be tragedy when society's needs no longer include what a person does best and has always done. After a certain age, some people cannot be expected to learn other jobs; to move to new places—an adventure or pleasure for some—is unthinkable for others. Society must take account of these facts and give them as much weight as it can without introducing too much rigidity into the economy. For the most part, fortunately, American labor has proved itself over the years to be highly adaptable and mobile; that has been one of the strengths of the American economy and one of the sources of the relatively high standard of living of American workers. Ironically, it is in part the benefits of past accomplishments—houses with mortgages, cars on time, pension rights—that increase the resistance to change. Parts of the labor movement probably rate security—or just the absence of change—over maximization of earnings (though they would prefer both). Frequently, an individual worker will be better off in the long run for making a change; but there can be no assurance of this, and often it is not true. But it is clear that to prevent change will in the course of time leave the majority of workers worse off than they would have been.

How to equip people for more rapid or frequent change in the future than in the past is a matter involving education, psychology, training, and the organization of work. To try to enhance adaptability while providing as much security as possible raises questions of social policy, social security laws, and industrial relations. All these are matters well beyond the scope of this book, but there is no reason to believe they are beyond the scope of what American society can accomplish. On a narrower basis, chapters 5 and 6 have sketched the

6. This, too, is not altogether new, as we have seen (chap. 6, pp. 180–81), but the worries of the late '20s on this score disappeared with the depression and the war.

main lines of policy. The first requirement is to recognize that there really is a problem to which the nation needs to respond more sensitively than before and more effectively. Thereafter quite a collection of measures may have to be employed in different ways and proportions at different times in order to help adjustment take place and to help those for whom adjustment imposes burdens. To the extent that investment abroad can in fact be shown to eliminate jobs in the United States—even if only temporarily—business should share some of the responsibility. To the extent that investment continues to be subject to a certain degree of government regulation (or at least influence), the employment implications of what is done or not done should be taken into account (without being made the sole criterion). But most of all, the aim of American policy should be to foster adjustment and to remove barriers to adaptation.

To make such a policy acceptable will not be easy. It will require much discussion and analysis to elucidate the real interests of labor, present and future. Preceding chapters have given some indication of how divided these are: against the wish of workers in some industries to be protected from import competition must be set the interest of workers in export industries for an enlargement of international trade; transport workers have an interest in the maximum movement, whether it is to or from ports or between inland points; in service industries there is more international trade than is often recognized, but much of it takes the form of American exports; where there is no import competition to speak of, workers should behave as consumers; the hard-hats and Ralph Nader are natural allies. These multiple interests sometimes conflict, but the only voice that is heard in the matter and plainly labeled "labor" is that of the AFL-CIO. It seems doubtful that the strong and hardly qualified protectionist stand taken by that body in the late '60s and early '70s really represents the true balance of interests of American labor as a whole.

To be sure, the AFL-CIO speaks for "labor" in a far fuller and more comprehensive sense than any organization speaks for "business." But some important segments of organized labor are outside it, notably the transport workers and automobile workers, and much labor is unorganized. Within the AFL-CIO there are conflicting interests, as we have seen, and it is doubtful if these are resolved by methods that carefully weigh all elements or seek a true evaluation of them. Within the organization, as in the public at large, those who feel threatened by import competition are heard much more loudly than those who have an interest as exporters or consumers. The decisions of the leadership reflect such pressures, along with the familiar kind of reciprocal granting of support (or a free hand) to someone for what he most wants, in return for his acquiescence in something else. One might even take the case a step further along these lines. The size and wealth of member unions play a major part in determining AFL-CIO positions; this distribution of power reflects a combination of industry size, union jurisdiction, extent of organization, and some historical (and of course personal) factors. Organizing lags behind the changes in the economy, most notably in not keeping pace with the rapid growth of the service industries. Consequently, there is a natural tendency of the AFL-CIO to represent a pattern of interests that is never altogether up to date and that has some inherent resistance to change.

This is the framework within which political leadership has to operate. A President who in the '70s wishes to pursue a forward-looking foreign economic policy has a special problem, but also a considerable opportunity, in dealing with this new set of labor issues. The effort to do so will engage both his function as teacher—to elucidate the general interest of a public that includes today's people and tomorrow's as well—and his function as politician—to fashion workable, if shifting, coalitions of private interests so that they serve the public good. His chances of success in doing these things in foreign economic policy will be greatly enhanced if his other policies promote employment and an expanding economy.

While labor presents the greatest set of problems in the early '70s, and the newest, it cannot be taken for granted that the support of business and agriculture for a liberal foreign economic policy will be as strong as in the past, for reasons discussed earlier. There is one new element in the political equation: a marked rise in concern about how the consumer is treated, the prices he pays, the quality of what he buys, and the recourse he has to avoid having bad (or false) choices foisted on him by manufacturers and sellers. People concerned with these matters ought to favor the lowering of import barriers (except those concerned with health, safety, quality controls, pollution, etc.) so as to increase competition and widen the consumer's choice. In some cases a specific connection has been discerned, as in the possibility that importing foreign cars with attachments that reduce pollution may hasten the pace of adaptation in Detroit. No doubt some gain in political support for a liberal trade policy can be found in this quarter; but, given the relatively small role of imports in the American economy, it seems clear that the main weight of consumerism will have to be on other concerns. There is also the old question about every reform movement, suggested by the remark of a New York low-life early in the century: "Virchoo's a sprinter; an' for one hundred yards it makes vice look like a crab.

But vice is a stayer, an' in th' Marathon of events it romps in a winner."[7]

POSSIBLE COURSES OF ACTION

The United States might, of course, face the challenges of the '70s in ways rather different from those suggested in this book. For one thing, instead of trying to anticipate future difficulties it might deal with problems as they arise. To some degree governments always do that, and the results can be good. But taking each case "on its merits" almost inevitably produces *ad hoc* settlements that formalize a specific and sometimes temporary balance of forces and are often dominated by considerations that have little to do with sound economic policy. Consistency is lost, breeding contradiction; the claims of domestic and foreign interests are dealt with in relation to immediate bargaining power, not real merit. Domestically, recalcitrance is rewarded; while internationally, retaliation becomes common and constructive approaches are rare. New problems remain unsolved and many of the gains of past cooperation are lost. Though the United States is economically and politically strong, it is not strong enough to win all the battles. Nominal victory can lose benefits for Americans as well as deny them to foreigners. Fred Bergsten, whose vantage point was in the White House, reports that because the United States is less dependent on foreign trade than other countries, several Congressmen say "Let a trade war come—we'll win it." He rightly points out that in such matters there are no "winners".[8] To be the strongest wolf among wolves is better than to be a weaker one, but it is not the height of human aspiration.

A second way of meeting the challenges of the future might be to give some direction to case-by-case pragmatism by a conscious decision not to try to push further along the lines laid down in the past. Further liberalization, it could be argued, is not worth the dislocation of domestic industries, much of which may have to take place anyhow, if at a slower pace, so long as barriers are not raised. The United States need not strain to make significant concessions to foreigners, who in the past have given so much less than they received. National interest in a conventional, mercantilist sense would provide the guidelines of such a policy. Most of the time there would be no good reason not to yield to domestic protectionism instead of running the political risks an administration usually incurs by resisting it.

7. A. H. Lewis, *The Apaches of New York* (New York: Dillingham, 1912), p. 173.
8. "Crisis in U.S. Trade Policy," *Foreign Affairs*, July 1971, p. 635.

In my view, a policy of this sort is not likely, in the long run, to serve true American interests. Fears about the balance of payments might lend support to such an approach, but it does not really offer much hope of improving even the trade balance alone.[9] The practical results of such a policy would probably be very similar to those of the first alternative. Like that one, it is less a policy than a way—a not very good one—of dealing with problems when they become inescapable, in preference to expending the energy and incurring the political costs required to promote policies that lead to a further opening of the economies of the industrialized countries to one another.

A third possible approach would be to try to avoid the difficulties of a universal or near-universal approach while reaping the gains of close cooperation with those most willing to move ahead with the United States. This is, essentially, the argument of those who would create a free trade association or some other kind of arrangement nominally "open to all" but in fact undertaken because some were known not to want to join. It is the kind of course that prefers a dollar area to compromises with countries of somewhat different monetary views, or that would build on the special relations among the countries of the hemisphere rather than work more laboriously to establish the widest possible area of understanding. Such a course has its attractions, especially those of shutting out some hard problems; it is not totally to be dismissed if some of those problems prove too hard. It is also a recourse that the United States has if other countries prove too nationalistic in their approach. It is not, however, a very promising way of coping with the biggest problems. The result would be at most second-best unless it was conceived as a device to induce progress toward a broader undertaking (a debatable approach), and it would be very misleading to think of this as an easily negotiated alternative that avoids major adjustments.

If the United States were to follow any of these courses, the Republic would survive. A rich country can afford some bad policies. Mistakes in other areas of national policy can be far more costly than those of a bad foreign economic policy. It would not be altogether unreasonable for a President who faced mountainous difficulties to decide that the slow, hard task of building a far-sighted foreign economic policy might well be deferred, especially if it threatened to undermine his narrow majority. Putting a low priority on foreign eco-

9. The trade balance might be temporarily improved by restraints on imports, but they could not long endure without stimulating retaliation against American exports. Foreign barriers to the expansion of American exports are not likely to be reduced without some American concessions. Import liberalization helps the competitiveness of the American economy.

nomic policy is quite understandable when other dangerous and urgent issues face the country. Such an approach would be tolerable for a time—but at increasing cost and risk.

Except as a very temporary expedient, this is the wrong approach, based on the wrong comparisons. The right question is not, What can we live with? but, What do we have to do to live better? There should be no need to have a poor or weak foreign economic policy in order to have strong and better policies in other fields. There is no incompatibility between a good domestic economic and social policy and a good foreign economic policy, or between a good foreign policy and a well-designed economic component of it. Indeed, there is much to be said for the advantages that a well-designed foreign economic policy can bring to both domestic economic policy and foreign policy in general. Properly conceived, they are mutually reinforcing, not separate lines of activity.

Doubt is thrown on these broad claims by the fact that foreign transactions are a smaller part of the American economy than that of any other industrialized nation except the U.S.S.R. Moreover, the amount by which the level of these transactions—and still more, the gain from them to the United States—can be significantly altered by foreign economic policy is probably quite limited at any given moment. Nevertheless, it does not follow that the difference between a wise and a foolish foreign economic policy is of only slight importance to the United States. Even in a trillion dollar economy, $65–$70 billion—on each side of the balance of payments—is not a negligible sum. For important parts of the economy, the foreign ingredient is a much larger share of the whole than the figures suggest, whether one looks at exports, imports, services, or investment. On top of that, it is clear that the stake of American business in the international economy is not easily expressed by a figure showing remittances, profits, total investment, or "international production." Nor do figures produce the final answer in other matters as well. Imports benefit the American economy by widening consumers' choices and through their influence on prices and competition. The long-run dynamic effects of measures of foreign economic policy are often far greater than the immediate, quantifiable results. The relative openness of the industrialized countries to one another has undoubtedly been an important element in making it possible for them to reach unprecedented heights of wealth, production, and growth. Barriers around the American economy put a burden on all, and the United States would be less well off if the others were less well off. The gains from the division of labor and the best possible allocation of resources are greater when the United States is fully in the world economy than when it is partly cut off. Only through a coherent foreign economic policy is it possible to improve the management of the international economy by limiting the inevitable conflicts arising from the conduct of national policies by independent states.

In both its "management" aspect and its "liberalizing" aspect, the kind of foreign economic policy recommended in this book repeatedly intersects with other national policies directed toward different ends from those of purely economic man—the nonexistent but very useful being who makes economic reasoning possible. No one in his right mind would suggest that the logic of foreign economic policy should always take precedence over society's interest in social justice, security, or the kind of activity that is nowadays summed up as improving the quality of life. But it is equally true that there is no lasting hierarchy that decrees that one of the other values should always override the economic. Quite often the choices are not at all clear-cut. The improved use of resources that is the continuing objective of foreign economic policy increases the means by which other needs can be satisfied, whether they be the need to reduce poverty, protect the weak, check pollution, or allocate a substantial fraction of national income to defense. Long-run compatibility may, of course, be accompanied by short-run incompatibility, not only of means but of proximate ends. To make choices or compromises is what government is all about. That fact has been taken for granted throughout this book and need not be elaborated here. The only need is to caution against a misunderstanding, so that positive statements about the desiderata of foreign economic policy are understood to be tacitly qualified in whatever way seems necessary to take account of other goals of national policy when they conflict.

Another source of confusion in the discussion of foreign economic policy concerns its relation with the rest of foreign policy. Here a good bit of the trouble is semantic. Concern with economic welfare is not unpolitical. Domestically, one of the first cares of a government is to be responsive to its people. Internationally, welfare is a major ingredient of relations among nations. If countries are not fighting with one another or solely concerned with insuring that they have a power advantage over others (and to some degree even then), a very large part of their relations with one another concerns what are usually called economic matters. While these relations can be conceived of as primarily instruments of power and are not free from conflicts of interest, the "normal" relations among the industrialized countries of the free world are not of this sort. Conflicts of interest are partial, not total; to reduce or remove them requires either a splitting of the difference or an adjustment; what one party loses or appears to give up in one respect is matched by something he gains in another. While there may be gainers or losers in any specific matter, it is possible in economic relations as a whole that both can gain—as is not possible in antagonistic power relations, except when the issue is avoiding mutual destruction. But that is only possible if there is the requisite degree of international cooperation, either in not interfering with a process or in regulating or shaping it in an agreed manner. We speak of these matters as the domain of foreign economic policy; that does not mean they are not also "political." If they were long neglected, the resulting deterioration could create acute problems for "foreign policy." Conversely, the willingness to cooperate to solve these "economic" problems may well depend on so-called "political" considerations.

The point is not that good economic relations make good friends or that good friends have good economic relations. Neither proposition is always true, though each has a touch of probability. Nor does it make sense to believe that by the proper manipulation of foreign economic policy one can go far toward persuading other industrialized countries to follow policies which the United States advocates but about which they have serious doubts. The attempt to buy cooperation and tax noncooperation is likely to be self-defeating for a number of fairly obvious reasons concerning self-respect, pride, economic strength, and the number of political and economic alternatives most countries have. The attempt to use economic measures to produce specific political results is also likely to damage economic policy, which requires a considerable degree of continuity and insulation from the pressure of day-to-day diplomatic differences.

Just because so much of the content of international relations is economic, those economic difficulties that are major, chronic, and unresolved are damaging to political relations. Within the free world there exists, in spite of all the differences, rivalries, and not infrequent disputes, a degree of understanding or harmony or recognition of a wide range of common interests. Perhaps best called solidarity—if that term is not taken to mean too much—this relation is basically different from the relations of the industrialized countries with the Communist countries and, with a few exceptions, the less developed countries. It is very difficult to imagine that a serious deterioration of economic relations would not damage that solidarity even if it did not really undermine the common interest in, for example, security. There are difficulties enough without adding to them those that would inevitably stem from the pursuit by any major partner, and especially the United States, of a policy that more or less consistently injured the others (even if unintentionally) and offered little or no prospect of improving matters. Conversely, policies that make for economic cooperation, the solution of common problems, and both the sharing and the maximizing of benefits which the rich countries are capable of producing are bound to contribute, in some measure, to an improved "political" atmosphere.

A broad concern for the strength and welfare of the non-Communist part of the world has been one of the driving forces of postwar American foreign economic policy. Since it was heightened by the cold war, the more narrowly "political" emphasis might be thought to have declined as the general level of tension between Communist and non-Communist countries was lowered in the late '6os. So it has in the sense that support for the kinds of measures advocated in this book could hardly be aroused by claiming that if they were not taken Europe or Japan would "go Communist." While the Marshall Plan gained support from precisely that fear on the part of some people, its real "political" justification rested on far more subtle and fundamental considerations than that limited risk. It was sound to argue during the early postwar period that the United States should pursue a liberal economic policy for "foreign policy" reasons; that kind of policy increased the solidarity of the free world. It was rational of the United States to agree to arrangements that were somewhat one-sided in the benefits they gave others because one of the aims of its policy was to strengthen the whole system. Has that time passed? The welfare of other industrial countries continues to be more dependent than that of the United States on good conditions in the international economy. A step of no great interest to the United States could be of great help to them. But the feeling exists that the United States has so many economic problems it can no longer afford a policy that takes account of the interests of others and that there are no real foreign policy gains in such measures. A rebuttal of these views can be found in the arguments throughout this book about the economic gains to the United States from the kind of policy it has followed. That policy has certainly contributed to openness and interpenetration. Whether the result is more of what I have called "solidarity" as well is a matter on which judgment should be reserved until there is a fuller political analysis than I know of. But there can be no doubt about the gain in foreign as well as American welfare. Indeed, the growth in economic and political power of Europe and Japan will undoubtedly alter the way many Americans think about foreign economic policy. The economic costs of foreign policy—heaviest and most obvious in military expenditure—have always been important but will be given more emphasis in the future. These and other links between foreign economic policy and foreign policy as a whole remain unbroken and not even badly twisted.

Matters are, of course, considerably more complicated than these generalizations suggest. For example, liberal economic treatment of Japan by the United States has a significance for Japan's domestic politics as well as its international policies. The dependence of Japanese and German security on American policy and the relations that have developed between each of those nations and the United States have a bearing on the part Bonn and Tokyo play in international monetary affairs.[10] President de Gaulle's foreign policy strategy contributed to the difficulties of the dollar in the '60s. American concern about the political future of Europe tempers what might otherwise be a more nationalistic American policy toward the economic effects of the enlargement of the European Community. The view that a united Europe would probably play a constructive part in the world economy depends to a significant degree on the assumption that the political orientation of the two powers on opposite shores of the Atlantic will not diverge too greatly. Nationalism is a major factor shaping Canadian economic policy toward the United States. European concern with "science policy" and measures to close what some call the technological and some the managerial gap with the United States is not prompted solely by economic motives. And so on.

So long as the United States does not believe it can live alone in the world, its "economic" relations have a "political" cast. Even if the United States considers that it can provide for its own basic security by itself, it cannot by itself alone make the kind of world it wants to be secure in. The range of opinions can be wide about just what kind of solidarity the so-called free world should have, just what its common tasks are, and how they are to be performed. But there cannot be any reasonable disagreement that measures which strengthen the free world economy improve its chances of carrying out those tasks and, perhaps, even of agreeing on what they are. To this end, foreign economic policy is essential, and in this sense the American stake in a properly conceived foreign economic policy is political as well as economic.

It would be foolish to claim that the only foreign economic policy for the United States that would serve these high economic and political purposes in the '70s is one embodying all the features and

10. When he was asked if the United States had threatened to withdraw troops to force Germany to agree to hold dollars instead of gold, Karl Blessing, the former president of the Bundesbank, said, "It was never an explicit threat, but the threat was always there." Interview in *Der Spiegel*, May 3, 1971, p. 82.

reasonably concrete prescriptions set out in the earlier chapters. My analysis has called attention to its own limitations and uncertainties. My suggestions have been couched more in terms of approaches than specific measures, of possible ways of dealing with problems rather than tight prescriptions for which sure results are claimed. There must be very many good ideas that have not occurred to me, many objections or difficulties I have overlooked or underestimated. The feasibility and relative importance of measures change with circumstances. I believe, however, that it is not too much to claim that a satisfactory foreign economic policy for the United States in the '70s must be of the general character set out here, and that the approach, if not all the specifics, points to both the problems that must be dealt with and the possibilities of doing so. If that is so, what remains for the final sections of this book is to say something about how the United States ought to proceed if it is to translate ideas into practice in spite of the very great difficulties and the unfavorable atmosphere of the early '70s.

How to Proceed

Often enough since the mid-'60s American leaders in and out of office have expressed the heartfelt hope that some other country would take a strong initiative, setting out major proposals for international action to deal with at least some of the key international economic problems facing the industrial world in the '70s, as the United States had so often done in the past. Usually the target of these remarks was Europe, and in economic matters it was certainly reasonable to suggest that the Community, which has become the biggest trading unit in the world, should begin to take a lead in shaping the world economy. The Community, however, had a different sense of priorities: first, its own integration, then British entry, and only third the world economy. Britain in turn was in no position to make major proposals about the reorganization of the world economy, being actively engaged in trying to enter the Community (and had that failed its stance would not have been that of a leader of a major new effort). Japan did not regard itself, and was not regarded by others, as the most fruitful source of new initiatives before it completed its lagging liberalization. While Canada and the smaller countries in Europe may have been as fertile in ideas as larger countries and as willing to move ahead, effective leadership in matters involving the whole world economy is almost always limited to countries above a certain size.

In these circumstances, it was not really surprising that there should have been no major initiatives for several years and that, when something was done to bring about change in the world economy, it should have been the strong American action of August 1971. The epilogue considers this effort in some detail; here our concern is with the time, sooner or later, when there will be a need for further initiatives, and again the United States may be the most likely leader. To fill that role effectively, American policy will have to satisfy two conditions, one external and the other internal.

Because economic power in the industrial world is far more evenly distributed than at the end of the war, or at the beginning of the '60s, it would be unwise of the United States to be too unilateral in its methods. Consultation and the engagement of other governments in the process of shaping a program of action should be normal procedures. Initiatives should deal with the problems that bother other countries, as well as those of special interest to the United States. While there may be times when a broad statement of purpose and objectives by the President, even a dramatic gesture, is the right tactical move, its results are likely to be better if other governments have a good idea of what the United States hopes to accomplish.

At the same time that American policy shows the rest of the world that it is other-regarding, it must show Americans that it is self-regarding. To many Americans, foreign economic policy seems to be made up of things we do for other people. Inaccurate as this view is, one can understand it as a hang-over from the days of aid to Europe, the reduction of American tariffs while the dollar-short countries continued to control imports, and the like. Though one can properly speak of a certain generosity in American policy in those days, it was the kind of altruism that coincides with an enlightened view of self-interest. The more recent idea that the trade bargains of the '60s have been one-sided, leaving the American market more open than those of other countries, is far from proved. Nevertheless, the formulation of American policy in the '70s has to take account of the feeling that past policy was one-sided and that weaknesses in the American trade balance and balance of payments reflect this fact. If the argument of this book is correct, it should be possible to do this by following a policy of actively attacking practices damaging to American interests while seeking to reach lasting solutions, which will, of course, have to serve the interests of others as well to be acceptable in the long run.

In the '70s it will be harder than in the past for any American President to achieve a persuasive and effective balance of the two elements of policy—the self-regarding and the other-regarding. For one thing there will be moments when these two requirements will conflict or lead to contradictions in policy, at least for a time. There will also be discrepancies between what is said and done. Verbally, the President will sometimes claim greater advantages for the United States than can really be found. Substantively, if not admittedly, general principles will be used to obtain benefits for the United States that are beyond the reach of other countries. Every so often there will be departures from principles—perhaps even violations of obligations. But American policy cannot succeed if it is too one-sided. Other countries have to be willing to respond and carry their fair share of the responsibility for the success of international economic cooperation. Just what that share is, is one of the most troublesome problems. Americans who stress the fact that the European Community is the largest trading entity in the world, and Japan the fastest growing, sometimes underestimate American power. Even if others could be said to have taken over the emporium of the free world village, the United States retains the arsenal and the mint. How the cost of the arsenal should be shared—and authority over the mint as well—are issues in dispute that have a bearing on all other issues. While the United States may be anxious to share responsibility for the international economic system even more than it is now shared, Washington cannot safely abandon that responsibility by adopting an altogether nationalistic policy of the familiar mercantilist cast. All these points were exemplified in one way or another in the events that followed the American declaration of August 1971.

The real national interest of the United States, it has been argued here, lies in moving toward a more open international economy and a higher level of cooperation than has existed in the past. Those who are worried—perhaps rightly—about the ability of the United States to compete in world markets should have to face the fact that protection offers no real prospect for improvement, while the best chance for the future lies in the best possible use of American resources and the maintenance of a high degree of flexibility in the American economy. No automatic consequences of liberalization, these are best achieved through an open international economy and a set of domestic policies that foster adjustment instead of inhibiting it.

Though it will serve its national interests by following this course, the United States will be at a disadvantage in facing the rest of the world since it will appear as the one who wants something more than others want it. To be the initiator was no great handicap in the days of Bretton Woods and the Marshall Plan because the need was so clear. By the time of the Kennedy Round and the measures of the '60s intended to reduce strains on the balance of payments, the position of the United States as *demandeur* was already a certain disadvantage. In the '70s, everything is less clear. Many Americans are bound to resent the idea that the United States should have to be the initiator once again because other countries are more interested in other matters. Partly to overcome the negotiating disadvantages of making a proposal, Secretary of the Treasury Connally reversed the position in August 1971 in the episode discussed in the epilogue. Whether the same technique can be used very often is open to doubt. Even in 1971 it became apparent that an absence of American proposals did not automatically induce others to make proposals, as a vacuum draws in air. And if it did, the United States might not like the result. A better course would be not to abnegate but to adopt techniques to changed circumstances.

If the United States again has to initiate a wide range of actions, one way to improve matters is to establish as much identity as possible between what the United States wants and what a number of other countries want. For example, much of what the United States asks of the Common Market can be shown to be of interest to all outsiders, and much of what is asked of Japan would benefit other countries as well as the United States. Equal treatment has a place in this approach both as a sound principle and as a pragmatic concept. The argument gains force that the strengthening of multilateral cooperation should be a central objective of American policy. Nevertheless, American economic diplomacy in the '70s has to steer a careful course if it is to be at the same time strong in pursuit of national interests, wise in conceiving those interests broadly, and effective in showing that a given line of action will also serve the interests of others.

Generalizations begin to sound hollow since everyone knows that concrete measures of policy have to be anchored in time. The program a President puts before Congress, the powers he asks for, the uses he proposes to make of them, and the proposals he makes to foreign governments must be geared to the here and now and shaped with an eye to what appears reasonable at the moment. Farsightedness in policy is no substitute for feasibility. The political compromises required to carry out concrete proposals may reduce their long-run value, but progress may in the end be greater if modest measures succeed one another over a period of years than if great leaps are attempted and fail. There is the opposite risk that proposals that are too modest may languish because they have failed to strike a spark of imagination and promise.

Vital as the calculation of the currently feasible is, it has no place in this book. The political and psychological assessments it entails must be made in known circumstances. An amateur's pulse-taking in 1972 tells nothing about what a President may be able to do in 1975.

But what a President does or does not do in one term (or even half of one term) will significantly shape the problems he or a successor faces in the next. This book has looked back over a long span to improve our ability to look forward. In the process it has dealt with issues that are already the subjects of negotiation, others that might reasonably be raised by any government on any day, and still others which can hardly become the subject of detailed policy formation for years though their eventual emergence can be foreseen. Though I have spoken frequently of "the '70s," the term is rather arbitrary. Many of the problems considered here will survive the '70s, since they are rooted in the nature of relations among the industrialized countries. Some may not even come to the point of being specific objects of policy by 1980. In these matters it is hard to know whether a decade is a long or a short time. International economic cooperation is usually a slow process; but the pace of economic life can demand immediate action as well, and the long run is a compilation of short runs.

Though it can be a fatal flaw in policy-making to neglect the short run, it is not sensible to try to conclude a book of this sort with a series of short-run prescriptions. Further, though policy must be concerned not only with where to go but with how to get there, there is a difference between the study of the proper direction and the art of choosing the right time. This book has been concerned with directions and with the kind of action best suited to certain problems. I have not tried to say just when certain actions should be taken or exactly what combination of measures would make up an acceptable compromise. It would, therefore, make little sense to try to draw up at this point a set of specific proposals for what should be done by the current U.S. administration or the next one. For similar reasons it is impossible to make a clear-cut choice between two flat alternatives: the launching of broad proposals for sweeping action by the principal industrial countries, or a step-by-step approach that deals with each problem according to its urgency. But something useful can be said about the nature of the choice.

The case for the step-by-step approach is easy to see. Few of the problems before us could be settled once and for all by agreements among governments. The problems go on; rules raise questions about their applications; the removal of one impediment to trade or payments reveals another; the essence of such issues as international adjustment is that they arise in different circumstances. It would be an illusion, therefore, to suppose that a "big push" some time in the '70s or some kind of comprehensive agreement would eliminate most of the problems with which we have been concerned or put economic cooperation on a wholly new basis. A sounder approach, according to this view, is to take each set of problems when it is ripe for action (a trite but meaningful expression) and push for as broad a solution to it as is realistic. Limited steps would be welcomed and might slowly pave the way for a broader agreement. There is no implication in this method that problems can in fact be sharply separated from one another or "solved" in isolation, only that progress can be made by taking bites instead of swallowing whole.

This approach suggests a pragmatic and largely depoliticized method of conducting foreign economic policy that is in many ways attractive. All parties would understand that what they were doing was managing the relations among open industrialized countries in ways that tried to find as wide an area of common advantage as possible. Each country would have to make some adjustments and show understanding of the difficulties others would have in making adjustments of their own. A sense of the quotidian and hebdomadal would replace the temptation to speak in language intended to ring through the centuries. The willingness to deal with the humdrum, though it lacks glamour, has the compensation that failures are not regarded as apocalyptic or limited successes as millennial.

The weakness of this approach is that it may not generate enough force to bring about change. After all, partial interests have to be sacrificed so that greater interests may be served; change is always chancy; politically it is usually easier not to do something than to alter existing arrangements. When problems are fragmented, each part can easily be dismissed as not worth fighting about, or at least can be put off to some more propitious tomorrow. The low priority that foreign economic policy often has is likely to fall still lower. To move great nations requires great promise or at least great hopes. Carefully calculated demonstrations of the gains of reallocating resources are not likely to stimulate the will to override the political strength of protected industries. If one is serious about the importance of foreign economic policy, it would seem better to dramatize the basic issues, show how much more is at stake than just short-run interests, and exhort the nations to action with the promise of what can be achieved by the right action and the threat of what failure would mean.

High expectations may stimulate action, but they may also encourage illusion and subsequently disillusion. It can be dangerous for a President to have promised too much—for he may have departed before all the returns are in. Even a successful action can suffer if expectations are too high, as we saw in the somewhat misguided disappointment in the Kennedy Round. But to reason this way may be to exaggerate the immediate and the subjective at the expense of the continuing and the substantive. The results of the Kennedy Round in tariff reduction are real even if there is no partnership with Europe. The Bretton Woods institutions have served us well, though they have not operated as they were expected to. Disillusion is not always fatal. The overselling of the British loan did not stand in the way of the Marshall Plan. Hope for which the basis is thin, and even illusions, may help produce good results. Would we have had the trade agreements program if Cordell Hull had not had exaggerated ideas about the relation of trade and peace?

The historical case for the big initiative is quite strong. The main steps forward in American foreign economic policy have been taken in the belief that drastic action was needed to deal with urgent problems. But where in the long agenda of foreign economic policy reviewed in this book are matters that can truly be said to be so vital that they will surely galvanize American opinion, or proposals so promising that a reasonable government will espouse them unconditionally in spite of the high risk of failure? While this book was in the press, it looked as if an answer to the question had been found in an unexpected place: the American balance of payments and the pattern of foreign exchange rates of the industrial countries. Certainly the steps taken by President Nixon in August 1971 give a strong political content to issues of foreign economic policy, at least for a time. How long that time may be and how much may be accomplished during it are matters for speculation. Over the long run, foreign economic policy-makers still have to make choices between the big initiative and the step-by-step approach and between a workaday emphasis and a more political attack.

It would be unwise to draw too sharp a distinction between these sets of alternatives. For one thing, issues that are not exciting on the surface can be shown to be politically significant. For another, it is not necessary to have a world economic conference to bring about major changes in international economic relations, as the Marshall Plan, the Treaty of Rome, the Kennedy Round, and the creation of SDRs and two-market gold have shown. The historical evidence is strong that major American initiatives are less likely to be carefully planned measures that someone is waiting to put forward when the time is ripe than responses (sometimes well thought out and sometimes not) to the need to do something about a major problem. The original framing of the Bretton Woods approach was in some ways an important exception; even so, it was only partly worked out in advance of a foreseeable need. The British loan, the Marshall Plan, military aid, and Point Four all illustrate the general rule. The sag in American foreign economic policy in the middle to late '50s was surely due in part to the fact that there was no general sense of a clear-cut problem that had to be dealt with. Then the Common Market provided the challenge which led to the Trade Expansion Act.

There is no doubt that similar opportunities will exist in the '70s. When, whether, and how they should be seized are questions to which a book with the perspective of this one can contribute little. There is, however, a way out of this aporia. Failure to deal with economic problems can have dangerous consequences—in the deterioration of international relations, the emergence of new difficulties, or the exacerbation of old ones. In these circumstances, perhaps the most significant thing governments could do would be to make clear their understanding that it is politically very important to come to grips with the problems arising from their economic relations. At a minimum, they should start by preventing further deterioration; their objective should be to find ways of dealing with a broad range of continuing issues; their hope should be to repair the old foundations of cooperation and lay new ones that can support open, interpenetrated economies in the '70s and '80s.

A declaration to this effect could avoid the objection of trying to deal with all problems at once or of demanding solutions where there has not yet been adequate analysis. Under its cover many different processes could go forward, some faster and some more slowly, each conforming to the requirements of its problem. Even the dustiest and most technical issues will have been recognized as being part of something that is politically significant. A sort of boundary will have been drawn, beyond which economic disputes are not to be carried or deterioration allowed to spread. Inside the boundary there will remain room for differences of view about how issues should be dealt with and even a good bit of friction, but a warning would have been posted.

ORGANIZATION AND POLICY

Except for some remarks on the role of Congress, I have not discussed the way the American government is organized to carry out foreign economic policy, because a useful analysis must be detailed and this book is full enough already. In the late '60s, some major deficiencies were obvious. Once upon a time, the State Department had a reasonably firm grip on foreign economic policy as a whole, shared with the Treasury in matters of monetary policy. Then other departments acquired increased authority over matters that greatly affect foreign economic relations and conducted their affairs without adequate regard to the needs of a coherent policy or the interests of other countries. The Office of the Special Representative for Trade Negotiations, created for the purposes of the Kennedy Round, continued in existence afterward without a staff adequate for either the prime operating responsibility for trade policy or its effective coordination. Authority over balance of payments measures was divided, and there was no clear locus of responsibility for policy about investment or international production. Except in certain cases, the machinery of coordination seemed to be weak, though sometimes it was elaborate.

This deterioration of the framework seriously hampered the work of the substantial number of able men in the U.S. government who were concerned with foreign economic policy after the end of the Kennedy Round. They accomplished a good deal but sometimes had to devote an inordinate part of their efforts to getting a response from their own government to what they saw as the needs of the day. Officials of international organizations observed an absence of American initiatives where they might well have succeeded, and even a lack of aggressiveness in pressing American rights. The White House has played an active part in foreign economic policy but even with excellent people on its staff has not been able to be prod, catalyst, and conductor on all issues when there have been too few strong points lower down in the bureaucracy. Early in 1971 President Nixon took a step with great potential for repairing these deficiencies. He established a Council on International Economic Policy, with himself as chairman and, as director, a new White House official, the Assistant to the President for International Economic Affairs. For the first time, foreign economic policy was given status comparable to foreign policy and domestic economic policy, both of which have similar councils. This is a promising step, which could do much to improve the conduct of American foreign economic policy, not least through ensuring presidential attention to important issues early enough to set a clear course and carry it through. That the change has not solved all problems was evident enough in late 1971, when the Secretary of the Treasury appeared as the dominant figure in shaping American foreign economic policy, regardless of the nominal responsibilities of other officials.

No doubt the concerns of the presidential assistant will include the organization and performance of the lower levels of the bureaucracy. Anything like the kind of active policy on many fronts proposed in this book will require a far nimbler apparatus than the U.S. government has deployed in recent years. The effective linking of short-run action—including disputes—with long-run aims is especially demanding. Good results may require not only better performance but some reorganization within the U.S. government. It is hard to believe that a single "right" method of organizing exists. Under any system there will have to be a balancing of bureaucratic interests and an overcoming of rivalries. The widened scope of foreign economic policy has been stressed in earlier chapters; one of its corollaries is that many agencies of government are inevitably involved in the conduct of foreign economic policy. Sharp distinctions between the domestic and foreign aspects of the activities of these agencies will often be impossible to make or self-defeating. No single system for dividing powers is likely to serve all purposes well. The recurrent idea of creating a department of foreign economic affairs would provide no escape from these problems and, while it might reduce some difficulties, would introduce new ones, not least in relating foreign economic policy to foreign policy as a whole. Emphasis on the latter point suggests re-establishing the primacy of the State Department, but the enlarged scope of foreign economic policy and its links with domestic economic management raise doubts about that course. Improved coordinating machinery is clearly essential, but to get certain things done it may be equally important to lodge responsibility for them in one place. Still another problem of reorganization is whether modest changes in existing arrangements, which will minimize disturbance and help preserve continuity, are to be preferred. Drastic changes in organization may open windows to new ideas and people and ultimately improve the chances of getting strong leadership, but the creation of new governmental bodies always introduces delay and confusion and may leave Washington in a poor position to deal with current contingencies while the new people are getting themselves established.

The commonplace observations that no organization is better than the men who staff it and that the right men, backed by the President, can accomplish significant results in spite of the deficiencies of the American way of government (many inherent) are certainly true. For the purposes of this book, a more significant conclusion is that even the best men with the best possible organization will not be able to accomplish enough unless they and the President have a clear idea of what they ought to be doing and why. The final test of any major change in organization, such as the creation of the White House council, may well be whether it stimulates the formulation and articulation of policy, provides ways of ensuring that action follows policy, and imbues both the bureaucracy and the rest of the community concerned with international economic relations (including other governments) with a sense that the U.S. government knows what it would like to see happen and how it proposes to bring about that result. (Getting Congress to act favorably is still another matter.)

Policy includes both means and ends, but the ends range widely. There are proximate solutions to current problems, improved ways of dealing with these or other problems on a continuing basis, and desirable but loosely defined general conditions such as greater openness of the national economies to one another as a way of bringing about more growth, more efficiency, and a better allocation of world resources. Between the general and the particular there are very clear and important connections. An immediate problem may be dealt with in a way that helps or hinders the achievement of long-run aims. There are other matters in which, so long as governments are moving in the right direction, it may not be vital that a particular step be taken this year or next, or whether it takes three years or only one to conclude certain negotiations. It is not even a bar to action to realize that the best agreement that can be reached at a certain moment deals with only part of a problem and will eventually fall afoul of its own insufficiencies in some predictable way. Nevertheless, it is of the greatest importance that the various moves, however timed, go in the same direction. Policy, in other words, must guide, though the pace of progress may be determined by expediency.

This imperative stems not only from the need for consistency, foresight, and the time required to prepare and conduct international negotiations, obvious and vital as those factors are. What policy does in guiding action is to establish both purpose and criteria, without which the choice of action in individual cases can only accidentally further the long-run national interest. In the absence of established policy, issues are likely to be decided on the basis of immediate political gains and losses. It is the inherent bias of government to give greater weight to the short run than to the long run and to protect the established pattern of interests against change. Together or separately, these tendencies are likely to resist progress toward greater openness among the industrial economies; or, when it takes place anyhow without the benefit of government action, to inhibit prompt action to deal with the new problems that result; or, when such problems are formally dealt with, to encourage compromises dictated by immediate circumstances rather than the working out of ways of coping with the broader implications of the problem and the issues that will arise in the future.

All of these things will happen anyhow, at least part of the time and perhaps often, even if a government has a professed policy that points in another direction. But without the policy it will have no direction and will lack both the intellectual and political spine-stiffening that is imparted by a sense of purpose, a set of reasonably well-defined objectives, and the consequent possibility of demonstrating that one choice leads toward the desired result and another away from it.

To have a policy, a country needs objectives. For a big country, whose actions affect the world, these objectives must add up to a picture of the world economy it would like to live in. In a comprehensive policy, objectives will be of three kinds: the retention of certain conditions, the creation of new ones of a fairly specific kind, and the finding of ways to deal satisfactorily with changing circumstances and the shifting conflict and convergence of interests among nations and other groups. For a long time, the Bretton Woods picture guided the shaping of American policy objectives. It can no longer do so because so much has changed in the world. But unless much that has been accomplished through the Bretton Woods approach can be retained—and some of the gains are constantly threatened—it will be difficult to fashion a new set of objectives that combines elements of liberalization, management, and cooperation in the rather complex fashion this book has suggested is necessary. In the absence of a new set of objectives derived from a conception of the world economy that it would be desirable to fashion, the natural dynamics of politics and economics will cause the United States more and more often to take a narrow rather than broad view of its interests, which will lead, in turn, to actions that are more nationalistic than liberalizing. And others will do what the United States does, for they are subject to a comparable play of forces.

It follows that an American policy that is adequate to the pursuit of global objectives must, as in the past, be a two-tier policy, which both serves American interests as conventionally (i.e., somewhat narrowly) conceived and looks after the needs of the international economic system as a whole. What this has meant in the past has been seen repeatedly in preceding pages. The specifics will be different in the future. An even more important difference compared to the '40s and '50s is that growth in the power of other countries, notably Japan and those of Western Europe, gives their actions much greater weight than ever before for making or breaking the system. It is vital to the success of any but the most narrowly conceived American policies to win the cooperation of these other powers. Unless they, too, incorporate concern for the system in their national policies, it is doubtful if cooperation in management and liberalization will survive the '70s. But an American policy with these objectives is essential if not sufficient, and so too, at least at the beginning of the decade, is American leadership. The determination of what objectives are to be sought has been the burden of this book. There seems no need for still another recapitulation. To be too concrete would be misleading. Our objective is less a specific pattern of relations among the industrial countries than of movement in the right direction.

*   *   *

Although a considered account of American foreign economic policy since the end of the war and the international economic cooperation it induced is a success story, there is no guarantee that the installments will go on forever, or that a sequel will not be different. The grounds for hope—not the least of which are rationality in the pursuit of ends and enlightened self-interest—were sketched in earlier chapters, though more often by way of showing what could be done than by way of guessing what would be. But the strength of the forces working the other way has been, I hope, sufficiently underlined to show that there is no basis for assuming that a desirable outcome is inevitable. There is perhaps one final way of making the argument that rises above the appeal to one or another version of the national interest of different countries and puts no special emphasis on a single segment of international economic relations, whether it be money, trade, investment, or agriculture. This way of putting the case reverts to the metaphor of pictures that has run through this book. What is depicted this time is not an altered version of the Bretton Woods world with clearly drawn objectives, institutions, and agreements. Instead there are two pictures in which we see not fixed plans or static patterns but two contrasting views of how the economy of the industrial world may move in the future. In one, a process of cooperation, liberalization, and management—in the sense in which these words have been used in this book—continues, however unevenly, haltingly, and accompanied by friction and disputes. In the other, every major country more often than not lets domestic interests have what they want, resists change except when its entrepreneurs initiated it, lets short-run considerations outweigh those of the long run, and proceeds accordingly. What these alternatives mean in the setting of the '70s is easily enough imagined in the light of the discussion that has gone before. All one need do, as so many have done before, is to follow Shakespeare and say, "Look here, upon this picture, and on this. . . ."

Epilogue: The System Challenged– August to December 1971

The behavior of the U.S. government in August 1971 was out of character. Never before in the postwar period had Washington taken such strong unilateral action with no advance notice and for the professed purpose of gaining a national advantage over other countries. Foreign governments were not invited to subscribe to American proposals or join in advancing some cooperative venture. Instead, they were confronted with a new state of affairs and more or less told they would have to decide how to adapt themselves to the conditions created by the United States.

This reversal of customary roles was, in part, a deliberate effort to startle people. It was intended to dramatize the fact that in the Nixon Administration's view the place of the United States in the international economic system had changed. The innovation was not one of manner only. By breaking the link between gold and the dollar, Washington opened new possibilities of monetary reform. Issues became immediate that had been thought hardly likely to arise until after long negotiation. Clearly, the world was again in one of those monetary crises out of which major reforms had come in the recent past. But whether a constructive result could be expected this time was far from clear on the morning of August 16. At first glance, at least, the American action seemed to threaten the whole pattern of cooperation among the industrial nations developed during the post-war period. Four months later, when major exchange rates were re-aligned, the danger seemed less great but the prospects of funda-mental reform remained obscure.

As one clear result, the American action and the reactions in the rest of the world imbued international economic relations with major political significance. Consequently, some of the obstacles to moving ahead set out in chapter 11 might be removed, but two large questions remained unanswered: Would the momentum created by the crisis continue to impart a sense of urgency to negotiations about money, trade, investment, and nontariff barriers that would run on through 1972 and 1973? More important, would the sharpening of the political issues lead, in the end, to more cooperation or more nationalism?

This epilogue is being written at the beginning of 1972. Its limited aim is to point out some of the main connections between this book and the issues raised by the events of August to December 1971 and the negotiations then set in motion. In this light, the present volume turns out to be a kind of guide to the understanding of these matters. To have written it helped me to appraise the events of late 1971. To have read it will, I hope, help others to assess those of the future.

What Happened

This is not the place for such half-history as can be written so close to the events. Neither can I yet provide a balanced evaluation of the American action; too much depends on what happens next. The em-phasis here is on the salient facts and a preliminary appraisal of the questions they raise.

In a television speech on Sunday night, August 15, 1971, President Nixon announced a series of major changes in economic policy. (He had been meeting all weekend with his principal economic advisers; no-tably absent were any high officials of the Department of State.) Faced with a record deficit in the balance of payments by all account-ing methods, the United States would no longer redeem dollars in gold (or any other reserve asset). This, it was expected, would cause the value of the dollar to fall in exchange markets unless other govern-ments accumulated dollars in sufficient amounts to preserve the exist-ing rate structure (which seemed most unlikely). A surcharge was to be imposed on imports into the United States.[1] This step, which could

1. Usually spoken of as 10 per cent, the amount of the surcharge was that large only if the resulting total duty was not higher than it would have been if no re-ductions had been made since 1934 under the President's trade bargaining powers.

be interpreted in several different ways, soon became one of the central problems of the negotiations set in motion by the American initiative.

Accompanying these steps was a drastic turnabout in domestic economic policy in the form of a ninety-day freeze on wages and prices plus a number of other measures intended to stimulate the economy, including some tax reductions and, rather surprisingly, some cuts in government spending. If successful, these steps would presumably help increase the competitiveness of American exports; damping down inflation would cut import demand, but the achievement of full employment would work in the opposite direction. One domestic stimulant turned out to be of special concern to the rest of the world. As a means of expanding employment, the President proposed to ask Congress for a tax credit on investment in new equipment, provided it was domestically produced. No new measures to promote exports were added to the Administration's proposal for deferring the tax on export earnings (see chap. 7, p. 251) which was already before Congress (and passed later in the year).

In addition to taking these specific steps, the President called on other countries to end the "unfair treatment" of American trade and to carry "their fair share of the burden of defending freedom around the world." It soon became apparent that the American tactics would be to avoid making explicit demands immediately, leaving it instead to others to suggest what should be done. Most other major currencies were either revalued or allowed to float, though not altogether freely. Uncertainty became the order of the day, not just in the currency exchanges but in foreign government bureaus where it seemed strange not to have an American proposal to react to. In some parts of Washington there was a certain hardly suppressed satisfaction that for once others were being pressed to play their cards before the United States did.

Was it really necessary for the United States to take such drastic action? Was the right action taken? Was it taken in the right way? Some day a definitive analysis of the American action can be built

---

Technically, the President was simply withdrawing some tariff concessions previously made. Consequently, the surcharge did not apply to imports on which no duties were levied or no concessions had been made. It was also not applied to products limited by import quotas and the cotton textile agreements. This curious arrangement seems to have resulted from the President's wish to act immediately and avoid going to Congress (which had been generally assumed would be the normal course of action for imposing any sort of import tax, a fact which had some bearing on the earlier unwillingness to try this measure, as is pointed out in chapter 5, p. 220n).

around these questions. For the present a limited commentary will have to suffice.

The unprecedented deficit, the strong feeling that "something had to be done," and the evidence that confidence in the dollar was shaken dispose most people to answer the first question affirmatively.[2] The continuing deterioration of the trade balance, though it may have been heavily influenced by short-run factors, undoubtedly added to the sense of urgency.

An argument that immediate drastic action was not necessary would depend in part on the answer to some further questions: How much of the deficit was still made up of the movement of short-term funds which had been so important in the previous year and which might be better dealt with by other methods than a fundamental readjustment of the position of the dollar? Was it certain that Europeans and others would try to convert so much of their increased dollar holdings into gold that confidence in the dollar would be further shaken? Was an effort made to persuade them not to do so? Would it have made sense just to let the gold go? Even if the United States was switching to an activist view of the balance of payments, could a new effort have been made to elicit the cooperation of others instead of taking unilateral action?

If one accepts the need to do something about the exchange value of the dollar, there is a good case for sudden action. Essentially it is the same case as that for the devaluation of any currency without delay once a decision has been taken. If some move was to be made in that direction, the "closing of the gold window" and, in effect, the floating of the dollar probably commended themselves to most people. Many felt that Washington should have stopped there since, in combination with the domestic measures, this step offered good opportunities to improve the international position.

Another, quite different, line of argument can be used to justify drastic unilateral action. It did more than anything else could have done to dramatize to the world—including Americans—the Administration view that times had really changed and the United States must improve its position in the world economy. Whether the United States was justified in this course will long be debated. Should there not have been more international consultation, more exploration of alternatives? It is true that other countries were not showing very much interest in the complaints coming from the United States about their trade practices and, in the case of Japan, investment restrictions.

2. The assumption here is that the timing was determined by the balance of payments, not by concern about the domestic economy (though, if drastic action were going to be taken in either field, it was logical to move in the other as well).

But, it is also true, one could hardly say that in its first three years the Nixon Administration had made such a dynamic effort to foster increased cooperation to deal with new problems that it was entitled to feel frustrated by the lack of response in the rest of the world. Neither internally in the working of the U.S. government nor externally in its economic diplomacy had there been much evidence that international economic policy was a matter of high priority.

International monetary reforms, we have seen, seem to require a crisis to become acceptable. That fact might itself be taken as a partial justification for Washington's precipitating a difficult situation. President Nixon spoke in his initial speech of "an urgently needed new international monetary system." Later Administration statements struck a similar note but seemed to put most emphasis on the realignment of exchange rates. The Europeans, for their part, talked mostly of an American "contribution" to the realignment in the form of a devaluation of the dollar in terms of gold. Not surprisingly, then, the first phase of the developments launched in August came to a close in late December when the Group of Ten agreed on new exchange rates, dollar devaluation, and a wider flexibility than before around the new parities (now called "central rates"). While not all parts of this agreement were put into effect right away, the assumption that it would be fully carried out made it likely that more general reforms of the monetary system would be discussed in a somewhat different atmosphere in the year to come.

The range of possible reforms is set out in chapter 7. For the long run, the central issue is whether the dollar will be replaced by something else as the principal reserve unit. Before, this had seemed likely to be a slow process; the events of 1971 may prove to have speeded it up if governments feel that the changes in the rules have destroyed the dollar's usefulness as a reserve unit and require them to create a replacement quickly. Should this happen, some device would have to be found to prevent existing dollar supplies from becoming potential threats to the American balance of payments.[3] The resolution of these two problems would, in turn, do much to determine whether in the future the United States will be subject to the kind of balance of payments discipline that applies to other countries and to what extent the dollar will remain different from other currencies.

During the 1971 difficulties, few people proposed doubling or tripling the price of gold so as to make the gold exchange standard work. Secretary of the Treasury Connally moved in the opposite direction

3. A range of interesting possibilities is explored and some strong recommendations made by C. Fred Bergsten in a forthcoming book prepared for the Council on Foreign Relations.

when he told the annual meeting of the International Monetary Fund that the far-reaching monetary reform needed in the long run would include "a lesser role, at the least, for gold." Nevertheless, one of the few points the European governments could agree on during much of the period was that the United States should raise the dollar price of gold. The increase of 8.6 per cent agreed on in the end was modest enough to permit sophisticated analysts to point out that by leaving the official price well under the free-market price (and continuing the separation of the two markets) the world's money managers had proved the gold speculators wrong and shown that the gold in the system was more like counters in a game than a store of real wealth. Americans could maintain the concession was primarily symbolic but there were others, and perhaps not just French officials, who claimed an important point had been scored. Clearly, the old beliefs about gold are not dead; if new monetary troubles are encountered, the United States may have to make even greater efforts than in the past to continue the progress already made toward limiting the place of gold.

Whether the sense that fundamental reform is urgent will remain pressing after the realignment of exchange rates has begun to take effect is not clear as this is written. If the balance of payments of the United States improves and its economy revives, some of the pressure for reform will ease. The objections to every alternative reform will be given weight. Even so, if the dollar remains inconvertible into gold or any other reserve asset for a long time, uneasiness about the implications of that situation may become the main prod for reform. But the transition may be slow with the dollar still the most important currency even if less used for reserves than before. New practices will develop and new perspectives will have to be explored in assessing the American balance of payments. Some observers think the greatest risk is of a repetition of the crisis of 1971. Others believe the newly provided flexibility in exchange rates will make a significant difference. In any event, the world is now aware that the dollar *can* be devalued and that the United States might again resort to unilateral action.

How these possibilities develop depends in part on the level of economic activity in the world, on inflationary and recessionary tendencies, and on the differences in their incidence among nations. A great deal will undoubtedly depend on a matter that has perhaps been given too little emphasis in this book, namely, the appropriateness of given exchange rates and whether the dollar was in fact overvalued or not. Another way of putting the point is to say that to the extent the problems of adjustment have been made less severe by altering the exchange rates, the sense of urgency about improving the mechanism will have been reduced. But other pressures persist. Altered and more flexible exchange rates are not likely to do a great deal to contract the volume of short-term capital movements or eliminate the need governments feel to exercise some sort of control over them.

As this book has repeatedly emphasized, the prospects for change in the world monetary system will be greatly affected by the degree to which the European Community moves toward monetary integration. The immediate effects of the 1971 difficulties were divisive. Not only did Paris and Bonn disagree as to the right way of dealing with the Americans, but the divergences between the exchange values of the mark and the franc reflected differences in the two economies and some real conflicts of interest. Eventually a common front against the United States on the devaluation of the dollar was achieved and also agreement on the mark-franc rate. Nevertheless, at the beginning of 1972, Europe seemed further from monetary integration than it had been a year earlier. When progress toward the distant goal could be resumed was hard to judge. Sooner or later there has to be either French-German agreement on how to revalue the Common Agricultural Policy's unit of account or a considerable change in the CAP. Efforts continue to narrow the margins of fluctuation inside Europe. The strongest inducement to move toward monetary integration—or at least to establish common positions on international monetary issues—is probably the wish to have a strong voice in whatever measures of international monetary reform are undertaken. Since the Six can now count on adding Britain to their number, their potential influence is greater than ever and so too their chance of playing a major part in the management of the world monetary system, an activity in which the City of London continues to have considerable skills if not the resources of former times. How far the Europeans move in this direction will greatly affect the speed and degree of international monetary reform.

TRADE, INVESTMENT, AND OTHER MATTERS

Though the international part of President Nixon's new program started with money matters, it was not to end there. Trade was important and one of the clear objectives was to remove "the unfair edge that some of our foreign competition has." Better exchange rates would do part of the job, but other countries were clearly expected to do something about the restrictions they imposed on American trade and investment.

The tone and the substance of the new approach were in accord with the fairly widespread mood and set of views described in chapter

11. It would be hard to document the propositions that past American trade policy consisted of doing things for other people that were contrary to the American interest or that the United States was more sinned against than sinning when it came to trade barriers (with a few clear exceptions like the lag in Japanese liberalization). Nevertheless, these views were held by many and assured the new policy of a good deal of domestic support.

The case for exploiting domestic dissatisfaction and sharply challenging foreign practices that seem particularly offensive to the United States has been made in chapter 11, where there is also a warning about the risks of this course and the great difficulty of balancing on the knife-edge between argument and retaliation. For some months at least it seemed doubtful if the new American measures satisfied the conditions set out in chapter 11, such as, that objectives be limited, that challenges be launched only when realistic prescriptions for solving problems are already in mind, and, above all, that the United States be prepared to make concessions as well as demand them. There was no doubt, however, of the risks in the strong course the United States was taking.

Not surprisingly, the focus of attention in this matter was the surcharge. The fact that other countries did not retaliate could be explained by the general realization that such a process, once begun, might gather momentum and lead to a trade war. Making a point of the fact that they were restraining themselves, other governments and the Commission of the European Community worked hard to create a situation in which the removal of the surcharge would be firmly linked with the realignment of exchange rates and not with some eventual set of trade concessions. This was akin to past practice when similar devices had been used by countries in balance of payments difficulties. The fear was strong (among Americans as well as foreigners) that if the surcharge remained in force for a long time other governments would find it increasingly difficult to resist domestic pressure for retaliation or protection. Moreover, the longer the delay and the more accustomed American producers became to what was in some cases a major increase in protection, the harder it would be to go back to the old state of affairs, especially in an election year. Statements from Washington referred to the temporary nature of the surcharge, but the bargaining tactic of leaving the precise conditions unclear suggested that the date of termination might be far off. When December brought the removal of the surcharge (and of the discriminatory features of the tax credit) along with the exchange rate realignment, there was a general feeling of relief, but uncertainty about the trade issue was not ended.

In mid-August the extent of American trade demands was not clear. Washington sometimes appeared to expect other capitals to take major steps quickly to remove restrictions on American exports and investment. Any such idea seemed unrealistic for reasons that will be familiar to readers of this book. For every foreign trade barrier offensive to Americans, there is some American practice that is offensive to foreigners. Governments are not inclined to remove their own trade barriers except as part of a bargain in which others do something in return. Most negotiations begin by treating different subjects separately, but in the end it may be necessary to link what is done in quite different fields so as to strike a balance. All this takes time. Moreover, the negotiators' tasks are increasingly complicated by the fact that many rules affecting trade and investment are rooted in domestic policies and practices. Sensing the dangerous dilemma in which their government would be put if it had to choose between holding out for concessions that others would not give or accepting a settlement that patently fell short of what had been demanded, many Americans recommended that Washington elicit from its principal trading partners firm commitments to negotiate, actively and soon, about a range of issues of concern to the United States rather than trying to make them give up something in advance and unilaterally.

The pre-Christmas settlement conformed in the main to this prescription, but Washington insisted that there should be at least a few concrete trade concessions as well. Without them, according to the official view, Congress might not act favorably on the bill to change the gold price of the dollar. Moreover, an earnest of good intentions would be welcome as an indication that other governments meant what they said about further negotiations and appreciated how seriously Washington now felt about these matters. What the initial concessions might amount to is unclear as this is written, but they will presumably be modest. There is no difficulty, however, in predicting the main issues that will arise in the negotiations with each of the United States's principal trading partners. One need only recall some of the points made in preceding chapters.

Japan was, naturally, one of the main targets of the American measures. Its restrictions on imports and investments and its resistance to the idea that an ever-growing export surplus was a sign that the yen was undervalued made that inevitable. A less justifiable spur was Washington's frustration at Tokyo's obduracy in the matter of restraints on exports of man-made textiles and woolens that the Administration wanted in order to fulfill one of President Nixon's campaign pledges. When Japan succumbed to the new American pressures on the textile issue, it was probably too late to gain much credit in

Washington. All in all, late 1971 proved to be a period in which (as chapter 3 suggested might be the case) many events increased friction between Tokyo and Washington. Economic disputes were exacerbated by other factors such as President Nixon's plan to visit China and the failure to consult Tokyo about it. There was little evidence of any departure by the United States from the old practice of singling out the Japanese for the restraint of exports. Whether in the end Japan is likely, as a result of the 1971 experience, to accelerate its adoption of the more liberal practices followed by other developed countries, only time can tell.

Like Japan, Canada had been a significant contributor to the disappearance of the American export surplus which seemed to weigh so heavily in Washington's thinking in the summer of 1971. But Canada had no restrictions on trade and investment comparable to Japan's, and for some time the Canadian dollar had been floating upward in relation to the U.S. dollar. "What more do you want us to do?" Canadians might well have asked. The answer, it appeared, took the form of a rather long list of American desiderata. Among the more important were those involved in the dispute over the automotive agreement reviewed in chapter 4. Trade-conscious Washington also argued that the tariff-free importation of defense supplies into the United States from Canada should be matched on the Canadian side by balancing purchases and an ending of "Buy Canadian" practices. Whether uncertainties about raw materials and the possibilities of a continental energy policy came seriously into the negotiations was not publicly known. Nor was there any suggestion that the Nixon Administration was trying to influence the course of the already troubled internal Canadian discussion about how far to go in setting new limits to foreign investment.

From the Canadian view, the big problem was the surcharge and the fear that, along with the appreciation of the Canadian dollar, it would depress exports at a time when unemployment was already high in Canada. Though only a relatively modest share of American imports from Canada had to pay the surcharge, other measures showed its impact to be greater on Canada than on the other industrial countries.[4] Many Canadians thought their country would be ex-

4. The surcharge applied to only a quarter of American imports from Canada compared to 87 per cent of those from the European Community and almost 94 per cent from Japan. However, since the American market is so important to Canada, the surcharge affected about 16 per cent of all Canadian exports, a figure double that for the United Kingdom, more than double that for the Community, but still well below Japan's 20 per cent. The key figure, in Canadian eyes, was the share of GNP represented by the trade affected by the surcharge. For Canada that came to 3.4 per cent, compared to 2.8 per cent for Japan and 1.2 per cent

empted from the surcharge as it had been from earlier American balance of payments measures, and the Canadian government reportedly asked for such treatment. Not all Canadians thought this wise. Some felt an exemption would underline their dependence on the United States in an undesirable way. Others feared that such an action by the United States would encourage discrimination in other parts of the world that might work against Canada. In any case, no exemption was granted, but whether that was because the Canadian offer did not go far enough to meet American demands or because the United States did not wish to do anything that might weaken its strongest bargaining weapon is not clear.

In summarizing the Canadian part in the 1971 episode in relation to the main themes of chapter 4, one can make several clear points. First, the extreme importance of the United States to the Canadian economy was underlined. Second, the United States seemed less disposed than in the past to consider that Canada, as the weaker party, needs exceptional safeguards or other forms of special treatment. And, third, the idea tentatively put forward in chapter 4 that in many respects Canada should be regarded as within the American balance of payments perimeter either has been not highly regarded in Washington or would be given weight only as the result of more elaborate understandings between the two countries.

The list of American complaints about Europe was predictably headed by the Common Agricultural Policy and the various kinds of preferential arrangements the Community had made or seemed about to make with nonmembers. Equally predictable was the clear unwillingness of the Europeans to contemplate any serious changes in the CAP. There were, however, some items on the American bill of particulars which edged into a realm sketched in chapter 8, namely, steps the Community could take which would be of value to the United States without flouting the principles of the CAP or undermining its central features. The best example was the American proposal that Europe should store a higher percentage of its large current wheat crops than it would otherwise have done so as to avoid a large increase in subsidized exports to third markets.

Another issue cut right across the domains in which the Com-

---

for the European Community. Figures from Canadian-American Committee, *The U.S. Import Surcharge and Canada* (Washington: Author, 1971), p. 5, and Organization for Economic Cooperation and Development, *OECD Economic Outlook 10* (Paris: Author, 1971), p. 14. Quite early the Canadians established a system for relieving their exporters of some of the financial pressures of the surcharge, a step which might have led to disputes with the United States about export subsidies if the surcharge had not been removed when it was.

munity was unified and those in which it was divided. Ever since the mark floated upward in the exchanges in the late spring, frontier adjustments had been made within the Community to equalize farm prices. When new exchange rates were confirmed in December, it became apparent that these interferences with the single agricultural market would continue indefinitely unless the unit of account (formerly linked to the dollar) was revalued. If it was revalued at the mark rate, agricultural prices in Europe would be even further above American export prices than before. If the Community chose the franc rate, the discrepancy would be smaller but German farmers would receive less in marks than before. What the United States would like was obvious, but the American negotiators went even further and suggested that a limit be put on the extent to which the variable levies should be allowed to compensate for the difference between American prices and European prices. Instead, the Europeans imposed new taxes over and above the variable levy and different for each country's imports from overseas so as to eliminate entirely the effect of the alteration of exchange rates on imports while they worked out their internal problems about the unit of account.

The monetary differences were, as has already been noted, a setback to European integration. Some people blamed the United States for this. But it was not difficult for Americans to reply that it was up to the Europeans to decide whether they were going to respond separately or together to what the United States did and that it was not the responsibility of Washington to pull its punches so as to make it easier for the French and Germans to compromise their differences about exchange rates. In some respects Germany was, like Canada, already doing what it was supposed to do to conform to the general thrust of the American initiative. Like Canada, it feared the recessionary impact of a fall in exports. Here and there a voice was raised to suggest that Germany should claim exemption from the American import surcharge, but other Germans quickly registered their negative reactions, fearing that any move in that direction would be a serious blow to European integration at a time when that process was already under considerable strain. It was also observed that, so far as the volume of trade was concerned, France and Germany were more important to one another than the United States was to either, so that in some ways the mark-franc rate was more significant than the respective dollar rates of either currency. Further evidence of the extent to which preoccupation with intra-European relations affected responses to what the United States was doing was the general quiescence of London throughout this whole affair, a fairly predictable reaction given the recency of the firm commitment to British entry into the

Community and London's need to feel its way toward common ground with its divided Continental partners.

This book has stressed the importance of equal treatment as a principle of foreign economic policy. One would not have expected the 1971 episode to be very edifying on that matter, but oddly enough a few points emerged that are worth thinking about. Again the focus is the surcharge. It applied to imports no matter where they came from and thus satisfied the usual criterion of nondiscrimination or most-favored-nation treatment. But as the surcharge did not apply to all products, countries were differently affected according to what they normally sold to the United States. Moreover, the proportionate increase over the previous tariff level resulting from the imposition of the nominally uniform 10 per cent surcharge varied greatly from product to product. All this is, of course, true of any given tariff structure or changes in individual rates. Nevertheless, the sweeping character of the surcharge, combined with the emphasis on its "across the board" character (which rather suggests "equal treatment"), brings sharply into focus some questions about the established conception of most-favored-nation treatment and the relevance for future policy of the distinction between nondiscrimination and producing equal results, which is pointed out in footnote 10 of chapter 10.

Nominally nondiscriminatory, the surcharge in fact hit Japan and Canada harder than Western Europe and so enhanced American bargaining power in relation to those countries more than with Europe. (Of course, other factors than the surcharge came into consideration.) As has been pointed out in connection with Canada and Germany, the question could never be very far below the surface whether the United States might remove the surcharge from imports for some countries but not others. This course could be advocated on bargaining grounds alone, or because all steps toward removing the surcharge were welcome. Some who disapproved selective removal thought it bad bargaining tactics to do anything that might throw doubt on Washington's willingness to hold onto the surcharge indefinitely. A more common argument was that the United States should not compound the felony of unilateral import restriction by violating rules about equal treatment.[5] Whatever the decisive reasons were, there was no selective removal and people seemed rather happy that this

5. Those of a theological turn of mind could pose the question whether, since the surcharge was illegal under GATT, its partial removal might not be said to make a net reduction in the amount of sin even though some was added by discrimination. A possibility that seems to have been considered was the selective removal by products, which could have been manipulated to benefit some countries more than others (as is done in tariff negotiations without violating most-favored-nation rules).

was so, in the United States and abroad. Is it stretching a point to suggest that one reason for this relief is that the heightened threat of competitive economic nationalism sharpened awareness of the advantages of the principle of equal treatment? It is, after all, a protection for the interests of each and a safeguard against general deterioration. Similarly, can one not see in the pattern of negotiations in late 1971 support for the view that the major economic problems among the industrialized countries can best be worked out on a multilateral basis, not through a series of separate bilateral arrangements or "special relationships"?

Investment had no prominent place in the discussions that followed the American measures (except, probably, the negotiations with Japan). Concern about their overseas holdings was, however, one factor leading some American businessmen to urge their government to work for a settlement of the monetary and trade issues as soon as possible. They feared that if the situation deteriorated and other governments sought ways of retaliating, they would not just restrict trade but also put pressure on American business abroad, perhaps rather subtly. One can interpret this worry as evidence that the influence of "international production" on national policies comes not just through "foreign control" of parts of a national economy but also through the investing country's giving "hostages."

A second connection between investment and the difficulties of late 1971 lay in the part capital outflows played in the U.S. balance of payments deficit. Many Europeans thought the Americans should have acknowledged that "buying up Europe" was a major cause of the deficits. Americans tended to deny or ignore the charge; no new restrictions on investors were included in Washington's plans, and there was once again the familiar suggestion that "soon" the "temporary" restrictions on capital exports might be liberalized. This would be made easier if the new exchange values slowed American investment (and perhaps stimulated the flow of European capital to the United States). Whether direct investment, which is so much an industrial rather than a financial process, would in fact be greatly influenced by the new rates rather than by other factors is open to question. With regard to portfolio investment and short-term capital movements, matters might be different. All that was clear was that nothing that happened between August and December 1971 seemed likely to alter seriously the major issues concerning the future of international investment set out in chapter 6.

IMPLICATIONS FOR THE SYSTEM

The newspaper cliché of late 1971 that "the Bretton Woods world is dead" was not true except in the most obvious sense. If it meant that monetary arrangements were no longer going to conform to the patterns and processes envisaged when the Articles of Agreement of the International Montary Fund were drawn, that had been true for a long time. If the statement meant that economic nationalism had displaced cooperation as a mode of behavior and that agreed rules would be flouted more than followed, that certainly was a great danger, but most of the activity in national capitals seemed to be aimed at guarding against that result. And if the cliché meant that any new arrangements on international monetary and trade affairs that might be agreed on would totally replace those already in existence, the statement will hardly bear scrutiny. As chapter 10 demonstrated, even if the industrial countries make great changes in their arrangements, so long as they are cooperating through international institutions to deal with common problems they will be building on the Bretton Woods system. Nevertheless, the events of late 1971 raised fundamental questions about the prospect of future cooperation. The possible answers depend very much on one's interpretation of the motives and consequences of the American initiative of August.

To an important degree, the American action was a response to the domestic and international changes in the world sketched in chapter 11. But the exact character of the response is not yet clear. Was it the aim of President Nixon and Secretary Connally to show the world that whatever might be said about the state of the American economy it still had great strength and others would not find it possible to manage the affairs of the world without relying heavily on the United States? That would be an understandable reaction of Americans who had been badgered by European finance ministers and central bankers to "do something" and were tired of reading oversimplified newspaper accounts of the plight of the United States and the iniquity of a policy of "benign neglect" of the balance of payments. Or had Washington, as President Pompidou suggested, made a virtue of necessity and "drawn from the weakening of the dollar a position of strength and galvanized American opinion?"[6] That answer adds little to what we already knew regarding the rise of power in the rest of the world and the risks of the American course.

6. Press conference reported in *Le Monde*, September 25, 1971. He also said that the surcharge was "a big stick which might eventually change itself into a carrot for those disposed to play the role of an ass."

The third possible interpretation is that Washington not only thought the time had come for others to do their share but believed that they were in fact in a position to take a good deal of responsibility for the management of the system. It would be disturbing to learn that this was the correct interpretation because it suggests a serious miscalculation about the other countries. What may eventually be adequate power in Europe to carry this kind of responsibility remained still inadequately mobilized in the early '70s. Despite extraordinary growth, the Japanese economy had not reached the levels ascribed to it in the somewhat exaggerated accounts that had become current in American folklore; moreover, the great economic advance had not been accompanied by a growth in psychological, bureaucratic, and political underpinnings adequate to take on greatly increased international responsibilities on short notice. For the industrial nations to act as a group when the United States is inert is very difficult not only because of specific conflicts of interest among them but because they differ so much in their relations with the United States. In the absence of American leadership, the likeliest road to cooperation would seem to be through forming a common front to persuade Washington to do something and of that there were only rudimentary indications in 1971.

Questions about American motives can be matched with questions about the consequences of the American action. Again there are at least three sets of answers. First, one could imagine that the discovery of the limits of what the other countries could do plus a sharpened awareness of the continued great weight of the American economy in the world would lead to the conclusion that the United States remains the dominant partner in the system and the one mostly responsible for its management. This conclusion would be highlighted if for a period of time it turned out that the world was living not only on a dollar standard but on one in which the dollar was inconvertible (or, after becoming convertible, retained something like its past central role). In short, both the system and the American position in it might have changed (and go on changing) but not radically.

The second set of possibilities is that even though the other countries had proved unable to take over anything approaching managerial responsibility for the system in the short run, the events of late 1971 would hasten the day when they could do just that. The mechanism would be something like the following: The proved undependability of the United States (a pejorative description of what Americans might call "acting like other nations") would give rise to a series of fears and worries about when another convulsion might be felt (and if it might be set off by a smaller stimulus than the first one, as can happen when a pattern of response is already established). Instinctive reaction strengthened by prudent calculation and abetted by a certain sense of shame at their failure to have risen to an opportunity would lead these countries to take a larger share of responsibility for running the economic system. It is easier to see what this might mean for Europe where integration is the key than for Japan and Canada. But for these more isolated countries as well there would be ways of taking on larger responsibilities in international organizations, of working out relations with Washington that gave them greater influence on events before they happened and in return for carrying an increased share of the burden, and of suitably adapting their own policies. Alternatively, the reaction might be, at least in the case of Japan, which has no obvious close partner in the industrial world, an increase in nationalism possibly accompanied by an attempt to plant deeper economic roots in some kind of Asian grouping.

This last possibility comes close to the third kind of outcome, one which many people would judge by far the most likely. The system has been badly shaken; repair may be beyond anyone's capability in the short run. The United States has proved, according to this view, that a country may do whatever it is strong enough to do. The United States has sought to gain an advantage by confronting others with new conditions to which they have to adapt. It has violated agreed-on rules and without consultation imposed restrictions which it will remove only when others have done what it wants. What conclusion can other governments draw except that they, too, are entitled to solve their problems in this fashion provided they can get away with it? A slightly milder version of the same argument is that the United States has now served notice it will no longer give the tending of the system the same priority it did during most of the last twenty-five years. It will not merely emphasize the pursuit of national interests but will construe them in a much more conventional and, therefore, rather mercantilistic fashion. The two-tier system of American policy (as it was referred to on p. 420) will come very close to having lost one of its tiers. There being no other system-tender in sight, international cooperation will be weakened and in some areas may well disappear. Unconstrained by past obligations or the fear that rules will be effectively enforced, each country will turn to a higher degree of nationalism. In many ways one of the most frightening aspects of the days after August 15, 1971, was the sense that when trouble accumulated and the established ways of doing things were judged to be unsatisfactory, a government's dominant reaction was not to search for new ways of improving cooperation but to reach for measures very close to old-fashioned economic nationalism.

As in other cases noted in this book, the ease with which a disastrous outcome can be envisaged may be the best insulation against its becoming a reality. In that case, there may still be a happy ending. After all the trouble—and in part because of it and the reactions it has stimulated—some elements of the first two possibilities may combine with other ingredients to give new vigor to the willingness of the industrial countries to cooperate in facing common problems. Things would be different from before, possibly better. The recent warning would make men less likely to take for granted some of the achievements of the Bretton Woods approach. Awareness that the system of cooperation did not work automatically would be combined with a new understanding on the part of other countries that they could not expect the United States to go on as before unless they were more responsive to its needs and shaped their own policies to show that they were taking their share of the responsibility for international cooperation. A complementary American reaction would be made up not only of a recognition of what others were doing but also of the realization that, although major damage had been averted, danger had not been eliminated and could be brought close again, by miscalculation if nothing else.

To speak of increased cooperation is not to rule out some increase in economic nationalism as well. The question, after all, is largely a matter of how national interests are perceived. I have argued in this book that, in order to make the most of the possibilities of their increasingly open and interpenetrated world, the industrial countries will eventually have to conceive their interests differently from the way they used to and shape their policies accordingly. But I have also recognized that the discrepancy between economic interdependence and the organization of political power along national lines creates a basic tension that dominates international economic relations. It is quite possible—for reasons set out in chapters 10 and 11 and elsewhere—that the '70s will see a shift toward more nationalism (in its old-fashioned sense) than existed in, say, the '50s or early '60s. In 1971 the United States was acting in a more nationalistic way than it had at any time in the postwar period. But it was not alone in its mercantilism. Perhaps it might be thought of as moving toward the others while they—at least in their initial restraint—might be somewhat closer to its earlier approach. That a system of cooperation for common benefit could be built at one level of nationalism as well as at another is hardly open to doubt.

Before there can be anything like a happy ending, a number of conditions have to be met. For one thing, the economic position of the United States has to improve. Undoubtedly the shift in exchange

rates will help. More important is a revival of production and employment. Even if the expansion of domestic demand increases imports, a
widely shared sense that the American economy has regained its
health will do more than statistical improvement in the balance of
payments to restore world confidence in the dollar so long as the
turnaround has not stimulated recession elsewhere. In these circumstances, it will again become possible to see the U.S. balance of payments in a more reasonable perspective than that of simple mercantilism. (Whether the line of argument set out in chapter 7 will remain
valid depends on the kind of monetary arrangements the world then
has.)

Economic improvement is not enough to insure that the United
States will again take a leading role in increasing cooperation among
the industrial countries to cope with common problems. Several other
things are needed, among them presidential leadership and enough
support in the country to make the leadership both effective and
politically attractive to a President. My reasons for not trying to pre-
scribe short-run programs and timing (set out in chapter 11) also rule
out making predictions for the short run. It is, however, worth noting
some of the ways the 1971 events may affect the setting in which
future foreign economic policy will be made.

A key question is how the United States appraises its own position
in the world. Will the confrontation of 1971 be seen as a "success," or
will it be said that the United States once again gave away more than
it gained, as is so often alleged about policy in earlier periods? The
latter case would be hard to sustain; how much of a "success" can be
claimed depends in part on expectations. As the preceding pages have
shown, the realignment of exchange rates plus the beginnings of
serious negotiations on monetary reform and major trade issues are all
that could reasonably be expected in the initial phase. In the matter
of burden-sharing, by the end of 1971 President Nixon could point to
agreements with Japan and Germany on American military spending
in those countries and a substantial increase in the contribution of
European members to NATO as significant steps toward altering the
condition in which, as he said at the outset, the United States had "to
compete with one hand tied behind her back."[7] He had also succeeded

---

7. How much the new American stance contributed to these arrangements,
which had been under negotiation for some time, is moot. There will undoubtedly
be further negotiations about military burden-sharing linked with security arrangements as well as economic problems. The case is strong that others ought to do
more and the United States less, but it is doubtful if the American share will be
greatly modified in the near future. So far as foreign aid is concerned, many other
countries are now ahead of the United States in the share of GNP they devote to
this activity.

in checking textile imports. In short, there was some evidence at the beginning of 1972 to sustain the claim that the Nixon Administration's policy had had an initial success which warranted moving actively into the next phase.

The shaping of American policy to deal with the uncertainties of that phase (discussed above) may benefit in several ways from the difficulties of 1971. For one thing, foreign economic policy has been raised to a level at which more thought, more governmental resources, and more political energy will be given to it than before. There has been a striking reactivation of American trade diplomacy. In addition to the flurry of activity over the immediate concessions demanded by the United States, there has been a building up of dossiers of proposals for longer-run negotiations in GATT, in the OECD, and to some extent bilaterally with major trading partners. New men were appointed to key positions and a direct link established between current activities and the process of thinking ahead that was to take place in the high-level group established by the OECD (page 354).[8]

Another potential advantage for the future was the heightened consciousness of the need to make the improvement of the competitiveness of the American economy in itself an objective of policy instead of regarding it as a natural by-product of the ordinary operation of the economy. This idea imbued a number of the President's statements in late 1971 and was set forth in a report by his Assistant for International Economic Affairs.[9] It was also reflected in much that was said and done about finding ways to encourage research and development and maintain the technological advantages which had always contributed so much to the United States's position in the world economy. This approach was, of course, closely linked with concern about inflation, price control, productivity, and wage levels on which domestic economic policy was focusing. While no one could be sure how great the results of this emphasis would be, they were potentially significant not only in their material consequences but in their impact

8. William Eberle was appointed both Special Representative for Trade Negotiations and American member of the OECD group. A businessman, he had served just before his appointment as chairman of a Committee for Economic Development group that made a forward-looking report about the implications for American policy of British entry into the European Community. Subsequently named as Deputy Special Representative for Trade Negotiations was William R. Pearce, a businessman with a firsthand knowledge of agricultural trade whose contributions to the report of the President's Commission on International Trade and Investment Policy showed him to be thoughtful and farsighted in trade matters.

9. Peter G. Peterson, *A Foreign Economic Perspective* and *The United States in the Changing World Economy: Statistical Background Material*, reports issued by the White House, December 1971.

on foreign economic policy. To put major emphasis on ways of improving competitiveness leads to different conclusions from deploring the United States' loss of competitive position because others have been given unfair advantages.

Improvement in the American economy plus advantageous exchange rates and a sense that the government was aggressively fostering national competitiveness might produce in the American business community attitudes that could favorably affect the making of foreign economic policy. For example, businessmen would find it easier to believe that the United States could benefit from greater openness in international economic relations than if gloom prevailed about the unfair competitive edge of other countries. Moreover, adjustment at home would seem natural and its difficulties, political as well as economic, could be faced with more confidence. All in all the difficulty of putting together a coalition to support a generally liberal foreign economic policy would be reduced.

There is, of course, a darker side. Each advantage can bring disadvantages. To endow foreign economic policy with increased political status is to risk overreaction to disappointments if, for instance, it takes a long time to see the results of complex trade negotiations. An emphasis on competitiveness slides easily into a simple mercantilism that justifies export subsidies, competitive devaluation, and the like. A sense of confidence about the economy can erode the willingness to make some hard decisions required to keep a competitive edge, excuse minor abuses that accumulate, and even blunt the sense of need to make adjustments. Related to all these is the danger that the "success" of the 1971 tactics will be so enhanced in memory that the temptation will be great to resort to them again when there are disappointments, failures, and delays, as there will be. The satisfaction of demonstrating that the United States is still the strongest, the sense that others are more vulnerable because they are more heavily dependent on international trade and finance, and the manifold lures of economic nationalism—inescapable in a world of nation-states—all draw men in this direction. Domestic popularity gained by defying foreigners or blaming "speculators" for the dollar's problems may often seem to a politician a solider return than the lower-keyed response elicited by a "statesmanlike" approach and a willingness to work steadily at a process that requires continuity, rests on compromise, and rarely produces spectacular results.

Also to be reckoned with are the domestic groups opposed to policies that would open the economies of the industrial countries further to one another. Since the end of the Kennedy Round, a good bit of American trade policy has been the effort to keep protectionist forces at bay. Bills that would impose sweeping controls received much support in Congress in the early '70s. In response to the AFL-CIO's concern about the "export of jobs," legislation was prepared to control foreign investment. Officials of the Nixon Administration said that their strategy for resisting these pressures was to make the economy strong domestically and internationally, and to make it apparent to all that they would press American interests actively in negotiations around the world. There was much to be said for this course (as is pointed out in chapter 11), but one could not take its success for granted. For one thing, it entailed some compromises where protectionist forces were strong; it might prove politically expedient to add other products to textiles, steel, and oil on the list of "exceptional cases." Another problem was potentially very difficult: To get much out of future trade negotiations the United States would have to make concessions itself. But if protectionist forces were strong enough, the United States would not be able to play its part and the negotiations would be likely to fail. Perhaps the first test of possibilities will arise when President Nixon or his successor goes to Congress, as he must, to get the power he will need to reach or carry out agreements with foreign governments about trade, investment, and related matters. Still another uncertainty that has to be taken into account is that if the American balance of payments improves too much or if other governments feel their positions are deteriorating (and their standards may be mercantilist ones), the structure of exchange rates agreed on at the end of 1971 may well give way to ones less favorable to the United States, thus further undermining the logic of the "strong policy through strong economy" strategy.

Some of these familiar points are worth recalling at a time when the sense is pervasive that "everything has changed." Everything has not changed. Important changes have been made, and they open opportunities to make still further changes that will better adapt the foreign economic policies of the industrial nations to the world they live in. But to overcome the obstacles to those changes governments must cope with problems that were clearly visible before August 1971 and in many cases seem hardly changed in January 1972. They are issues dealt with in this book and considered in the report of the President's Commission on International Trade and Investment Policy,[10] which

10. The Commission was appointed by President Nixon in the spring of 1970. A sizable body with a good staff, it produced a thoughtful report and many recommendations not incompatible with the main line of argument of this book. I have not tried to take account of its specific points in my revision. My assessment of the report appears as "Timely Advice from the Williams Commission," *Columbia Journal of World Business*, November-December 1971.

lost none of its interest or relevance by being submitted to the White House in July 1971 instead of, say, September. What has changed are the immediate prospects of dealing with a number of issues, not the long-run requirements for an effective American policy.

A notable requirement that was neither met nor removed by the events of late 1971 was for a set of objectives and a long-range policy for achieving them. These must rest in turn, as has been argued throughout this book, on a conception of what kind of world economy is desirable. About that objective there has not been a wide area of agreement in the United States or internationally. This book has tried to suggest some of what is needed so far as relations among the industrial countries are concerned. Happily there are signs that others, confronting the same problems, have come to somewhat similar conclusions,[11] so perhaps a consensus is beginning to form which after further work and argument—and without ever being given what could be called "final form"—will serve as a guide to policy. But sound analysis and general agreement are not guarantees of good policy, only prerequisites for it.

11. For example, the majority of the Williams Commission just mentioned; a report made in 1971 by the Committee for Economic Development, *The United States and the European Community: Policies for a Changing World* (New York), and one by the National Planning Association, *U.S. Foreign Economic Policy for the 1970s: A New Approach to New Realities* (Washington); and a report released by an international group of economists brought together by the Brookings Institution, *Reshaping the International Economic Order* (Washington, 1972).

Index

Note: *In addition to the conventional listing of topics, this index provides a guide to some of the main themes of the book that are not reflected in chapter titles or subheads. It should be used in connection with the Table of Contents. Not all key words are listed; the entry under "international economic system" indicates directly or by cross reference most of the relevant topics. Since the emphasis is on concepts, passages in the text may use different words from those under which they are indexed. Because the whole book is about U.S. policy, entries under that heading are confined to history and a few topics that would otherwise escape notice. References are selective rather than exhaustive, especially when countries, products, industries, etc., are used as examples. The index also provides a list of abbreviations.*

COUNCIL ON FOREIGN RELATIONS

Recent Publications

FOREIGN AFFAIRS (quarterly), edited by Hamilton Fish Armstrong.
THE UNITED STATES IN WORLD AFFAIRS (annual), by Richard P. Stebbins.
DOCUMENTS ON AMERICAN FOREIGN RELATIONS (annual), by Richard P. Stebbins with the assistance of Elaine P. Adam.
AMERICAN AID FOR DEVELOPMENT, by Paul G. Clark (1972).
THE CARIBBEAN COMMUNITY: Changing Societies and U.S. Policy, by Robert D. Crassweller (1972).
INDIA, PAKISTAN, AND THE GREAT POWERS, by William J. Barnds (1972).
CONGRESS, THE EXECUTIVE, AND FOREIGN POLICY, by Francis O. Wilcox (1971).
THE REALITY OF FOREIGN AID, by Willard L. Thorp (1971).
POLITICAL HANDBOOK AND ATLAS OF THE WORLD, 1970, edited by Richard P. Stebbins and Alba Amoia (1970).
JAPAN IN POSTWAR ASIA, by Lawrence Olson (1970).
THE CRISIS OF DEVELOPMENT, by Lester B. Pearson (1970).
THE GREAT POWERS AND AFRICA, by Waldemar A. Nielsen (1969).
A NEW FOREIGN POLICY FOR THE UNITED STATES, by Hans J. Morgenthau (1969).
MIDDLE EAST POLITICS: THE MILITARY DIMENSION, by J. C. Hurewitz (1969).

The Economics of Interdependence: Economic Policy in the Atlantic Community, by Richard N. Cooper (1968).

How Nations Behave: Law and Foreign Policy, by Louis Henkin (1968).

The Insecurity of Nations, by Charles W. Yost (1968).

Prospects for Soviet Society, edited by Allen Kassof (1968).

The American Approach to the Arab World, by John S. Badeau (1968).

U.S. Policy and the Security of Asia, by Fred Greene (1968).

Negotiating with the Chinese Communists: The U.S. Experience, by Kenneth T. Young (1968).

From Atlantic to Pacific: A New Interocean Canal, by Immanuel J. Klette (1967).

Tito's Separate Road: America and Yugoslavia in World Politics, by John C. Campbell (1967).

U.S. Trade Policy: New Legislation for the Next Round, by John W. Evans (1967).

Trade Liberalization Among Industrial Countries: Objectives and Alternatives, by Bela Balassa (1967).

The Chinese People's Liberation Army, by Brig. Gen. Samuel B. Griffith II U.S.M.C. (ret.) (1967).

The Artillery of the Press: Its Influence on American Foreign Policy, by James Reston (1967).

Trade, Aid and Development: The Rich and Poor Nations, by John Pincus (1967).

Between Two Worlds: Policy, Press and Public Opinion on Asian-American Relations, by John Hohenberg (1967).

The Conflicted Relationship: The West and the Transformation of Asia, Africa and Latin America, by Theodor Geiger (1966).

The Atlantic Idea and Its European Rivals, by H. van B. Cleveland (1966).

European Unification in the Sixties: From the Veto to the Crisis, by Miriam Camps (1966).

The United States and China in World Affairs, by Robert Blum, edited by A. Doak Barnett (1966).

The Future of the Overseas Chinese in Southeast Asia, by Lea A. Williams (1966).

Atlantic Agricultural Unity: Is It Possible?, by John O. Coppock (1966).

Test Ban and Disarmament: The Path of Negotiation, by Arthur H. Dean (1966).

Communist China's Economic Growth and Foreign Trade, by Alexander Eckstein (1966).

POLICIES TOWARD CHINA: Views from Six Continents, edited by
A. M. Halpern (1966).

THE AMERICAN PEOPLE AND CHINA, by A. T. Steele (1966).

INTERNATIONAL POLITICAL COMMUNICATION, by W. Phillips Davison
(1965).

ALTERNATIVE TO PARTITION: For a Broader Conception of America's
Role in Europe, by Zbigniew Brzezinski (1965).

THE TROUBLED PARTNERSHIP: A Re-Appraisal of the Atlantic Alliance, by Henry A. Kissinger (1965).